# WHAT THE CRITICS ARE SAYING ABOUT PREVIOUS EDITIONS OF
## *HOW TO SURVIVE YOUR FRESHMAN YEAR*

"Hidden gem."
—*INGRAM LIBRARY SERVICE*

"Ten Good Books for Grads."
—*DETROIT FREE PRESS*

*"How to Survive Your Freshman Year* provides student viewpoints and expert advice on virtually every topic pertaining to first-year students from moving in to finding meals....After reading this book, students will be aware of the realities of college life and be better prepared to shape their own unique college experience.
—*JOURNAL OF COLLEGE ORIENTATION AND TRANSITION*

"A guide full of fantastic advice from hundreds of young scholars who've been there… a quick and fun read."
—*BOSTON HERALD*

Winner - Best Book on Adjusting to College Life.
—*READERS' CHOICE AWARDS*

"The perfect send-off present for the student who is college-bound. The book manages to be hilarious and helpful. As an added bonus, it's refreshingly free of sanctimony."
—*THE POST AND COURIER, CHARLESTON, SOUTH CAROLINA*

"Explains college to the clueless."
—*COLLEGE-BOUND TEEN*

"The advice dispensed is handy, useful, and practical. This book will make great light reading for an incoming freshman."
—*VOYA*

"A great tool for young people beginning an important and often daunting new challenge, with short and funny, real-world tips."
—*WASHINGTON PARENT*

Visit www.howisurvived.com to learn more.

# How to Survive Your Freshman Year

**This Guide contains differing opinions. Hundreds of Heads will not always agree. Advice taken in combination may cause unwanted side effects. Use your Head when selecting advice.**

# How to Survive Your Freshman Year

## Sixth Edition

ALISON LEIGH COWAN, EDITOR

Created by
MARK W. BERNSTEIN & YADIN KAUFMANN

Illustrations by
LISA ROTHSTEIN

**Hundreds of Heads Books, LLC**

NEW YORK, NY

Cover photograph Jupiter Images
Cover design by Katelyn Rivera
Book design by Elizabeth Johnsboen

Library of Congress Cataloging-in-Publication Data on file

HUNDREDS OF HEADS® books are available at special discounts when purchased in bulk for premiums or institutional or educational use. Excerpts and custom editions can be created for specific uses. For more information, please email sales@hundredsofheads.com.

HUNDREDS OF HEADS BOOKS, LLC
info@hundredsofheads.com

ISBN: 978-1-933512-99-0

Printed in Canada.

0 9 8 7 6 5 4 3 2 1

# CONTENTS

# THE HEADS EXPLAINED

Look for these special symbols throughout the book:

 Remember this significant story or bit of advice.

 This may be something to explore in more detail.

 Watch out! Be careful!

 We are astounded or delighted by this one.

 Here's something to think about.

*—THE EDITORS*
*AND HUNDREDS OF HEADS BOOKS*

# Introduction

First off, congratulations on the exciting days ahead and on being one of nearly 2 million lucky souls to be starting college this year in the United States. You've worked hard to get this far, and you have every reason to feel proud.

We know you're anxious. You're not wrong to think that college is harder today than it was when your parents and teachers may have attended. Certainly, it is more nerve-wracking than the zany days when Lisa Rothstein, the book's illustrator, and I each settled in to our first dorm rooms. (Lisa with her art posters, me with my electric typewriter.) The art of the job hunt has changed. Stress is lurking everywhere, and the glare of social media only magnifies the pressure to be perfect, one reason why we created an all-new chapter in this edition all about "Coping."

But here's a secret the elders in your life may not appreciate. The Straight-A Life is highly overrated. Success depends on so much more than compiling that perfect GPA, as new research keeps finding. Failure has never been more fashionable – or helpful to your career. Robert F. Scott's perpetual daydreaming may have made him look lackluster as a student, though that same restless curiosity about what lay beyond his classroom walls also led him to Antarctica. Steve Jobs', George W. Bush's, and J.K. Rowling's spotty grades in college never held *them* back, either.

So, remind yourself to breathe, and give yourself permission to have some fun. College may or may not be the best four years of your life, but for sure it shouldn't be the dullest, either. Sample new foods. Make some unlikely friends. Try out for an extracurricular group you think is way out of your league. You may surprise yourself (and the doubters back home who said you never could.) I tried out for an *a cappella* group, which quickly showed me the door. (To this day, I can't even believe the group did not burst out laughing upon hearing my first off-pitch note.) But I also auditioned for a dance troupe that I was sure I had no chance of making, only to be stunned when I got in. That ended up being one of the more thrilling experiences of my college years.

By all means, take basic statistics because it's good for you, and maybe a course in computer coding. But mostly take the courses that interest **you.** Yes, even philosophy majors can land big jobs out in the real world. Just ask Robert Rubin, the former Treasury Secretary who credits the time he spent studying philosophy at college for much of his success. Or Megan Rooney, the classics major who went on to write speeches for the White House. Challenge yourself, when you can, but if a subject proves too much, take it pass-fail. Worry less about having all the answers, more about asking the best questions.

Oh, one more thing. Try not to leave college without getting to know some professors. To their credit, most American colleges encourage this kind of up-close exchange. Take advantage of all those office hours. (Wish I had.) Your teachers could end up being your greatest mentors and champions.

Most of all, relax.

This book has your back. Hundreds of people have generously drawn from their experiences so you have the benefit of that. The chorus of voices you'll hear in the book will not always be singing in perfect unison (any more than I was years ago.) But the multiplicity of views represented will help you make more informed choices and take on ticklish situations with fewer surprises. Meanwhile, we'll be continuing the conversation over at www.HowISurvived.com. So, please check us out there, too. We'd love to hear about your new adventures and what's on your mind.

*Alison Leigh Cowan*

When we published the first edition of How to Survive Your Freshman Year fifteen years ago in 2004, we were in uncharted territory. We believed – strongly – that kids going off to college would enjoy hearing from hundreds of others who have lived through freshman year and come out with something interesting to say about it all. But the enthusiasm with which readers responded surprised even us. The book quickly became the year's best-selling college guide, and its following has only grown since.

Other advice books, no matter how smart or expert their authors, are generally limited to the knowledge of a single person. But, as the old saying goes, two heads are better than one – and hundreds are better by far. So we interviewed lots – and we do mean lots – of students and graduates from big schools, small schools, Ivies and state universities to bring you the latest intelligence from the hundreds of campuses we scoured.

Greeks, geeks and jocks sat down with us and trusted us enough to weigh in on everything from dorm life and roommates to college parties and dating; from choosing a major to improving your study habits; from battling homesickness to avoiding fashion faux pas – all gathered here for your benefit.

When viewpoints on an issue were mixed, or even contradictory, as they often are, we have not held back. Are fraternities and sororities a good choice or not? How close should you try to stay with your high school friends? And, of course – should you party or not party? By all means, make your own decisions on these hairy topics, but do it armed with the collective insights of the people featured on these pages. You might also discover that things you fret about deeply are common concerns shared by others.

And now we're on to the sixth edition of this indispensable guide, our most ambitious yet. This new version has been smartly edited by Alison Leigh Cowan, a former reporter and editor for the *New York Times*, who by now has sent four children of her own off to college. (All different ones, too!) So, she's seen first-hand how much college has changed and keeps changing. This edition features new interviews with hundreds of students across the country – thanks to the journalistic efforts of Alison and her team of reporters. You'll also find timeless advice from previous editions – where we believed the wisdom of earlier years' graduates is relevant for current students. And we're pleased to include new sections on issues that have come to the fore of the college experience for many students in recent years: accommodations for students with special needs of one kind or another; the dangers of hazing; free speech on campus; and sexual harassment/"#MeToo."

The new illustrations that provide some extra commentary and whimsy along the way are from Lisa Rothstein, an award-winning cartoonist whose irrepressible artwork has appeared in the *New Yorker*.

As before, this one-stop guide features not only updated wisdom from your peers but also invaluable expert advice from a bevy of pros in the know (check out the back of the book for their bios).

You're embarking on one of the best experiences of your life. Have fun. Study hard. And know that you've got hundreds of friends to show you the way.

MARK W. BERNSTEIN
YADIN KAUFMANN

## A Personal Reflection from a Former Reader (and Now Contributor)

The lead-up to when you leave for college is one of those magical times when it seems like your parents are willing to buy you just about anything.

They're freaking out just as much as, or more than you are, and they want to be absolutely sure you have everything you need to be comfortable and successful. At least that was my experience. I was in the university's bookstore in the summer of 2011, with my mom, following my overnight orientation in Flagstaff at Northern Arizona University, about a month before the start of school, and she was in the midst of one of these pre-going-away, compulsive-stress shopping moods.

I would only be about 150 miles away, but I was nervous. Almost like I was about to venture into the darkest, most unknowable future I'd ever face. I felt like I was about to jump off the high-dive with my eyes closed, with no idea how far away the water was below. I saw *How to Survive Your Freshman Year* beckoning from the store shelf and in it, saw a flickering hope that it might alleviate my panicked, racing mind. The candid, diverse stories and fresh advice within the book seemed to shine a light on the intimidating darkness that loomed ahead. With minimal effort, I convinced my mom that it would be a valuable purchase, and it was thrown in with the rest of the haul.

I remember devouring the thing on the two-and-a-half-hour drive home. Within it, was a dizzying, bizarre, entertaining, and sometimes contradictory, collection of anecdotes and advice that I found enlightening – but not always clarifying. I realized that there were more challenges and wacky possible predicaments than I had even imagined. All of which I found strangely reassuring: I saw there would be no way to know the future and the only thing I could do was surrender to the uncertainty.

So I went to college. I jumped blind off that high-dive and lived to tell the tale, progressing from one-time reader of this humble book to one of its many proud contributors. As an undergraduate, I faced hurdles big and small, serious and ridiculous – things I could have never prepared for or predicted. I worked through them all without my parents, without my high school friends, and without the security blanket of home. The world opened up to me and I learned things about it and myself that I'd never previously considered. I grew up.

I went to college as a product of upbringing, a cog in the machine of my hometown community and, I'd like to think, I returned something closer to my true self. I learned to see things more objectively, to shed the thick cultural biases that had accumulated in the bubble of my youth. There is a wealth of beauty and wisdom and information that the wide and ancient world has to offer, and universities exist to preserve those things and pass them on to future generations. They are exhilarating places to be.

So don't take your years there lightly. College is, like its more brutal predecessors, a turbulent time of growth.

For me, this book was valuable because, not that long ago, it helped me realize a hard truth: sometimes, there is no elegant way to avoid roadblocks that will mar your path or blunders that will befall you. At college, there's no way to predict what those will be like for you, and no single way of handling them. How you tackle them will make you who you are, and that is the goal: becoming the person you want to be.

*Anthony Wallace is a Phoenix-based writer who recently left a college campus with a degree in Philosophy from Northern Arizona University in snowy Flagstaff.*

"I don't think you'll be needing that in Ithaca."

# Get Ready: What to Take to College

The world is full of lists of things incoming freshmen should bring with them to college. But dorm rooms are small, and you can't afford every gimmicky gizmo Buzzfeed brings to your attention. What you need is unfiltered advice from those who have been there before and who aren't trying to sell you anything – and, look, here it is!

Legend has it that when Alexander the Great left to conquer the world, the only thing he packed was a copy of *The Iliad*, annotated by his teacher Aristotle, which he tucked under his pillow each night. Of course, there's no shame in bringing your teddy bear, if that's what you prefer. Just know, no matter what you forget at home, you can survive on a good attitude and a few extra bucks to buy things once you get there.

**BRING SOME GOOD PAJAMAS.** It's uncomfortable sleeping with other people in the same room, but one thing that helps is to have good pajamas that cover most of your body parts. You can lounge around in them without worrying about how you look.
—S.G.
COLUMBIA UNIVERSITY, SENIOR

**MY PHOTOS. THEY KEPT ME GROUNDED.**
—HANNAH SMITH
HARVARD UNIVERSITY, JUNIOR

- Make a list of what you need to bring. Let your mom and dad make a list. Use these lists to pack.
- Don't forget to take some things that remind you of home – pictures, your favorite pillow, etc.
- What you *don't* bring is also important – do you really need all those sweaters and shorts?
- Don't forget: blankets, pajamas, a towel.
- Remember, this isn't a camping trip in the wilderness. If you forget something like toothpaste, you can always buy some.

**MY JOURNAL.** It's a companion when you don't have one. It sounds cheesy, but I used mine a lot.
—STEPHANIE
UNIVERSITY OF PENNSYLVANIA, SENIOR

• • • • • • • •

**A HUSBAND PILLOW.** I would always try to sit up in bed – regular pillows could only lift you up so much and sitting up hurts.
—DANIELLE
SUSQUEHANNA UNIVERSITY, SOPHOMORE

• • • • • • • •

Bring your blanket. Make sure it's comfy.
—CHANA WEINER
BARNARD COLLEGE, SOPHOMORE

**BRING LOTS OF BEDDING.** The mattresses at my school are covered in rubber in case you wet the bed or something, so I got a feather bed, and lots of people have simpler foam things, such as egg crates. Then, you can get a good night's sleep.
—EDITH ZIMMERMAN
WESLEYAN UNIVERSITY, SOPHOMORE

• • • • • • • •

**A CASE OF NO-DOZ,** Pop-Tarts, and several extra room keys.
—S.L.M.
INDIANA UNIVERSITY, GRADUATE

**DON'T GET BED LIFTS.** They are scary. I know people who refuse to have sex on lifts because it's so unstable. I guess you can fit more shit under your bed but what's more important?
—*ANONYMOUS*
*DARTMOUTH COLLEGE*

**BEST GIFT TO ASK FOR FROM YOUR PARENTS:** One really great sleeping bag. You'll use it for everything, from spring break in a hotel room with 20 other people, to backpacking across Europe or the U.S.
—*WENDY W.*
*UNIVERSITY OF GEORGIA, GRADUATE*

**BRING EXTRA LIGHTING** for your dorm room and an air mattress in case a friend comes over.
—*JESSICA*
*BARNARD COLLEGE, JUNIOR*

**AN EXCELLENT PAIR OF STUDIO-GRADE** headphones for those times when you want to jam but your roommate wants to snooze. You cannot get through college without your music.
—*MARGOT CARMICHAEL LESTER*
*UNIVERSITY OF NORTH CAROLINA AT CHAPEL HILL, GRADUATE*

**EARPLUGS.** There's a lot of noise in the dorm.
—*RICK SHILLING*
*PENNSYLVANIA STATE UNIVERSITY, GRADUATE*

**WAIT TO BUY YOUR BOOKS.** I found out that I didn't really need a book that I spent money on and just needed to buy the access code – the password that is often sold separately to buy the online version of the textbook and related materials.
—*DANIELLE*
*SUSQUEHANNA UNIVERSITY, SOPHOMORE*

# LESS IS MORE

**TRAVEL LIGHT.** You can always have something brought to you or buy it. Have a mini-fridge and microwave, it makes breakfast a lot easier. Don't put out expensive TV's or stuff like that until you know you can trust your roommate.
　　—*R.S.*
　　　*GUILFORD COLLEGE, GRADUATE*

• • • • • • • •

**PACK ONLY WHAT YOU NEED.** My first-year packing philosophy was to bring just about everything I owned to school – or at least what could fit in the car. (That way there was no way I could forget something at home.) After making it through half the semester without using more than one of the dozen water bottles I brought, unpacking half the boxes shoved in the closet, or ever touching the golf clubs, skis, or bike that had been shoved under my bed, I realized that I didn't need any of it. All it did was clutter my room and make returning home an absolute pain. Only pack what you use regularly.
　　—*DANIEL GRUMBLES*
　　　*LEHIGH UNIVERSITY, SOPHOMORE*

• • • • • • • •

**DON'T LOOK AT YOUR CLOSET WHEN IT'S TIME TO PACK.** Look at your everyday dressing pattern for the last two seasons. Yeah, you *are* sort of moving, but that doesn't mean you should take all your clothes with you. I took all 40 of my T-shirts with me, for instance, but I ultimately ended up cycling through about 10. Because those are the shirts I really like.
　　—*ANONYMOUS*
　　　*DARTMOUTH COLLEGE*

• • • • • • • •

**LEAVE "HIGH SCHOOL" AT HOME.** Don't pack too many clothes, shoes, notebooks, folders and such. So many things are digital now, it's insane. As for old high school T-shirts, it's time to move on. You'll get plenty of new college tees and your wonderful "I'm a freshman" shirt!
　　—*ABBY*
　　　*SOUTH DAKOTA STATE UNIVERSITY, SENIOR*

**IF YOU ARE FEMALE, YOU ABSOLUTELY DO NOT NEED MORE THAN 2 PAIRS OF HEELS.** Don't be the girl that thought her 10 pairs of wedges and heels would actually be worn to class. Most college campuses (even small ones) cover a fair amount of ground. Long walks across campus and heels do not go together!
—*MARISSA LICURSI*
*JOHNS HOPKINS UNIVERSITY, GRADUATE*

**IT'S NOT WORTH TRYING TO SAVE TIME** by buying your books early. My friend and I were told that the first days of college are really crazy, and the advice was to "buy all your books right away to avoid lines!" We bought $400 worth of books (each), including a hardcover dictionary. We realized we had done it all wrong the next day, when we looked at our schedule, which needed some revisions. Make sure your classes are totally lined up before buying your books.
—*JANNA HAROWITZ*
*MCGILL UNIVERSITY, GRADUATE*

**I HAD A BATTERY-CHARGED, PORTABLE BLENDER.** It was super. It cost $50. I was dorm shopping with my dad, and I said, "I need that blender." He was like, "You don't need a portable blender for college." I was like, "No, no, Dad, I need that. Take the comforter out of the cart. I need that." So we got it. And I made everything in it. A blender helps make friends.
—*CASEY*
*GEORGETOWN UNIVERSITY, SENIOR*

**HAVING A PRINTER** in my room is really helpful. I can print in my room without going to the computer center or waiting until the next day.
—*ANNIE THOMAS*
*UNIVERSITY OF MICHIGAN, SENIOR*

# WHY OVERPAY FOR BOOKS?

Typical college students spend about $157 on average for course-specific materials for each class taken, according to the latest study from the Student Public Interest Research Groups. Even if you buy used textbooks and e-books from popular sites like Amazon, these outlays add up. Access codes, which are often bundled into the purchase and add to the cost of the book, make the situation even trickier to navigate.

Access codes are essentially passwords that give you access to online supplements such as practice questions or homework with your textbook. You can't reuse access codes or share them among friends. They're like workbooks that someone has written on in pen. If someone claims you can reuse an access code they're selling, don't bet on it.

Nobody wants to spend money when they don't have to. So, check out these smart ways of saving money before splurging on your required reading for the coming year:

1.  **Ask your professor what to do.**
    Some professors allow students to buy just the textbook without the access code – or the reverse. Your professor also may cut you some slack by making the textbook available online or pointing out other ways students can find the materials for less money.

2.  **Go to the library.**
    Your college librarian may have a mystery solution to your textbook needs. Professors sometimes ask the library to put their required textbooks "on reserve" so they can be loaned for a couple hours at a time by their students. Those few hours should be enough to take pictures or scan pages of the chapters that you need. Some libraries also have access to more than one college catalog and can retrieve the books you need from other libraries in the area if your own library is out of them.

3.  **Search prices using textbook price comparison sites and apps.**
    Instead of checking every listing that comes up in a Google search, use textbook price comparison sites like Campusbooks.com. These

websites can help you compare prices for different formats and options (e-book, renting, etc.) for your textbook. A new textbook might set you back $134 on average, while the same one bought used from a reseller might be closer to $56, the Student PIRGs study found.

4. **Consider online textbook subscriptions and rentals.**
Some companies offer a subscription service to online materials. Cengage, for instance, offers year-long unlimited access to its digital library for only $179.99. Chegg is another platform that offers students affordable e-book prices, rentals, and online learning services. Some libraries are more limited than others, so search their catalogs for books you need before subscribing.

*Jessica Reyes graduated with a B.A. in English Writing from the University of Pittsburgh but considers herself an adventurer first and writer second.*

I WAS WORRIED I WOULDN'T BE ABLE TO AFFORD A LAPTOP with all the specs I needed for class, since I pay for college completely on my own. My adviser directed me to the financial aid department, which loans out laptops for free to students who either automatically qualify for one based on their financial needs or can apply for one. Score.
—ANONYMOUS
NORTHWESTERN UNIVERSITY, GRADUATE

BRING SOMETHING THAT YOU USE OR DO CONSISTENTLY AT HOME. Skating has always been my rock. I feel the same on my board no matter where I am. It centers me. There's something really nice about that. I ended up using my skateboard a lot more than I thought I would my freshman year. It helped bridge the gap between home and college, especially when I was homesick.
—OLIVER MENKEN
TUFTS UNIVERSITY, SOPHOMORE

**MY PLANNER.** I didn't use one in high school. But when I got to college, I had so much going on that I couldn't afford NOT to use one. With all the deadlines for papers, applications and tests, no one can keep everything straight in their head. So, to encourage myself to stay organized, I bought a cute, visually appealing planner/calendar that I would want to write in. It is my life! From dates for schoolwork, to clubs, to social activities and even just little notes to myself about things I need to remember.
—*MERELISE HARTE ROUZER*
*GEORGIA INSTITUTE OF TECHNOLOGY, SOPHOMORE*

**AIR FRESHENERS;** you can make your dingy room smell like apples and cinnamon. When I got to my dorm room it smelled like sweat and smelly socks. Most first-year dorms don't have air conditioning, so be prepared and bring something that smells good.
—*Y.H.*
*UNIVERSITY OF VIRGINIA, JUNIOR*

# 5 BACKPACKS THAT SAY, "I WILL PROTECT MY VIRGINITY AT ALL COSTS"

1. The Strap Trapper (featuring four front straps)
2. The Cargo Shorts Backpack (with 100 khaki pockets)
3. The One with "Finding Nemo" on it
4. The Adult Sippy Cup (with a storage unit and straw for easy access juice)
5. The Giant Turtle Shell (huge, for all your books, you nerd!)

*Val Bodurtha is a Chicago-based writer and comedian.*

**A NICE WATERPROOF BOOK BAG.** If it rains, your books get wet and there's not a lot you can do to fix them. It hurts the sell-back value, too.
—*B.M.*
*UNIVERSITY OF MARYLAND, JUNIOR*

• • • • • • • •

**GET A KICKASS MOUNTAIN BIKE** to ride between classes – and an even more kick-ass lock.
—*J.G.*
*FLORIDA STATE UNIVERSITY, GRADUATE*

• • • • • • • •

**A GUITAR.** It's something that relaxes me, and it helps socially. You can always pull out your guitar and play on the lawn or wherever, and other people will come up and talk.
—*LEAH PRICE*
*GEORGETOWN UNIVERSITY, SOPHOMORE*

• • • • • • • • •

**GET A FRISBEE.** It will help get you out and hanging out with other people. And that is a great way to find out where people are living and what classes they are taking.
—*DAVID*
*KEAN UNIVERSITY, JUNIOR*

• • • • • • • •

**A MECHANICAL PENCIL WITH A BIG ERASER.** If you're like me and you'd rather pay attention in class than do a bunch of reading, a good mechanical pencil is great for taking clean, concise notes.
—*J.S.*
*UNIVERSITY OF GEORGIA, GRADUATE*

• • • • • • • •

**A TENNIS BALL.** It's great to toss around the lounge and in the hallway, and it is a great conversation starter. As you throw the ball around, people come in to toss and the camaraderie begins.
—*DAVE BANVILLE*
*AMERICAN UNIVERSITY, GRADUATE*

# PEACE OF MIND AT A SMALL PRICE

All your life you've relied on the comfortable security of home, but now you're leaving the nest. Most schools do a fine job protecting their students from danger, but sometimes criminals sneak through the cracks of the best defenses. The good news? Simple devices can help keep you and your things safe from campus prowling lowlifes. Bonus: these are all items that'd be easy to convince your worried parents to buy for you.

**Vigilant 130dB Personal Alarm**                 **Approx. cost: $15**
This frighteningly powerful little alarm is cleverly disguised as a car fob and clips on to a keychain. At the touch of a button, this deceptively small and humble device unleashes a deafening 130 dB alarm. That's the equivalent of a military jet taking off an aircraft carrier from 50 feet. Plenty loud to scare off attackers who still have their hearing.

**BlingSting Pepper Spray**                 **Approx. cost: $20**
If you've been reluctant to add pepper spray to your keychain because it's not cute and sparkly, you're now out of excuses. This bedazzled can of pepper spray will WOW the average observer and scare the hell out of any would-be attacker. This ingenious bit of chemical warfare can stun any-sized bad guy long enough to make a getaway. Just check the laws where you live before buying.

**SentrySafe Security Safe, 0.31 Cubic Feet,  X031 Approx. cost: $55**
No matter how cool your random roommate or suitemates seem during the first month of school, you would be wise to acknowledge the possibility that they might have sticky fingers or harbor some Marxist notions about personal property. You probably haven't yet acquired a mountain of gold bars or similar treasure, but you might have some cash (remember that?) lying around for emergencies and maybe prescription meds that ought to be stashed for safekeeping. A small safe might be just the solution. This model comes with keys and can be bolted in to keep someone from swiping the whole thing. Other safes are available that simply require a combination.

**Home Dictionary Diversion Metal Safe Lock    Approx. cost: $15**
Do you like the idea of having a place to lockup your valuables, but
afraid the big black safe might come across as a little paranoid or
shady to your new friends? If so, this sneaky thing is just the safe for
you. Disguised on the outside as a dictionary, with room inside to stash
valuables, the safe comes with a key and, with any luck, it'll blend right
in on the shelf with all your other books, *assuming you have books*.
The only way you'd be found out is if someone went to borrow your
dictionary – but who uses a hard dictionary anymore anyways? Don't
be the weirdo with the safe. Be the weirdo with the dictionary!

**FEENM Door Stop Alarm, Set of 3    Approx. cost: $14**
Suspicious that a roommate is tiptoeing into your room to steal your
cash or toothpaste? Don't trust the old dorm room locks? Ease your
paranoia with these doorstop alarms, primed to blare at a volume of
120 dB – that's equivalent to a chainsaw. Perpetrators who sneak into
your room will now wake up the whole floor.

**Kryptonite 2079 Heavy Duty Bicycle U Lock
w/ 4' KryptoFlex Double Loop Bike Cable    Approx. cost: $58**
The sad truth is – if you leave your bike unlocked on campus, your
bike will get stolen. The sadder truth is – if you use a low-quality lock
or don't use it correctly, your bike will get stolen. The college campus
is heaven on earth for bike thieves. Some locks are better than others,
and good ones are a decent investment. According to the product
reviewers at Wirecutter, this lock is the only one in its price range that
can withstand anything but noisy power tools.

**Kensington Cable Lock    Approx. cost: $18 to $30**
At this stage of life, your laptop may be your most valuable possession.
You may not know this, but most of them come with a Kensington
security slot. Take advantage of it with this ultra-durable cable that
secures to a stationary object and locks into your laptop with a four-
digit code. It's like a bike lock for your computer. If you have a fancy
new laptop that's eliminated ports of any kind, they sell adaptors that
can stick to any device.

*Anthony Wallace is a Phoenix-based writer and thinker.*

**A BOX FAN** of reasonable torque and a bath towel, preferably damp. The fan directed out the dorm window was to create an exhaust vacuum effect while the damp towel, covering the gap at the foot of the door, prevented the escape of any extraneous, ahem, smoke.
> —*A.D.*
> *UNIVERSITY OF NEW HAMPSHIRE*

> " Communal showers are gross, so bring shower shoes. Everybody wears them, except my roommate. But at least she took showers! "
> —*SIERRA*
> *CALIFORNIA POLYTECHNIC STATE UNIVERSITY AT SAN LUIS OBISPO, JUNIOR*

**A NICE TOWEL IS REALLY IMPORTANT.** People see you in your towel and you need to look good. Douglas Adams said the towel is the most important piece of equipment in the universe, because you can do so much with it.
> —*TIM JOYCE*
> *GEORGETOWN UNIVERSITY, SENIOR*

**A FOLD-OUT CHAIR.** Visitors will constantly be stopping by your dorm room. Plus, the chair can double as seating for a tailgate!
> —*LINDSEY WILLIAMSON*
> *VANDERBILT UNIVERSITY, GRADUATE*

**BANISH TUMBLR POSTS AND THE TEEN POTTERY BARN CATALOGUE FROM YOUR DECORATING PLANS.** Guys don't do this so much. But I swear, I walk into so many girls' dorm rooms that look exactly the same. They have the wall covered with photos of high school parties, Christmas lights strung up, white furry pillows and white furry rugs. It basically says nothing about you other than the fact that you aren't confident enough to create a space of your own.
—*ANONYMOUS*
*DARTMOUTH COLLEGE*

Stuffed animals...I brought mine!
—*CATHERINE G. BARRETT*
*BRYN MAWR COLLEGE,*
*SOPHOMORE*

. . . . . . . .

**ALL THOSE POSTERS YOU THINK YOU WANNA BRING** for freshman year? Burn them. Don't even think about it. No one cares about your Bob Marley poster. Everyone's seen a thousand of them, it's not gonna get you laid or anything. Just don't bring them. You're better off with a blank wall, buddy.
—*NAF*
*NEW YORK UNIVERSITY, GRADUATE*

. . . . . . . .

**TAKE PEPPER SPRAY OR AIR HORNS, JUST IN CASE.** In states where pepper spray is legal to purchase, you can get it on Amazon for $10 or so. It's the size of your palm and is generally on a key chain, so you can carry it anywhere. Just make sure you don't get anything military grade since that's illegal.

If you prefer air horns, you can usually get small ones to put in your purse. All you have to do is press on it and it makes a really loud sound. If someone creepy comes up and tries to harass you and you need a quick getaway, it's a great thing to have, point it toward their ear, press on it quick and just run. The sound is so loud, it will disarm them.
—*SHARMAINE*
*UNIVERSITY OF NEW MEXICO, GRADUATE*

# KILLER PACKING LIST

By all means, take all your favorite clothes and shoes with you to school, from those lived-in jeans to your comfiest sweats. But here's a list of other easy-to-forget extras that you might also want to toss in to your suitcase or send ahead.

- ☐ Detergent and fabric softener
- ☐ Laundry basket, hamper, or bag
- ☐ Shower caddy
- ☐ Shower shoes
- ☐ Robe
- ☐ First-aid kit that includes a thermometer, ace bandage and reusable gel pack for your fridge and contact info for your doctor back home
- ☐ Sewing kit
- ☐ Small toolkit
- ☐ Hangers
- ☐ Extra-long sheets
- ☐ Pillow and favorite comforter
- ☐ Towels
- ☐ Batteries
- ☐ Cell phone charger
- ☐ Computer cables
- ☐ Computer printer and paper
- ☐ Desk lamp
- ☐ Electric cords
- ☐ Flashlight
- ☐ Surge protector
- ☐ Laptop lock
- ☐ Laptop
- ☐ Extra chargers and batteries for your phone
- ☐ Power strip
- ☐ Small fan
- ☐ Cup, bowl, plate, silverware
- ☐ Can opener
- ☐ Microwave
- ☐ Mini-reading light
- ☐ Egg-crate mattress pad
- ☐ Tupperware
- ☐ Snacks
- ☐ Acetaminophen, aspirin, ibuprofen
- ☐ Band-Aids, Neosporin
- ☐ Condoms and other contraceptives
- ☐ Brush and comb
- ☐ Cough drops
- ☐ Dental floss
- ☐ Hair dryer
- ☐ Hairstyling products
- ☐ Lotion/moisturizer
- ☐ Nail clippers, tweezers
- ☐ Pepto-Bismol, Benadryl
- ☐ Razors, shaving cream, aftershave
- ☐ Shampoo, conditioner
- ☐ Soap, antiseptic wipes
- ☐ Toothbrush and toothpaste
- ☐ Vitamins
- ☐ Mechanical alarm clock
- ☐ Ziploc bags, especially small snack-sized ones for dining hall leftovers

- ☐ Electric kettle and a small hand-powered frother (think of all the money you will save by staying out of overpriced coffee shops)
- ☐ Laundry marker, to put your name on everything you bring, or else you'll be dressing your entire dorm
- ☐ Instant coffee, packets of cocoa, powdered milk, power bars and microwave popcorn
- ☐ Mini-fridge for drinks and snacks. (You may be able to rent one, once you are on campus.)
- ☐ Lamps that help you work and sleep. (They are likely to be more expensive if bought from the university store.)
- ☐ Envelopes and stamps
- ☐ Stapler and binder clips
- ☐ Scotch tape and duct tape
- ☐ 3M Command tape or double-sided tape to mount things, if your school does not allow nails
- ☐ Hooks for a robe and coat
- ☐ Corkboard for the space above desk plus pushpins
- ☐ Small whiteboard that can be hung on your door for messages, plus markers

- ☐ Ear buds and noise-cancellation headphones if you have them
- ☐ Drinking straws if you are the kind of kid who still needs them even though they are being phased out.
- ☐ Battery-powered votives if you really can't leave your candles behind.
- ☐ Eye mask that might help you sleep if you turn in before your roommate
- ☐ A raincoat or rain poncho, and small umbrella
- ☐ Boots for rain and snow
- ☐ A spare winter coat, if you can swing it, in case your coat goes missing. Many do.
- ☐ A deck of cards and some favorite board games like Boggle, Scrabble, MadLibs, Scattergories, Cards Against Humanity, Werewolf and CodeNames.
- ☐ Frisbee – easiest way to meet people when you arrive
- ☐ Long underwear or thermal skiwear for those really cold days. Really.
- ☐ Key chain for your new room key and mailbox

# AND DON'T FORGET THE INTANGIBLES...

**BRING GOOD JUDGMENT.** Having good judgment will help freshmen start off in the right direction.
> —*KAMALI BENT*
> *CORNELL UNIVERSITY, GRADUATE*

• • • • • • • • •

**A SENSE OF SELF:** You always have to see where you are and where you want to be in the future. It's something that's always changing.
> —*RUTHANN*
> *MOUNT HOLYOKE COLLEGE, GRADUATE*

• • • • • • • • •

**FRESHMEN SHOULD TAKE** a blank slate with them to college; a fresh and clean start. If they did poorly in high school or were nerds, college is the time to change all of that. In college, you determine your future.
> —*VIVIAN ORIAKU*
> *UNIVERSITY OF MIAMI, GRADUATE*

• • • • • • • • •

**IF I COULD BRING ONE THING** to college, it would be maturity. But I suppose that's what college is all about...living and learning!
> —*ANONYMOUS*
> *INDIANA UNIVERSITY, GRADUATE*

• • • • • • • • •

**FRESHMEN SHOULD BRING** a plan for the future and a positive attitude with them to college. And ... stunna shades! LOL.
> —*SHAQUEENA LE'SHAYE LEWIS*
> *UNIVERSITY OF MIAMI, GRADUATE*

• • • • • • • • •

**PATIENCE IS ABSOLUTELY KEY.** You will undoubtedly be faced with a variety of people, classes, rules and requirements over the four years of college that will test your patience, so starting off with a healthy dose is good.
> —*REBECCA*
> *HUNTER COLLEGE, SENIOR*

**BRING A SHOWER SPEAKER.** A lot of people would try to use their phones to play music on the other side of the door and it's kind of sketchy. It's all about learning to be comfortable in your private space. For your whole life, you've had the luxurious privacy that comes with living in your parents' house and now you have to shower around 50 people. Ignore all the unspoken social boundaries and just bring your speaker, play it loud, and be comfortable.
—*MEGHAN WALLACE*
    *NORTHERN ARIZONA UNIVERSITY, SENIOR*

**A TRUNKFUL OF COMFORT.** There are many things to fill your old leather trunk with before heading off to college. Comfortable bedding is a must. A soft comforter and a substantial pillow will make your dreams of calculus and Shakespeare that much sweeter. A microwave, some Pyrex, and a few packets of cocoa will help to make cold winter study sessions more bearable. Moreover, a rug or two can help to add a bit of warmth to a dorm room. The greatest things to bring to college, however, won't fit in your trunk. These are things like self-confidence, composure, and respect. Don't be afraid to stick to your guns, hold your morals, and be yourself. College can be a time of becoming someone new, for sure, but that doesn't mean you have to become someone else. If you have respect for yourself, people will have respect for you. Respect for others is also essential.
—*DREW HILL*
    *COLBY COLLEGE, JUNIOR*

Bring your mom's credit card.
—*J.G.*
    *GEORGE WASHINGTON UNIVERSITY, SENIOR*

**A HOT POT.** I hated the food at my college, so every other meal I made Oodles of Noodles. You can make tea, coffee, soup – anything, really – in a Hot Pot.
—*ALYSSA*
    *JAMES MADISON UNIVERSITY, SOPHOMORE*

**BRING A FULL-LENGTH MIRROR.** I think a lot of people just assume it's something that comes on the backs of most bedroom doors. I picked mine up at Target and it came with something that let me hang it really easily. Everyone was always coming into my room to check themselves out. It actually helped make my room a bit of a gathering place.
—*ZOE*
*JOHNS HOPKINS, GRADUATE*

· · · · · · · · ·

**IF YOU'RE MOVING TO A COLD CLIMATE, BRING A SEASONAL AFFECTIVE DISORDER LAMP** and keep yourself busy and active with schoolwork and working out. Coming from Arizona, I was not prepared for the weather in Chicago. From November to the last week of school it was very gloomy, grey, cloudy, windy, rainy, snowy almost every day. It was definitely a shock. When it gets cold out, a lot of people just drink, and it can be depressing.
—*ANONYMOUS*
*LOYOLA UNIVERSITY IN CHICAGO, SOPHOMORE*

· · · · · · · · ·

**BRING AN UMBRELLA.** Yes, it rains at college, too.
—*PHIL*
*UNIVERSITY OF VIRGINIA, SENIOR*

· · · · · · · · ·

**ORANGE-FLAVORED GATORADE.** More Gatorade is consumed to relieve hangovers than while playing any sport. And stay with orange, because red can stain when it comes back up.
—*ANONYMOUS*
*UNIVERSITY OF FLORIDA, GRADUATE*

· · · · · · · · ·

**A GEORGE FOREMAN GRILL.** Those grills are so fast and easy, and everything is pretty good, from steak to grilled cheese. No college kid should be without one.
—*JEFF*
*BOWLING GREEN STATE UNIVERSITY, GRADUATE*

# SHIP, DON'T SHLEP

What comes to mind when you think of move-in day? Cramming all of your belongings into oversized suitcases? Stuffing the back of your car until you can't see out the rearview mirror while you drive? The stress and anxiety of last-minute shopping?

Well, what if we told you that it didn't have to be this way?

Lucky for you, there are many stores including Bed Bath & Beyond that have come up with ways to make life easier.

Bed Bath & Beyond's Pack and Hold program is simple. All you have to do is go to your local store and choose all the items you need for your dorm. The chain can even provide recommendations on what to bring and what to leave home, tailored around your particular school's requirements. Then, the store will ship everything on your list to the branch closest to your school to be picked up at your convenience.

Bed Bath & Beyond also offers plenty of student discounts, but don't forget to look out for store coupons to save even more on your purchases.

Many other companies like Pottery Barn and its corporate sibling, Williams-Sonoma, are also beginning to provide this Ship-to-Store type service. They vow to "make the move easier" by letting you pick up orders placed online at one of their catalogues at the brick-and-mortar store nearest your destination.

Pottery Barn will also add a monogram or Greek Letters to your belongings, if you want to personalize them. Enter your school email address to get 15 percent off the purchase.

Target has also piloted a similar program that allows college students to order items online that can be picked up later at stores near campus. In select cities, you can even sign up for a Shipt membership, which costs $99 a year or $14 per month. Then, seven days a week, excluding holidays, during Target's store hours, you can order anything you want and it will be brought to your dorm.

Between new student orientation, saying goodbye to family and making new friends — you already have plenty to worry about during your first few days of college. Moving in and outfitting your dorm doesn't have to be one of them.

*Catherine Oriel is a student journalist at George Washington University in Washington, D.C. who is originally from Los Angeles, California. She stuffed all of her belongings into nine suitcases and found move-in day extremely stressful.*

# WHAT NOT TO BRING

**DORMS ARE SMALL. ESPECIALLY AS A FRESHMAN.** Don't buy too much stuff.
The checklists at stores like Target and Bed Bath & Beyond are
a good start, but you don't want to overbuy. Laundry turns into a
pain pretty quickly when you're on your own, so a lot of socks and
underwear will make your life a lot happier.
    —*MICHAEL CUMMO*
     *BOSTON UNIVERSITY, SENIOR*

**I JUST DIDN'T KNOW WHAT TO BRING,** so I kept packing
every little thing I might need or want to have with
me. I would have brought my bathroom and bed,
too! When I got to school I had no place to put
anything. I ended up bringing back as much stuff as I
could each time I went home. After break, I came
back up with only the things I really needed.
    —*ILANA COOPERSMITH*
     *RUTGERS UNIVERSITY, GRADUATE*

**DON'T BRING YOUR HIGH SCHOOL YEARBOOK** with you.
Yes, I missed high school but I was so busy
that I did not even open the book. It is a
major dust collector.
    —*DAVID*
     *KEAN UNIVERSITY, JUNIOR*

**DON'T BE THE ONLY PERSON IN YOUR DORM** with a car,
and if you are, don't let other people borrow it.
If you do, there will be trouble.
    —*HANNAH*
     *EMORY UNIVERSITY, JUNIOR*

# TOP 5 THINGS TO LEAVE BEHIND

1. **Your childhood trophies,** merit badges or anything else that screams that you were popular in high school.
2. **Your jewelry collection:** You don't need it all, and you definitely don't need the stress of making sure it doesn't get stolen.
3. **That big wall hanging displaying the family crest** and your favorite pair of Nantucket-red trousers.
4. **Candles of any kind, incense and lighters:** They're against the rules. Don't go down in history as "that *@#%& freshman who burned down our dorm." Besides, you can buy electric candles nowadays for those special occasions when mood lighting is in order.

5. **Your pink Easy-Bake Oven** from childhood. Fun, yes, but you won't have the room.

**FIGURE OUT IN ADVANCE WHERE YOU'LL BE FILLING YOUR PRESCRIPTIONS.** My doctor warned me that if I mail-ordered my Adderall, my meds could get stolen. Then, it turned out that the CVS closest to campus didn't have a pharmacy. I actually have to drive to a CVS to get my drugs. That would be a problem if I didn't have a car. Also, it's not paranoid to lock up your meds. I've seen kids pick up weed and pills from other people's desks in their room. What's to stop them from taking your Adderall? This is especially true on really social floors where people are walking in and out of dorm rooms all the time. I bought a lockable little safe on Amazon that looks like a book and I keep it on my shelf. It was 10 bucks and worth it.
> —ANONYMOUS
> SYRACUSE UNIVERSITY, SOPHOMORE

# CLASSIC ROCK 101

The music we listen to in college is the stuff we hold on to for life. What will the soundtrack of this four years of your life sound like? You'd better pick carefully. This is the music that your kids will associate with you, the music that will determine your definition of 'good music', the music that you will revere as sacred as you grumpily proclaim, "they don't make music like they used to!"

There's good reason to be familiar with the culturally approved canon of musical greatness. Music can be enlightening. Sociology class might give you some alarming glimpse into how poor Compton, Ca. is, but it's never going to make you *feel* what it's really like to live in that world like Kendrick Lamar's *Good Kid M.A.A.D. City* can.

Music can be moving. It can give you feelings you didn't even know you possessed. People don't love Pink Floyd's *Dark Side of the Moon* because music writers decided it was important. They love it because it's blown their mind -- an invaluable process of expansion and growth.

Music can be bonding. A basic awareness of and appreciation for the most universally revered records will not only make you wiser and more culturally aware. It'll give you something to talk about. When you inevitably see a Kurt Cobain poster on a dorm room wall, it can be taken as a tribal marking, a warm welcome to fellow Nirvana fans, and an invitation to throw on *Nevermind* and excitedly discuss the legend.

But don't freak out, music is for fun, too. It's for passing the time, putting you to sleep, waking you up, informing your crush of your feelings and consoling you when they're not reciprocated. It's for finding your friends, your heroes, your ideals, and your conception of beauty. Music permeates all those moments we find genuinely important and fulfilling. As with friends, you can't choose the music you love; it kind of chooses you. And as with friends, the music you love, especially at this time, has a massive impact on whom you become, what you prioritize, and how you fundamentally see the world. All you can do is open your mind and try it all.

Here is a decidedly non-exhaustive list of 25 albums, in no particular order, that have stood the test of time and earned a reputation as quintessentially "collegiate." Their impact and lessons are indispensable, as important as any you will learn in a classroom. Give them a shot. They've shaped your parents, professors, older siblings, favorite musicians, and future bosses before you. They could change your life, too.

Radiohead, *OK Computer*
The Beatles, *Magical Mystery Tour*
Pink Floyd, *The Dark Side of the Moon*
Bruce Springsteen, *Born to Run*
Kendrick Lamar, *Good Kid M.A.A.D. City*
Nirvana, *Nevermind*
Johnny Cash, *Live at Folsom Prison*
2Pac, *Me Against the World*
The Strokes, *Is This It*
Amy Winehouse, *Back to Black*
Beach Boys, *Pet Sounds*
Bob Marley, *Exodus*
Paul Simon, *Graceland*

Brian Eno, *Apollo*
Grateful Dead, *Europe '72 Live*
Bon Iver, *22 A Million*
The Flaming Lips, *Yoshimi Battles the Pink Robots*
Kanye West, *My Beautiful Dark Twisted Fantasy*
Rolling Stones, *Exile on Main St.*
Joni Mitchell, *Blue*
Alanis Morissette, *Jagged Little Pill*
Ms. Lauryn Hill, *The Miseducation of Lauryn Hill*
Cocteau Twins, *Heaven or Las Vegas*
Prince, *Purple Rain*
Bob Dylan, *Highway 61 Revisited*

*Anthony Wallace is a Phoenix-based writer and thinker.*

**A CLIP-ON READING LAMP.** Or just a light you can shut off from your bed.
> —AMANDA
> WELLESLEY COLLEGE, SENIOR

• • • • • • • •

**DO NOT BUY A TRASHCAN WITH A LID,** because once it is full you will turn it into a table. You may think you're better than that now, but so did I.
> —BARRY LANGER
> OGLETHORPE UNIVERSITY, JUNIOR

• • • • • • • •

**HAVING A FRIDGE** was really nice, and if you're a coffee person, a coffee maker makes life much easier. Also, I'm very glad I didn't have a game console freshman year as it forced me out of my room and to be more social.
> —CONOR MCGEEHAN
> NORTHWESTERN UNIVERSITY, SENIOR

• • • • • • • •

**MAKE SURE TO TALK TO YOUR ROOMMATE** to see what you need to bring and what you don't. I talked to my roommate before I moved in but we did not discuss everything and ended up having doubles of some things, and then there were many things we forgot to bring so we had to go out and buy them. And, get a rug – it's a good investment for a dorm. The floors are usually dirty and a rug at least looks cleaner.
> —E.M.G.
> UNIVERSITY OF SOUTH FLORIDA, JUNIOR

**Underwear.**
> —WALTER
> UNIVERSITY OF
> MARYLAND–COLLEGE
> PARK, SOPHOMORE

• • • • • • • •

**I GOT A LIST FROM THE UNIVERSITY** on what to – and what not to – bring with me. If your college or university offers something like this, make sure you use it.
> —DAVID
> KEAN UNIVERSITY, JUNIOR

I CAME HERE WITH MY DAD'S STATION WAGON and a minivan filled with my stuff. About a week ago, my parents came back and we packed the station wagon back up and sent stuff back home. It was too much. I brought my notes from my classes in high school. I brought my books from home. I didn't even want to look at a book or notes unless it was from a current class.
—*H.D. BALLARD*
  *UNIVERSITY OF VIRGINIA, FRESHMAN*

KNOW YOUR SPACE before you pack up and arrive. One family came with a U-Haul full of stuff – a bed, desk, everything—and saw there was no room for any of it. They turned around and drove it right back home.
—*TOM SABRAM*
  *CARNEGIE MELLON UNIVERSITY, SOPHOMORE*

I WOULD DEFINITELY BRING THAT ONE DVD OR BOOK that you can't live without. Last semester was pretty stressful and being able to curl under the blankets and marathon a favorite show from high school probably kept me from burning all of my papers in a manic bonfire. It sounds silly, but grab onto that DVD or book like it's a lifeboat, because it very well may be (not to be overly dramatic or anything.) Plus you can lend it to friends if you want to let them have access to a part of your brain.

Also, socks. You can never have enough socks.
—*SHANNON KELLEY*
  *KENYON COLLEGE, JUNIOR*

"Wasn't it just last week she wanted us to get out of her life?"

# Get Set: Leaving Home – and Arranging Accommodations

*L*eaving home – what a daunting concept: that epic moment when young ones leave home and finally must fend for themselves. Rest assured, almost no one manages to get from home to college with perfect dignity and grace, and departing for school is never as bad, nor as easy, as you think. As the big day approaches, stay busy, savor the time you have left with friends and family, and enjoy the present instead of just worrying about the future.

If all else fails, watch Planet Earth. It's full of inspiring displays of newly grown beings getting their first exhilarating taste of independence. Sure, you might return home for short roosts over the holidays, and maybe some longer stays after graduation. But for now, you are leaving, and that's a big deal.

**DON'T FREAK OUT ABOUT** saying goodbye. Keep in mind that you will see them again soon, probably in just a few months. You can call, email, write, and get care packages to stay in touch.
— *ELIZABETH*
   *CORNELL COLLEGE, FRESHMAN*

**SAY GOODBYE, KISS THEM, AND MAKE THEM DRIVE AWAY QUICKLY.**
—*C.H.*
   *UNIVERSITY OF VIRGINIA, FRESHMAN*

**HEADLINES**

- Leaving home is harder than you think.
- Say goodbye to parents, siblings and pets quickly – it will be easier on all of you.
- Once you adjust to the shock of being away from home, you'll have a great time.
- It can be harder to leave your friends than your family – you know you'll see your family again.

**A FEW DAYS AFTER MY DAD DROPPED ME OFF** at college, I found out that he had mailed me a letter telling me everything that I'm assuming that most parents tell their children when they leave them at college. It was really nice because I now have a physical reminder of my dad, in his handwriting, and it let him give me advice without the drama of the big college good-bye.
    —*LIZZIE*
    *BOWDOIN COLLEGE, FRESHMAN*

• • • • • • • •

**LEAVING HOME IS ALL ABOUT** you and your parents each having more sex, more frequently and more easily. C'mon – the 'rents act all weepy to see their little chick flying the coop, when in reality they can't wait to turn their bedroom into a steamy den of *coitus parentalis*. And you feign maturity, eager to take on the responsibilities of living on your own and furthering your education, when in reality you are ecstatic that at the end of a night, instead of having to do it in the back of your car in the school parking lot, you can finally take a special someone home to the (relative) privacy of your dorm room.
    —*JOHN*
    *UNIVERSITY OF WISCONSIN AT MADISON, GRADUATE*

**LEAVING FAMILY IS A BIG ADJUSTMENT.** I got lonely my first year and my parents were pretty strict about keeping me at school until I got over it. It was very hard but I grew from it. When I joined the football team, they came up for games, which was great. But the way I fought it mostly was by keeping busy; that's the best way. It's still hard.
—*R.S.*
*CARNEGIE MELLON UNIVERSITY, JUNIOR*

. . . . . . . .

" I was expecting my mom to be sadder. She was like, "All right, see ya." I was like, "Is that it? That's all I get?" But I was the third one to get dropped off. They were sad the first time. "
—*M.A.S.*
*UNIVERSITY OF VIRGINIA, GRADUATE*

. . . . . . . .

**I LEFT GUAM AND FLEW** to Georgia by myself and stayed with my extended family before school started. It was tough leaving my family, and there definitely were tears and lots of hugs. Saying goodbye to your parents is going to be tough no matter what, especially if you are close to your family. But before leaving home, it's important to be open with your parents and let them know how much you'll miss them, and how often you plan to call them. It's a tough time for them, too.
—*MICHELLE*
*EMORY UNIVERSITY, SENIOR*

ONLY TWO MORE FLIGHTS!

**I THOUGHT I WAS GOING TO HATE COLLEGE.** My parents dropped me off my first day and were leaving me there, and I looked at them and said, "I don't think this is going to work out. Can I just come back to the hotel with you guys?" They were just like, "Nope, sorry." My mom got in the car and started crying. And my dad was like, "She'll figure it out." I stayed and I ended up having a great time in school.

    —J. DEVEREUX
       GEORGETOWN UNIVERSITY, GRADUATE

● ● ● ● ● ● ● ●

**WHEN MY PARENTS MOVED** me to college, the dorm didn't have elevators, so they helped me carry my stuff up four floors. After that, we went back to the hotel where they were staying and I burst into tears. I said, "Please take me with you. I want to go home. I'll go to school there." My dad looked at me and said, "I would take you, but I just moved all of your stuff up four flights of stairs. Stay a semester and then see what you think." That was great advice.

    —ERIN
       CENTRAL BIBLE COLLEGE, GRADUATE

● ● ● ● ● ● ● ●

SORRY!

**DON'T BE AFRAID TO LEAVE HOME,** no matter what. When it was time for me to start college, leaving my mom while she was fighting breast cancer was one of the hardest things I ever had to do. But if I had stayed home, I wouldn't have met my husband, whom I am still gaga over after six years of courtship and three years of marriage. And Mom was the prettiest breast cancer survivor and mother of the bride ever.

    —ERICA LANGE-HENNESEY
       TEXAS STATE UNIVERSITY, SENIOR

**IT'S OKAY TO CRY.** As an only child who is very close to my parents and extended family, I was totally terrified when I moved to college! I acted tough, but when my parents left me at the top of the Jackrabbit Den stairs, I bawled like a baby. I don't care if you are a boy, girl, only child, or you have 15 siblings – it's okay to cry. It's a scary time, and it's okay to let your emotions out every once in a while.

> —*ABBY*
> *SOUTH DAKOTA STATE UNIVERSITY, SENIOR*

· · · · · · · ·

**SOMETIMES, THE ANTICIPATION** of the good-bye is more painful than the real thing! As someone very close to my parents, I had a pit in my stomach at the thought of saying goodbye to mom and dad. But once they left, and I ran off to the next orientation activity, I felt as though a weight had been lifted off my shoulders. That being said – don't make a big deal of saying goodbye and make sure you have plans for right after.

> —*STEPHANIE DREIFUSS*
> *DUKE UNIVERSITY, SENIOR*

· · · · · · · ·

**LIVING WITHOUT YOUR PARENTS** for the first time is a bigger deal than many of us want to admit. For the first few days after they dropped me off at the dorms, I called them every day, just to make sure everything was going smoothly at home since my departure. After I got settled in, the phone calls reduced to a couple a week. Maintaining a close relationship with your parents is vital to succeeding freshman year. You're going to experience a lot of ups and downs, and it's always nice to have your parents' support through the good and the bad.

> —*ILAN GLUCK*
> *UNIVERSITY OF MARYLAND, JUNIOR*

**MAKE SURE YOUR COMPUTER IS WORKING REALLY WELL BEFORE YOU LEAVE.** Get rid of unnecessary junk on it, and if yours is on its last legs, think about getting a new one. (A lot of schools offer good deals on them.) Then treat it like a serious tool and think twice about what you're putting on it. My computer ended up crashing the first day of school.
—*OLIVER MENKEN*
*TUFTS UNIVERSITY, SOPHOMORE*

. . . . . . . .

**SAYING GOODBYE TO MY PARENTS** was really hard. My mom, dad and sister brought me up to school and we all spent the day setting up my dorm room and decorating it. At the University of Michigan, we have a new student ceremony that all new students go to. I went with my hall and by the time I came back, my parents were gone. We had said goodbye before I left for the ceremony, but it really set in when I came back and they weren't there. My sister left me a really cute note about how she was going to miss me and I could come home soon. That's when the tears started.

Being sad about your parents leaving is totally natural. I think many students have a lonely feeling the first couple of hours after they leave, but do something to get your mind off of it. Open your door and keep setting up your room. Wander down your hall to see if anyone needs help, or call someone you know. The feeling will pass really quickly and you will get into the groove of your new college life.
—*ANNIE THOMAS*
*UNIVERSITY OF MICHIGAN, SENIOR*

# LEARNING TO COPE, EVEN BEFORE YOU LEAVE

Starting college can be an exhilarating experience. At the same time, it can be anxiety-provoking to leave behind a familiar high school and old friends for a new school setting where you hardly know anyone. The good news is there are quite a few things you can do in advance to limit or handle these feelings and challenges:

- Life Skills: This may sound simple or even silly, but living on your own for the first time can present you with a lot of challenges if you are not prepared. Making sure you are comfortable managing your eating, sleep, basic health needs, time and money can go a long way. Even knowing how to do your laundry can make it easier for you in the transition. These are all things you can learn to do before you leave.
- Make a connection: Many schools share contact information for roommates before you come to campus. Get in touch and get acquainted. If you are not dorming, but receive information about an academic adviser or peer mentor, reach out to them as well to say 'hi' before you arrive. They will be a ready-made connection once you arrive.
- Have a conversation in advance with your friends and family about how you plan to keep in contact. You'll probably want to be in more frequent touch when you first get to campus, and you should need this less as you begin to settle in.
- Make your new home familiar and comfortable: bring familiar posters or linens (a teddy bear or favorite toy is okay, too) – anything to make your dorm homier when you move in.
- Familiarize yourself with campus resources using the college website: Learn, for instance, where freshmen live in relation to the rest of campus. Also, find out where you'll be having class and where the gym, health service, counseling services, library, dining halls and advising office all reside.

*Dr. Victor Schwartz is the chief medical officer of The Jed Foundation, which works to support mental health in teens and young adults and helps prepare teens for college.*

# PLANNING FOR ONGOING CARE

It is not unusual for young people to have medical or mental health problems in high school that may require continuing care in college. If this applies to you, here are some things to consider:

*What care can your college be counted on to provide?*

Many colleges provide only short-term primary care for students. To learn about the range of services at your school's health and counseling service, consult their websites. See whether you will be able to continue care with clinicians back home (in person if you will be coming home often enough) or through a remote service such as Skype. Otherwise, you may need to find professionals in the community near your school. Also, some colleges do not have clinicians who can prescribe medications.

*What health insurance will you need?*

Most students can stay on a family health insurance plan while in college. Some have good coverage in the state where the plan is written but only limited coverage outside the plan's home state. Check your plan's coverage and also the fees for care at the college health or counseling service. Many are free for basic care but charge if your case is complicated.

Bottom line: If you have a condition that will require care as you move to college, make sure to:
- research resources at your school and in the local community before you go
- understand your insurance coverage and make sure your needs will be properly covered
- discuss with your family and home-based clinicians how ongoing care and prescriptions can be handled
- make a plan for handling crises and urgent problems that might arise.

For more info on transitioning to college, visit, https://www.settogo.org/transition-of-care-guide.

*Dr. Victor Schwartz*

# GETTING YOUR ACCOMMODATIONS IN PLACE

*Everyone has unique challenges and setbacks in life. If yours just happens to be one that requires extra help or consideration from your school, not to worry. Colleges have fielded these kinds of requests before. Universities now have whole departments dedicated to "disabilities services," whose job is helping you succeed and graduate, such as Hunter College's cleverly titled, Office of Access Ability.*

*But even in this relatively warm and welcoming environment, obtaining the specific accommodations you need can be a struggle. Push comes to shove, know this: universities are required by law to make "reasonable" accommodations for students with physical and mental infirmities, whether or not those disabilities are visible to others. So, learn your rights, and learn from the resilient souls in the following pages who fought for their rights before you.*

**CAMPUSES ARE VERY OPEN TO ACCOMMODATIONS.** If you plan to request them though, request early! There are only so many spots available. Colleges are becoming accommodating to therapy and emotional support animals, too, but not general pets. The best thing to do if you want a pet is to get a betta fish honestly.

 —MOLLY
  COLLEGE OF SOUTHERN IDAHO, GRADUATE

**YOU HAVE A <u>LEGAL</u> RIGHT TO ACCOMMODATIONS – WHY WASTE THAT?!** Be open to your school's policies, and work with the administration to find a situation that will benefit you the most. A fish can't be expected to climb a tree. So, make sure you're in a position where you can thrive and show your genius.
 —ANONYMOUS
  GEORGETOWN UNIVERSITY, JUNIOR

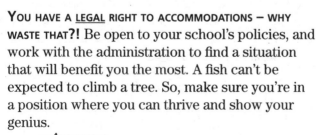

**DEAL WITH ALL THE LEGWORK AND PAPERWORK FOR ACCOMMODATIONS LONG BEFORE YOU THINK YOU NEED TO.**
I have dyslexia and got time-and-a-half for tests in high school. But when I got to college, I learned that I still had to ask the resource center to send letters to my professors about my testing needs. That ended up taking way longer than I expected. So, if you wait until one week before class to get the ball rolling, you may spend weeks in class before you get what you need. If I had known all of this, I probably would have reached out to the resource center over the summer and asked what I needed to do to make sure my accommodations were in place right when I got to school.

Also, your resource center might fully support your accommodations but that doesn't mean your professors will. Most of my professors were more than happy to give me the extra time I needed because of my dyslexia. They wanted to see me succeed. But I had a computer science teacher freshman year who was strictly by the book. I had studied really hard for a test, knew the material but still couldn't finish in the time and a half I was given. He basically told me it was my fault I didn't finish and that I should have studied harder.

After spending my childhood mortified when my mom had a problem at the cash register and asked to see the store manager, I decided to take a page out of her book. I went to student resources and told them what had happened. They went back to the professor, and I ended up getting an extra half hour and doing fine on the test.

If something is bothering you or not working for you, you can be as annoying as you want about getting the school to help you out. You're paying for your education and they should be doing what they can to make it work for you.
        —OLIVER MENKEN
         TUFTS UNIVERSITY, SOPHOMORE

**TIME-AND-A-HALF WAS KIND OF HARD FOR ME TO GET** because I had to first get tested for dyslexia and ADHD. I went to a doctor who was a specialist. He gave the school this paper saying, 'She does better when she's not anxious and can sit quietly to think.' The testing cost about $250, and we paid out-of-pocket because insurance didn't cover it. But it was so worth it. And I'm sure the school would have helped if I had asked but I didn't know at the time to ask. My kernel of advice would be, fight for yourself because no one else will.
—*LILLIE REITER*
*GUILFORD COLLEGE, GRADUATE*

**IF YOU BELIEVE YOU HAVE A SLEEPING DISORDER,** consult a sleep specialist and ask for help. I have Type 2 narcolepsy, which is known as narcolepsy without cataplexy, and I didn't find out until I fell asleep behind the wheel and totaled my car. I went to the school to ask for accommodations, so I could register earlier for classes later in the day, and they were totally helpful. All my professors have been very understanding and don't think I'm lazy if sometimes I just fall asleep. You don't realize how much it impacts your life until you get help. It's just a matter of actually talking about it and saying, maybe this isn't normal and I need accommodations to make this better for me. No one can properly help you if you don't ask.
—*KATHERINE*
*GEORGE WASHINGTON UNIVERSITY, SOPHOMORE*

**DON'T JUST MEET DEADLINES FOR ACCOMMODATIONS PAPERWORK, BEAT THEM BY A LONG SHOT.** No college professor, even if you have a disability, is going to respond well to an email from your mom asking for help because you're having a hard time. Being a good self-advocator is definitely a quality you need to have if you are going to need accommodations in college. If you don't do it for yourself, no one will.
—*ANONYMOUS*
*SYRACUSE UNIVERSITY, SOPHOMORE*

# WHAT TO DO WHEN YOUR DISABILITY IS TEMPORARY

THANKS TO A SHOULDER INJURY THAT'S COMMON AMONG FOOTBALL PLAYERS, I had to undergo surgery during Christmas break after my freshman football season was over. My shoulder had to be immobilized in a brace that wrapped around my waist and was suspended out in front of me for eight weeks. I was lucky that it wasn't my writing hand, but there was no way I could carry my bag or use my laptop to write papers. Student Services was incredibly helpful and offered the use of a special device that allowed me to use a microphone connected to my laptop and I could give my laptop commands and tell it what to type so I didn't fall behind in my homework. I still struggled sitting down at a desk, so I ended up sitting in an open chair. So, if you ever have an injury or need surgery while at college, use Student Services for help in adjusting back to class.
—LUKE
UPPER IOWA UNIVERSITY, SOPHOMORE

USE YOUR DISABILITY AS AN EXCUSE TO BUILD RELATIONSHIPS WITH PROFESSORS. On the first day of every class, I'd wait until the room had pretty much cleared out and then go up and introduce myself to the professor and talk a little about my ADHD and how it might affect me in his class. (For example, I take Adderall and it makes it very difficult for me to speak out or get cold called.) I'd go to office hours so I could get clarification on stuff I didn't pick up during lectures. I also sat right up at the front of the class. All of these things helped me academically. But they also showed my professors that, even if I did have setbacks, I really cared and was making every effort to learn. I ended up becoming very close with many – I ate dinner at their houses, babysat their kids, and did research for them. I think that if I didn't have ADHD or some other learning disability and hadn't felt compelled to reach out, I might not have bothered getting to know them. Instead of seeing my disability as a weakness, I used it as an opportunity.
—ANONYMOUS
COLBY COLLEGE, GRADUATE

# SEEING THE PERSON BEYOND THE WHEELS

AS A STUDENT WITH A DISABILITY ENTERING BROOKLYN COLLEGE AS A FRESHMAN, I experienced nervousness, anxiousness, and excitement, all at the same time. I was prepped in advance about some of the differences that would occur during the transition from high school to college, but it's another thing to actually experience them.

For starters, no more yellow buses picking you up and taking you back home throughout the week for free. I was now in charge of my own means of transportation, which, in my case, meant working with a door-to-door, paratransit service that provides transportation for individuals with disabilities.

The biggest change, though, was that I would no longer be entitled to the services of a paraprofessional – helpers who had been assigned to me throughout the school day before college. Being in a wheelchair, I found that daunting at first, but I also viewed it as a challenge, and I asked myself, "Can I be my own advocate?" As nervous as that made me, I knew that I could rise to that challenge. I also knew that it wasn't going to be easy. But as they say, the things that are worthwhile in life usually aren't.

Looking back, I'm reminded of one of my favorite quotes by Robert M. Hensel, the world record holder for the longest, continuous wheelie. He said, "There is no greater disability in society than the inability to see a person as more." Everyone at Brooklyn College whom I encountered and interacted with saw past my wheelchair, and just focused primarily on me as an individual, and that was an amazing feeling. They saw my potential, both in and out of the classroom, which has helped me in becoming the student leader that I am today.

—LEONARD BLADES
BROOKLYN COLLEGE, FRESHMAN

# HOW ONE STUDENT GOT HIS SCHOOL TO HELP

Nicholas Astor had only been a freshman for a few weeks at SUNY Purchase College in New York before the outgoing 19-year-old had put his upbeat stamp on the place.

He gets around with the help of a scooter, a walker and round-the-clock aides because of cerebral palsy. Yet, only a few weeks into college, he was busy sampling classes in politics and government in preparation for a possible career in law. He tried out new material for a comedy routine, in which he quips about the number of people it takes to get him on stage. "It's like having your own personal stalker," he joshes.

He even went on a kind of date, according to his father and #1 champion, Michael Astor. "He wants to have a girlfriend," said the father, who has his son's dry sense of humor. "And I don't know how to tell him to do it: it's hard to make the first move when you can't really move."

None of this happy tableau, however, came without a fight. Which is why college students with physical or mental infirmities who might someday need accommodations from their schools might wish to familiarize themselves with the Astors' story.

Nick, as he is known, had always been a stand-out student. Nonetheless, because of his need for round-the-clock care, someone to help him climb in and out of bed, use the bathroom and get around, Nick's father thought his son might prefer to attend college someplace near home so he could commute and sleep at home.

Nick wanted none of that. He wanted the traditional college experience of going away from home, nothing less. "I hate this stay-in-your-lane mentality," he told one news outlet.

He happily accepted an invitation to enroll at the State University of New York's campus in Purchase, N.Y. But the state-owned school did not make it easy for him to attend. Three weeks before orientation, Purchase was still refusing to assign Nick an adjoining room for the primary aide who would be accompanying him on his daily rounds. Administrators insisted that the best they could do was to allow Nick to share a one-room "double" with that aide, an arrangement that prospective hires found unacceptable.

Advocates for the disabled, who had seen these impasses before, advised Nick to consider a gap year, to give himself time to budge the administration.

He and his family instead mobilized an army of supporters by posting an online video clip about Nick's story. Soon, 5,000 people had signed a Change.org petition urging SUNY to provide the extra room.

Their grass-roots campaign caught the eye of New York Governor Andrew Cuomo, and things finally flipped. He applauded Nick for his achievements and urged SUNY Purchase to accommodate the request.

Administrators now offered to cough up a compromise it deemed "reasonable," the standard that colleges must meet under federal law. Administrators now offered to place Nick and his aide in separate rooms inside a suite that ordinarily housed four people, but wanted to bill Nick's family an extra $13,000 for that second room.

The hard-to-stomach surcharge required Michael Astor to raid his 401(k) retirement account. "Now I'm broke," said the father. "But my son is happier than he's ever been. He's making friends. He's integrated in the community." Plus, he said, "I'm not just doing this for Nick. It's time for people to stand up and say I don't care what the intricacies of the law says. This is not decent. This is not the way we should behave."

His best advice to others girding for battle: "The strategy is to go to the top, as high as you can and make them aware of your needs and your situation and make them aware that you are not going away until you get that," he said.

*The Editors*

# WHAT TO KNOW IF YOU WILL BE NEEDING ACCOMMODATIONS

Whether your disabilities are physical or mental ones, highly visible or hard for others to see, colleges often have a dedicated office that could be a valuable resource for you. Its purpose is partly to advise and partly to collect the documentation you need to qualify for accommodations.

Colleges are subject to many of the same laws as K-12 schools. But they have no obligation to offer *specialized instruction* for students with disabilities. So, expect less monitoring of your case and fewer evaluations to determine whether you are being well-served.

Institutions that receive federal funding do, however, need to make reasonable *accommodations* under the Americans with Disabilities Act and Section 504 of the Rehabilitation Act of 1973 so you have an equal opportunity to obtain an education. The Fair Housing Act also dictates the kinds of accommodations that might be reasonable to expect from university housing.

Accommodations run the gamut but can include anything from furnishing extra time and a quiet setting on tests to allowing someone with diabetes to snack in class to manage glucose levels.

According to the National Center for Education Statistics, 11 percent of undergraduates last surveyed reported having a life-impairing disability. No surprise, really, when improved laws in Washington have enabled many children to get crucial support through their high school years, which in turn helped prepare them for college.

The proportion may even be higher at private colleges. According to a Wall Street Journal analysis, the number of college students considered disabled has been swelling sharply, partly due to the surge in diagnoses for anxiety and depression, to the point that one in four students are now classified as disabled at many elite colleges in the United States.

That means that the percentage of students on many campuses who have physical or mental disabilities is larger than the slice of students

– thought to be about 10 percent – involved in Greek life, or the 10 percent of students in varsity sports. The number is that big.

That does not mean that colleges make it easy for students in need of help. Many schools take the unfortunate attitude that "we do the minimum possible under the law," nothing more, according to Michael Astor, the father of a college freshman with cerebral palsy. So, students and their families may have to lobby administrators if they want more.

While parents may be accustomed to helping, students should expect to advocate for themselves at college. Carnegie-Mellon's Office of Disabilities plainly warns parents that the Family Educational Rights and Privacy Act applies to college-age students and students will need to give "explicit, written permission" for "the university to share any information about a student's academics, disability accommodations, or other aspects of their college experience" with parents.

So, get acquainted with the school's disability center, and the folks who staff it. Take notes when you meet with them. If you've already registered with the center, and suspect you need more support and guidance than you are getting, ask professors, residential life counselors and your advisors for help. Don't forget campus clergy – they often know what's available on campus and may be able to intervene.

College students are expected to bear the cost of any documentation required to secure accommodations. Consult the staff at the disabilities center if cost is an issue. They may be able to refer you to a nearby clinic, staffed by grad students, or some other low-cost provider.

Most importantly, know that lots of students struggle with anxiety, learning issues and physical disabilities. If your school does not offer the services you need to succeed, you can mount a fight, but think, too, about transferring to a college with more support programs and a better attitude. They exist.

*Kristin Hussey lives in Connecticut with her husband and children. She almost didn't graduate from college because she flunked gym.*

*Additional Resources listed in Appendix.*

# WHO LET THE DOGS IN? HOW COLLEGES LEARNED TO WELCOME EMOTIONAL SUPPORT ANIMALS

Nearly every college allows traditional service animals such as seeing-eye dogs for the blind to accompany their owners all around campus, and many allow fish in small tanks.

But if you cross paths at college with people who have "emotional support animals" bunking with them in their dorms, you can thank Butch, a 4-pound miniature pinscher, and the Fair Housing Act for that.

Butch's owner, Brittany Hamilton of Bellevue, Nebraska, left for college in August 2010, expecting to live in university-owned housing, as most freshmen do. Except that her college, the University of Nebraska at Kearney, refused to allow Butch, her medically prescribed pooch, to live on campus, causing her to withdraw from school.

For most purposes, emotional support animals are one notch below "service animals," a designation generally reserved for dogs that have been trained to perform specific tasks for someone disabled.

Nearly any type of animal can qualify as an "emotional support" animal, and they are not required to perform specific tasks. They are, however, expected to have some therapeutic value, and they must be approved by a licensed medical provider for a recognized malady.

Civil rights lawyers at the U.S. Department of Justice sued the University of Nebraska at Kearney on behalf of Butch's owner and another student who claimed she, too, was denied the chance to attend school because of the school's refusal to accommodate her medically-approved animal.

Colleges were put on notice by the consent decree that ultimately resulted from that lawsuit that they could no longer delve into a student's medical history when weighing requests for reasonable accommodations. All that mattered was establishing whether the applicant has a diagnosed disorder – *which one* is not their concern – and confirming through simple means, such as a doctor's note, that the animal was therapeutically necessary for the individual to use and enjoy university housing.

Colleges do have some wiggle room to withhold an accommodation as "unreasonable" or revoke it later if the animal imposes an "undue" burden on the school, poses a threat to the health and safety of other residents or causes substantial property damage.

No surprise, though, that requests at many schools are zooming. Northern Arizona University fielded 75 requests for emotional support animals one year, many times what it used to get. Posted on its website is a commitment not to "limit room assignments" for those who qualify and a pledge not to levy surcharges in anticipation of damage caused by the animal. It also promises not to retaliate against anyone who seeks accommodations.

St. Mary's College in Maryland has also made a visible effort of late to be more welcoming. Even so, it expects owners of "comfort animals," as it calls them, to be considerate of people with allergies by doing laundry in designated machines.

Most of the requests schools get are for cuddly critters. But some have also entertained requests for lizards, tarantulas, ferrets and marsupials.

Western Washington University accommodated a student who wanted to bring a six-foot-long snake to school. Washington State University allowed a freshman to bring a 95-pound pig. That creature had its own litter box to minimize outings. But when the smell began to irk the neighbors, its owner moved off-campus.

*Anthony Wallace graduated from Northern Arizona University with a degree in philosophy. Jessica Reyes graduated from the University of Pittsburgh with a B.A. in English Writing. They both like other people's pets but prefer not to have their own.*

# ANIMAL TIPS:

For students determined to bring an emotional support animal with them to school, here are some tips:

- You may need to register with the campus' Disabilities Center and provide documentation from a healthcare professional stating that you have a qualifying disability that would benefit from living with an emotional support animal.
- Don't wait till the last minute to ask. Schools warn that they need at least two weeks – and sometimes as much as two months – to process requests. Nor will the animal be permitted to move in while the application is pending.
- Understand, too, that such animals are generally not allowed everywhere their owner goes. That is a big distinction from a traditional service animal that can accompany its owner almost anywhere. Emotional support animals may also be evicted if they are off-leash, not in a carrier, or are otherwise disturbing the "peace and quiet" of a residence.
- Some schools require animal owners to accept singles, forfeiting the chance to have roommates, if other residents have animal-related allergies or phobia.
- Studies show animals often help relieve stress. But caring for them can cause stress, too, and the responsibility will be yours alone at school. So, make sure that you are equipped for having a plus-one in your life. Otherwise, you may end up needing stressbusters for the stressbuster.

*Anthony Wallace and Jessica Reyes*

I LOVE HAVING AN EMOTIONAL SUPPORT ANIMAL ON CAMPUS, BUT IT'S NOT FOR EVERYONE. I wouldn't say it was hard, but there were definitely a lot of steps and protocols to follow because it's not common to have an animal living with you in the dorms.

I did not apply to have my dog freshman year. I did not even know that I could apply to have her with me in the dorm until I learned of accommodations for emotional support animals in dorms during my freshman year of college.

It's definitely something that shouldn't be abused. And it's not something to do if you're not going to take care of the animal. For example, I live in an N.Y.U. dorm, but I am originally from Cleveland and my dog Roxie was not accustomed to living in the city. So, I had to make sure that she adjusted well. I have to take her to dog parks. I have to make sure that her water bowl is always full and that she has food, and that I come back periodically throughout the day to walk her.

So, it's just something to always be cognizant of. There's someone else depending on you. It's not fair to the animal if you aren't willing to accept that responsibility.

Barking has not been a problem with her being in the dorm, and she does spend time in my dorm without me. I have not received any complaints about her since she moved here with me.

—FAITH MARNECHECK
NEW YORK UNIVERSITY, SOPHOMORE

"Hi, I'm Justin, and I have absolutely no idea what I'm doing here.
What about you?"

# 3 Go: Starting Out

It's true, you have (at least) four years of college ahead of you. But, as the Chinese philosopher Lao Tzu says, "every great journey begins with a single step." It just so happens that the first step of this college journey can be pretty hectic. You're probably feeling a lot of things right now: intense excitement, nervousness, maybe, even overwhelming anxiety. Whatever it is, it's okay – and you're not the only one!

Your organization apps are maxed out with tasks and checklists, your Mom is constantly asking you if you're done unpacking, and you can't seem to figure out how to swipe yourself into campus buildings. Believe it or not, if you keep your head down and make it to October, things will start to chill out. Take a deep breath, remind yourself that there's no way to know the future, and read the accounts below of students who have survived – and thrived.

**DON'T TRY TO FIND A GROUP OF FRIENDS.** First, meet as many people as possible and wait until later to find your group.
— JENNIFER A. SICKLICK
GEORGE WASHINGTON UNIVERSITY, FRESHMAN

**STARTING OUT, EVERYBODY IS BASICALLY LOST.**
— JOHNNY
GEORGETOWN UNIVERSITY, JUNIOR

■ Arrive on campus early, if allowed, to learn the layout of the campus before classes start.

■ The first few days can be overwhelming, but the adjustment comes quickly.

■ Be outgoing, meet as many people as you can those first few weeks of school.

**Smile. It helps.**

—CASEY
GEORGETOWN
UNIVERSITY, SENIOR

**THE LIVING IS COMPLETELY DIFFERENT.** At home, my parents took care of everything. It's a big adjustment: doing laundry, cleaning dishes, going out and getting food. I get back to school from a vacation and I forget – I'm kind of expecting my friends to be making food.
　　　—MATT MONACO
　　　　GEORGE WASHINGTON UNIVERSITY, FRESHMAN

• • • • • • • •

**THE HARDEST THING ABOUT LEAVING HOME** was getting used to the freedom. I went from a setting where everything was controlled by my parents to one where I could do whatever I wanted. You have to balance things; have fun, but don't go crazy!
　　　—CANDACE LA PAN
　　　　UNIVERSITY OF NORTH CAROLINA AT GREENSBORO, SOPHOMORE

• • • • • • • •

**GET TO THE DORMS EARLY** on the first day! I was in a triple my freshman year, and by the time I got to my dorm at 7:30 A.M. (it supposedly was not going to open until 8 A.M.,) a local girl was already there and had claimed the best spot. It all worked out fine, though. My roommates and I arranged our room in a way that gave us all some individual space.
　　　—MAYA NEWMAN
　　　　COLUMBIA UNIVERSITY AND JEWISH THEOLOGICAL SEMINARY,
　　　　GRADUATE

THAT FIRST DAY OF COLLEGE felt like a grown-up version of summer camp. Some of us hadn't realized that kids really did grow up in these faraway places. It was not odd to hear, "No really, c'mon, Iowa?" or, "Kalamazoo is a *real* place?!"
— MICHAEL
GRADUATE

" The first days of college are the best: For a few brief drunken moments, there are no cliques, no caste, no class, and no classes. It's a big, egalitarian, drunken orgy. At least, that's the way I partially remember it; I could be wrong. "
— JOHN
UNIVERSITY OF WISCONSIN AT MADISON, GRADUATE

BEFORE CLASSES START, take a walk through campus and get acquainted with the buildings. That way, you can recognize some of the buildings and sites later, through the chaos. On my first day, there were so many people running around that it was fairly intimidating for me, and it was difficult to find my classes.
— MICHAEL ALBERT PAOLI
UNIVERSITY OF TORONTO, GRADUATE

**JUST GIVE IT TIME.** At first, I would call or message some of my old buddies from high school, talking with old friends. It was good to have some close friends as a sounding board for the things I was going through.

> —WONNIE RYU
> EMORY UNIVERSITY, SENIOR

The teachers are going to try to scare you the first week or two and you'll feel overwhelmed. But just keep on track.

—GREG
JAMES MADISON
UNIVERSITY, JUNIOR

**COLLEGE IS NOT SLEEPAWAY CAMP!** I thought college life would be a breeze freshman year. I had gone to sleepaway camp since I was seven, so I was very independent.

My first freak-out moment was when I met our community adviser and she told me to unpack and then meet up with the floor outside to play a game. Um…excuse me? I just told the group of eight-year-olds I had left behind at camp to wake up and brush their teeth mere hours ago. I am the authority figure, not you! I am a camp counselor. But I wasn't anymore. I was just a scared college freshman.

I spent most of Welcome Week staying in my room. I didn't go out to any of the activities because I was tired from working for the last two months. I felt the Welcome Week friendships were fake. People weren't showing their true colors because they just wanted friends. There were three other Rebecca's on my floor, so no one bothered to remember me. I was miserable.

> —REBECCA
> COLLEGE OF NEW JERSEY, SENIOR

**WHEN YOU MOVE IN,** choose the bed where people will see you when the door is open. While you are moving in, people will walk by and see you setting up your room and will stop and say hi.

> —B.K.
> CORNELL UNIVERSITY, GRADUATE

I DID A PRE-ORIENTATION PROGRAM on the arts. I'm glad I did. I made some great friends, and it was great to be on campus early. But I don't think that the content of the program was that important. It was just great to have people that I recognized once school started, and any programs would have been good for that.
    —CATIE
      HARVARD COLLEGE, SENIOR

 

> Find a campus map. The weekend before classes begin, figure out where all your classes are. You'll feel much more at ease on the first day.
>     —SIERRA
>       CALIFORNIA POLYTECHNIC STATE UNIVERSITY
>       AT SAN LUIS OBISPO, JUNIOR

 

I DID A SUMMER SESSION which was about a month and a half before freshman year and I took three courses; it was mostly just to get you adjusted to school. It was probably the best thing I could have asked for – I got a head start, I learned all about my school, things like where everything was. I figured it out before most people got to school, so I didn't feel as much like a new kid on the first day of freshman year. I definitely suggest doing that if it's available.
    —TAYLOR PETTIS
      BLOOMSBURG UNIVERSITY, JUNIOR

# EMILY, MEET EMILY

Some people have common names, we get it. But, still, it gets confusing to hear "Jessica"and see four people turn around. Sometimes, it's not a big deal. Maybe it's a big class, and you're not going to talk to even half of those Jessicas. But, sometimes, you can't avoid a couple of them in your college circles. According to the Wall Street Journal, the University of Washington recently found itself scrambling after its football team ended up with four quarterbacks and a tight end, all named "Jacob," plus a linebacker named "Jake."

So how do you avoid confusion? Alternatively, if you're a person with a common name, how can you help others distinguish you from others of your kind?

1.  For people who have multiple friends with the same name, ask them: What do you want to be called? Is it okay if I call you this nickname?

2.  If you have a common name, consider adopting a nickname. It doesn't even have to be a derivative of your actual name. It can be the name you always wanted. I have a friend named Cody, who happens to have another friend named Cody. So, he asked his friends to call him Yoda. Pretty good trade, in my opinion.

3.  Sometimes, people won't even ask. They'll just inform you, "Okay, you're 'Jessica,' and she'll be 'Jess.'" If you're okay with that, problem solved.

If you are college-bound, here are the names you're most likely to encounter among your new classmates, assuming that they, too, are around 18 years old. The list is based on baby names that Americans favored most in 2001, as determined by the Social Security Administration. My name is there at #11. What about yours?

*Jessica Reyes graduated with a B.A. in English Writing from the University of Pittsburgh.*

| Rank | Male name | Female name |
|:---:|:---:|:---:|
| 1 | Jacob | Emily |
| 2 | Michael | Madison |
| 3 | Matthew | Hannah |
| 4 | Joshua | Ashley |
| 5 | Christopher | Alexis |
| 6 | Nicholas | Sarah |
| 7 | Andrew | Samantha |
| 8 | Joseph | Abigail |
| 9 | Daniel | Elizabeth |
| 10 | William | Olivia |
| 11 | Anthony | Jessica |
| 12 | David | Taylor |
| 13 | Tyler | Emma |
| 14 | John | Alyssa |
| 15 | Ryan | Lauren |
| 16 | Zachary | Grace |
| 17 | Ethan | Kayla |
| 18 | Brandon | Brianna |
| 19 | James | Anna |
| 20 | Alexander | Megan |

**DON'T SETTLE DOWN TOO FAST** with your friends. It's great to make some friends off the bat, but don't let that limit you during the course of the year; you have a lot of time to get to know a lot of people, so keep making friends beyond the first couple of days.
> —CATIE
> HARVARD COLLEGE, SENIOR

**BE WARY OF BECOMING THAT FRESHMAN WHO FRIENDS EVERYONE.** Yep, every class has one, and yes, I promise you that you will be remembered that way for your entire college career. Wait until you actually have conversations with people until you go on a friending spree.
> —SOPHIE STONE
> FRANKLIN AND MARSHALL COLLEGE, JUNIOR

**GO WHERE NO ONE ELSE WILL.** I went to a career fair, having no idea of what I wanted to do later. I noticed that there was absolutely nobody at the entrepreneurial studies table, and I figured I'd check it out because I'm from a small town and I'm kind of afraid of large groups. It was a newer major for my school, so class sizes were small, and they were just trying to get it started. That intrigued me, because I graduated from a high school with 14 kids, so I really like small classes. It ended up being a good fit.
> —ANONYMOUS
> UNIVERSITY OF SOUTH DAKOTA, GRADUATE

Don't be afraid to go up to people and introduce yourself.

—MANI
UNIVERSITY OF
MARYLAND,
FRESHMAN

**TRY TO BE AS OUTGOING AS YOU CAN.** All the people that I'm friends with now, I met the first two or three weeks. You end up being closest with the people that you meet early on – because you're all in the same situation, going through the same thing. You're all in a new school, no one knows anyone.
> —CHIP JONES
> HAMILTON COLLEGE, JUNIOR

**THINGS WON'T BE PERFECT AT THE BEGINNING.** You're going to have a couple of rough months when you're trying to find your niche and remember why on earth you came to college. But give yourself time to integrate, to decide how you want to spend your time, who you want to spend your time with, and what kind of people will complement those objectives. You can drive yourself crazy trying to do everything with all sorts of people or you can try to figure out what makes you happy and whom you're comfortable with. But that won't happen immediately. It takes at least a year, maybe a little longer.

    —ANONYMOUS
      UNIVERSITY OF VIRGINIA, SENIOR

**FRESHMAN YEAR IS ABOUT LEARNING HOW TO LIVE ON YOUR OWN FOR THE FIRST TIME.** How to do your own laundry. How to wake up for an 8 A.M. lecture class. How to deal with annoying roommates or others in your dorm. And how to drink responsibly since the allure of alcohol seems woven into the college experience.

    Success in freshman year is 50 percent about being a good student, going to class, writing papers and meeting deadlines. And 50 percent is learning how to live with other people from diverse and fascinating backgrounds different from your own.

    And you never know what will happen. My senior year at Princeton I was a resident adviser for a rambunctious group of freshmen and one of them turned out to be David Kelley, who later wrote me into one of his TV shows, *"Ally McBeal."* You might not become a minor TV star, but the people you meet and the relationships you form freshman year will impact your life forever.

    —MICHAEL MCCURRY
      PRINCETON UNIVERSITY, GRADUATE

# CAN I GET SOME CREDIT?

You may be starting college with a few credits already under your belt if you took Advanced Placement or International Baccalaureate exams in high school or completed other college-level work before enrolling. If so, don't forget to check in with your adviser to make sure that you get full credit for those credits!

*Frances Northcutt*

IF YOU'RE NERVOUS ABOUT THE FIRST DAY, take a walk around the campus a day or two before and find your classes. Some campuses are huge; mine was actually divided into two campuses with a highway running through the middle. I went to the entirely wrong side of campus on Day One, so a lot of time was lost.
—*COREY*
*SAN DIEGO STATE UNIVERSITY, JUNIOR*

. . . . . . . . .

IF YOU COME FROM A SCHOOL that sends a lot of kids to your university, it is okay to hang out with them for the first few weeks. If you have a few people that you know, it is much easier to make new friends. Not only that, but the group that you know will always bring along people you don't know, and vice versa.
—*ANNIE THOMAS*
*UNIVERSITY OF MICHIGAN, SENIOR*

. . . . . . . . .

THE FIRST FEW MONTHS WERE EASIER than I thought they would be. But everyone I knew hit a patch right before they went home, after they'd been here for a couple of months. It was easy to come here, but after a couple of months you start to miss the security of home. Especially when the tests start.
—*D.F.*
*NEW YORK UNIVERSITY, SENIOR*

**TALK TO RANDOM PEOPLE** everywhere you go. I met everyone that way freshman year. In my orientation group I met the bassist and the keyboardist from one of the bands I play in now. Most people think freshman orientation stuff is annoying and just blow it off – but I made really good friends there.

—*PETER*
*TUFTS UNIVERSITY, SOPHOMORE*

Keep your Social Security number handy for the first several days.

—*BRIAN TURNER*
*UNIVERSITY OF GEORGIA, GRADUATE*

**EVERYONE EXPECTS THAT YOUR FINANCIAL AID PACKAGE** is a done deal when you get it, but depending on the school, it's not. Northwestern allowed me to file an appeal for more funding before I officially committed, which gave me the chance to barter for a better financial aid package and make a more informed decision before I committed myself to anything. Dealing with the financial aid office is definitely a pain, but if you want the help badly enough it's worth it. Be persistent and be annoying. Appeal multiples times. At N.U., you're almost guaranteed to get a couple thousand dollars added to your aid package each time you appeal, so don't drop the issue right away.

You should also expect your financial aid package to change based on your expected family contribution or EFC, which is calculated each year after you submit the FAFSA. If your EFC goes up, your aid decreases and vice versa. Accept this now and appeal once you get a decision if you're not happy with what they offer you. Just know their first offer rarely has to be their final offer.

—*ANONYMOUS*
*NORTHWESTERN UNIVERSITY, GRADUATE*

**AS CORNY AS IT SOUNDS – BE YOURSELF.** You'll never be happy if you're trying to please other people.

—*AMANDA*
*UNIVERSITY OF MIAMI, JUNIOR*

# JUST DO IT: ORIENTATION

ORIENTATION IS WHEN THE SCHOOL tells you things that they really told you previously in tours and in the pounds of literature that they send to you in the mail – but with more detail and a little bit more application of how you can use it.
   —BARRY LANGER
   OGLETHORPE UNIVERSITY, JUNIOR

ORIENTATION IS A SCARY TIME and an awkward time. It is too short to get really comfortable, but enough time to get an introduction to the school. It is important to be really outgoing during orientation and try to meet at least a couple of people. This way, you have two or three people to call during welcome week to go out with, grab lunch, explore campus or get books. You will feel a lot more confident if you tackle the first couple of days with a friend rather than by yourself!
   —ANNIE THOMAS
   UNIVERSITY OF MICHIGAN, SENIOR

ENJOY ORIENTATION. First of all, it's more like summer camp than school – every day is full of activities, BBQs, music, and entertainment. Second, at no other time will everyone be so open to new people. Take advantage of this friendly climate by stepping out of your comfort zone. Say "hi" to a stranger, go get dinner with random people from your dorm, and go to as many of the events offered as you can (even though some will sound lame.) It's funny how the people you meet during orientation turn out to be your best friends when you graduate. At that point, you can look back and reminisce about the mildly embarrassing things you did or said when you first got to college!
   —STEPHANIE DREIFUSS
   DUKE UNIVERSITY, SENIOR

# DIS-ORIENTED

**I SKIPPED ALL THE ORIENTATIONS.** My sister told me I didn't have to go to them if I didn't want to. So I took that as, "Go to the bar instead." But that's not the best advice. I never knew the other three-quarters of our class that didn't go to bars.
    —CASEY
      GEORGETOWN UNIVERSITY, SENIOR

• • • • • • • • •

**THE FIRST WEEKEND OF ORIENTATION,** I felt really homesick. Not because I'd been away from home for long – obviously! – but because I felt out of place. My floor was entirely made up of freshmen and many of them, to me, seemed to have found their "group" right off the bat. I'd met a ton of nice people, but it takes me a little while to open up, and I felt like I had no real connections yet. After calling up my older brother crying, he told me that no matter what it seemed like, no one had found a "group" yet. It turned out he was right. The people who seemed to be best friends the first week didn't necessarily stay that way. And people who I thought I had no connection with eventually become some of my best friends at college (e.g., my roommate!). The friends that matter take time to find.
    —EMMA
      HAMILTON COLLEGE, JUNIOR

# LEARNING TO COPE, ONCE THERE

Starting out in college can be lots of fun but you may naturally feel some anxiety about this big step once you arrive. As uneasy as you may feel about your new setting, keep in mind that all your classmates are in the same situation as you. Here, too, are some additional ways to make those early days easier to manage:

- Orientation: attend as much of the orientation programming as possible. This is an unparalleled chance to meet students and faculty in an informal setting before the work begins, and don't worry if you don't digest everything. You can always fill in the details later.
- Get involved: Most colleges hold a club fair as part of orientation. Find a club, intramural sport, religious or political organization and get involved. These activities are a great way to meet other students. But be careful about over-committing until you have a sense of what your academic workload will be. Much as a lot of really valuable learning also happens outside the classroom, remember, you are primarily in school to learn.
- Use your supports: Most every college has a broad array of support services. These include things like academic advising and peer advising services/tutoring, student finance, veterans support, religious communities, and health education, nutritionists, health care and counseling and support for students with a range of disabilities or other challenges. These programs are there to be used. Many students (especially when you might be the first in your family to attend college) don't like to admit a problem or ask for help. But, asking for help before a problem becomes serious can help prevent trouble and is the sensible thing to do.
- Take good care of yourself: This might be the first time in your life that you are responsible for your self-care. You will adjust faster and feel better if you take care of your body. Getting enough sleep, exercising regularly and eating well will all help.

*Dr. Victor Schwartz is the chief medical officer of The Jed Foundation.*

**The first few days of college are weird;** you're bombarded by cheesy campus groups and pressured to commit to a thousand things that aren't even cool. Take time to relax. Don't worry about jumping into anything too soon.
—*Katie*
*Baylor University, Junior*

. . . . . . . .

**The first few weeks,** freshmen move around in packs. Try to make friends with some upperclassmen. You're more likely to get into parties without a herd of freshmen around you.
—*Kevin*
*Georgetown University, Sophomore*

. . . . . . . .

**Test out of as much science and math and other generals as you can,** because it saves money, and it saves time. Test out of the ones you can, and the rest, suck it up, because you have to do it.
—*Anonymous*
*South Dakota State University, Graduate*

. . . . . . . .

**Surrender to "YES."** There's this Jim Carrey movie called *Yes Man* where the main character says "yes" to everything people ask. Obviously, in college you should say "no" to really dangerous stuff. But don't say "no" to experiences because they sound too weird, too nerdy, too cool, too intimidating or because you're just feeling lazy. Go to that party or that robotics club meeting or that show and if it goes poorly, it will be a story to laugh about. Or you could meet someone great. One weekend, I had a friend from high school visiting and we went out to the bars. I was ready to go back to the dorm after a while but a group of people invited us out with them. I pushed myself because I wanted to show my friend a good time. I ended up meeting this guy named Pat who is now one of my best friends.
—*Anonymous*
*Syracuse University, Sophomore*

Be brave; be the one to initiate the conversation.
—*Aleksandr Akulov*
*Macaulay Honors College at CUNY Hunter, Sophomore*

# Expectations: College Dreams & Campus Reality

*S ocial media, pop culture and Hollywood all seem to conspire to create a culturally accepted version of the college experience and the quintessential freshman. If you've watched movies, or followed older friends on Instagram, you've probably been treated to tales of wild pranks, alcohol-fueled frat parties, and nail-biting all-nighters. How seriously should you take any of it? And how seriously should you try to conform?*

*The truth is, there is no "right" way to go through college and its gauntlet of challenges. Even if college seems bewildering at first, you'll figure it out. You might even have some fun and learn a thing or two along the way, as each of the following students did.*

IT'S FUNNY; I think if I'm not in class I must be late for something or missing something. I'm so used to being in school eight hours a day!
—TOBIAS
HARVARD COLLEGE, FRESHMAN

BE PREPARED FOR CHANGE.
—MICHAEL A. FEKULA
UNIVERSITY OF MARYLAND, GRADUATE

- Sometimes, it takes a while to find your group of friends.
- Be patient.
- The constant need to define yourself can be very stressful.
- If you feel like transferring, hang on. Try harder to join groups and meet more people before making any big decisions.
- Lots of students worry about adapting to a very different culture when going to a school in a different region of the country, not to mention a different country altogether.

**YOU'RE GOING TO BE LONELY.** I wish someone would have warned me about move-in weekend a little bit more. Everyone said it was going to be a big moment in my life, and I knew that, coming from a small town with 12 kids in my class all my life. I was mentally prepared for that, but nobody warned me that when you got dropped off at college and you hugged your parents and they were leaving, that you were going to bawl for 20 minutes, in the most ugly cry ever. And nobody warned me about the loneliness that came with that first night.
—*KENDRA KLUMB*
*UNIVERSITY OF SIOUX FALLS, JUNIOR*

• • • • • • • •

**THE BIGGEST DIFFERENCE BETWEEN** high school and college is that professors do not treat you like babies. They rarely give "busy" homework on a daily basis. Instead, there are only a few papers to write, in which you must demonstrate what you have learned in class or how extensively you researched.
—*KANU*
*HUNTER COLLEGE, SOPHOMORE*

I WAS CONCERNED ABOUT adapting to a Southern school and its culture, since I came from San Francisco. But I soon realized that while the culture might be preppy and Southern, the minds of the students are more progressive. Professors are also just as open, so I felt more at ease as my freshman year went on. At first you might feel alienated, judging by the cliques around the students and the huge presence of Greek life. Regardless of your personality, you'll find your own group of friends who share the same interests.

—*ANONYMOUS*
*UNIVERSITY OF VIRGINIA, JUNIOR*

. . . . . . . .

COLLEGE IS A TIME TO EXPLORE AND BE SELFISH. Remember that it's *your* path, *your* college experience – not what someone else has drawn for you. Ever watched "Dancing with the Stars" and thought you could be pretty good? Then, go to a meeting for the Ballroom Dance Club. It could be your passion. Ever thought you were funny? Try stand-up comedy – you could be the next big thing. You'll regret so much more the things you didn't do than the ones you did. So, get out there and do – you never know what could happen. I would advise my friends to put their hesitations aside and really ask themselves what they want, not what the popular thing to do is. It's hard to make the distinction sometimes, but in hindsight, you'll be glad you did.

Incoming college students – you have the whole rest of your life to stick to one path. So, while you can, get a taste of all of them. Make sure when you do settle down and pick a career, it's because you've ruled out all the others and found your best fit. Live large, spontaneously and loud before the world tries to confine you into something more quiet.

—*HANNAH BENSON*
*ELON UNIVERSITY, SENIOR*

**DO NOT THINK YOU CAN "DO IT ALL" JUST BECAUSE YOU "DID IT ALL" IN HIGH SCHOOL.** Learn your drinking limits before your first night in the dorms, and don't eat so much shit 24/7 and think you won't gain the Freshman 15.

I graduated from a college prep school with pretty good grades and a knack for over-achieving. I took on a hefty fall semester because I didn't know any better. I thought that's what all freshman did. At the time, I was a biology major, so I loaded up on courses I knew would be challenging, but I could handle it because I was a kick-ass student from an expensive private school. Freshman year would be a breeze. Wrong. I barely squeezed by being put on academic probation and got my first ever D. Spring semester called for a change in major and more realistic expectations. I went from teetering on the tightrope of freshman delinquency to Dean's List.

I also drank way too much lemonade and vodka my first few nights as a college student which resulted in hugging the toilet. And to top it all off, I gained a minimum of 15 pounds that first semester. It's what happens when you introduce beer and pints of Ben & Jerry's at 2A.M. into your diet and are no longer a varsity athlete.
> —*JONNA*
> *GEORGE WASHINGTON UNIVERSITY, GRADUATE*

· · · · · · · · ·

**I'M NOT TOO BIG** on the drug/alcohol thing: in fact, I abstain from both altogether. My biggest fear for college was that I wouldn't fit in: that people would find me "lame;" that I wouldn't make friends, being an abstainer and all. However, I found that other kids were really not as shallow as I thought. I had no problem making friends. Drinkers, non-drinkers, math nerds, ice-climbers, Trekkies... you name 'em, I befriended 'em. As clichéd as it sounds, people liked me for who I was.
> —*DREW HILL*
> *COLBY COLLEGE, JUNIOR*

MY BIGGEST MISCONCEPTION about college was that I would be 100-percent free of parents, and I definitely wasn't. I had to force myself to become more independent by getting a job and not calling home every day.

—CHIDIMMA UCHE ETO
DUKE UNIVERSITY, GRADUATE

• • • • • • • •

EVERYONE TALKS ABOUT how college is an opportunity to start over…but no one ever mentions how to recover from horrendous first impressions. What if I came off as completely socially inept? How could I recover from that? I felt a little "off" in terms of language. I'd been used to speaking a mixture of Chinese and English – Chinglish, if you will – so suddenly switching to pure English was an adjustment. I'd often be talking and have to wave my hands around trying to translate a word into English. I don't think my fears ever turned into reality, since I have a fair amount of friends now. Chalk that one up to worrying way too much about a new, unknown situation.

—MEL
UNIVERSITY OF VIRGINIA, SOPHOMORE

• • • • • • • •

IN THE BEGINNING OF FRESHMAN YEAR, everybody is looking for the party and making friends as fast and easily as possible. You get sucked into doing things that you might not want to do, like, you're hanging out with a crowd during orientation and they want to go to some frat party, and you might not really want to do that. You have to not be afraid to stand apart and not participate in something that you don't really want to do. That way, you find the friends who are really like you. The people who are not doing the things that you don't want to be doing are waiting to meet people just like you.

—MOLLY
BROWN UNIVERSITY, SOPHOMORE

**YOU ARE FREE TO BE** who you want to be, and you don't have to be the prom queen or band geek that you were in high school. It's a time to explore who you are, what you want in your life, and what path you will take. You're free from conforming to what your group of friends is interested in; if you don't want to be in a theater class or an economics class, you don't have to be. In the end, everyone in college is working toward life after college, whether that means business school, pre-med, or liberal arts.
—*MICHELLE*
*EMORY UNIVERSITY, SENIOR*

• • • • • • • •

**COMPARING YOURSELF TO OTHERS IS JUST NOT A GOOD IDEA IN COLLEGE.** I grew up in a small town and I always got straight A's. I didn't even need to work hard, and you just had this very high image of yourself. Then, you get to college and you take your first classes and you're like, 'Oh my god. I'm not smart. I'm actually probably average, and all these other people around me look absolutely on track. They know what they're doing. They're putting in 100%, and I'm over here putting in 10%.'

It made me feel like there was nothing I could do anymore. Business seemed hard. Math seemed hard. Science, impossible. Computer programming? Heck no! Nothing felt even remotely possible for me. Eventually, I studied a language – Japanese! – but I felt bad that I wasn't in computer programming or medicine or law or all these other things that everyone around me looked like they were getting so much smarter for taking.

From the minute you step foot on campus, just stop comparing yourself to others. You'll be able to work on yourself so much more. Everyone might look like they're on the right track, but everyone is faking it.
—*JESSICA*
*UNIVERSITY OF PITTSBURGH, GRADUATE*

**GET SOME SLEEP.** Don't feel like your life needs to be like *Animal House.* Our chancellor said something in his speech at the beginning of the year that stuck with me: 'there are three things you can do in college: party, study, and sleep, and you can choose two of those, because you don't have time for all three.' I picked studying and partying and it was so unhealthy. I felt like I had to have a certain experience in college. I had to go to parties, I had to do this or that because I was in college and you're only in college once and I didn't want to miss out on what everyone says is the best time of your life. I felt like I had to go out every night because that's what you do. I had insane expectations for what college would be. That year was one of the worst years of my life, also one of the coolest years of my life.

— *ANONYMOUS*
*UNIVERSITY OF COLORADO, GRADUATE*

**YOU BECOME *YOU* IN COLLEGE.** My whole life, I had the same small class. But when I got to college, I completely re-created myself. I found new friends and interests and hobbies that I never knew I would enjoy. You start with a blank canvas and you get to paint it to be whoever you want it to be.

— *SARA*
*SOUTH DAKOTA STATE UNIVERSITY, GRADUATE*

**COLLEGE ISN'T LIKE HIGH SCHOOL;** you have to actually try to get good grades. When I was a freshman I would write a paper with no thesis and think that I would still get an A on it (which happened in high school.) Then you get the paper back and you get a B-minus and it says, "You don't have a thesis." It's hard to slip things by professors; they know the tricks.

— *KIM*
*STANFORD UNIVERSITY, SENIOR*

# FOLLOWING THE RULES?

Do you even know what the rules are? Your college's policies and regulations are listed in several places. Here's an overview to get you started and help put things in perspective.

## FINANCIAL POLICIES

Pay special attention to policies that pertain to registration and tuition and fees. In general, students may register and add or drop courses without penalties before the first day of classes. However, most institutions hold registered students responsible for percentages of tuition and/or fees once the semester has started – even if they never attended a class. On the other hand, after a certain point in the semester, students may be restricted from officially withdrawing from a class. Thus, you should always consult an academic adviser or the student service center before deciding not to continue with courses.

Financial aid, too, may be affected if you add or drop courses, as the level of aid generally depends on the number of credits you take per semester. You also may need to maintain a certain GPA in order to continue receiving aid.

Make sure to pay any and all outstanding tuition and fees by your college's deadlines, since students are routinely dropped for nonpayment. Should this occur, you may find it difficult to secure your original course load or to register for a subsequent semester.

## BEHAVIORAL POLICIES

The Student Code of Conduct primarily addresses behavioral concerns. These concerns go far beyond lying, cheating, or stealing. Certain institutions formulate a Code of Conduct to generate a unified message against inappropriate behavior within the community. The code almost always discusses academic integrity issues. Academic integrity is a term used to describe ethically sound behavior that relates to educational endeavors. The most notable academic integrity issues pertain to plagiarism and to cheating on exams. Schools have also updated their codes to include bans on discrimination, harassment, and sexual misconduct. If students are found responsible for engaging in these prohibited behaviors, sanctions might be issued.

## RESIDENTIAL POLICIES

Residential campuses normally develop policy manuals with focused policies. This helps to establish parameters for circumstances that relate directly to living in the residence halls. Topics covered may include prohibitions such as unauthorized guests, drugs, and other banned substances. Some campuses restrict overnight guests, while others may permit overnight guests only over a weekend. While it may seem like common knowledge to steer clear of drugs and alcohol, some campuses even ban drug-related paraphernalia or imagery. Could you imagine getting dismissed from the halls because you had a particular picture of Bob Marley on the wall, although you truly loved his music?

## ACADEMIC POLICIES

Your academic program may have its own academically related policies, and your professors will certainly have their own policies as stated in each course syllabus. Familiarize yourself with the most important academic policies before you begin your studies. If this time has passed, consult with the appropriate departments before making serious decisions.

**Where can you find these policies?** On your college's website, or within the respective department. Here are the most relevant sources:

- The Student Handbook or webpage
- The Student Code of Conduct or Community Standards
- The Academic Policies and webpage
- The Course Catalog
- Residence Life Handbook and webpage
- The Office of Financial Aid
- The Office of the Bursar
- The Office of the Registrar

*Tatum Thomas, Ph.D.*
*Senior Associate Dean of Student Affairs*
*Columbia University*
*School of Professional Studies*

**THE MOST DIFFICULT THING** freshman year was the constant need to define yourself in every conversation, in every new person you meet, and in every class you attend. You're in a totally new environment and no one knows who you are. That was kind of unnerving. It took me a while to embrace it, but I found my best friends in the middle of my first semester, and that helped me. I found them when I was rappelling off the football stadium. I found my niche. Here I get to be the crazy hippy outdoorsy rock-climbing adventure-racing person, which is really great.
—*DENALI*
*PRINCETON UNIVERSITY, JUNIOR*

● ● ● ● ● ● ● ●

**THINGS ARE LESS STRUCTURED IN COLLEGE.** Professors don't bother taking attendance at most lectures, you don't have the same class (or sleep) schedule every day, and you can have breakfast for dinner. With all of this increased flexibility, you will find that you have more responsibilities – keeping up with class material, maintaining healthy sleeping and eating habits, and budgeting your time appropriately. Getting used to college life is all about understanding and fulfilling these responsibilities, while still enjoying yourself!
—*STEPHANIE DREIFUSS*
*DUKE UNIVERSITY, SENIOR*

● ● ● ● ● ● ● ●

**IN HIGH SCHOOL,** the school you attend, your friends, and your parents primarily dictate your direction in life. College is a time when you can do WHATEVER YOU WANT! Take classes that interest you. Join clubs that seem interesting. Work out when you want and get drunk when you want. It's up to you whether you sink or swim.
—*ILAN GLUCK*
*UNIVERSITY OF MARYLAND, JUNIOR*

# WELCOME HOME!
# TIPS FOR VETERANS

As a veteran who may have spent time away from friends and family in highly challenging circumstances, you bring a perspective to campus that is vastly different from that of most students. Here are some success strategies with you in mind:

- **Access your GI Benefits:** Your tuition can be substantially reduced with GI benefits, but these benefits are not granted automatically. You have to apply for them. Check out http://gibill.va.gov/apply-for-benefits/.

- **Apply for Financial Aid and Scholarships:** There are scholarships specifically created to support veterans.

- **Find your campus office to support student veterans:** Some schools even offer priority registration for vets.

- **Complete the College Level Examination Program (CLEP):** Taking these exams may help you get academic credit for things you learned during your service. For more information, check out http://clep.collegeboard.org/.

- **Remember, you are not alone:** Consult http://www.studentveterans.org to find other veterans groups and leads on resources.

- **Political viewpoints and perspectives about the military may differ widely from your own:** This could be frustrating and at times agonizing, particularly if your peers are vocal. Be patient, especially if you are also grappling with post-traumatic stress or anxiety. Campus resources may be able to help.

*Scott C. Silverman, Ed.D., is the Associate Dean of the Emeritus Lifelong Learning Program at Santa Monica College.*

I DIDN'T THINK THAT I, a kid from Flatbush, who was kicked out of his first high school for low attendance and mischievous behavior, would be a candidate for college. However, to my surprise I was.

I figured this would be just like high school, a few years of minimal effort and I'd pass. I was sadly mistaken. Once the semester started, I was immediately overwhelmed. To me, it seemed like everyone already knew each other, everything was moving way faster than I expected. I was shocked by the pace of the campus, the fact that I was in a new city so far from home and the structure of the classes. As a result, I felt paralyzed. I stopped going to classes, I didn't wake up on time and only left my room to eat in the cafe. By the end of my first semester, my mother got a letter saying that I was in danger of losing my financial aid, because of my low grades, which meant going back home without a degree. That letter was the biggest eye-opener for me.

That next semester, I barely missed a class and ended up earning a 3.75. I started becoming more outgoing because I realized that this campus and Buffalo were my home for the next four years and I could either sit in my room all day or make the most out of this experience. I realized that I was in a privileged place. I was the first in my family to earn a college degree and first to go away for school. I knew that I couldn't afford to jeopardize all those things again. By getting involved, I was able to establish a network of peers, faculty and advisers who cared to see me succeed. I realized the importance of time management. I discovered that I wasn't alone and that other students experienced shock just like I did. Making these connections was what helped put me on track to be successful.

—OLIVER W. COLBERT
STATE UNIVERSITY OF N.Y. - BUFFALO, GRADUATE

**ONE PARTICULAR FEAR** that I had coming into Rice was that I would no longer stand out in the classroom or in extracurricular, since practically everyone who comes to Rice was a standout in her high school. I thought everyone might be really competitive in classes or cutthroat about getting leadership positions. My first few years, I applied for jobs, internships, and leadership positions and was rejected for practically all of them. Rather than get discouraged and give up, I just kept trying and continued to develop good relationships with supportive members of the faculty.

 —*EMILIA*
  *RICE UNIVERSITY, JUNIOR*

- - - - - - - - -

**EXPECT ANYTHING AND EVERYTHING!** Expect toiletries to go missing, especially if kept in the public bathroom. Expect to find random fliers for a hundred different clubs under your door every day of the first week. Expect to have R.A.'s who care, and those who don't even know your name. But above all, expect to be sick at least once during your first year in a dorm, no matter if you were healthy as a horse in high school. Just make sure to have the basic medicines with you so if you can't go home easily, you can at least take care of yourself without having to leave your room.

 —*MERELISE HARTE ROUZER*
  *GEORGIA INSTITUTE OF TECHNOLOGY, SOPHOMORE*

- - - - - - - - -

**THE BIGGEST DIFFERENCE** between high school and college is basic: You are on your own. You can do whatever you want, whenever you want, however you want. If you want to stay up until 3 A.M. for three weeks in a row, that's fine. But you need to learn what plan and schedule works best for you. (I promise that eating pizza, drunk, at 2 A.M. every weekend, isn't best for anyone.)

 —*ANNIE THOMAS*
  *UNIVERSITY OF MICHIGAN, SENIOR*

IN COLLEGE, NO ONE WILL EVER CALL YOU OUT on skipping class, being uninvolved, going crazy on weekends, etc. I'd heard this, but it didn't really sink in until I got here and I realized that nobody cared if I didn't attend EVERY orientation event. If I thought it was better that I went to sleep rather than attending the social events that lasted until midnight, then it was my decision. However, most events (especially classes) are important enough that you're cheating yourself if you don't go. In college, you have to be entirely self-motivated rather than relying on requirements to get you involved.
—LIZZIE
BOWDOIN COLLEGE, FRESHMAN

· · · · · · · ·

UNLIKE HIGH SCHOOL, where most of the homework is due the next day, the workload in college comes in waves. Some weeks there will only be some reading and other times you might have two papers and a test in the same week.
—KANU
HUNTER COLLEGE, SOPHOMORE

· · · · · · · ·

MY FRIENDS AND I WERE HORRIBLE at managing our time to meet our class requirements. This was a whole new experience for us and we tackled the situation just as we did in high school. We waited until the last minute before actually doing the required work. The problem with that: Last minute in high school meant the day the assignment was given; last minute in college meant a month after it was given. There's not enough time to accomplish a month's worth of work in just a few days. Freshmen need to learn that they must schedule their own academic calendar. This is one of the most crucial adjustments to be made by freshmen.
—RAJ MATHEW
MACAULAY HONORS COLLEGE AT CUNY HUNTER, JUNIOR

# 3 DIFFERENCES BETWEEN HIGH SCHOOL AND COLLEGE

1. You have to rely on yourself.
2. You learn to become self-sufficient pretty fast.
3. Your time is less scheduled. Managing your time is key.

—*LINDSEY WILLIAMSON*
*VANDERBILT UNIVERSITY, GRADUATE*

**SO MANY PEOPLE SAY THAT HIGH SCHOOL** is some of the best years of your life, when in actuality, college is way better. It's like sleep-away camp: you live with these people for four years. You pick and choose the activities that interest you. You create memories with these people that you'll never forget. You meet these people during a time when you're trying to figure out your future.

A lot of people get bogged down with choosing the "right" college. College is what you make of it, regardless of where you go. It's going to be a wild (however you personally define that word) experience. And like everything else in life, it does go by pretty damn quickly, so enjoy it.
—*JONNA*
*GEORGE WASHINGTON UNIVERSITY, GRADUATE*

**THE BIGGEST DIFFERENCE,** undoubtedly, is the independence students have in college. It's a great feeling knowing that you are free to go anywhere, sleep anytime, and eat as much as you would like. Just make sure that you schedule time for studying.
—*JONATHAN LIU*
*UNIVERSITY OF TENNESSEE AT KNOXVILLE, FRESHMAN*

# GET A MENTOR!

Of course, you're excited to be in college, but the newness can also be intimidating or confusing at times: the way classes are scheduled, for example – or how to decide which classes to take. How do professors grade? What is really expected of you?

One way to get your questions answered and feel more confident about the transition, is to get a mentor. A mentor, in this context, is someone with first-hand knowledge of the college experience, the expectations of college, and how to be an effective student on the campus. A mentor is someone who can either give you the correct answer to your questions or point you to someone who can.

So where do you find a mentor? Anywhere, really: on campus, in your community, at your place of worship, or at your place of employment. A mentor can be a helpful professor or counselor at the school or a more experienced student on campus. The key is to choose someone who has first-hand knowledge about college, and how to be a good college student. Does s/he know how to study? Can s/he give you advice about social life on campus, financial aid, life issues that may arise, etc.? Choose a person who is easy to talk to…someone you feel comfortable asking questions of, and someone you trust and think you can look up to. Is that person in the career that you would like to be in? Is that person a model student? Has that person been to college, and was s/he successful?

After you decide on someone you think would be appropriate, it's as simple as asking that person to help you with your college experience. People are usually very willing to help when they can.

Once you get a knowledgeable mentor, your college experience will never be the same.

*Michelle T. Williams, Ed.D., has developed retention and support programs for academically at-risk, first generation, and minority students at the high school and college levels.*

**MY NUMBER ONE WORRY** was gaining the "Freshman 15." So I went to the gym three times a week, I joined the dance team, and I became a vegetarian. That's a lot of stuff, but it worked.
> —*M.T.*
> *GEORGIA STATE UNIVERSITY, SENIOR*

**IT'S OKAY TO DO THINGS ALONE.** As a freshman, I went without meals because I couldn't find anyone to go with me to them. When I first started college, I equated doing things alone to not having friends to do them with. It was only after I convinced myself that I still needed to eat and have fun, even if it meant doing those things alone, that I actually began to enjoy and even look forward to alone time. You are constantly surrounded by people in college, so having time for yourself is extremely important.
> —*EMMA*
> *UNIVERSITY OF PENNSYLVANIA, GRADUATE*

**STRICT PARENTING EQUALS NOT DOING WELL** in college. Strict parenting doesn't prepare kids for the overload of freedom they will experience in college. Relaxed parents bring up kids who can balance school work and social life. Don't expect to go to college to have fun. Do the work first and enjoy yourself later.
> —*DAVID*
> *KEAN UNIVERSITY, JUNIOR*

**I WASN'T EXPECTING TO SPEND** as much time sitting up and talking to people, going to people's dorms and talking until 3 A.M. That was pretty cool. It didn't help with sleep habits or work habits but it was definitely worth it, looking back.
> —*EMILY*
> *HARVARD COLLEGE, SENIOR*

# FIRST-GENERATION STUDENTS

As the first in your family to go to college, how do you talk to your family members about college? And how much can you lean on them for tips about how to succeed? Here are three that are especially relevant for the "first-generation" college experience:

1) **Attend New Student Orientation:** You'll learn more about your campus resources, get a thorough tour, make a four-year course plan and register for your first classes. You'll get your bearings and figure out how best to tap into resources available to you on campus and in the community, especially if your campus has programs geared specifically around the needs of first-generation students. Plus, you'll make your first new college friends!

2) **Involve your family:** your family will be proud that you are in college and will want to celebrate every success with you. Some parents of first-generation students may not understand that you have to dedicate so much time to college, so you may have to convince your family that the resources and tips you are getting from campus will help you thrive. For instance, if they know that going home is not an option the week before exams, then they may feel as though they are contributing to your college success. Invite them instead to visit at a time that works for everyone and introduce them to people you've met on campus. And if there is a family orientation, bring them.

3) **Find a mentor:** Upper division students or peer mentors will be a great help, particularly if they, too, are first-generation college students.

*Scott C. Silverman*

**DON'T FORGET THE REASON YOU'RE THERE.** I went into college thinking I was going to be this new person with a new style, new friends, new everything. I soon realized that I was the same person who graduated high school a few months ago. I befriended the same kind of people and did the same things I did in high school. Broaden your surroundings and meet new people but don't go so far you miss the kind of people you know you love. Most importantly, don't forget you're there to study and get a degree. Looking back at freshman year, classes were so easy compared to now. Get those easy A's while you can.

    —*REBECCA*
    *COLLEGE OF NEW JERSEY, SENIOR*

• • • • • • • • •

**YOU MIGHT START OUT LOWER,** but that'll force you to get up to where everyone else is. I came from a public high school and the level of stuff that we did was subpar compared to what is taught at many prestigious high schools. So, when I came here to Princeton, without the background that others came in with, I felt kind of inferior and dumb because everyone just knew this stuff that the professor was discussing.

The first quiz I took at Princeton was one of the worst tests I've ever taken. It had three questions and it was timed for 50 minutes. I only completed one question, and it wasn't even done correctly. That first grade was a wake-up call. After that, I did some reflection and changed my habits up a little bit.

It levels out. Know that the first semester will be an adjustment and don't be intimidated. You had the drive to get to college and you're going to make it through. Just focus on yourself, instead of comparing yourself to other people.

    —*ANONYMOUS*
    *PRINCETON UNIVERSITY, JUNIOR*

# HOW TO SUCCEED ACADEMICALLY, FROM A PRO IN THE KNOW

For you, along with the overwhelming majority of the hundreds of students I see in my capacity as a dean in a college advising center, the first year of college will be a transitional one, on many fronts. Your professors will introduce you to ideas and views that may be different from your own, and they will challenge you to meet higher academic standards. You will set your own academic and co-curricular schedules, and you will be solely responsible for meeting your responsibilities on campus. Because this new setting and your newfound independence present both challenges and opportunities, here are a few strategies (not intended as a comprehensive list) for successfully navigating Year One.

1. **Show up**. As people have often noted, 80 percent of success in life is just showing up. So, go to class, and, I would add, show up prepared. Do the reading, the problem sets, whatever task has been assigned to you. If you are confused by an assignment or if you are nervous about participating in a discussion, jot down a few observations or questions. Thoughtful questions are often just as productive and valuable in class as answers and commentary.

2. **Ask for help.** Reach out to faculty when you are struggling with class material. Reach out to them with questions when you're not struggling, too. It's perfectly appropriate to seek instructors' guidance on a topic raised in class, their thoughts regarding a broader academic discipline, their advice on a prospective major, etc. Professors and TAs hold office hours, which are times earmarked for students with precisely these types of concerns. Academic advisors and other university staff are also on call to help with any other issues that arise – but they often do not know if there is a problem unless you reach out. You should feel emboldened to do so.

3. **Rethink your notions** about what constitutes academic success. What is "academic success" anyway? As a high school student, you worked hard, earned top grades and rightfully earned your spot at a selective college. I often find myself trying to disabuse students of an unhealthy fixation on their GPAs, and of avowed striving for the "perfect" 4.0. This mindset, in which a GPA is often unduly viewed as validating (or impugning) not only a student's intellect, but also his or her overall worth, is pernicious, largely because it overlooks the tremendous importance of making mistakes. When students regroup after a stumble, they learn resilience and grow intellectually. So, rather than chasing that elusive 4.0, I urge you to prioritize assimilating the material you are being exposed to, and expanding and improving your skills as a critical, quantitative, or creative thinker.

I'll end with a story recounted to me by one of my most successful advisees, because it encapsulates all three of my recommendations. My student – let's call him Nathan – earned a grade of D on his first exam in a challenging class. He was used to getting better grades. Disappointed, but determined to improve, he visited his professor to review his test and figure out what he had missed. During that meeting, the professor, who was at that point a tenured expert in his field, told Nathan that he, as an undergraduate, had also received a D on his first exam in the identical class.

Nathan ended up earning a B+ in the class, a mark he takes more pride in than in the several A's he racked up during his undergraduate years. Since graduation, he has enjoyed considerable success – and fulfillment – both professionally and in his graduate studies. This is as much a product of his undergraduate academic record (solid, but not a 4.0) as it is to his commitment to showing up, asking for help, and learning from his mistakes.

*Erica Siegel is the Assistant Dean of Communications and Outreach at Columbia University's James H. and Christine Turk Berick Center for Student Advising.*

# GET ENGAGED

Research shows that the more engaged students are during college, the higher their level of success throughout college and in their careers. Engaging in campus activities will help you build skills and experiences, and make you a well-rounded candidate for jobs once you graduate. Your involvement also supports your college and makes it a better place to go to school.

**Things To Do During Your First Year on Campus**
- ☐ Find one or two student organizations that interest you and join them.
- ☐ Attend at least two big campus events: This is one of the coolest things about college that you won't get anywhere else in life: Convocation, Welcome Week, Homecoming, or a Fall Festival/Block Party/Spring Splash events, etc.
- ☐ Attend a sporting event for at least two different sports.
- ☐ Go to a professor's or TA's office hours and ask a question.
- ☐ Explore your college town with roommates and hall mates.
- ☐ Take a picture with your university's mascot. Maybe later you can try out to be the mascot.
- ☐ Explore some of the hidden gems of your campus – a botanic garden or a courtyard that's tucked away.
- ☐ Read your campus newspaper. If you want, try to write for it.
- ☐ Listen to your campus radio station.
- ☐ Attend at least one meeting of your student government. You may really enjoy the topics discussed and get motivated to help create positive change on campus.
- ☐ If you have the opportunity to meet someone important or famous on campus, or just hear them speak, do so. Grades are important, of course – for future employers, grad schools, etc. But when people ask you what you did in college and what you learned, getting involved on campus will help you best answer those questions – and that probably means a lot more than simply getting great grades.

*Scott C. Silverman, Ed.D.*

**I** SOMETIMES WISH THAT PEOPLE DIDN'T TELL ME HOW MUCH FUN COLLEGE WOULD BE. I think I went into college with a little bit of a heightened expectation of the fun that I would have and all the new things I would experience and whatnot, and in a way, it kind of set an unrealistic perception of college life in general. Don't get me wrong – college is definitely a lot of fun, and maybe sometimes *too* fun – but there are also a lot of late nights spent at the library that people don't show off on their Instagrams.
—*CHRISTINE*
*DREXEL UNIVERSITY, JUNIOR*

**FOR** MANY PEOPLE, COLLEGE IS THEIR FIRST OPPORTUNITY to experience life without the filter set up by their (surely well-meaning) parents. That can be exhilarating and scary, and everyone handles it differently, some more productively and healthily than others. If you understand your peers' sometimes inexplicably stupid behavior through that lens, things make a little more sense. And it's okay to be inexplicably stupid sometimes – it's how you learn how not to be.
—*MAX*
*DARTMOUTH COLLEGE, GRADUATE*

**THE** THING THAT STANDS OUT THE MOST about my freshman year is the fact that I was completely responsible for my learning. No one cared if I came to class or not; no one cared if I took notes or studied for a test. I remember thinking that it was wonderful to have so much freedom, and if the professors didn't care, why should I? I took full advantage of having no attendance phone calls, no conduct grades, no authoritarian instructors. By the time I figured out that I was wasting my time (and my parents' money) and that I had to take responsibility for my education, it wasn't too late, but my GPA never fully recovered.
—*S.A.S.*
*UNIVERSITY OF SOUTH FLORIDA, GRADUATE*

*"Pottery Barn again? Don't these kids have any imagination?"*

# Dorms: On- and Off-Campus Options

Y our parents tell you that your dorm is a hundred times fancier than the dorms they had when they were college students – you just wish they could see what your hall looks like on Sunday mornings. And even at the very best of times, five minutes after the custodial staff tunnel their way through, there are still plenty of interpersonal adventures to face: The neighbor who steams broccoli every single night at 6:45. The neighbor who stays in shape by kicking a soccer ball against the wall for hours. And then there's you – wanting to have fun and hang out, but sometimes craving just one moment of peace and privacy. Try not to get too hung up on the poor hygiene and see this for the opportunity it is: never again will you live in a building teeming with so many people your own age. Read on to see what else you might be in for – and what to do about it!

GROW ACCUSTOMED TO SEEING some things in the bathroom that you just wouldn't at home. You will learn to cherish personal space and privacy in ways you never could before.
—J.V.
THE COLLEGE OF WILLIAM & MARY, GRADUATE

IF YOU PUT A THOUSAND FRESHMEN INTO A BUILDING, ANYTHING CAN AND WILL HAPPEN.
—B.
GEORGE WASHINGTON UNIVERSITY, SENIOR

**HEADLINES**

- Be respectful of your roommates and clean up after yourself.
- Set a monthly cleaning schedule with your roommates, and stick to it.
- Try to meet all the people on your floor – it makes sharing a bathroom easier.
- Dorm life means adjusting to living with a lot of other people in a small space.

Dorms are a good place if you can deal with living in a box with another person.

—*K.M.*
  *Northwestern University, Graduate*

YOU ARE AN ADULT. SO, YOU DO HAVE TO TAKE SOME RESPONSIBILITY FOR BEING CLEAN because it can get out of hand and other people are going to see your space. This very friendly guy who worked at a restaurant I liked gave me his number on my receipt one night, and I texted him. He invited me over, and when I got to his place, I thought: 'this cannot be true.' It could literally have been on the show *Hoarders*. The door barely opened because of all the stuff that was everywhere. It smelled like B.O., old food, bathroom, and musk. I was expecting a rat to come out of the pile of clothes. I haven't talked to him since.
—*Greta*
  *Northern Arizona University, Graduate*

• • • • • • • •

GIVE YOURSELF UP TO THE CABIN FEVER that sometimes comes with dorm life. Never again will you have the opportunity to run around in your pajamas, darting into the open doors that line the halls. Once, when it was snowing, my roommate and I opened our door, blasted music, ran to every one of our friends' rooms, did a little dance, then moved on to the next. It's one of the goofiest memories I have of my freshman year.
—*Allison Greco*
  *Montclair State University, Graduate*

**THE SHOWERS ARE GROSS.** I was raised with boys, and I always thought they were smelly and disgusting, but girls are equally gross, but in very different ways. Nobody was like, "Oh, you're going to share a bathroom with 48 other girls, and there's always going to be garbage and toothpaste and hair *everywhere*." The custodians are underpaid.
—KENDRA KLUMB
UNIVERSITY OF SIOUX FALLS, JUNIOR

**BRING HEADPHONES INTO THE DORM BATHROOM.** The hardest adjustment for me moving into the dorms was learning to live without privacy. Communal bathrooms scared the crap out of me. You can't dance around times or try to wait for someone to take a shower for the noise. Just go in there, put headphones on, and do what you need to do. I think a lot of people have a hard time pooping in public. It was the elephant in the room when there were four girls in a stall and it was pin-drop silence for ten minutes because everyone was scared to drop their first dump. I started putting on headphones so I could block out all the social rules and all the social norms and just not care and do what I needed to do, fully and openly.
—MEGHAN WALLACE
NORTHERN ARIZONA UNIVERSITY, SENIOR

**SET MONTHLY CLEANUP TIMES** and stick to them. Failure to do so might result in an infestation of dust bunnies.
—KHALIL SULLIVAN
PRINCETON UNIVERSITY, JUNIOR

**FRESHMEN WHO PULLED THE FIRE ALARMS** in the dorms were never caught - but you can definitely get arrested for that.
—SHELBY SMITH
GUILFORD COLLEGE, GRADUATE

**I'M AN ONLY CHILD** and I lived with three girls in one big room. It was a pretty big adjustment the first semester. I remember being kind of miserable. You don't get much sleep and there's a lot of work to do. But you get through it.

—*ANNE*
*GEORGE WASHINGTON UNIVERSITY, SENIOR*

· · · · · · · ·

**LIVE IN THE DORMS WITH FRESHMEN** in small ratty rooms. It doesn't sound right, I know, but it's what I wish I had done. My school had a variety of dorms that ran from old, predominantly freshman dorms with tiny, two-person rooms, to newly renovated, upper classman dorms that were like six-person apartments. I chose the middle of the road; a mostly upperclassman dorm with large rooms. Big mistake. These types of dorms aren't conducive to meeting lots of people, which is what freshman year is all about. Through a classmate in one of the older dorms with tiny rooms, I discovered a social wonderland. Everyone in the building was a freshman, everyone kept their doors open, and everyone wandered around meeting and greeting. There was pretty much a family or little town atmosphere; everyone hung out and did lots of stuff together. This is what the freshman experience was supposed to be.

—*JEFF*
*BOWLING GREEN STATE UNIVERSITY, GRADUATE*

· · · · · · · ·

**IF YOU'RE GOING TO LIVE IN THE DORM,** I hope you like noise. Dorms are what they are advertised to be: a place to meet people and have lots of fun. Some of my best friends to this day are people I met and bonded with while trying to survive dorm life. So, if you opt for living in the dorms, expect a lot of fun and interesting experiences; just don't count on getting a lot of studying or sleep.

—*K. HARMA*
*WESTERN WASHINGTON UNIVERSITY, GRADUATE*

# OFF-CAMPUS FOLLIES

I thought living in a dorm would be stifling and stupid, so I got an apartment next to campus with three other roommates. Now *that* was stupid. Friends from the dorms – and their friends – considered our place Party Central, since they had no other place to go and were too young to get into bars. There was a parade of people in and out of the place almost every night – not to mention an abundance of alcohol and drugs. The police came four different times, warning us to quiet down. Regulars included the entire trumpet section of the marching band, a five-piece rock band of bare-chested guys, and a torch-juggling pharmacy student. The apartment was trashed and I was always afraid of getting in big legal trouble. I tried to kick everyone out, but my roommates refused to back me up. At the end of the year, I packed up my stuff and moved into the dorms.

—*W.*
*University of Georgia, Graduate*

**MOST RESIDENTIAL ADVISORS IN COLLEGE AREN'T THERE TO "GET YOU."** I was an R.A. They're not there to be narcs. Instead, they just want that sweet, sweet financial aid, and free housing in some places.

—*Naf*
*New York University, Graduate*

**I CHOSE A DORM ROOM WHERE WE HAD OUR OWN BATHROOM;** that was a huge mistake. It got destroyed. You have a roommate and you think, "Well, maybe I'll wait for him to clean it up." But it never happens. By the end of the year, I didn't even go in there.

—*Johnny*
*Georgetown University, Junior*

# ADVICE FROM A FORMER R.A.

- **MAKE FRIENDS WITH YOUR RESIDENT ASSISTANTS.** They know most of the professors and staff on campus and can put you in touch with people a lot more easily than if you had to just walk in or cold-call an office.

- **IF YOU HAVE ROOMMATE PROBLEMS,** handle them right away. If you wait, you might get stuck with someone who already had a roommate move out, so you'll probably end up with a worse roommate.

- **IF YOU DRINK UNDERAGE,** be quiet. You're far less likely to get caught if you're quiet.

- **IF YOU SMOKE POT,** don't do it in your room. It is very easily smelled and tracked down.

- **IF YOU DAMAGE YOUR ROOM,** report it immediately. The staff likes students who are up-front and appear apologetic. If we find it when you move out, you will definitely get a bigger bill, and your parents will be mad.

- **FIND OUT THE DORM RULES UP FRONT.** Some schools can call your parents for offenses, some schools can revoke your housing for getting in trouble, and so on. You don't want to have to explain to your parents mid-semester that you got kicked out for playing your stereo too loud.

- **DO ANYTHING YOU CAN TO MOVE IN EARLY.** Moving in with everyone else is a nightmare.

- **YOUR RESIDENCE DIRECTOR CAN ALSO BE A GOOD RESOURCE** to talk to about classes, professors, what to take and what to avoid, and other campus tips. Many students avoid the hall staff, but if you drop by on occasion, they will go out of their way to give you good information and help you.

    —*MELISSA*
      *GRADUATE*

I LIVED IN AN ALL-GIRL DORM, and for the first two weeks, everyone was happy. But then we all started getting our periods at the same time, and everyone became bitchy all together. It was terrible. And the dorm was filthy. You'd think an all-girl dorm would be clean, but girls are definitely dirtier than guys. Our bathroom was disgusting. And the end of the year was ridiculous. We had garbage cans spilling into the hallways. Living off campus now is like a slice of heaven.

—*S.L.*
*EMORY UNIVERSITY, JUNIOR*

It's much more fun living with other people than living by yourself.

—*MATT LACKNER*
*PRINCETON UNIVERSITY, GRADUATE*

IF YOU'RE MISSING YOUR ROOM AT HOME, try and personalize your side of the dorm room. Within a few weeks, you'll feel like it's where you belong. What's weird, though, is when I went home for a few days, I felt like I wasn't home, and I wanted to go back to my dorm room. I've talked to multiple people about this, and lots of other freshmen have this same feeling.

—*JONATHAN LIU*
*UNIVERSITY OF TENNESSEE AT KNOXVILLE, FRESHMAN*

# EARLY TROUBLEMAKER MAKES GOOD

Washington & Lee College in Lexington, Va. may have the distinction of having hosted the first college streaker. Back in 1804, one of its seniors, George William Crump, got himself suspended for "running naked through the streets." Crump, no worse for the wear, eventually graduated from Princeton, studied medicine at the University of Pennsylvania, and went on to become a U.S. Congressman and Ambassador to Chile. President Andrew Jackson even appointed him chief clerk of the Pension Bureau in 1832.

**WHEN I CAME TO SCHOOL, I KNEW NO ONE.** I entered an all-male dorm and everyone thought we were dirty, stinky guys – and we were. With no girls around, there was no need to really focus on hygiene. But because we were so isolated, we bonded super tight and have great friendships for life. We have the last laugh: Now we can bathe, but the other folks don't have our strong friendships. All-male dorms are a good idea.

—*JUSTIN PEABODY*
*CARNEGIE MELLON UNIVERSITY, JUNIOR*

* * * * * * * *

**No matter how nice your R.A. is, don't date him. It always turns out to be a bad thing.**

—*KYM*
*SAN JOSE STATE UNIVERSITY, SOPHOMORE*

* * * * * * * *

Make sure you have good music coming out of your room, since that's a good conversation starter.

—*B.K.*
*CORNELL UNIVERSITY, GRADUATE*

**CONSIDER RENTING A FURNISHED APARTMENT.** I did that when I first started at a community college. It was awesome, and the price difference was very small. I didn't have to put in any money to buy my own gear, and when it came time to move, I didn't have to worry about selling my stuff or putting it out on the street corner. Sometimes the furniture inside the apartment was a bit cheap; my bed had these horrible wooden planks keeping the mattress up, and if I shifted too much the planks would fall and the bed would sag. I still felt like it was a good way to save some money, and it was nice to just have everything there.

—*COREY*
*SAN DIEGO STATE UNIVERSITY, JUNIOR*

**MAKE IT A POINT** to get to know everyone on your floor at the dorm. Invite everyone to a weekly pre-dinner cocktail party. Play some icebreaker games so that everyone gets to know everyone else. Without their old high school cliques and social circles to fall back on, most people are truly eager to meet new people and make new connections. My dorm years were phenomenal, thanks to all my fantastic floor mates.

> —*LAURA WOLTER*
> *UNIVERSITY OF TEXAS AT AUSTIN, GRADUATE*

**RESPECT YOUR ROOMMATE** and don't leave pizza in the room for a week. It's not your roommate's job to throw it out. The room stinks; it's not livable. People don't want to come in your room because it stinks. And don't try to blame the bad smell on the fact that your roommate's clothes are on the floor. That is not what's causing the nasty, rotten smell in your room. That would be the pizza box that you left there for a week.

> —*ANONYMOUS*
> *UNIVERSITY OF VIRGINIA, SOPHOMORE*

# REMEDY FOR HOMESICKNESS:

1. Keep busy. Go to campus events.
2. Decorate your dorm room; that can definitely make it feel more homey. A comfy bed with lots of padding and sheets will be your best friend.
3. Call home. It's okay to call multiple times a day, especially when you just want to hear Mom's or Dad's voice. I still do it as a sophomore.

By second semester, you'll be calling the dorms your home.

> —*SHEILA CRAWFORD*
> *NORTH CAROLINA STATE UNIVERSITY, SOPHOMORE*

# HIGH-CLASS DORMS

College students and their families expect to spend $940 on average on back-to-school items each year, according to the National Retail Federation. Planned purchases range from $229 in electronics on average to $109 on household furnishings and $52 on college-branded gear.

**REACH OUT IMMEDIATELY** to people living on your floor. It didn't thrill me to know that I would have to share a bathroom with 40 other girls. But I ended up having the most fun. Bonding with my roommates and floor mates, going to floor events, and even playing pranks were all memories to be cherished.
> —*RAE LYNN RUCKER*
> *BIOLA UNIVERSITY, GRADUATE*

66 Living in the dorm, everyone knows about everyone else. If you do something dumb, everyone knows about it. 99
> —*MAUREEN S.*
> *GEORGETOWN UNIVERSITY, SOPHOMORE*

**GET A ROOM NEAR THE SHOWERS.** My dorm was always so cold in the mornings, especially in the winter. I hated that long walk down the hall while I was practically naked.
> —*ANONYMOUS*
> *YOUNGSTOWN STATE UNIVERSITY, SENIOR*

# DORM ADVENTURES

**WE HAD MICE.** We had a sewer pipe break in our building, and all these little mice were running around. So we set traps. Our hall worked together to catch them; it was teamwork.
—*LAUREN WEBSTER*
*BARNARD COLLEGE, JUNIOR*

**DORM LIFE CAN HAVE A BAD REPUTATION,** but don't knock it. Everyone should have the experience. We had a blast in the freshman dorms – we had a grill on the patio, so we'd barbecue at night sometimes, especially if the cafeteria food was creepy. It's a great way to meet people – and after this year, you have the rest of your life to pay your own electric bill.
—*J.I.*
*SONOMA STATE UNIVERSITY, JUNIOR*

**MAKE FRIENDS WITH PEOPLE** who are not on your hall. That way, when you need a break from your dorm or your roommate, you can call those people and say, "I need to get out of here, I'm coming over!" I would usually completely leave my dorm during the day. I wouldn't return to my room until the evening. That way my life didn't revolve around my hall. Find something to do by yourself outside your dorm, like biking, running, or singing; whatever it is that will get you out.
—*SUMMER J.*
*UNIVERSITY OF VIRGINIA, SENIOR*

**I TRY TO HAVE A** "low impact" on the room – meaning, I try to keep the volume down on music or television when my roommate's clearly doing work or sleeping, and I generally clean up after myself.
—*MANNY*
*GEORGE WASHINGTON UNIVERSITY, SENIOR*

I HAD TO SHARE A BATHROOM with about 20 girls and a kitchen with about 40 girls. That took a bit of an adjustment; there were some "whoa" moments. But I feel that is part of the college experience. Just be as clean and polite as possible.
—REBECCA
HUNTER COLLEGE, SENIOR

* * * * * * * *

ONE OF THE MOST IMPORTANT THINGS about surviving freshman year is that if you live in coed dorms like I did, you're going to see people in all states of life. You're going to see them on the can, you're going to see them before they've painted their face on, and you're going to have to get over the shock. I've met long-term friends in the dorms. Everyone bonds in a totally different way when you live there. People go through difficult times – separation from family, separation from friends – and you all have that in common.
—ZACH FRIEND
UNIVERSITY OF CALIFORNIA AT SANTA CRUZ, GRADUATE

* * * * * * * *

GO NUTS ON THE DECORATING. Be tacky, be shocking. This is the only time in your life you can get away with hanging a beer sign in your window or assembling a Buddha shrine in your bathroom. I actually had an Elvis shrine in my bathroom.
—WENDY W.
UNIVERSITY OF GEORGIA, GRADUATE

* * * * * * * *

ONE OF MY FRIENDS LIVED above a group of guys who would blare music until one or two in the morning. She would go down in her pajamas and ask them to turn the music down, but they never did. So, one morning when she got up at six, she opened up her windows and blared country music until she could hear them stirring and cursing.
—ANONYMOUS
WESTERN WASHINGTON UNIVERSITY, GRADUATE

# SOME HOME AWAY FROM HOME

- Springfield College (Massachusetts) has an 57-acre "campground and outdoor adventure area."
- Southern Vermont College boasts a 27-room Edwardian mansion.
- University of Chicago is said to be the college campus most like Hogwarts.

**GUYS, KEEP YOUR ROOMS CLEAN,** because there will be girls in your room and they'll be turned off if you have disgusting rooms.
> —*REID ATTAWAY*
> *JAMES MADISON UNIVERSITY, SOPHOMORE*

• • • • • • • •

**THERE'S A LOT OF ANNOYING THINGS ABOUT BEING ON-CAMPUS** – like their strict guest policy. That can be a really good thing to think about when you're choosing to live on-campus or off. But I'd definitely recommend living on-campus at least your first year so that you can get used to college before having to pay bills and stuff!
> —*NINA*
> *TEMPLE UNIVERSITY, JUNIOR*

• • • • • • • •

**SPEND TIME MAKING YOUR ROOM** a place you would want to hang out in and study in. If you don't feel comfortable in your room, which is basically your college home, where are you going to feel comfortable?
> —*JULIE*
> *PRINCETON UNIVERSITY, SOPHOMORE*

# DON'T TRY THESE AT HOME

**MY ROOMMATE SECRETLY RECORDED** my cacophonous shower singing and played it for our hall. Another time, my friend hid under my bed making scratching noises until I was terrified that I had mice.
—*STEPHANIE DREIFUSS*
*DUKE UNIVERSITY, SENIOR*

. . . . . . . . .

**DURING FINALS WEEK,** I was studying in the common area of my floor. The elevator opened and I saw that the elevator had been fully furnished with a chest of drawers, a few books sitting on its top (along with a vase of fake flowers), a chair, a bookshelf, a bowl of popcorn (which I found to be the most odd), and a few posters that were hastily taped to the wall.
—*REBECCA*
*HUNTER COLLEGE, SENIOR*

. . . . . . . . .

**BUY A LOT OF DAWN** or dishwashing soap and pour them down the drain of a water fountain that people use. Let the soap bubbles begin! The fountain turns into a bubble bath.
—*G.L.*
*GEORGE WASHINGTON UNIVERSITY, SENIOR*

. . . . . . . . .

**IF YOU HAVE ANY MEANS OF GETTING AHOLD OF SAND,** find a way into your victim's room and cover everything with sand. Having a beach-themed dorm room might sound sweet. But there is nothing more time-consuming and irritating to get rid of than sand. Water turns it to mud, and you will never be able to vacuum it all up.
—*J.V.*
*THE COLLEGE OF WILLIAM & MARY, GRADUATE*

I LIVED IN A CO-OP MY FIRST YEAR, so I wasn't pampered by the dorms. It's chaos 100 percent of the time, but it's worth it. It's about self-sufficiency. We don't go to the army after high school, like they do in Israel. Here we go to college, so here is where we need to learn independence, develop a thick skin, and learn how to balance life.
　　　*—KATE L.*
　　　　*UNIVERSITY OF CALIFORNIA AT BERKELEY, JUNIOR*

· · · · · · · ·

TAKE MEASURES TO MAKE YOUR DORM COMFORTABLE AND BEAUTIFUL. You reflect the space you're in, and you're not going to make a new home if you're feeling apathetic about your dorm. Put up pictures, invest in a nice throw rug, and design it the way you'd like.
　　　*—VALERIE BODURTHA*
　　　　*UNIVERSITY OF CHICAGO, GRADUATE*

· · · · · · · ·

IT'S IMPORTANT TO FIND TIME to be by yourself in your room. Living in the dorms is always hectic. We all need time to relax alone, and this is often hard to come by in the dorms. Don't be afraid to shut your door and relax alone.
　　　*—ILAN GLUCK*
　　　　*UNIVERSITY OF MARYLAND, JUNIOR*

· · · · · · · ·

MAKE FRIENDS WITH SOMEONE WHO HAS A CAR. Without transportation, it's hard to get snacks or even toiletries, especially if the dorms are far from town. Sometimes you just need to go to Walgreens. It's also nice to have someone to take you on an In-N-Out Burger run at midnight when the dining halls aren't an option and you're hungry.
　　　*—ANDREW*
　　　　*UCLA, SENIOR*

**AT THE END OF MY FRESHMAN YEAR,** the carpets literally had to be pulled up and replaced. We wrecked them. It happens if you plan on being the social center of your building.
—*BARRY LANGER*
*OGLETHORPE UNIVERSITY, JUNIOR*

* * * * * * * *

**I highly recommend you loft both of your beds. The amount of floor space you get is killer.**
—*ELISE*
*WESTERN CAROLINA UNIVERSITY, GRADUATE*

* * * * * * * *

**YOU WILL LEARN THAT** there are two kinds of people when it comes to food and drink – the moochers and the moochees. Moochees get the respect, but moochers eat and get drunk at their expense.
—*J.V.*
*THE COLLEGE OF WILLIAM & MARY, GRADUATE*

* * * * * * * *

**TAKING THE TIME TO DECORATE** your room and make it homey is extremely important, especially freshman year. Bring a stuffed animal or set up curtains in your room. Things like that make your room feel more like a home. Having a plant in your room is a huge bonus, potted plants or flowers... It's nice to have something to care for and look after! Getting a carpet and changing the curtains made my room so much homier and really changed the feel of the room completely.
—*CATIE*
*HARVARD COLLEGE, SENIOR*

## ASK A GRAD... OR MAYBE NOT

# 10 BRO MOVIE POSTERS, LESS MANLY THAN A BLANK WALL, THAT STILL MAKE IT CLEAR HOW COOL YOU ARE:

1. Scarface
2. Fight Club
3. Step Brothers
4. Clockwork Orange
5. Wolf of Wall Street
6. Wedding Crashers
7. Rambo
8. Anything with boobs on it
9. Eat, Pray, Love
10. Saturday Night Fever

*Val Bodurtha is a Chicago-based writer and comedian.*

**EXPECT TO LIVE IN** a diverse environment. Expect to be independent. Expect to have a lot of fun. Expect to procrastinate, but learn to prioritize.
—*ALEKSANDR AKULOV*
*HUNTER COLLEGE, SOPHOMORE*

• • • • • • • •

**DEFINITELY GO THE DORM ROUTE** your freshman year. That's where I met all of my friends, including the girl I live with now! You meet the most people by sharing the bathroom, waiting for a shower stall or while brushing your teeth. My friends and I would have shower parties! We'd all make a plan to meet at 9 P.M., bring in a radio and blast the music while singing in the shower. I think establishing a clique your freshman year is really important, and the dorm is the place to do it. Stay longer than one year if you can.
—*JESSICA DOSHNA*
*UCLA, GRADUATE*

# TIPS FOR COMMUTERS

Maybe your parents want you close to home, or you have to help take care of younger siblings or keep expenses low. That's okay; a lot of students choose to live off-campus. Here are some tips that can help you succeed:

1. **Schedule your classes to maximize your time efficiently:** Maybe you want to take all of your classes back-to-back, or fit all of them in fewer than 5 days a week, to reduce your commuting days. You won't always be able to make your schedule work out as smoothly as you want, but that's okay, too.

2. **Take advantage of your "down time:"** Commuter students can find great things to do on campus in between classes – beyond just going back to your car to take a nap between classes. You can spend that time reviewing your notes for the next class or working on assignments.

3. **Transportation tips:** If you drive to campus, leave plenty of time to get to campus and find parking. You can't use traffic or a lack of parking spaces as an excuse for being late to class or exams. If you bike to campus, register your bike with campus police in case it ever gets stolen. (And get a great lock – like the one we describe in Chapter 1 – to reduce that possibility.) If you walk, pay attention to your surroundings and don't walk with your earphones in... Finally, however you commute, plan ahead so you can run your errands on the way home rather than making separate trips.

4. **Make friends with people living on campus:** It's going to happen: There will be a late-night program on campus that you really want to attend, and if you have a friend on campus, you can go to the event with them, and hang out afterwards. It keeps you off the freeway late at night when you're tired and builds your social circle.

*Scott C. Silverman*

**WHENEVER YOU LEAVE YOUR DORM ROOM,** bring your key with you. My friend woke up late one day and half-unconsciously took a shower in the dorm bathrooms. He only had a towel on, and flip-flops. After his shower he returned to his dorm room to find it locked; he was locked out. Everyone was in class, even his RA. He had to run to the other side of campus in his towel to our friend's laundry room to borrow some clothes so that he could go to lunch and to class.

—*E.F.*
*CLAREMONT MCKENNA COLLEGE, SOPHOMORE*

. . . . . . . . .

**FRESHMAN DORMS ARE LIKE A BIG,** happy family. Once you get to know everyone, you'll have people you can rely on for anything you need. Broken computer? Your trusty technology genius is just upstairs. Can't sleep? There are always a few dorm night owls in the common room. Wondering about a class for next semester? Chances are you'll find someone who already took it. Be ready for people to count on you for something, too! By earning a reputation as a master stain remover, I subjected myself to an entire year of removing people's unconquerable stains.

—*STEPHANIE DREIFUSS*
*DUKE UNIVERSITY, SENIOR*

*"I get it that inspiration struck, Krystal...but does it always
have to strike at 3 AM?"*

# Roommates: Living With Perfect (and Not-So Perfect) Strangers

Y ou have friends – sure, but have you ever tried living with them? This is a whole new ballgame and it doesn't always work out as expected. There's no better way to learn all there is to know (and smell) about a person than to live with them. Living with a good friend from high school or a random classmate from the other side of the world can come with a host of unanticipated conundrums and faux pas. You might have to learn to deal with personality traits or lifestyle choices you didn't even know existed.

The classic clash of personalities and cultures make for some of the most hilarious and memorable stories known to man, and even to some life-long friendships, but in the moment, it can be seriously stressful. The interpersonal lessons you learn in these sardine-like years may just be the ones that stay with you the longest.

TRY TO HAVE AN OPEN MIND about your roommate. It makes a difference.
—DAVID
KEAN UNIVERSITY, JUNIOR

FEEL FREE TO AVOID YOUR ROOMMATE IF YOU NEED TO.
—JOHN BENTLEY
TRINITY UNIVERSITY, GRADUATE

HEADLINES

- Be honest on your roommate form or you may end up with someone you don't get along with.
- Don't live with your high school friends; meet new people.
- Having a roommate you click with can be the best part of college life.
- If you and your roommate are at odds, don't be afraid to request a room change.

**GO OUT OF YOUR WAY TO BE MINDFUL OF YOUR ROOMMATE'S PERSONAL SPACE IN THE BEGINNING.** Dorms are notoriously tight-living spaces, especially freshman year. So, go out of your way to keep your mess on your side, or under your own bed. Go out of your way to adjust your routine for your roommate in the beginning – maybe eat breakfast a little earlier with them if they have morning class, or eat dinner a little later to meet up with them for lunch or dinner. Or just simply wear headphones when you watch something on your computer to be mindful of the noise or go to bed when they do. If your roommate can sense that you are doing these little things for their sake, more often than not, it gets reflected back to you. It's when you're not mindful of these little things that roommates tend to take notice.
—*ANONYMOUS*
*BOSTON COLLEGE, GRADUATE*

• • • • • • • •

**I LOVE MY ROOMMATE.** She's my closest friend here. We talked the day after we got the rooming information and we clicked on the phone. Don't come on too strong with your roommate, and don't think you have to be friends right away. But if you do, that's great.
—*M.D.*
*BOSTON COLLEGE, FRESHMAN*

**YOU CAN BE INDIFFERENT TO PEOPLE** you pass on your walks around campus, but if you're indifferent to your roommate, silence turns into coldness, and coldness turns into animosity, which might turn into hatred. So continue to cultivate your relationship with your roommates. Also, if you know that you are a naturally introverted person, go for a single. Many upperclassmen choose to have singles, so they must know something.

—*SEAN CAMERON*
*PRINCETON UNIVERSITY, SOPHOMORE*

* * * * * * * *

**I'M IN A TRIPLE.** What happens in a triple is that two people combine and go off together. And that's what happened with me; I'm the odd one out. But I don't feel bad about it because they're not my kind of people.

—*AMY HOFFBERG*
*UNIVERSITY OF DELAWARE, FRESHMAN*

* * * * * * * *

**IT'S BETTER TO TALK IT OUT THAN LET IT BE.** My freshman year roommate was a germaphobe. I'm a neat person, but he was on another level. He had this weird obsession with Lysol. It started with his spraying it around the room, which bothered me because I don't like the smell of chemicals and our room was so small. It evolved to his spraying his clothes and other belongings with Lysol. And then eventually, he began to spray it on himself. He really had an issue. I waited way too long to talk to him about it and ask if he could stop spraying so much Lysol since it became hard to breathe. He stopped for about three days and started using it again like he did before. I never talked to him about it again, because I didn't want to start a conflict since I would be stuck with him for another semester.

—*ANONYMOUS*
*FORDHAM UNIVERSITY, JUNIOR*

# FINDING YOUR MATCH

**BE REALLY HONEST ON YOUR ROOMMATE FORM** or you might end up with somebody you don't get along with. It's hard to share your personal space with someone else. The space tends to be really small.
—*RUTH FEINBLUM*
*BRYN MAWR COLLEGE, JUNIOR*

**IT'S HARD TO TELL YOU WHAT TO EXPECT** after filling out the roommate survey – half the kids who say they like neat rooms actually do like neat rooms, and the other half only say that in order to snag a neat roommate who will do all the cleaning.
—*J.V.*
*THE COLLEGE OF WILLIAM & MARY, GRADUATE*

**USE YOUR INGENUITY** to get a good roommate. When you are listing what you are like in the application for roommates, be honest. I know a guy who pretended to be a "stay in and study" kind of guy, and he got stuck with a roomie who never left the room and had a sleeping disorder. If he had been honest and said he liked to party, this would not have happened. If you get a bad roommate, get out of it before it gets worse. The longer you wait, the harder it is.
—*JUDSON KROH*
*CARNEGIE MELLON UNIVERSITY, JUNIOR*

**THE ROOMMATE-SELECTION SURVEYS NEVER ASK** questions that are meaningful enough to give you insight into how it's really going to be like to live with someone. So just expect the unexpected and get ready to be flexible. According to the survey, my freshman-year roommate appeared to be a conservative who liked country music. She turned out to be a very dynamic and wild gal who kept me laughing throughout the year.
—*K. HARMA*
*WESTERN WASHINGTON UNIVERSITY, GRADUATE*

# FRIENDS – OR ROOMMATES?

SOME PEOPLE MAKE GREAT FRIENDS, AND SOME PEOPLE MAKE GREAT ROOMMATES. I had arranged to be roommates with a high school friend – and the adage that you don't know someone until you live with them really applies. They may do things that you find bothersome, and if you weren't living with them, these characteristics may not have been revealed. So I recommend not rooming with someone you've known previously.
> —YALDA A.
> UNIVERSITY OF CALIFORNIA AT BERKELEY, GRADUATE

I LIVED WITH MY BEST FRIEND and it was the worst thing I did my freshman year. We didn't speak for a year after that. It was like a competition, rather than a partnership, always seeing who could make plans to do something cool, seeing how high the dishes could stack up. At first, we did everything together, but then learned we didn't like each other's company that much and almost never talked. That's not easy when you live with someone. When the year was finally over, it was a relief. We'd had enough of each other; there was no reason to hang out.
> —IRVING BURNS RAMSOWER III
> UNIVERSITY OF FLORIDA, GRADUATE

DON'T BE ROOMMATES with your old high-school friends because then you just bond together and you don't meet other people. But if you live with a new person she'll introduce you to a whole bunch of other aspects of life. She'll open you up to a whole world you wouldn't have expected. It worked for me. It was a good experience with my roommate and I learned a lot.
> —KYM
> SAN JOSE STATE UNIVERSITY, SOPHOMORE

# THE MESSY TRUTH

**CHECK UNDER YOUR ROOMMATE'S BED** for old, moldy food. For two weeks our room completely stunk. People were avoiding my room and I was wondering, "What's going on?" I never thought to look under my roommate's bed. When I did, I found an old can of salsa and moldy bread.
—*SIERRA*
   *CALIFORNIA POLYTECNIC STATE UNIVERSITY AT SAN LUIS OBISPO, JUNIOR*

**I ENDED UP ABSOLUTELY ADORING** my roommate's personality. But her tidiness, on the other hand, was an issue. My friends would joke that you couldn't even see my side of the room because of her stuff overflowing onto it, and my parents were horrified at the mess. But she turned out to be one of my best friends, so the best thing I could do was joke about it and try to give subtle hints. It wasn't even close to the worst scenario possible for a random roommate, but it was a challenge! I'm proud to say that we're still friends to this day.
—*MERELISE HARTE ROUZER*
   *GEORGIA INSTITUTE OF TECHNOLOGY, SOPHOMORE*

**MY ROOMMATE THINKS I'M MESSY** and I think she's too neat. We argue over that. And we have a division going down the middle of the room; her stuff on one side and mine on the other.
—*WHITNEY*
   *YALE UNIVERSITY, FRESHMAN*

**THE SCHOOL ASSIGNED ME A ROOMMATE,** and we didn't get along at all. She was completely my opposite – she smoked, she swore, she was messy. It was very uncomfortable anytime we were in the room together. Eventually we avoided that situation, except to sleep. As soon as the semester was over she asked for a transfer, and I was never happier.
—*JENNY PRISUTA*
   *YOUNGSTOWN STATE UNIVERSITY, SENIOR*

**I AM A MESSY PERSON.** Mess just doesn't bother me! But most of my roommates were not like that. The best advice I have is to just keep your mess to yourself! Be as messy as you want in your room, but do your best to keep the communal areas clean. I know it can be hard (it certainly was for me!), but it will help your relationships with your roommates. If you are a clean person, it is important to realize that you might live with a messy person! Be patient, as cleaning and being clean might not come naturally to your roommate.
—*ELIZABETH*
*UNIVERSITY OF ILLINOIS AT URBANA-CHAMPAIGN, GRADUATE*

. . . . . . . . .

**A GOOD ROOMMATE IS DIFFERENT** from a good friend. He or she should have about the same sleep schedule as you do, practice good hygiene, and not be too messy. I rarely talk to my roommate outside of the dorm room, but he's a great roommate who always makes the room smell nice.
—*JONATHAN LIU*
*UNIVERSITY OF TENNESSEE AT KNOXVILLE, FRESHMAN*

. . . . . . . . .

**SOME PEOPLE THINK IT'S BETTER** to live with someone who's just like them. But I learned that's not always the case. During my freshman year, I was paired with someone who was like me: a "clean freak." We got along fine, but surprisingly enough, we never became close friends. After she moved out at the end of the first semester, I moved in with Veronica. I knew she was a little more cluttered and messy than I was, but we became best friends. She is easy to talk to, and living together was a blessing.
—*EMILY TUCK*
*CALIFORNIA STATE UNIVERSITY, GRADUATE*

. . . . . . . . .

**YOU MAY NOT APPRECIATE IT ON DAY ONE,** but you'll be happy with a soft-spoken, class-attending roommate. It's tough to find someone in sync with you. You may think you want to room with someone who on paper appears to be like you, but it could be misery living with him or her.
—*J.*
*COLUMBIA UNIVERSITY, GRADUATE*

**ASK A GRAD...OR MAYBE NOT**

# DÉCOR TIPS FOR KEEPING YOUR ROOMMATE'S UGLY SHIT ON HER SIDE OF THE ROOM

a.  A line down the center of the room
b.  An ant infestation on your side
c.  A "Soviet Union" theme
d.  A whole lotta bear traps

*Val Bodurtha is a Chicago-based writer and comedian.*

**IF YOU NEED IT AND YOUR ROOMMATE IS REASONABLE,** just be honest and ask for some privacy. I had a roommate who would never tell me when he was bringing girls over. There were at least four different girls he would bring in on a schedule. I was on good terms with all of them. I knew their names and wasn't sure if I should mention the other girls or not because I didn't know what kind of pyramid scheme he had going on. He'd be on his bed with a different girl each day watching a movie or something, with me sitting at my laptop with headphones on trying not listen.

I went home at the end of the quarter and when I came back, I half-expected him to be going at it already with some girl. But when I opened the door, all his stuff was gone. The only sign he had been there was three individual socks. That's how I got out of the roommate situation.
—*NATHAN*
*DEPAUL UNIVERSITY, SOPHOMORE*

# HOPE FOR THE BEST, BUT EXPECT THE WORST

When I moved into the dorms, I was expecting that the college would pair me up with someone who shared my interests and who would become my new best friend. Boy, was I in for a surprise! I had *five* other roommates:

- A girl from San Diego who was some kind of singer. She would sing constantly…and I mean *constantly*. She was extremely bossy, annoying, and required a lot of attention.

- A smoker who would sit on the patio, smoke a pack of cigarettes an hour, and cry about how some girl had screwed her over.

- A girl who wore black lipstick and drawn-in eyebrows. We only saw her when she answered the door for her homeys and then they would lock themselves in her room and smoke pot for days on end.

- A girl who told her father she was living in the dorms, but was actually living with her boyfriend. I think I saw her six times in the whole year. (One of those times, she asked to borrow a pair of my underwear!)

- And Julia. She was the roommate I needed. She was like me and became my best friend.

Ultimately, I learned to accept people for who they are; you will find that there is something to love about each of them.

—*HEATHER POLLOCK*
*CALIFORNIA STATE UNIVERSITY, GRADUATE*

**FRESHMAN YEAR WAS CRAZY.** It was tough to get adjusted to school life; there was a lot of partying and a lot of girls. Just say no – to everything. And if your roommate can't say no, change roommates. My roommate couldn't say no, and I couldn't say no; we just played off each other. It wasn't good.

—*KENTON*
*UNIVERSITY OF VIRGINIA, SENIOR*

• • • • • • • •

It is probably better to come up with a chore rotation sooner rather than later!

—*N.W.*
*UNIVERSITY OF PENNSYLVANIA, SENIOR*

**I AM VERY GOOD AT AVOIDING CONFLICT.** I had a roommate freshman year who kept stealing my food and using my stuff. I came back one time and he was using my measuring spoon for spices. I was finally like, "Okay, you can't use my stuff unless you ask me first." Because at first when I showed up I was like, "Oh you want to borrow something? Whatever." So, don't be a pushover if someone is taking your stuff. Actually sit down and say, "Yo, you can no longer do this and no, you don't have a right to just eat my oranges whenever you feel like it."

—*ABE KENMORE*
*GUILFORD COLLEGE, GRADUATE*

• • • • • • • •

**ONE SUBLETTER WE HAD WAS A SWEET QUIET SORORITY GIRL** – none of us really knew her. The weekend she was supposed to move out, none of us saw her and we just assumed she had left without saying goodbye. On Monday, she burst in and started packing – we learned that she and her friends had spray-painted a building while they were drunk, been caught by the police and held in an army holding cell for the entire weekend, because it was a military base they had vandalized... That same girl also left behind a vibrator on the bed.

—*SARAH COLVIN*
*NEW YORK UNIVERSITY, GRADUATE*

**WHEN IN DOUBT, PUT ON A MOVIE AND WATCH IT WITH YOUR ROOMMATES.** It promotes bonding and seems to make any problems fade away.
—*RAE LYNN RUCKER*
*BIOLA UNIVERSITY, GRADUATE*

**CONSIDER "GOING RANDOM."** I 100 percent recommend going random. If you go random and you like your roommate, great, it works out. If you go random and you don't like your roommate, who cares? You didn't choose them, and you're not going to see them again. But I know people who chose their roommates and it didn't work out, and it was so bad because they chose each other and had mutual friends. My random roommate and I had different majors, no classes together, no real mutual friends. We had separate lives.
—*BRIANNA*
*GEORGE WASHINGTON UNIVERSITY, JUNIOR*

**COMPLETELY RANDOM IS NOT THE WAY TO GO WITH ROOMMATES.** We just needed a roommate for the summer and we found this random guy on Craigslist. We watched a boxing fight at my house. He told everyone he would buy it, and everyone could Venmo him. My other buddy was the one who paid the cable bill, so the charge just went to his bill, like $200! The guy from Craigslist never paid my buddy back and he kept the contributions from everyone else. In total, it got to where he owed us over $1600 and we told him he had to pay. He gave me false bank information and left in the middle of the night. We tried to contact him, but we eventually gave up, it was a lost cause. We should have made him pay his rent the first day he moved in. Lesson learned.
—*RILEY HOFFMAN*
*UNIVERSITY OF CALIFORNIA AT SANTA BARBARA, GRADUATE*

# PASSIVE-AGGRESSION ALERT!

**THE WORST THING THAT HAPPENED** with my roommate: She decided to tap dance at 7 A.M. to get back at me because I kept her up at night.
—*MELANIE*
*PENNSYLVANIA STATE UNIVERSITY, SOPHOMORE*

**LET'S CALL MY NEW ROOMMATES POLLY AND JESSICA.** Not sure I recall the exact incident that made Jessica and me despise Polly, but there was one incident I remember: Polly went away one weekend, the same weekend Jessica's boyfriend was visiting. Once Polly was gone, Jessica and I checked out her bedroom, which was separated from ours. Her bed looked lumpy, so we pulled back the covers to see all of her textbooks lining her bed with a note that read "STAY OFF MY BED." Okay, weirdo, Jessica and I laughed. Jessica then spent the evening with her boyfriend, while I hung out with friends. The next morning, Jessica couldn't stop laughing. When I asked why, she showed me Polly's bed. Underneath the covers, on top of the textbooks, on the blank side of Polly's note read: "I HAD SEX IN YOUR BED. GET OVER IT."
—*JONNA*
*GEORGE WASHINGTON UNIVERSITY, GRADUATE*

**IN ORDER TO DEAL WITH MY ROOMMATE** and the guy with whom she was cheating on her boyfriend, I found ways to vent my frustration, like blow-drying my hair in the middle of the room at 8 A.M. while they were still asleep, or coming back to the room unexpectedly to catch them at awkward times. These things were pretty harmless but they made me feel somewhat better.
—*ALLISON GRECO*
*MONTCLAIR STATE UNIVERSITY, GRADUATE*

**BE UPFRONT WITH YOUR ROOMMATE RIGHT OFF THE BAT.** My freshman-year roommate and I spent the year passive-aggressively adjusting the thermostat when the other left the room. You don't want to harbor any issues with your roommate, or your room will be a stressful place to come back to – when it should be the exact opposite. Creating a chore chart and keeping a calendar of both of your exams/interviews/important events are great ways of maintaining accountability, order, and thoughtfulness when living with another person.
—*L.G.*
*BUCKNELL UNIVERSITY, GRADUATE*

**IN ORDER TO SURVIVE YOUR ROOMMATES,** you have to be friendly and considerate. If you are nice, you will get treated the same way (and if you don't, then you have a reason to be treated like a jerk.) Some people like living alone in singles, but I enjoy a crowd. Sure, it makes hooking up tricky (and hilarious) sometimes, but it also expands your social circle, and gives you lifelong friends – or enemies! It all depends on what kind of person you are.
—*PETE*
*PRINCETON UNIVERSITY, SOPHOMORE*

**YOUR ROOMMATES SHOULD KNOW WHAT'S GOING ON IF YOU HAVE REAL PROBLEMS.** My sophomore year, we got a house with four guys, and one of our roommates, whom we were friends with the year before, just didn't show up. Everyone was like, "Where are you?!" A few weeks passed by, and we got an eviction notice, and that's when I realized he hadn't paid his rent. I ended up covering his ass, but he left us all hanging. It turns out he failed out the semester before. We had no idea. We all thought he was a pretty good student. He should have just told us.
—*HANK*
*NORTHERN ARIZONA UNIVERSITY, GRADUATE*

# WHICH IS WORSE: GETTING SEX-ILED OR HAVING ROOMMATES WHO JUST GET IT ON WHILE YOU'RE THERE?

**DON'T GET "SEX-ILED";** set ground rules with your roommate right away. One month into freshman year, my roommate's 26-year-old boyfriend moved in, and I found myself sex-iled for an entire week. When I tried to get into my room to get some books, it was locked. These kinds of situations can be avoided by talking about the possibility in advance.
— *LAURA*
   *HAMILTON COLLEGE, JUNIOR*

**THE OTHER DAY, MY ROOMMATE ASKED ME TO LEAVE THE ROOM.** I asked why. He said, "You know." He wanted to be alone, if you know what I mean. So I left, for like an hour. That's one of the things you have to put up with when you have a roommate.
— *C.*
   *COLUMBIA UNIVERSITY, JUNIOR*

**I WALKED IN ON MY ROOMMATE AND HER BOYFRIEND HAVING SEX** in the middle of our floor. Another time, they did it in the room when they thought I was asleep. Not cool!
— *CHAVON MITCHELL*
   *XAVIER UNIVERSITY, GRADUATE*

**I HAD A ROOMMATE WHO HAD SEX** in the room while I was sleeping. I thought they were just lying there; I would hear whispering and I thought they were just talking. Nope, they were porking. They told me later, when they were drunk.
— *SEIJI YAMAMOTO*
   *STANFORD UNIVERSITY, GRADUATE*

**IT'S GENERALLY BAD PRACTICE TO DATE YOUR ROOMMATE** because if something goes wrong, I've seen what happens: the problem becomes getting a new roommate. In a lot of schools, you have to go to mediation with your soon-to-be ex. Then, if you don't work it out, there is another step and another, until you finally get to the point where they approve a move-out. It's very difficult, like getting a divorce. So, just don't do it in the first place.
— *J.G.M.*
*GUILFORD COLLEGE, GRADUATE*

• • • • • • • • •

**THE KEY TO HAVING A GOOD RELATIONSHIP** with your roommate is the first two weeks of school. You will have to judge if you think this person has the potential to be one of your closest friends, or your complete opposite. If you think you will have a rough time being friends with your roommate, there is no need to force the issue. Obviously, you should be courteous, but if you are not the greatest friends you can still have a livable situation.
— *ANDREW OSTROWSKY*
*PENNSYLVANIA STATE UNIVERSITY, JUNIOR*

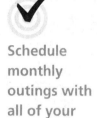

Schedule monthly outings with all of your roommates.
— *K.S.*
*PRINCETON UNIVERSITY, JUNIOR*

# 5 THINGS NOT TO SAY TO YOUR ROOMMATE

1. "I just know we're going to be best friends." (Pressure!)

2. "Sure, I don't mind if your boyfriend/girlfriend sleeps here." (You'll regret it later.)

3. Wow. Your accent is so cute!

4. "Borrow whatever you want." (Don't say it if you don't really mean it.)

5. "You want to major in WHAT?"

# GUESTS WHO DON'T, UM, LEAVE

**I WAS TOLD I WOULD HAVE JUST ONE ROOMMATE** my freshman year. Little did I know I'd also have a permanent visitor: my roommate's boyfriend. He was like "the guy on the couch;" he would stay Friday to Wednesday, always on the couch, on my computer, or even on my bed when I came home from class. Although I was open to guests, I had to tell my roommate I was sick of having a dude in my space all the time. It didn't go down well. Soon, she moved down the hall into a single; she set up her very own love nest.
　　—*LISA G.*
　　　*NEW YORK UNIVERSITY, JUNIOR*

**WE HAD A PROBLEM WITH A ROOMMATE** and her boyfriend sleeping over non-stop, almost every other day. I'm not comfortable with guys sleeping over like that, and we agreed that she would at least notify me about when people would stay over so I could get dressed in my room before he came back. She didn't do that on the night of Valentine's Day. So, we ended up screaming and almost fighting, and a friend needed to break it up before it really got ugly.

Especially if this is your first year, discuss rules within the first week to make sure that you guys are on the same standing point so no bullshit like that happens and, if it does, you have rules to fall back on. And sometimes, if you don't feel comfortable talking to your roommate about the problem or if they're just not listening and keep doing the same bullshit all over again, don't hesitate to get an RA involved. Don't feel like you're snitching or feel like 'oh this is going to make things worse.' It's already worse! How much worse could it get?
　　—*C.O.*
　　　*UNIVERSITY OF PITTSBURGH, GRADUATE*

**IF YOU'RE NOT OKAY WITH THEM HAVING GUESTS OVER, LET THEM KNOW!** They aren't mind-readers, and they don't know you super well yet. You won't always have great roommates...my freshman-year roommate had people over a lot and I even came home after midnight to someone else sleeping in my bed! Awkward! She also clipped her toenails freely on her bed, letting them fly all over – gross!!!! The key for roommates is communication.. And be careful living with friends. You may want to lay out your expectations and boundaries that first week of living together.
—*NATHALIE*
*RUTGERS UNIVERSITY, GRADUATE*

**I TALKED TO MY ROOMMATE ON THE PHONE** and I was totally convinced that I wasn't going to like her. She sounded like a person who was very different from me, but now she's one of my best friends.
—*SIERRA*
*CALIFORNIA POLYTECHNIC STATE UNIVERSITY AT SAN LUIS OBISPO, JUNIOR*

**MY ROOMMATES WERE ALL** from the deep South. One of them was the daughter of an Episcopalian minister. We got into some clashes. She told me that I was going to hell, in all seriousness. She was concerned for my soul. So, I didn't have anyone to talk to about that. But other than that, it was fine. I had some friends who went to a bigger college nearby, and I would drive an hour and a half to hang out with them there.
—*HANNAH SMITH*
*HARVARD UNIVERSITY, JUNIOR*

**IF YOUR ROOMMATE IS NOT GOOD** – for instance, steals your food, throws dirty laundry on your bed, etc. – get out as soon as possible because your life will be hell. It's easy to do, just go to your R.A.
—*K.*
*NORTHWESTERN UNIVERSITY, GRADUATE*

**YOU DON'T HAVE TO BE BEST FRIENDS TO GET ALONG.**
You'd think, both growing up in the Midwest, my
roommate and I would have a lot in common,
but we couldn't have been more different. I grew
up on a farm in South Dakota and was on the
shy side. She grew up in Wisconsin, in a big city,
and was big into hockey and boys. She was very
nice, and we got along for the most part, but our
interests were very different, and she was very
blunt. Within the first week, she told me that I
had a "hick accent." I was so offended! From
that moment on, I always held a bit of a grudge
against her. Sometimes opposites attract, but in
this instance, they did not. We were civil and nice
to one another, but we never saw a reason to be
friends.
—SARA
SOUTH DAKOTA STATE UNIVERSITY, GRADUATE

❝ I went from never having to
share anything in my whole
life, including my bedroom,
to moving into a triple with
two girls who were my
complete opposite. How did I
manage to survive? Flexibility
and compromise. ❞
—RAE LYNN RUCKER
BIOLA UNIVERSITY, GRADUATE

# CLASSIC COLLEGE FLICKS

One of the great traditions of college is watching movies about college – specifically, movies that glorify college or make the whole experience out to be a hilarious R-rated romp. Below is a list of some classics in this vein.

| | |
|---|---|
| Love Story | 1970 |
| National Lampoon's Animal House | 1978 |
| Porky's | 1982 |
| Revenge of the Nerds | 1984 |
| The Sure Thing | 1985 |
| Back to School | 1986 |
| PCU | 1994 |
| How High | 2001 |
| National Lampoon's Van Wilder | 2002 |
| Old School | 2003 |
| American Pie Presents: Beta House | 2007 |
| Road Trip: Beer Pong | 2009 |
| Adventureland | 2009 |
| Life of the Party | 2018 |

**DON'T WORRY IF YOUR ROOMMATE** is from a different world. I moved in with a gal from small town Ontario, Canada, who had never met a Jewish person. When she found out I was Jewish, she asked me all sorts of funny questions. On one occasion, when I explained that Lay's potato chips were kosher, she worried that she'd be converting to Judaism by eating a bag! We never became close friends, but she was a perfect roommate for me. We kept the place clean, were respectful of each other's stuff, and had a perfectly nice relationship.
—*A.S.*
    *QUEENS UNIVERSITY, GRADUATE*

**DURING MY FRESHMAN YEAR** I lived with an Orthodox Jew, a practicing Seventh-Day Adventist, and an atheist/agnostic. We survived – in a room made for two people, with four beds and four alarm clocks – by learning to leave God out of it!
—BRIAN ROSEN
    PRINCETON UNIVERSITY, GRADUATE

. . . . . . . . .

**IT'S HARD BEING SICK WITH A ROOMMATE.** You have to share this really small space. I once had this health-nut roommate who was a germophobe. That was really bad. Every time I got sick, she would open doors with a Kleenex. What was I supposed to do? I couldn't go home.
—KAIT DUNTON
    UNIVERSITY OF VIRGINIA, JUNIOR

# NOT A VERY 'COOL' ROOMMATE

My freshman year roommate was a genuinely awful person to have to live with. He walked around without a shirt on 95 percent of the time, woke up for crew at 4 A.M. and blew his hair dry after showering. He never said anything even remotely funny that didn't end up also making people horrendously uncomfortable. And all he contributed to the room was a fridge. While this was an essential item to someone like me that liked to host pre-game parties four nights a week, I hated having one that he'd purchased. He was of the opinion that because the fridge was his, he could eat or drink anything inside of it, despite the fact that he never bought anything. Ever. He claimed he couldn't buy alcohol because his parents would see it on their credit card statement, but he never threw in cash to help. He would bring the most awkward friends to the room. They also helped themselves to all the food and drink, without asking. Usually, I would tell you that the best way to deal with such a person would be to drink. Having done this myself, know that it will only aggravate the situation.
—J.V.
    THE COLLEGE OF WILLIAM & MARY, GRADUATE

**MY ROOMMATE IS MY TWIN SISTER.** I get along with her. We know how to live together; my sister does the laundry and I clean the room.
—*MANI*
*UNIVERSITY OF MARYLAND, FRESHMAN*

• • • • • • • •

**MAKE SURE EVERYONE IS ON THE SAME PAGE.** Establishing expectations for cleanliness, noise levels, and guests is important. I can be passive-aggressive when something is done to my distaste, but it didn't help anyone when I sent pictures of a dirty sink and a message about how it was gross. Talking things out, in person, is the way to go.
—*EMMA*
*UNIVERSITY OF PENNSYLVANIA, GRADUATE*

# ASK THE ADVISER

*Why won't Res Life let me switch roommates?*

It's not because they want you to be miserable. And it's not because they don't care, either. But while some housing offices will process change requests with no questions asked, others are far more interested in helping students learn to *work through* their differences. It's part of the college mission to expose you to new ideas, new cultures, and new ways of interacting with the world. So be prepared to sit down with your roommate and your RA for some mediated sharing and negotiation. "I" statements will be viewed more favorably than statements that blame your roommate. Try these: "I have trouble sleeping when music is playing at 4 A.M." "I'm curious about the occult symbols that have been appearing on the ceiling over my bed." "I have a very sensitive nose and strong odors are a problem for me..."

*Frances Northcutt, Ed.M., is the coordinator for academic advisement and exchange programs at the Cooper Union School of Art.*

# MAGNET FOR OVERSEAS STUDENTS

Roughly 1.1 million international students
– equal to 5 percent of all those enrolled – attended U.S.
colleges and universities or were staying on under the terms
of their student visas, as of 2017. One in three were pursuing
their studies in California, New York or Texas, with New York
University pulling in the most students of any school: 17,300.
One difference: while Iran had been the biggest sending
country back in 1980, China is now the clear leader. Its students
accounted for one-third of all visiting students.

**I HAVE A TERRIBLE ROOMMATE.** He plays video games
all the time. He stays up until six in the morning.
Needless to say, I lose a lot of sleep.
—*ANONYMOUS*
*ST. JOHN'S UNIVERSITY, FRESHMAN*

· · · · · · · ·

**MY ROOMMATE AND I** have a big difference in music
tastes. I listen to rock and alternative, and she
listens to this really bad R&B all the time. Whoever
gets to the room first gets to choose the radio;
sometimes it's a dash from class back to the room.
—*ANONYMOUS*
*YALE UNIVERSITY, SOPHOMORE*

· · · · · · · ·

**I HAD A ROOMMATE WHO SNORED** and I had to go to the
study lounge to sleep. I would take my blanket and
comforter and sleep on a couch or chair at two in
the morning. I got out the second semester. I didn't
have the heart to tell him. Other than the snoring,
we got along great.
—*RICK SHILLING*
*PENNSYLVANIA STATE UNIVERSITY, GRADUATE*

**MY ROOMMATES AND I SAT DOWN** in the beginning of the year and talked through all of our habits, which was really helpful; both of my roommates were very quiet so I'm not sure if I would have known how they felt about having guests staying over (male and female!), doing chores, and that kind of thing, otherwise. And then we also talked about it again halfway through the year, because at that point we could re-evaluate how things were going and if something came up that's upsetting, there's a place to talk about it without making a really big deal out of it.
—*EMILY*
*HARVARD COLLEGE, SENIOR*

• • • • • • • •

**I WALKED INTO MY ROOM** for the first time freshman year to see that my roommate had decorated my side of the room with posters, a hanging thing over my bed, and the quote "God is dead" on the eraser board. My survival was pledging a sorority, so I was never there.
—*M.*
*AMERICAN UNIVERSITY, FRESHMAN*

# LET'S CLEAR THE AIR

I had a terrible roommate experience. Our personalities clashed, we came from completely different backgrounds and had different values. But one thing that bothered the most: She would fart all the time. I tried using Febreze, perfuming my side of the room, leaving the window open, asking her to excuse herself outside. It got to the point where I was never in the room during waking hours, and the library became my best friend. Moral of the story: Expect the unexpected. My roommate's bowel problem wasn't even on my list of things to worry about college life.
—*MICHELLE*
*EMORY UNIVERSITY, SENIOR*

**Give your roommate his space, and he should give you yours.**

—*DANIEL RUSK*
*UNIVERSITY OF*
*MARYLAND,*
*SOPHOMORE*

**MY ROOMMATE CAME WITH ONE BAG** to school, he didn't have any sheets for his bed, and he had this long beard that he used to cut in the sink and it got everywhere. He was a wreck. He couldn't be more different from me and the other guys in our suite. I tried to be friends with him, but it became clear that we were opposite personalities. So we agreed to disagree. He wasn't so bad that I couldn't live there, but I spent a lot of time out with my friends and every once in a while showed up there to sleep.

—*JOHN BENTLEY*
*TRINITY UNIVERSITY, GRADUATE*

• • • • • • • •

**DON'T ROOM WITH SOMEONE YOU ARE VERY CLOSE WITH.** I went random my freshman year, and my roommate and I decided to live together again sophomore year. We needed two other people to live in a suite with us, so I asked two of my close friends. At first everything was great. But then one of my friends ended up getting a boyfriend none of us liked. He was always in our dorm, even though we had talked to her about having more personal space and giving us more notice about when he is coming over, but she never listened. It got to the point where she would start leaving us passive aggressive notes. But then one night, she went to a party and ended up sleeping with my other suitemate's boyfriend while my roommate was in the room next to them. Her actions created an extremely hostile environment in the room for the rest of the year. Coming home to your room, you want to be somewhere with people you feel safe with and that you could talk to about things going on in your personal life. If your best friends and your roommates are the exact same people, then sometimes it's not so great of a situation.

—*ANONYMOUS*
*GEORGE WASHINGTON UNIVERSITY, SENIOR*

We had a roommate in my suite my freshman year that we ended up asking to leave. It was not an easy thing to do, especially because the three of us who were asking him to go just did not want to initiate the confrontation. We asked for advice from one of the heads of student affairs, and then approached him one night about it. We had our laundry list of reasons ready, and it makes it much more effective if you have that set up and ready before you approach them about it.
—Barry Langer
Oglethorpe University, Junior

"Yeah, I thought about majoring in Comp Lit, but there
was too much reading."

# Filling Daytime Hours: Choosing (and Attending) Classes

*C*hoice can be thrilling and stimulating, but it can also be *paralyzing. How do you know if you like Geology? The only geologist you know of is Stan's dad from "South Park." What requirements should you tackle first? What if you're interested in everything and it won't all fit in your schedule?*

*Here's another shocker: now that you're in college, school isn't just from 8 A.M. to 3 P.M. anymore. Nope. In college, classes can run from early morning well into the night, and the responsibility of sticking to the schedule rests entirely upon your sleep-deprived shoulders. But don't fret! You will not be alone if you let your academic advisers and the wisdom in this chapter guide you.*

**TAKE CLASSES THAT YOU ACTUALLY LIKE,** that you're actually interested in. Everyone I know is taking all these intense classes in subjects that they're not interested in, and they're miserable. But I'm having a great time.
— LUCY LINDSEY
HARVARD UNIVERSITY, FRESHMAN

**ASK PEOPLE WHAT THE BEST CLASS THEY'VE EVER TAKEN IS.**
—SUMMER J.
UNIVERSITY OF
VIRGINIA, SENIOR

**HEADLINES**

- Avoid early-morning classes if you don't want to sleep through lectures.

- Experiment – take a class or two outside your desired major.

- If you think the first class of the semester is boring, drop the course – it won't improve.

- Talk to students who already took the class you're interested in to see if the professor is any good.

- Don't choose your major too soon – and don't be afraid to change it once you do.

I WOULD RECOMMEND that during your first year, you take a class that is outside what you think you want to do. You'll meet other people, and freshman year is a really good time to meet a lot of people. Take the P.E. classes; it's something active. If you're in a very academic school, go out and have something active in your life. It's a good release. I did martial arts – Tae Kwon Do. That was really fun and you meet a lot of different people there. And kick some ass.
—*JASPER*
*UNIVERSITY OF CALIFORNIA AT BERKELEY, JUNIOR*

• • • • • • • •

DURING YOUR FRESHMAN FALL, PICK COURSES THAT TRULY INTEREST YOU. When you study for exams and write papers in each of those courses, begin to notice the way you feel during those study sessions. Notice when you are annoyed by having to study for a particular subject. Notice when you are neutral about studying. Notice when you are excited. In your freshman spring, start to narrow your course selection to the subjects that excited you most in your first semester.
—*MARISSA LICURSI*
*JOHNS HOPKINS UNIVERSITY, GRADUATE*

**IF YOU'RE GOING TO TAKE A CLASS THAT YOU'RE NOT LOOKING FORWARD TO,** you might as well take it with all your friends. My freshman year, everyone on my coed floor signed up for the same class at 9:30 A.M. on Tuesdays and Thursdays. It was literally 13 of us, and every morning we would bang on each other's doors until everyone was ready, and we would roll out to class in a mob. It was just about the worst class I took in college. It was so dull and dry, and the professor had the most monotone voice in the entire world. It was a great way to make going to a class that was painful really, really fun. Those days, I actually looked forward to waking up at that nightmarish hour of 9 A.M., so I could be with all my friends.

—*MARY*
*UNIVERSITY OF ARIZONA, GRADUATE*

• • • • • • • •

" Try to make connections with professors, and show interest early on. They may be more likely to give you permission to take their class if all the spots fill up. "

—*SAKIYA GALLON*
*UNIVERSITY OF THE SCIENCES IN PHILADELPHIA, GRADUATE*

• • • • • • • •

**JUST BECAUSE SOME PEOPLE** don't go to class and still get A's doesn't mean you can skip class and still get A's. You can try it, but I wouldn't recommend it.

—*J.D.*
*EMORY UNIVERSITY, SENIOR*

# CHOOSING CLASSES BASED ON THE PROFESSOR? YEAS & NAYS

**GO FOR THE GOOD TEACHERS** and the bad times instead of the good times and bad teachers. I took calculus the first semester at 8 A.M. and that time just sucked. But I had a good teacher and I got an A. Second semester, I took a class at 1 P.M. and it was a hard teacher, and I got a C.
—AMY SCEVIOUR
GEORGIA INSTITUTE OF TECHNOLOGY, SOPHOMORE

**TALK TO OLDER STUDENTS.** If your school has an internal ranking website or system, trust that. My advice was always to choose the class by professor, not by subject matter. Great professors can make any subject the most fascinating and stimulating thing in the world; bad professors can ruin anything.
—MAX
DARTMOUTH COLLEGE, GRADUATE

**DON'T BELIEVE PEOPLE** when they tell you a professor is really good. They're probably wrong. I've taken about three classes because someone told me the professor was so cool and so good, and those are the three classes I hated the most. Then I hated the people that recommended the classes to me. Find the classes that interest you, and you'll be fine.
—EBELE ONYEMA
GEORGETOWN UNIVERSITY, SENIOR

**SEE PAST SOME OF THE NEGATIVE REVIEWS.** More often than not, negative reviews are for professors who tend to be more challenging and 'hard' graders. With that in mind, maybe drop out of college if you don't want to challenge yourself and elevate your intellect.

Other than that, pick every class intentionally. Topics are more important than teachers or time slots. Take things you care about waking up at 8 A.M. for or staying out until 9 P.M. for.
—ANONYMOUS
BOSTON COLLEGE, GRADUATE

# REFLECTIONS FROM A COED CODER

I THINK THERE IS STILL A GENDER DIVIDE IN SOME CLASSES, like in computer science and physics where you'll notice, some people walk in like they own the place. And feeling like they just came out of the womb a computer science or a physics expert. First of all, that's not true, and second, you don't have to think about physics or about coding every second of your life to be good at it and enjoy doing it. Some people have work and hobbies that are completely aligned, and some people don't. Like, I'm a physics major and a medical student, and in my free time I try to avoid those things as much as possible and only read about history. And I think there can be pressure in those really specific disciplines to be obsessed with that subject. And if you are, that's great. You'll probably find a lot of advantages. But I wouldn't want anyone to be discouraged into thinking that they can't be good at math or physics or coding just because it's not their hobby as well as their academic focus.

I really enjoyed the first project I ever did in a class where I was learning how to code. There was a lot of satisfaction in being able to come up with a project and figure out ways to solve problems along the way, and having something at the end that really worked and you could be proud of. Besides that, I just loved being able to work on that project with a group of friends. One day second semester freshman year, we had on a C++ project and we sat in our dorm for a couple days, just working on it together. I was sick, and had only eaten key-lime pie for two days straight. I think those are the moments that, in hindsight, are type-two fun. It's hard in the moment, but once you're done, you're like, "that was really wonderful." That was how I made some of my best friends. And that was how I learned so much about what I love to do.

—*ALISON*
  *GRADUATE*

# OFFICE HOURS: THE PROFESSOR WILL SEE YOU NOW

**TO GET THE MOST OUT OF YOUR CLASSES, YOU NEED TO GET THE MOST OUT OF YOUR PROFESSORS.** I always go to office hours. I make an effort to go to each of my professor's office hours at least twice during the semester. It lets the professor get to know who you are and where you excel. Office hours before a test are always helpful since you can ask, "What kind of questions will be on the test?" Going to office hours after a test helps too. You can go over it with the professor and learn what you did wrong. This also lets the professor know that you're serious about the class and your education. Although no one will probably say this, a professor would change a student's B+ to an A- if that student went to practically every office hour. It looks good, and to me, it feels good to go.
—*REBECCA*
  *COLLEGE OF NEW JERSEY, SENIOR*

• • • • • • • •

**I HAVE ONE STANDOUT 'NEGATIVE PROFESSOR' STORY.** I started school as an accounting major, and first semester sophomore year I was taking an upper-level accounting class and struggling. I went to my professor for help on an assignment, and he told me "Accounting isn't for everyone, you should consider switching your major." Coincidentally, I had already switched my major at this point, but I often think about how I would have felt if I hadn't. I can only imagine how devastating it would be to hear from someone that you are perceived as not good enough or smart enough to pursue the path you were planning to take.
—*L.G.*
  *BUCKNELL UNIVERSITY, GRADUATE*

SOMETIMES IT'S JUST NOT REALISTIC FOR PROFESSORS TO MEMORIZE ALL 500 OF THEIR STUDENTS' NAMES. The good news is regardless of whether or not they know your name they are there to help you and want you to succeed. But it's up to you to make the first move. My biggest piece of advice is to prepare some questions and take them to the professor after class or to their office hours if they have them. This not only shows your initiative to succeed but will also allow you to interact with them on a much more personal level. Chances are next time you're in class, that professor will recognize you in that crowd of strangers.
—SOLANA
DREXEL UNIVERSITY, SENIOR

GO TO PROFESSORS' OFFICE HOURS, the 1 to 3 hours every week when professors get paid to sit in their office and answer student questions! I was in a math class freshman year, and the first month was absolutely brutal. When I heard that my teacher had office hours, I decided to finally go there after bombing my first exam. When I first walked into the office, he was almost in shock that someone actually showed up, as he had been sitting there week after week with no one ever showing up! It was actually quite funny. But through office hours, you get to know and create relationships with your professors, who may even write you recommendation letters later on! The best part about office hours was that he'd sit and help us through the homework AND the same problems were on the exams. So, I ended up doing way better in the course.
—NATHALIE
RUTGERS UNIVERSITY, GRADUATE

**DON'T AVOID AN INTRIGUING COURSE** just because it is notoriously difficult. It's much easier to study something interesting that is challenging than it is to study something dry that is simple. You'll surprise yourself when you end up doing better in the difficult class that inspires you!

　　—STEPHANIE DREIFUSS
　　DUKE UNIVERSITY, SENIOR

• • • • • • • •

Take the most interesting and easiest classes you can find, have a good time, and try not to flunk out.

—JUAN GONZALEZ
CLEMSON UNIVERSITY,
GRADUATE

**DON'T TAKE CLASSES THAT ARE IMPORTANT** for your major that first quarter. I entered school as a chemistry major, so I took a chemistry class right away and it totally kicked my butt. In high school I was so into science, and I had a great, hands-on science teacher, but lectures in college were nothing like that. It's fine to have a major in mind, but be open to the fact that it might change. You need time to adjust to college life, to being on your own, to having no one telling you what to do. If I could do it over again I'd only take general education requirements for a quarter or two.

　　—JESSICA DOSHNA
　　UCLA, GRADUATE

• • • • • • • •

**WHEN REGISTRATION COMES, BE READY.** If registration opens up at midnight, then by 11:30 P.M., you should be logging on, with the classes you want written down in front of you. If you can, log in to a computer at the library (those are usually faster) and have your laptop open to the registration page next to you as a backup. Check to make sure the university has not placed holds on your ability to register for classes because of unpaid bills a week in advance in order to make sure you have time to clear anything up if need be.

　　—R.S.
　　GUILFORD COLLEGE, GRADUATE

IF THE FIRST CLASS of the semester is boring, drop it! If a professor can't make the first twenty minutes of the first class exciting, it is going to be a long semester. Go into add/drop week with a list of possible classes to take. Go to seven or eight classes in a week, or more. Then choose the best of those. It makes for a hectic week, but it will make the semester so much better.

—SUMMER J.
UNIVERSITY OF VIRGINIA, SENIOR

# THE 7 HOGWARTS PROFESSORS YOU COULD HAVE IN COLLEGE

**Prof. Dumbledore** – the nice old white man who runs your school (who gets replaced by a nearly identical old white man at some point while you're there)

**Prof. McGonagall** – the professor who's both very strict and very sweet, whom you will accidentally call "Mom" at least once

**Prof. Snape** – the former nerd who got bullied when he was in college, and now takes out his frustrations on his students

**Prof. Lupin** – the "cool" professor whom the students love, but the teachers don't trust – mostly because of how wild he goes on his nights off

**Prof. Trelawny** – the hippie who uses "non-traditional" teaching methods that make assignments even MORE confusing

**Prof. Lockhart** – the arrogant, half-capable professor who makes his students buy all the books he ever wrote

**Barty Crouch, Jr.** – the creepy TA who acts like he's the professor

*Jon Barr is an LA-based writer & comedian.*

**MAKE THE MOST OF COLLEGE CREDITS OFFERED DURING HIGH SCHOOL.** I had taken a number of advanced placement courses, which enabled me to start a little ahead when I arrived as a freshman. This is an opportunity that does not come around too often, and with the rising price of tuition, it is one that should be fully taken advantage of.
—*ANONYMOUS GRADUATE*

● ● ● ● ● ● ● ●

> **❝ Fall in love with someone in your class right away; student, T.A., professor, whomever. You'll be hard-pressed to skip class. If there is no one in your class to love, then pick someone to hate and show up every day to make his or her life a living hell. ❞**
>
> —*S.P.*
> *UNIVERSITY OF GEORGIA, GRADUATE*

● ● ● ● ● ● ● ●

**ACADEMICALLY, TRY TO GET TO KNOW YOUR PROFESSORS.** They're not some guy in the Emerald City hiding behind the curtain. Your professor is just a person.
—*PHIL UNIVERSITY OF VIRGINIA, SENIOR*

**WHEN REGISTRATION COMES, BE READY.** If registration opens up at midnight, then by 11:30 P.M., you should be logging on, with the classes you want written down in front of you. If you can, log in to a computer at the library (those are usually faster) and have your laptop open to the registration page next to you as a backup. Check to make sure the university has not placed holds on your ability to register for classes because of unpaid bills a week in advance in order to make sure you have time to clear anything up if need be.
—*R.S.*
*GUILFORD COLLEGE, GRADUATE*

**ALL THE GOOD STUFF YOU DO ACADEMICALLY,** you do in your junior and senior years. So, try to do all the crap in your freshman and sophomore years. Get it out of the way so you can enjoy your last two years.
—*ANONYMOUS*
*JOHNS HOPKINS UNIVERSITY, JUNIOR*

**LEARN A LANGUAGE.** If you've taken a language in high school, take more of the same and become fluent. If not, learn a new language, but think about one you might actually use. Even if you aren't thinking about a term abroad, pick a language and go for it.
—*ANONYMOUS*
*UNION COLLEGE*

**EVERYBODY'S SMART IN COLLEGE.** At least give yourself a semester before you dive into the hard classes. I was in the top 10 percent of my high school class and I felt really good about myself. But it took me the first year of college to realize I had to work real hard to make good grades.
—*JONATHAN COHEN*
*EMORY UNIVERSITY, SENIOR*

**I'M A VERY ORGANIZED PERSON.** So, as soon as I got to college and picked my major, I actually wrote a schedule for the next three and a half years... which changed around a lot but actually did help me figure out what classes I wanted to take, what classes I maybe had time for later, and it kept me on the path towards graduation. I would say don't stress yourself out, but also there is definitely a benefit to looking ahead.
—*NICOLE ZELNIKER*
*GUILFORD COLLEGE, GRADUATE*

• • • • • • • •

" Share your school supplies with fellow classmates. Believe me, there's going to be a time when you forget something in the future, so volunteer your extras. "
—*J.S.*
*UNIVERSITY OF GEORGIA, GRADUATE*

• • • • • • • •

**IF YOU PLAN TO WORK** for Goldman Sachs in four years, your entire future seems to rest on whether you secure a seat in Accounting 101. But this is a misguided approach. You should use your first few semesters to take the courses most dissimilar to your goals. If you plan to major in business, take a course in French New Wave Cinema or British Lit. If you think you're a chemist, take physics. If you want to speak Hebrew, take Arabic.
—*DOUG*
*WAKE FOREST UNIVERSITY, GRADUATE*

# CRACKING THE ACADEMIC CODE

Choose one course from Category 3A and two from Category 2E. This applies only to students matriculating before Fall 2019. All others should consult the 2019-2020 Bulletin. We apologize for the delay in printing the 2019-2020 Bulletin. It should be available within six months. In the meantime, questions may be directed to the Dean of Arts and Sciences. Although this position is currently vacant, the new Dean should be selected…in around six months.

Are they kidding???

Navigating the academic requirements of your college can be as mind-twistingly complicated as filing taxes for the average multinational corporation. But don't despair; help is here.

- Does your college offer an online degree audit system? Use it! But whatever you do, don't be fooled into thinking that requirements are just a series of boxes to fill in, or annoying tasks to "get out of the way" so that you can go on to the good stuff. Your general education courses might turn out to be the good stuff you've been waiting for all these years.

- All those confusing letters, numbers, and symbols actually represent something: the range of skills and knowledge that the faculty of your college think every student ought to have. If you take half an hour to read up on the purpose and design of the general education curriculum, you'll start to see some method to all the madness. (Hint: Try the first few chapters of your college catalog and the Mission Statement online.)

- Still stumped? Go see your academic adviser or favorite faculty member. They will be happy to let you in on the secrets cleverly concealed behind the baffling charts and lists.

*Frances Northcutt*

**USE EXCEL SPREADSHEETS TO KEEP YOURSELF ON TRACK** when other students are panicking. Freshman year, I outlined all of my requirements and when I would need to take each class for the rest of college. This was a great reference when picking classes each semester, so I knew exactly how I could balance what I needed to take versus what I wanted to take. None of my requirements slipped through the cracks. Second, I made charts for every class of each assignment expected and its impact on my final grade. This helped me keep track of every assignment, how much something would affect my grade, and gave me an idea of how I was doing in the class.
—*L.G.*
*BUCKNELL UNIVERSITY, GRADUATE*

" Figure out the social scene of your school before you make any schedules. It's no fun going to class hungover on Friday mornings! "
—*ERIN*
*SUFFOLK UNIVERSITY, GRADUATE*

**ESTABLISH REAL RELATIONSHIPS WITH YOUR PROFESSORS.** At Colby, I went to dinner at professors' houses. That changed the game for me. They made me more curious. Trusted me. Some even hired me to do work for them, which was huge. I didn't think I was capable. They made me feel like the work I was doing was legit.
—*ANONYMOUS*
*COLBY COLLEGE, GRADUATE*

**BEGIN REGISTERING FOR CLASSES** as soon as your registration time opens up – a few minutes can cost you a seat in the class that you really want to take.
—*ALEKSANDR AKULOV*
   *HUNTER COLLEGE, SOPHOMORE*

* * * * * * * *

**DON'T WAIT TOO LONG TO CHOOSE A MAJOR.** I didn't declare until my third year, and I ended up needing to take four classes per quarter. It was intense, and not very fun when you're nearing the end of college and you want to have a good time with your friends.
—*JESSICA DOSHNA*
   *UCLA, GRADUATE*

* * * * * * * *

**I'M USUALLY THE TYPE OF PERSON** who does all his work, but now, I actually have to think. The workload isn't harder, but it's different. I take a lot more notes now. I'm in a study skills class and they suggest a system for taking notes – dividing the page into three sections, writing notes in one part, cues for main ideas in another, and summaries in the other. I don't like that system, but it helps to try different things.
—*DUSTIN CAMAC*
   *UNIVERSITY OF DELAWARE, FRESHMAN*

# HOW TO TAME BUREAUCRACY

1. "I'm so sorry to bother you ..."

2. "I read all the information on your website and I just have one more small question ..."

3. "Hello, how are you today?" (So obvious, yet so rarely used!)

4. "My R.A. said you were a good person to talk to about ..."

**DON'T OVERLOAD;** don't take too many classes. I did. I was staying up to five and six o'clock in the morning, missing classes that morning. That's not fun.

—ALBERT SO
GEORGIA INSTITUTE OF TECHNOLOGY, SOPHOMORE

• • • • • • • •

**WHEN LOOKING FOR AN EASY ELECTIVE,** ask a few athletes. As a former student-athlete who usually had taxing courses for my major, I was pretty good at finding less taxing electives, GPA-boosters, blow-off classes, etc. This allowed me to keep my sanity. Also, ask around to find out if your chosen elective is as interesting as it sounds. I almost signed up for "Costumes Through the Ages." It sounded like it might be a good elective to take. After asking around, I found out the class is boring and difficult.

—HASSAN
UNIVERSITY OF TULSA, GRADUATE

• • • • • • • •

**THERE'S NO HARM TAKING A CLASS YOU'VE TAKEN ALREADY IN HIGH SCHOOL.** Because freshman year is about getting used to your environment, and if you're studying all the time, it's harder to do that.

—NATASHA PIRZADA
GEORGETOWN UNIVERSITY, SOPHOMORE

• • • • • • • •

**ONE OF THE MOST IMPORTANT THINGS** in college is to have a good relationship with your academic adviser. Meet with him/her a couple times a semester to work out your four-year plan and choose your classes for the upcoming semester. They have a wealth of knowledge and will make your time a lot less stressful. They appreciate involved students and are always willing to help you get the best schedule possible.

—ILAN GLUCK
UNIVERSITY OF MARYLAND, JUNIOR

# MILTON & ME

Once, I gave a big speech to the whole class, while hung over. That was a bad idea. I had an economics professor who picked out a few people to give speeches; to teach his class, basically. The night before, I got pretty drunk. The speech was on Milton Friedman's theory on something or other.

I was so hung over when I tried to give the speech, I couldn't talk; I just mumbled. The professor asked me questions: "Do you mean this means that?" I said, "Yeah, yeah, that. Yes, of course." And so we got through the whole thing, and afterwards he pulled me aside and said, "Wow, I've been teaching this class for 20 years, and that is the worst description I've ever heard." And yet, I passed the class. I talked to the professor. I realized I screwed up, and I made up for it. So the moral is, if you screw up, talk your way through it. Don't let it lie. People understand.

—ANONYMOUS
UNIVERSITY OF TEXAS, GRADUATE

ONE OF MY STRANGEST MEMORIES is attending a class taught by a dead man. One of the freshman-level psychology courses consisted of videotaped lectures from a professor who died in the 1960s. I don't remember his full name but his first name was Fred, so everyone called him – you guessed it – Dead Fred. I wish I had a picture of 500 students all staring at small monitors streaming a flickering, grainy, black-and-white, talking head three times a week. Maybe it was all just one big psychology experiment.

—SCOTT WOELFEL
UNIVERSITY OF MISSOURI, GRADUATE

# TIME MANAGEMENT

Managing your time is a lot like managing your money. Once you spend it, it's gone, so you have to make it all count. With 24 hours a day multiplied by seven days a week, you've got 168 hours a week to spend.

**Step #1: Figure out how you use your time each week on each activity:**

_____ Class time (# of hours in class each week)
_____ Studying (Most colleges suggest three hours for every hour you're in class.)
_____ Job/Work
_____ Commuting/transportation time
_____ Athletics/physical fitness (team sports, working out, etc.)
_____ Co-curricular activities and other hobbies
_____ "Family" responsibilities (cleaning, cooking, shopping, communication, time with relatives)
_____ Socializing with friends and other hobby time
_____ Screen time
_____ Sleeping
_____ Eating
_____ Personal hygiene (bathing, hair, make-up, etc.).

**Step #2: Assess your use of time:**

a) Add together the totals for the above       SUBTOTAL = _____
   lines for your week:
b) Now subtract your subtotal from       TOTAL = _____
   168 hours per week:

- If the number in your TOTAL line is negative, you have committed more time than there is in a week. YOU ARE IN TROUBLE. Time to cut back in certain areas.
- If you have time left over, ask yourself what choices can be made. Do you have time for more sleep? Volunteering? Friends? Relaxation?

- If your time used equals 168, you are off to a good start. Still, you may want to consider adjustments that might make you more effective.

**Step #3: Determine a goal and action plan for better time management/use:**

What would you most like to do to better manage your time? Consider buying (and USING) a planner, which can help you keep track of time, projects, assignments and be more efficient. Some tips: Color-code your calendar/planner by the activities listed above, and once you make a schedule, do your best to stick with it.

*Scott C. Silverman*

**DON'T BE AFRAID TO SAY** what you need to in class. One time, a kid across the table from me and I got in a heated debate over the validity of fart jokes. I really care about that subject. They're a legitimate source of humor! And the teacher wasn't fazed, since it was a class called Theory of Comedy. Plus, she had just explained a very inappropriate (and highly unprintable) joke that Shakespeare made in "A Midsummer Night's Dream," so everything was fair game. That class was a blast. I got a pretty nice grade and am still friendly with many of my classmates.
—*SHANNON KELLEY*
*KENYON COLLEGE, JUNIOR*

**GEOLOGY (A/K/A "ROCKS AND JOCKS")** is much harder than the course description would lead you to believe.
—*LYNN LAMOUSIN*
*LOUISIANA STATE UNIVERSITY, GRADUATE*

# ASK THE ADVISER

*If one of my classes isn't going well, can I drop it?*

You'll probably need to see your real-life adviser to discuss the particulars of your situation, but here are some general principles to get you started.

Before classes begin, check on two things:

1. How many credits do you need in order to be considered a full-time student? (Financial aid, health insurance, and your eligibility to live in the dorm can all be linked to full-time student status.)

2. What is the last day to drop a class without receiving a 'drop' or 'withdrawal' notation on your record? One "W" is not terrible, but you don't want your transcript to be littered with them. Once classes begin, if you want to drop a class and you're sure that dropping won't affect your full-time status or your transcript, ask yourself:

- 'Will dropping this class throw me off track for my major or pre-professional sequence?'

- 'Is dropping the class my only option? Can I switch sections, take the class pass/fail, or get help with difficult material?'

Your adviser can help you sort through all of this.

*Frances Northcutt*

**GET TO KNOW YOUR TEACHERS,** because when it comes down to getting a better final grade you might need a little help. And if your professors know you, they might be willing to help you.
—*MATT BURLESON*
*UNIVERSITY OF TENNESSEE AT MARTIN, GRADUATE*

**LOOK UP REVIEWS ON PROFESSORS** before you sign up for classes. I took a math class once that was really bad; the final was so hard that most of us failed it. Had I looked at his profile on ratemyprofessor.com, I would have known to avoid him. Don't go too far and avoid every professor, of course. Sometimes, you won't be able to get around having a bad teacher.
—*ANDREW*
*UCLA, SENIOR*

**BE WARY OF CLASS TITLES** like "Frodo's Epic Nightmare," "American Humor," and "Introduction to Comparative Politics." They might sound interesting, but the professors could be dry and boring.
—*JACKIE*
*STATE UNIVERSITY OF NEW YORK AT BINGHAMTON, GRADUATE*

**THE WORST MISTAKE YOU CAN MAKE IS TRYING TO MAJOR IN SOMETHING THAT YOU ARE NOT INTERESTED IN AT ALL.** Sometimes, students choose their majors and classes based on their parents' preferences or what they think will make them the most successful down the road. If you're not interested in a subject, you're not going to do well in the classes and it's going to make your time at college much less enjoyable.
—*T.B.*
*BOSTON COLLEGE, GRADUATE*

# THE EARLY BIRD… IS TIRED AND COLD?

**TRY TO STAY AWAY FROM** early-morning classes as much as possible. Even if you think you can do it, it'll start to take a toll on you halfway through the semester, when you are staying up late studying for midterms, and you have to get up at 8 A.M. after getting three hours of sleep.
   —*MICHELLE*
      *EMORY UNIVERSITY, SENIOR*

**IF YOU HAVE AN 8 O'CLOCK** followed by classes until the afternoon, make sure to eat breakfast. Even if you think you can power through a few hours of class without eating, you should still grab a quick granola bar or Pop-Tart on your way to class. It definitely gives you enough energy to participate in labs and stay awake in lectures.
   —*JONATHAN LIU*
      *UNIVERSITY OF TENNESSEE AT KNOXVILLE, FRESHMAN*

**COMING FROM HIGH SCHOOL,** starting class at 9 A.M. seems like a vacation. But only for the first couple of weeks. Waking up at 8 A.M. becomes legitimately painful after a while, especially if you go to school in the north.
   —*ANNIE THOMAS*
      *UNIVERSITY OF MICHIGAN, SENIOR*

**NEVER SIGN UP FOR A 7 A.M. CLASS.** Yes, you did it in high school, but Mom was always there to keep waking you up, and if by some miracle you do make it to an early class, you will sleep through the lecture when you get there.
   —*J.T.*
      *UNIVERSITY OF FLORIDA, GRADUATE*

**LOOK THROUGH ALMOST EVERY SINGLE DEPARTMENT** of classes and pick the ones that are really cool-sounding. Don't be afraid to take a class early in the morning... especially if it's only one day a week. You'll be okay. Probably.
—*PETER*
*TUFTS UNIVERSITY, SOPHOMORE*

**IN COLLEGE YOU HAVE TO STAY UP** a lot later working, pretty much everyone does. So try to schedule your classes a little later. When I was a freshman, I ended up taking an 8:30 class, and I thought that wouldn't be so bad because in high school I had to get up at 6:30. But I ended up not making it to class a lot of days because I stayed up so late, a lot later than I would have in high school, and I found it really hard to wake up.
—*MATTHEW GUTSHALL*
*ST. JOSEPH'S, JUNIOR*

**TALK TO YOUR COUNSELOR,** especially if you're not certain what major to choose. A counselor can look at your interests and help you pick classes that apply to multiple majors, rather than to just one major. They also have a better understanding of when classes are offered; I had to wait a whole year for a required class once because I didn't know it was only offered in the fall, and I didn't sign up in time.
—*COREY*
*SAN DIEGO STATE UNIVERSITY, JUNIOR*

**GO TO EVERY CLASS;** that's half the battle. If you do, you'll pass. I went to the majority of classes freshman year, but I would've done so much better if I had gone to all of them.
—*KRISTIN THOMAS*
*JAMES MADISON UNIVERSITY, JUNIOR*

# HOW TO CATCH SOME ZZZzzz

Freshman year is one of radical changes: sharing a room with a stranger; an irregular, hectic schedule; sudden, seemingly limitless freedom, and an overwhelming array of brand new temptations. Sometimes, sleeping can feel impossible. Few things in life are as stressful as restlessly lying awake as you ponder how bad tomorrow will be if you can't get any sleep. There are ways to avoid this nightmare; here are a few that actually work:

## 'Sleep Hygiene'

Many college libraries flaunt the fact that they stay open 24 hours a day for those pulling all-nighters. But scientists who study the brain are now finding all kinds of reasons why you really do need 7 to 8 hours of solid sleep a night.

Among the more frightening stats: one sleepless night makes you much more prone to catastrophic accidents, catching a cold, and poor mental performance the following day, while a lifetime of inadequate ZZZ's may increase your risk of cancer, Alzheimer's and heart disease. Studies also show that sleep quantity and quality equal or outrank alcohol and drug use as a predictor of students' grades and chances of graduating.

After being awake 16 hours in a row, brain function starts to decline, and after 20 hours, you perform as if legally drunk, according to Dr. J. Roxanne Prichard, an expert on college students' sleep issues at the University of St. Thomas in Minnesota. Each additional day per week that a student experiences sleep problems makes you 10 percent more likely to drop a course and lowers cumulative GPA by 0.02, according to a recent paper she co-wrote in *Sleep Health*.

So, if you're serious about giving your brain the nightly rest it deserves, here are some ways to go:

- Maintain a consistent sleep regimen and resist the temptation to pull all-nighters.

- Avoid screentime within an hour of bedtime. (And no falling asleep with the TV on!)

- Sleep in a dark, cold, quiet room. (Combat ambient room noise with comfy ear plugs or a white noise machine.)

- Avoid caffeine late in the day, say, after 2 P.M.

- Eat a modest snack before bed. Don't lay down too hungry or too full.

### Sleepytime Apps and Podcasts

If your problem is a racing mind, meditation might be the antidote. There are a number of great meditation apps to get your practice started: *Waking Up With Sam Harris*, *Headspace*, and *10% Happier* are all perfect for beginners and highly rated by users.

*Sleep Cycle* uses your phone's motion sensor to 'feel' you toss and turn and uses the data to graph your sleeping patterns and even wake you up at the most optimal time in your cycle.

Maybe you just need a distraction? The podcast *Sleep With Me* is bizarre, wildly popular, and strangely effective. It will make you laugh one second and snore the next.

Listen to all of this wonderful relaxing audio on *CozyPhones*, brilliantly designed headphones embedded in a comfy headband you can wear all night. Best part? They're only $20 on Amazon.

If all of this sounds a little too complicated for your tastes, maybe you'd like *Count Sheep HD*. For just 99 cents, this app offers an infinite stream of sheep to count. As its description boasts, "it sure beats staring at the ceiling."

*Anthony Wallace, a recent graduate of Northern Arizona University, and Jessica Reyes, a recent graduate of the University of Pittsburgh, are both fairly sure they did not sleep through the best parts of college.*

**BEFORE SIGNING UP FOR ANY CLASS,** find out who is teaching it, and go talk to them. At the beginning of the year, most professors are just sitting around waiting for students to drop in. You can learn way more about a class, and the professor teaching it, by spending 10 minutes with the professor, one-on-one. You'll get a sense of what will be required and how much of a hard-ass the teacher is going to be.
—*DON WAZZENEGER*
*YOUNGSTOWN STATE UNIVERSITY, SENIOR*

* * * * * * * *

**IT'S ESSENTIAL THAT YOU BUILD** up a grade cushion in your first year. That way when you're a junior or a senior and things get tough, you don't have to worry as much about your GPA.
—*YAP*
*NEW YORK UNIVERSITY, JUNIOR*

* * * * * * * *

**I WISH I'D HAD A BETTER IDEA** of the classes I wanted to take. When you get here it's a bit of a scramble; you have so many options. You have a course book that's 3,000 pages and you have to flip through it and find stuff.
—*TOBIAS*
*HARVARD COLLEGE, FRESHMAN*

* * * * * * * *

**ONE OF MY BIGGEST REGRETS** about freshman year is that I let a lot of my peers pressure me into taking classes I wasn't interested in. That was a bummer because I didn't get to take the classes I should have taken, and also I didn't do as well, because I wasn't as interested, and that brought down my overall GPA. Make sure the classes you take are the ones you personally want to take. You'll make new friends in your classes so you don't have to sign up for classes with friends.
—*CATIE*
*HARVARD COLLEGE, SENIOR*

**USE THAT FIRST YEAR** as your sandbox year. It's really important. It's okay to screw off. It's okay to go out and experiment.
—*W.J.F.*
*GEORGETOWN UNIVERSITY, JUNIOR*

**DON'T BE AFRAID TO CHANGE YOUR MAJOR.** My friend thought he was going to be an engineer and now he's going to study philosophy.
—*PETER*
*TUFTS UNIVERSITY, SOPHOMORE*

**STAY LATE AFTER CLASS** and ask questions. It's good to be known by your professors; later on you'll need recommendations from them. It's important that you did more than just get a good grade, that your professor remembers you.
—*JAWAN AYER-COLE, M.D.*
*FLORIDA A&M UNIVERSITY, GRADUATE*

**TAKE ADVANTAGE OF THE LIBERAL ARTS EDUCATION SYSTEM TO TAKE CLASSES OUTSIDE YOUR MAJOR.** As someone pursuing a bachelor's of science diploma, I've also been taking creative writing. I'm not the most creative person, but I thought it would be fun to exercise that muscle and create these fictional characters. Our professor, Joyce Carol Oates, has been doing this for fifty years, and it's incredible to see how in tune she is with how to write a novel. Someone will read something they've written, and she'll say, "I hear this ventilator, maybe we can talk about that. Hospitals are always cold because they want to keep the germs away so your character would be shivering when she wakes up. She wouldn't have a jacket." She sees the whole scene in her head. And she knows what details are important enough to put in the story.
—*CHARLIE BAGIN*
*PRINCETON UNIVERSITY, SOPHOMORE*

# ALARM CLOCKS THAT WON'T LET YOU DOWN

Waking up is hard to do, especially if you've been up late studying or doing crazy college-student things.

It may seem like the once ubiquitous alarm clock has gone the way of the tape recorder, standalone GPS device, and digital camera as products supplanted by the smartphone. But the truth is – that wimpy phone alarm just doesn't cut it for some of the sleepiest among us. Some of us need the snooze button to be a bit more challenging, which is one reason there are now apps out there like FreakyAlarm that make you solve a logic puzzle before they will shut up. Other people simply need a louder noise to penetrate the depths of their sleep, and conversely, some people prefer to be aroused more gently than by brute noise.

If the simple phone alarm and its spinoffs aren't cutting it, find your perfect solution here within this list of high-tech, low-tech, obnoxious, hilarious, and naughty options:

**Sonic Alert SBB500SS Sonic Bomb Extra-Loud Dual Alarm Clock with Red Flashing Alert Lights and Bed Shaker        $35 or so**
If the name of this alarm clock alone doesn't fill you with fear, we don't know what would. Amazon user LoveAmazonAZ describes it quite eloquently: "Imagine someone putting a jackhammer to your bed and the loudest alarm you can imagine going off. If you can sleep through this, then you may not be alive." By all accounts, this thing is very loud. If you sleep through alarms, this is your solution. The bed shaker provides added insurance. It slides under your pillow or mattress and quakes until you make it stop.

**Clocky, the Original Runaway Alarm Clock on Wheels   $40 or so**
This fashionable alarm clock is the cute and creative answer for those who can't resist hitting the snooze button. At your specified wake-up time, this wailer on wheels springs to life, jumps off your nightstand, and rolls around your bedroom making a ruckus. There's

no way around it. You need to get out of bed to shut this thing up. With its anthropomorphic 'face,' cute name, and alarm sound that's been compared to R2D2, it is the most droid-like alarm clock money can buy.

**Peakeep 4" Twin Bell Alarm Clock**                    **$14 or so**
As the vinyl revival has taught us, digital technology can be a little lifeless and unreliable. Sometimes, analog is the way to go. This is the classic alarm clock. It looks like the alarm clock emoji and the alarm clock on Blue's Clues, before the color was added. Lauded by deep sleeping users as impossible to sleep through, this thing is very loud. This is a time-tested design; affordable, functional, minimal, and stylishly retro.

**MOSCHE Sunrise Alarm Clock**                    **$30 or so**
Maybe loud and scary is not at all what you are looking for in a bedside buddy. Maybe you need something kinder. This line of clocks takes advantage of your sensitivity to light to simulate the natural bliss of rising with the sun. You wake naturally without having to be jolted awake by a screeching alarm. By lighting up gradually in the 30 minutes preceding your alarm time to mimic the growing intensity of the rising sun, the device aims to coax you soundlessly out of slumber with the loving touch of a mother. It can reverse the process at night to simulate a sunset, and comes preloaded with 6 relaxing nature sounds and white noise sleep aids. Not for hard-core sleepyheads, though.

**Little Rooster Alarm Clock** VIBRATOR                    **$102 or so**
Okay, this one is pricier than the others, and only the half the population can enjoy its innovative design. But here is the twist: Set the alarm, carefully position the device in your undies before turning in for the night, and look forward to a pleasant awakening. Some complain that keeping the device in place is impossible, but others claim it's changed their lives. Apparently, the natural flood of happy chemicals that come with an orgasm are even better than caffeine. Fear not, men. The designers claim they are working night and day on one for you, too.

*Anthony Wallace and Jessica Reyes*

# CHOOSING A MAJOR

What's it going to be – Accounting, Art, Geology, History, Math, Nursing, Pre-Law, Psychology, Social Work, Spanish – or are you still undecided? If it's the latter, you just might be one of the smartest new students entering college this year.

Believe it or not, you simply don't yet know enough to make such a critical decision. Here's why: First, you may have the impression that your choice of academic major will dictate your career path as well. In reality, most people with college degrees will change careers 2 to 10 times in the 40 or so years they work, and often those careers are not in the major they chose when they started college.

Second, your decision might have been made due to pressures from others – for example, your family, your peers, and even yourself in the search for the "right" major for you. By giving yourself more time to decide, you might make a better choice.

Third, you are about to experience an academic and social environment in college that will provide you with many fields of knowledge, experiences, and opportunities that are completely new to you – and that may influence your decision.

So, how should you plan? Colleges often ask for your major when you apply and you might have to choose something. However, if the "Undecided" or "Exploratory" option is available – take it! It's okay to be undecided at this stage. But even if there's no such option initially, don't worry; you'll have the option to change your major later if you want.

But how will you know what to choose, especially when some colleges offer as many as 1800 majors and academic programs to choose from? There's a very simple answer: major in what you enjoy studying. As you complete your courses during your freshman year and after, you will learn which subjects you like to think, read, listen to lectures, talk, do research, and write about. This should greatly influence your ultimate choice of a major.

*"But what can I do with a major in _____?" you ask.*

Another good question, but it shouldn't dominate your choice of a major. Most psychology majors do not become psychologists; most math majors do not become mathematicians; most history majors do not become historians. Whatever your choice, be sure that you develop the skills that graduate schools and employers need, want, and expect when you graduate. These include: writing, speaking, using technology, and other more directly applied skills, as well as those that are more generic and that students often underestimate – including demonstrating leadership, responsibility, collaboration, a strong work ethic, and integrity. All of these can be developed in your college experiences both in and out of the classroom through student clubs and organizations, service learning, internships, volunteerism, work experiences, and more. Most importantly, these skills can be learned in any and all majors, if you choose your related options strategically and wisely.

*Thomas J. Grites, Ph.D.*
*Assistant Provost*
*Stockton University*

**DON'T TAKE MORE THAN ONE CLASS** that has a lot of reading. I picked some classes that had too much reading, so I am always reading. I average four hours a day, maybe longer. I go to class, take a break, go to dinner, and then go to the library. I'll be in the library until 1 A.M.
—*BAYLESS PARSLEY*
*UNIVERSITY OF VIRGINIA, FRESHMAN*

"*Explain to me how partying tonight could be any worse for his future career than studying lyric poetry.*"

# Hitting the Books: Why, When & How to Study

*However you may have gotten through high school, college is a new ballgame and there's no way around it: you're going to need to study. Effective studying is a learned skill, polished over time, not something you pick up overnight or fake. Your ability to focus and get stuff done is also likely to influence anything you pursue after graduation.*

*Sure, college is an endlessly tempting smorgasbord full of fun and adventure. So, it might require some serious discipline to leave the shenanigans behind even for a second to insist on some peace and quiet and focus on studying. But let's not forget – the primary reason you went to college was to get an education. Those college admissions officers let you in because they knew you had the chops. This chapter should help, too.*

FRESHMEN COME IN AND EXPECT TO GET AN **A.** But then you realize you were a big fish in a small pond in high school, and in college there's a bunch of other big fish and you've got to step it up a notch.
—*K.K.*
  *NORTHWESTERN UNIVERSITY, GRADUATE*

SLEEP A LOT. AND ALWAYS GO TO CLASS.
—*SARAH*
  *GEORGIA INSTITUTE OF TECHNOLOGY, GRADUATE*

**HEADLINES**

- Find a place where you can study without interruption – most likely not your room.
- Don't skip classes – it makes the work that much harder.
- Self-discipline is the key to academic success.
- Don't wait until the last minute to get your work done – you'll only regret it.

**COLLEGE IS NOT HIGH SCHOOL.** You are responsible for doing your homework and making sure you are ready for the next class. Invest the time and go to class.
> —MICHAEL
> RUTGERS UNIVERSITY, JUNIOR

- - - - - - - -

**NO MATTER HOW SICK YOU MIGHT BE** during finals week, do not take any cough medicine. And read the labels on any cold medication you take for any reference that the medicine will make you drowsy. I was sick as a dog my first finals week, but I made the mistake of taking medication that made me so tired I couldn't stay up to cram. And no amount of caffeine can overcome the depressants in that medication. Just put up with the runny nose and drink coffee.
> —ANONYMOUS
> YOUNGSTOWN STATE UNIVERSITY, SENIOR

- - - - - - - -

**IF YOU GET A B OR A C, DON'T WORRY.** When you're going into the job world after graduating, there's no company that's going to say, "Well, you didn't do well in Western Civilization."
> —RHIANNON GULICK
> GEORGETOWN UNIVERSITY, SENIOR

**STRIVE FOR GOOD GRADES DURING YOUR FIRST SEMESTER,** but don't beat yourself over the fact you may receive your first C or D. That doesn't necessarily foreshadow your future unless you allow it to become your reality.
—*LORENZO DOZIER*
   *ST. FRANCIS COLLEGE, GRADUATE*

. . . . . . . .

" Don't read in your bed; you'll fall asleep. When you're in your bed, that's what you do. And then you start to associate reading with sleeping, so anytime you try to read anywhere, you fall asleep. "
—*BETHANY*
   *JAMES MADISON UNIVERSITY, SENIOR*

. . . . . . . .

**DON'T MISS EVEN ONE DAY** of homework. If you fall behind, it's so much harder to catch up.
—*NATASHA PIRZADA*
   *GEORGETOWN UNIVERSITY, SOPHOMORE*

. . . . . . . .

**A WEIRD TRICK** I've seen that I've tried a couple times was at the end of each page, have a little treat. Put an M&M at the bottom of the page and once you finish reading it, you get that M&M. That was one trick that I tried. It wasn't 100 percent successful because I just ended up eating all the M&Ms.
—*LILLIE REITER*
   *GUILFORD COLLEGE, GRADUATE*

# THE FLIP SIDE OF FREEDOM

**THE PROBLEM I HAD WAS THE PRIORITIZATION.** I don't know anyone who wasn't behind. You tend to forget to study when you first get here. You have parties, freedom from parents – you almost forget that you're in school. Freshman year, people would go to 60 to 70 percent of classes, at best, because they would stay up late and then miss morning classes. You almost forget how important education is. You worked for 12 years to get here, but just because you're here, the work doesn't stop.
    —*ZAK AMCHISLAVSKY*
    *GEORGETOWN UNIVERSITY, SENIOR*

**IT WAS STRANGE.** Freshman fall, I had the fewest hours of class of any semester so far. In high school, I was used to getting up early in the morning and staying at school all day, sometimes coming home late, depending on athletics or rehearsals, so it was so strange to find myself with five free hours in the afternoon. Which of course is the time you should be getting your work done, but I was excited about getting tea, and going biking on the river! After the first few weeks, once I started getting bigger assignments, I realized that if I wanted to get any sleep, I had to work during the day.
    —*HALEY*
    *HARVARD UNIVERSITY, SENIOR*

**THE BIGGEST CHALLENGE IN COLLEGE SO FAR HAS BEEN FIGURING OUT HOW MY WEEK IS GOING TO GO.** I have a class that ends at 8:30 A.M., and my next class isn't until noon. I have this whole gap where I have to figure out where I'm going to study and what I'm going to do with my time. If you don't figure that out, you end up wasting a lot of time and then you're up at 2 A.M. doing your homework. To prevent that from happening, I found places that are near my classes – nice, quiet places like the library, that I know are going to be there and that I know I can get to without being late to class.
    —*SIDDHARTH NATHELLA*
    *PURDUE UNIVERSITY, FRESHMAN*

KEEP EVERY SINGLE COURSE AT THE SAME LEVEL OF IMPORTANCE so that you're not slacking off in any specific one. Coming in as a freshman, I was like, 'Oh, man, I got so much free time. I could do whatever I want.' There was one course where I was just like 'Oh, I could do this tomorrow' or 'I could do this later.' I didn't really care because I only had class once a week. Then I forgot about an assignment for that class because I had other assignments to do, and then when the day for that specific course happened, I realized, 'Ah man, I forgot to do it!'
　　—JAIRO MARTINEZ
　　FAIRLEIGH DICKINSON UNIVERSITY, GRADUATE

KEEP A SCHEDULE. Have a really good calendar. I always kept mine on me, so I'd know what's going on. Set phone reminders if you have to. It impresses employers, too, when you actually show up on time for everything.
　　—TAYLOR ELLINGSON
　　NORTHERN STATE UNIVERSITY (S. DAKOTA), SENIOR

I HAD STAYED UP UNTIL 4 A.M. studying for my art history final and was confident that I would get an A. I awoke the next morning to the horrifying realization that my alarm clock had not gone off and I had already missed the entire exam. I was so disappointed and angry at myself. And I got a zero on that exam. To avoid this disappointment in the future, I make sure to set a backup alarm, and sometimes even a backup-backup alarm, on important test days.
　　—MAXWELL
　　STATE UNIVERSITY OF NEW YORK AT ALBANY, SOPHOMORE

IT'S NOT SO MUCH TECHNOLOGY that interferes with studying as it is the notion of procrastinating. You will find the most ridiculous excuses to put off studying. But that's really what college is all about – learning to do the best job in the smallest amount of time because you were an idiot. Every year, you will convince yourself that you won't allow yourself to fall behind. And every subsequent year, you will learn that you are more full of it than the year before.
　　—J.V.
　　THE COLLEGE OF WILLIAM & MARY, GRADUATE

**MAKE SURE YOU SPEAK UP IN CLASS.** If you have a question, ask it! Nine out of ten times, there's someone sitting in the same class with the same question but they're too afraid to ask. Don't listen to that little voice in your head telling you, "That's a dumb question!" I repeat, ASK THE QUESTION! Nothing beats the feeling of knowing exactly what's going on in class and the confidence of knowing you're going to ace that course in the end.

     —MEGAN BAEZ
       *CUNY BROOKLYN COLLEGE, GRADUATE*

> " The workload in college is like shoveling snow. If you do a little bit every day, you'll get by. If you wait until everything piles up, it becomes an impossible task. "

     —NICHOLAS BONAWITZ
       *UNIVERSITY OF ROCHESTER, GRADUATE*

**STUDYING WITH MUSIC** works for some people. It does not work for me. I wish I could focus on my work as well as I can focus on the songs on my iPod. For me, it definitely interferes with what I am trying to study or get done.

     —ANNIE THOMAS
       *UNIVERSITY OF MICHIGAN, SENIOR*

**Easybib.com or any sort of citation websites save lives!** I've always used sites like those to generate my citations for the many papers I've written. Towards the end of my time at college, I remember multiple classmates talking about how they've been struggling for years making sure they're writing the citations up correctly. I don't think the Internet is always right, and you should always have a critical eye. But for most papers, especially freshman year, you can definitely use those sites to make life easy! Also, using grammarly.com helps give you a fresh look any grammatical errors. (It's way better than spell check!)
—*Nathalie*
*Rutgers University, Graduate*

Watching the sun come up while studying is not a good thing.
—*Jamese James*
*University of Tulsa, Graduate*

**Get old tests** from previous semesters; old tests and notebooks. There's a code name for this at most schools; find this out the first week of school.
—*Sebastian*
*Georgia Institute of Technology, Graduate*

**I made a Spotify playlist out of movie scores,** which are designed to help you focus on the action in a movie, so they're the perfect study companion.
—*Valerie Bodurtha*
*University of Chicago, Graduate*

# A LITTLE (TAT)TOO CREATIVE...

At the University of Central Florida, a recent case of cheating had nothing to do with the Internet, cellphones or anything tech-related. A heavily tattooed student was found with notes written on his arm. He had blended them into his body art. The same university prohibits gum chewing during exams, because it might "disguise a student's speaking into a hands-free cellphone to an accomplice outside."

# PARTY ON?

IF YOU'RE QUESTIONING whether or not to go to a party, you better not go. Kids in college don't have good judgment. That's how you learn responsibility, learning how to listen to yourself. Some kids are like, "You think I should go to that party? Because I've got a midterm." It's like, "Keep your ass inside and study. You just answered your question." Learning how to answer your own questions; that's a big part of college.
> —ANONYMOUS
> BROWN UNIVERSITY, SOPHOMORE

I GO TO SCHOOL IN A BIG CITY, and there's always the temptation to go out and do something. You can't escape it. You have to realize, when nighttime comes, you're going to want to go out. So you have to do your work in the day; otherwise, your work won't get done.
> —CATHY
> COLUMBIA UNIVERSITY, SENIOR

GO OUT TO PARTY ON THURSDAYS, Fridays and Saturdays, but stay at home on the other days. I don't have classes on Friday; you should try to schedule that. And I don't study on Sundays; that's for watching football. During the week, I go to class and then study about two hours a night.
> —FRED
> UNIVERSITY OF RHODE ISLAND, JUNIOR

NEVER, EVER GO TO THE LIBRARY ON SATURDAY, unless it's during finals. Take a break one day a week and have fun.
> —STEVE DAVIS
> FLORIDA STATE UNIVERSITY, GRADUATE

DON'T TRY TO STUDY ON A FRIDAY NIGHT. DON'T EVEN TRY.
> —NOURA BAKKOUR
> GEORGETOWN UNIVERSITY, SENIOR

**DON'T KID YOURSELF** thinking that you are going to work on a project or do any studying at all on weekends; it ain't gonna happen. I used to think like this: okay, test Tuesday. Today is Thursday. That means I have five days to prepare. But it never worked out like that. What really happened is that Friday was Friday (party day) and on the weekend the party continued. Monday was for recovery. You have to factor reality into your planning.
—*KEN KEEL*
*UNIVERSITY OF VIRGINIA, SENIOR*

**DON'T CLOSE YOURSELF OFF FROM UNEXPECTED OPPORTUNITIES BECAUSE YOU'VE 'MADE YOUR MIND UP.'** I went into college wanting to minor in Chinese, and signed up for a class called Intro to Chinese Civilization for my first semester. I walked into my first class and the teacher did the whole lesson in Mandarin! I hadn't studied any Chinese and was completely lost. Needless to say, I went back to my dorm and immediately switched out of that course!

I found that by keeping my options open and taking classes that interested me, such as theater electives and psychology courses, I was not only able to understand the lessons, but I was a lot happier going to class and was offered opportunities I would have never known about otherwise.
—*NATHALIE*
*RUTGERS UNIVERSITY, GRADUATE*

**PAY ATTENTION TO STUDY GUIDES.** Those were very beneficial. For physics, the sample questions would be the same ones on the test. So, you need to study the study guide.
—*NICOLETTE*
*RUTGERS UNIVERSITY, SENIOR*

**I'VE ACTUALLY HAD T.A.'S CHANGE MY GRADE** because they read the paper again and realized that they graded it too harshly. I had it happen twice. I showed them that I knew the material, even if it didn't come out in the paper.

—*EVELIN OCAMPO*
*UNIVERSITY OF CALIFORNIA AT SANTA BARBARA, JUNIOR*

• • • • • • • •

**PROFESSORS ARE OFTEN VIEWED AS BEING VERY DISTANT** from students, and in a sense they are, compared to what most students are used to in high school. As a freshman, I took a class with a certain professor who is practically villainized on campus; students are terrified of him before even meeting him. I was one of those students.

One day, I saw him walking his dog down the street, wearing normal clothes. This was a strange moment, that made me realize that my professor lived a relatively normal life outside of the classroom. I decided to go up to him and we ended up having a great conversation. It is very important to remember that professors are human, like we all are, and that they are very often more than willing to talk.

—*AAVO*
*UNIVERSITY OF PENNSYLVANIA, JUNIOR*

• • • • • • • •

**AS A SENIOR IN COLLEGE** there are a lot of things that I wish I could tell my freshman self. Partying and other activities may seem important but ultimately your grades are what defines you as a scholar. I would tell myself that math tutoring doesn't make you dumb. It helps you more and don't let anyone stop you from believing that you can do anything. Math was a big struggle for me, and still is. but I'm going to tutoring and I put way more time and effort into my studies.

—*JASMINE*
*LONG ISLAND UNIVERSITY, SENIOR*

**TALKING TO YOUR PROFESSORS IS REALLY HELPFUL** because you gain insight into what they're looking for. That helps guide the way you study and how you organize information.
—*JOSE CISNEROS*
     *UNIVERSITY OF NORTH CAROLINA AT CHAPEL HILL, GRADUATE*

● ● ● ● ● ● ● ● ●

**GET A LAPTOP LOCK.** I've heard stories where people get up from their computer for a minute – to go to the bathroom or get a drink – and a minute later, their computer is stolen.
—*DIANA SHU*
     *UNIVERSITY OF CALIFORNIA AT BERKELEY, SOPHOMORE*

# MEMO TO MY FRESHMAN SELF:

**IF I COULD GO BACK TO MY FRESHMAN SELF,** I would probably slap her in the face and tell her to open up a book.

A very big motivator for me was not being able to find a job when I took a break from college. I was able to find a lot of entry-level positions, but I needed to take on three at the same time to save up to pay back the money that I owed in order to get back into school. So, I needed to work hard, and then I realized how expensive school actually is and, looking back, I realized that I took it for granted and I didn't actually put in the effort that I should have.

Now I'm back and I'm part-time, and still working on the side. I work for the university, so I interact with the kids quite frequently, and I'm seeing my past self, reflected in them, and I see that they procrastinate too. I hear people in the elevator all the time and their friends are saying, 'You don't wanna study today, you wanna come out and have fun with us.' And then they all agree and they all go with it. I used to do that too, so the fact that I see it right in front of me – it's actually kind of shocking for me. They take out all these loans but they don't understand how much money, and how much time and effort, they're going to need to put in for that education.
—*AMANDA*
     *UNIVERSITY OF PITTSBURGH, SOPHOMORE*

# THE COMPANY YOU KEEP

**CREATE STUDY GROUPS WITH PEOPLE WHO SHOW UP TO CLASS AND TAKE NOTES.**
This way, if you ever miss a class you have someone to grab notes
from. It makes studying a lot easier and gives you motivation to go
to class to see those people. Record your lectures, and make sure
you introduce yourself to the teacher so they know who you are.
This way, if you ever miss class or something crazy happens and you
fail a test or have to turn something in late, they are more likely to
help you out since they know who you are and that you're a good
student.
> —NATHALIE
> RUTGERS UNIVERSITY, GRADUATE

**GET INVOLVED WITH PEOPLE** who are taking classes with you. When you
have friends who are doing the same thing with the same goals, it's
easy to work together, and you can build off each other, rather than
trying to do everything by yourself.
> —COURTNEY WOLFE
> GEORGIA STATE UNIVERSITY, JUNIOR

**SOME OF MY MOST PRODUCTIVE STUDY SESSIONS** were studying in groups.
Find a classroom that's empty in the evening, write notes and
questions on the chalkboard, quiz each other, and have fun with it.
> —K. HARMA
> WESTERN WASHINGTON UNIVERSITY, GRADUATE

**DATE A GOOD STUDENT.** Being around people who study and care a
good deal about their grades is going to rub off. If the people you
hang out with are less liable to ditch a study session to hang out,
chances are you'll crack down and study – if for no other reason
than a lack of available buddies to procrastinate with. This holds
doubly true for dating.
> —AMANDA
> UNIVERSITY OF COLORADO AT COLORADO SPRINGS, SOPHOMORE

**STUDY WITH FRIENDS WHO ARE ALSO TRYING HARD TO STUDY.** Don't study alone and don't study with the ones who struggle with distractions.
—*LI*
*UNIVERSITY OF TORONTO, GRADUATE*

**GET SOME FRIENDS WHO CAN EDIT A PAPER.** They'll come in handy. And for every hour you study, do 15 minutes of fun stuff. It helps keep a balance.
—*CONOR MCNEIL*
*EMORY UNIVERSITY, SOPHOMORE*

**BY 9 P.M. ON THE NIGHT BEFORE I HAD TWO PAPERS DUE** the same day (for the first time ever), I hadn't started either of them. I was freaking out, I was not prepared. I was sure I wasn't going to finish everything in time. I called my mom close to tears on my way to the library, saying "I don't know what to do, how did I let myself get to this place?" And she said, "Emily, I know what you're saying, but it's time to put on your big-girl panties and get to work." Basically, freaking out wasn't going to help. I say that to people now, "put on your big-girl panties" …. even though I'm not really sure what that saying means!
—*EMILY*
*HARVARD COLLEGE, SENIOR*

**YOU ALWAYS THINK YOU HAVE MORE TIME THAN YOU ACTUALLY DO,** and then it comes up and bites you. The deadline is right in your face. I ran into that a few times and realized that it's really inefficient. It causes a lot of undue stress, so you've got to start things days in advance. You can never, ever wait until the last day for something. Never.
—*AARON*
*PURDUE UNIVERSITY, JUNIOR*

# UH, WHAT TIME IS IT?

**YOUR FIRST ALL-NIGHTER WILL BE HORRIBLE,** but there will be many of them.
    *—ABBY*
        *SOUTH DAKOTA STATE UNIVERSITY, SENIOR*

• • • • • • • •

**I PULLED MY FIRST ALL-NIGHTER LAST WEEK,** two nights in a row. I was up
from 5 A.M. on Tuesday morning to 3 P.M. on Thursday afternoon. It
was tough. I went to class to turn in my second paper on Thursday;
I got there, sat down, and hit the desk. I fell asleep and someone
woke me up at the end of class and I turned in my paper. Diet Coke
with lemon pulled me through.
    *—WHITNEY*
        *YALE UNIVERSITY, FRESHMAN*

• • • • • • • •

**ALL-NIGHTERS WILL NOT HELP YOU FOR ANYTHING.** When you're so tired, your
brain doesn't function properly, so it doesn't work. You might think
it works – and I thought it worked, especially when I was hyped up
on energy drinks and trying to read. But when I woke up the next
day, I realized I didn't remember anything that I spent time on that
night.
    *—AMANDA*
        *UNIVERSITY OF PITTSBURGH, SOPHOMORE*

• • • • • • • •

**MOUNTAIN DEW AND CAFFEINE** pills help you get through all-nighters.
    *—ANONYMOUS*
        *UNIVERSITY OF RHODE ISLAND, SOPHOMORE*

• • • • • • • •

**I ONCE STAYED UP THREE NIGHTS** back-to-back. It was fairly intense. I
drank coffee, but also ate chocolate-covered espresso beans. They
taste good and give you a little boost.
    *—B.*
        *MASSACHUSETTS INSTITUTE OF TECHNOLOGY, GRADUATE*

THIS IS SOMETHING MY DAD TOLD ME: You should look at college like a 9-to-5 job. Wake up and do all your work from 9-to-5 so you're not stuck doing your work at 3 A.M., like I always am. Then you're tired and you end up sleeping through your first class, like I always do. So, get your work done early and then you have time to socialize.
—JENNA
BOSTON COLLEGE, FRESHMAN

. . . . . . . .

" In classes with required reading, if you just actually do the reading, you will be leagues ahead of the average student in the room who did no more than quickly skim. This is especially true in literature courses. "
—CONOR MCGEEHAN
NORTHWESTERN UNIVERSITY, SENIOR

. . . . . . . .

IN ENGLISH LITERATURE, don't watch the movie instead of reading the book. I didn't read all of A Clockwork Orange and I had an exam on it, so I watched the movie. I didn't know how obvious it would be that I substituted the book with the film. Never rely on the movie rendition or, for that matter, what you find online! Your professor makes you read the book for a reason.
—VERONICA
QUEENS UNIVERSITY, GRADUATE

# SEE THE MOVIE – BUT YOU'LL STILL HAVE TO READ THE BOOK!

No matter your major, there will be books in college that you would rather skip, and you may be tempted to search for shortcuts. But before you turn to a movie adaptation as a way to pass for having done the work, be warned: Hollywood takes liberties. Six cautionary tales to consider:

**"A Clockwork Orange" by Anthony Burgess**
Stanley Kubrick's 1971 movie adaption relied heavily on a controversial American version of this classic British novel, which omitted the crucial 21st chapter. In that chapter, the book's main character redeems himself.

**"Jurassic Park" by Michael Crichton**
More main characters die in the 1990 book than they do in the 1993 movie that Hollywood's Steven Spielberg directed. Also, a runaway T-Rex does not save the day.

### "The Scarlett Letter" by Nathaniel Hawthorne

A guilt-burdened man who impregnated a woman out of wedlock seemingly drops dead from shame at the end of this 145-year-old novel. But the 1995 movie version of the story, starring Demi Moore, has the couple simply flee from town to escape judgment and begin anew. Even older silent film versions of this tale stick more closely to the author's harsh vision.

### "Robinson Crusoe" by Daniel Defoe

This 300-year-old novel has its hero, Robinson Crusoe, stranded on an island for more than two decades, while the 1997 movie starring Pierce Brosnan deposits him there for a mere six years. Also, the end of the movie deviates sharply from the book by killing off the hero's buddy, Friday. In the novel, Crusoe saves Friday's life.

### "Fahrenheit 451" by Ray Bradbury

HBO 2018 movie adaptation of this dystopian classic eliminated the main character's wife and turned a teenage character into an older, sexier love interest for its star, Michael B. Jordan. Unlike the 1953 book, HBO also did not allow the protagonist to make it out alive.

### "Frankenstein" by Mary Shelley

A 1931 version of this tale is considered one of the best movies ever, but it is only a "loose adaptation" of the 200-year-old novel. It changes the name of a main character and casts the monstrous Frankenstein as a more mindless, zombie-like figure than the book. A later 1994 film version received less fanfare from critics but is a more faithful adaptation of the book.

*Anthony Wallace*

# STUDY "AIDS" THAT PUT YOU AT RISK

**PRESCRIPTION STUDY AIDS, PARTICULARLY ADDERALL, WERE EXTREMELY COMMON** at my university. A lot of students felt overwhelmed, especially around midterms and finals, and felt like the only way they could succeed was to take something. This made a lot of students dependent on study aids and, I would imagine, feel like they were unable to succeed on their own. I didn't take them, and I think that has helped me substantially in the long run. While other students were relying on study aids to complete assignments, I was learning how to study effectively and build on my time management skills.
—*L.G.*
*BUCKNELL UNIVERSITY, GRADUATE*

**ADDERALL SHOULD NO WAY, NO HOW, BE YOUR FIRST LINE OF DEFENSE FOR SCHOOLWORK.** Obviously, the best thing is not to use it at all. But I use it very occasionally in emergency situations, like when I have two papers to write in two days or maybe during finals. I have friends, though, who got to school and literally started using drugs to do their first papers. After that, it was like, who *wouldn't* want to spend $10 and be laser-focused for a few hours? They never developed the confidence that they could do their work without drugs. They became psychologically dependent upon it and then, eventually, physically dependent upon it. Not a good situation.
—*ANONYMOUS*
*DARTMOUTH COLLEGE*

**BE GREEDY ABOUT YOUR MEDS.** People ask me all the time for my Adderall. "C'mon, just one. It's finals, I really need it." I just flat-out say "no." I could get into serious trouble and lose my prescription if I got caught doing it. Plus, college is competitive. I'm a competitive guy. I take my meds to catch up with everyone else. I don't need someone taking my pills so they can do even better.
—*ANONYMOUS*
*SYRACUSE UNIVERSITY, SOPHOMORE*

**KEEP YOUR MORALS, EVEN IF IT MEANS IT'S HARDER TO KEEP UP YOUR GRADES!** Drugs and prescription aids to study are very popular in college – even with the kids you would think never would do that. They were great kids who never drank in high school and got straight A's. Guess what! They do it, too. I am very proud to say that I never did that in college. I called my mom a few nights, crying and so frustrated that I wasn't doing as well in some classes while I felt other people were "cheating" their way through a class by taking these prescriptions when they were not actually prescribed them. My mom was like, "If you study and fail, we'll be more proud of you just for not doing it."
    —*TAYLOR*
    *UNIVERSITY OF SOUTH DAKOTA, GRADUATE*

• • • • • • • • •

**THERE IS A PREVALENCE OF ADDERALL USAGE ON CAMPUS,** especially with majors that require you to stay up really late, like mine, Mechanical and Aerospace Engineering. It's almost kind of accepted that sometimes people feel forced to use it and thus the culture is hush-hush. If someone uses it, they don't mention it to anybody. I also know people who want to use it and have been asking me, "Should I?" Princeton's very tough. I don't know if I can handle it any more. I think I need to use Adderall. Otherwise, I'm not going to make it. There are just a ton of very rigorous classes that require a lot of work, and if I use Adderall, I'm going to be able to concentrate better in class.
    —*ANONYMOUS*
    *PRINCETON UNIVERSITY, JUNIOR*

# RISING USE OF "STUDY AIDS"

In a recent nationwide poll, as many as 6 percent of undergraduates reported taking stimulants such as Ritalin or Adderall that had not been prescribed to them, while another 3 percent reported taking anti-depressants such as Prozac or Zoloft that were not prescribed.

# IT'S ALL IN THE NOTES

**TAKE NOTES BUT DON'T TRY TO BE A STENOGRAPHER.** Use class notes to enhance your understanding of the course; for example, flagging areas for follow-up in text or with the instructor.
—*SCOTT WOELFEL*
*UNIVERSITY OF MISSOURI, GRADUATE*

• • • • • • • •

**I'VE LEARNED TO LISTEN TO THE PROFESSOR** and what he's saying – not just scribble down everything that he says – and then try to summarize his thoughts in my notes. Not word-for-word, but the main points.
—*JOSH*
*PRINCETON UNIVERSITY, SENIOR*

• • • • • • • •

**DO NOT USE LAPTOPS TO TAKE NOTES IN CLASS.** The research at this point is overwhelming: laptops are terrible for learning. Your job when taking notes is not to transcribe what the professor said; it's to synthesize, comprehend, and put it in your own words. Taking notes by hand forces you to do that.

Also, be organized. Even if you aren't an organized person, it's pretty easy to do. Keep your notes all together. Date all of your class notes so you can easily cross-reference them later. Keep an eye on the syllabus so you know when exams and papers are coming up. It's actually pretty easy to be organized once you put your mind to it.
—*MAX*
*DARTMOUTH COLLEGE, GRADUATE*

• • • • • • • •

**AVOID PUTTING STUDYING OFF** until the last minute. After a lecture, I would always go back and go through my notes and rewrite them. If the professor says something more than once, that is a strong clue that it is important. In high school, I could get away with cramming the night before; that changes in college.
—*SARAH*
*WESTERN ILLINOIS UNIVERSITY, SENIOR*

**WHILE SOME PEOPLE PREFER** to take notes on their computers, most of them also decide to surf the net while in class. Not only does it distract from your lectures, but it also distracts your peers. Plus, teachers know – I've seen plenty of people get busted.
—*MAYA NEWMAN*
*COLUMBIA UNIVERSITY AND THE JEWISH THEOLOGICAL SEMINARY, GRADUATE*

**TIME MANAGEMENT IS KEY!** You can do so many amazing things while in school but you have to be on top of all your own stuff, there's no one there to remind you to do your homework or when your next assignment is due. There are websites and apps such as focusme.com that help keep you on task and in control over your assignments and deadlines, as well as reducing distractions while you try to work!
—*NATHALIE*
*RUTGERS UNIVERSITY, GRADUATE*

**TRY TO TEACH SOMEONE ELSE THE MATERIAL.** That's the best way to make sure you understand it.
—*R.S.*
*GUILFORD COLLEGE, GRADUATE*

**DON'T BITCH ABOUT GRADES.** Professors are not out to get you. They expect a lot of you. I loved a screenwriting class I took, studied a lot, and ended up getting a B on the midterm – which I was sure I had aced. So, I politely asked the professor in an e-mail if I could meet to discuss it. He met with me and simply said, "a B is a great grade. It was one of the highest in the class. You have nothing to worry about." It really put into perspective about how to look at grades.
—*ANONYMOUS*
*BOSTON COLLEGE, GRADUATE*

# TECHNOLOGY AND STUDYING

**IN ONE OF MY CLASSES,** all my homework was online. You couldn't forget homework, it was due at midnight. It kind of sucked because I would get lazy about it, and copy/paste the question into Google. While I got good grades on the homework, I wasn't learning and was screwed for exams.
>—*TINA*
>*MARIST COLLEGE, SENIOR*

**KNOW HOW TO ACCESS** all the teachers' information. Most professors expect you to be able to download syllabi, assignments, labs, things to write up. Your grades are online. It's more difficult if you can't do these things. It's not impossible, but it's more difficult.
>—*LEAH PRICE*
>*GEORGETOWN UNIVERSITY, SOPHOMORE*

**MY COLLEGE USES BLACKBOARD** and it's actually pretty good. It organizes your classes and keeps you updated about your grades in detail. But if a project is due at midnight through Blackboard, DO NOT wait until the last five or even 10 minutes to send it, because everyone in your class is sending it at that time, and the site will crash!
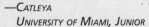
>—*CATLEYA*
>*UNIVERSITY OF MIAMI, JUNIOR*

**TURN OFF YOUR CELL PHONE IN CLASS!** One student forgot to turn his phone off in one of my classes, and the professor made this particular student hold a normal phone conversation in front of the entire class. At the end of the conversation, the student had to say "I love you" really loudly, so that everyone could hear. Professors frown upon cell phones in class.
>—*LINDSEY WILLIAMSON*
>*VANDERBILT UNIVERSITY, GRADUATE*

# THE POWER OF THE FRONT ROW

I took Introduction to Business and panicked when I got 7 out of 10 on the first quiz. One of my friends said to go to the T.A.'s office hours, because it was a huge class and the professor didn't know who you were. My friend also suggested I sit in the front row of the class. I then went to the T.A.'s office hours and she said, "Sarah, don't worry about it. I am happy that you are showing dedication by coming to my hours." A few minutes later, the professor walked in and said to my T.A., "How are your students in the section?" She said, "They're fine, and by the way this is Sarah; she was concerned about her quizzes." My professor said, "Oh, I know who she is. She sits in the front of my class. And by the way, don't worry about the quiz, just keep sitting in the front row."
—SARAH F.
AMERICAN UNIVERSITY, FRESHMAN

**HAVE YOUR SCHOOL'S WRITING CENTER** help you edit first drafts of your papers. I learned this later, but if I had started freshman year, I would have had a much smoother experience, believe me.
—MAYA NEWMAN
COLUMBIA UNIVERSITY AND THE JEWISH THEOLOGICAL SEMINARY, GRADUATE

- - - - - - - -

**IF PROFESSORS GIVE OUT EMAIL ADDRESSES,** use them! Don't send anything raunchy, even if you are in love with your English professor. Use it to communicate about class work. Email them if you happen to have skipped class and want to know what you have missed. This is a sure way to win points with them. By humanizing them, you make them a friend. I have done this a few times and they seem to like it when you are involved in school, even when you are not.
—E.S.
KINGSBOROUGH COMMUNITY COLLEGE, SENIOR

Be careful when buying used books. The person who had the highlighter before you may have been an idiot.
—J.T.
UNIVERSITY OF FLORIDA, GRADUATE

# TIPS FOR ACADEMIC SUCCESS

You are probably used to getting good – maybe even excellent – grades in high school. Well, we have news for you…college is harder than high school! To get (more or less) the same grades in college, you'll have to work harder, despite dealing with enhanced opportunities and distractions, and taking care of yourself, perhaps for the first time. How do you get a leg up? Try any combination of these:

- **Sit in the "inverse T" of the class:** If you sit in the front two rows of class, or directly down the center (see, it makes an upside down "T" from your professor's point-of-view), you'll be in his or her line of sight. So you'll be forced to be more attentive in class and caught up on the material, and your professor is more likely to get to know you and take an interest in you. When you have a question, she or he is more likely to see your hand go up. Of course, this also means that if you skip class, someone's going to notice.

- **Don't skip class:** You are paying far too much money for every hour of class. Skipping even one lecture is like flushing wads of money down the drain.

- **Go to office hours:** Your teaching assistants and professors are required to hold a certain number of office hours every week. Many times, these go by without anyone stopping in to visit or ask questions. When you go to office hours, your instructors will appreciate your interest and the fact that you're taking full advantage of your education. Try to go with a great question in mind – even if it's one you think you understand but you want to comprehend more fully.

- **If your college offers supplemental services, check them out:** There is probably a department called the Learning Center, Study Skills Center or Academic Resource Center. In addition to study skills workshops (note-taking, time management, exam review tips), they may offer 1:1 tutoring for various classes. Or an upper division student who has excelled in that class may hold regular review sessions or help you work through homework.

- **Don't cheat:** You may not realize it, but there are many – many! – different forms of cheating beyond simple plagiarism and copying someone's answers on a test. For many assignments, your professor may not allow you to collaborate with others. You can even plagiarize *yourself* if you use any portion of work you had submitted for another paper, without citing yourself as a source! Don't violate any of these forms of cheating. You'll get caught, plain and simple.

- **Stress less:** Stress can either empower you (meaning you overcome it) or devour (overwhelm) you. You can tap into resources from your Wellness Center or Counseling/Health Centers. Work out regularly, go out with your friends once in a while, and otherwise, find ways to de-stress or unwind, or you may find yourself getting sick or irritable.

- **Study before you party:** Suffice it to say, doing things in the reverse order will NOT be productive. Plus, where are your priorities? Look, we get it, college involves lots of opportunities to have fun, but you have a job right now: your education, and you may very well have some actual paying jobs as well. This may be the most important 'job' you ever have, as it will pave the way for most, if not all, of your future opportunities. Do not squander this chance. Above all else, be successful in your coursework. There's nothing worse than repeating a class that you didn't enjoy the first time but need to graduate…except, of course, for not graduating at all.

*Scott C. Silverman*

**DON'T PARTY TOO MUCH** and then cram. I did, which resulted in my very low GPA my freshman year. As a result, I had to work very hard to make up for it.
—*JESSICA TAYLOR*
*STATE UNIVERSITY OF NEW YORK AT GENESEO, GRADUATE*

• • • • • • • •

**DON'T WORK IN DORM COMMON ROOMS.** Crazy things will happen, people will pass through and you will get sidetracked. Everyone has different methods and preferences, so figure out what works for you. I always opted for somewhere with natural light, either holed up in my room or in the library.

Leave your phone on 'do not disturb' while you work. This year, I started keeping notifications off from when I get up in the morning until I am done with class, studying and working out for the day, and it's made a drastic improvement in my productivity and in the quality of my work.
—*CONOR MCGEEHAN*
*NORTHWESTERN UNIVERSITY, SENIOR*

• • • • • • • •

**WAKE UP EARLY AND STUDY.** Even if you're not a morning person, make yourself one. It's the quietest time in the dorm and you'll be so productive.
—*SEAN CAMERON*
*PRINCETON UNIVERSITY, SOPHOMORE*

# THREE WAYS TO BE A BETTER STUDENT – FAST

1. Sit in the front of every class. Now, you'll stay awake.
2. Buy a different notebook or set up a separate binder section for each class – and use it! Now you'll keep up with the material.
3. Reread (or read for the first time, as the case may be!) all your class syllabi. Now the semester holds no unpleasant surprises

# FOMO: THE MOTHER OF ALL DISTRACTIONS

Ever heard of **FOMO**? Social Media can't exist without it. FOMO, or the Fear of Missing Out, is anxiety – often aroused by posts on social media – that an exciting or interesting event may currently be happening elsewhere. And it exists wherever social media does.

Allow me to paint you a picture. Let's say you have a lot of work coming up and want to get ahead on your Media Law reading on a Saturday afternoon. Back in the day when my parents went to school, this would've been a breeze – when they'd take a little reading break, maybe they'd stroll around the library, get some water, and not dwell on whatever fun things their friends were doing at a frat house off campus at the moment. But today, Snapchat is our biggest obstacle.

If you see any diligent students in the library on a Saturday afternoon (a rare sight where I come from), I guarantee their study break will feature them opening Snapchat and browsing through their friends' stories. Maybe a close girlfriend is doing a keg stand, maybe a boyfriend is facilitating a Slip n' Slide. These little glimpses into the lives of people who are spending their afternoon differently are enough to make diligent students wish they were somewhere else, with friends and (more often than not) alcohol. It's not necessarily that this is what the students would rather be doing – after all, they made the choice to go to the library, when they were just as free to go to the party if they had wanted to. A lot of times, what really irks isn't that there's something you'd rather be doing, but rather that everyone else seems to be there doing it – without you. You didn't exactly want to attend the party, but you certainly don't want people to party when you're not around.

If they hadn't opened Snapchat or Instagram or Twitter in the first place, they wouldn't have seen this content and wouldn't be experiencing FOMO. It's that ability to have someone else's life at your fingertips that makes the longing so much more visceral.

—*Hannah Benson*
*Elon University, Senior*

# THE LIBRARY: YOUR PARTNER IN ACADEMIC SUCCESS

Now that you're a freshman, it's time to begin getting to know your library. College and university libraries are very different from your high school or local public library. Known as academic libraries, they are teaching libraries, and genuinely so. Most academic librarians are faculty members with masters or doctoral degrees. Their purpose is simple and yet very important – to provide you, the student, with the research and information tools needed for your chosen profession so that by the time you graduate, your library skills will be developed enough to strongly support the research and information tasks in your profession. Academic librarians won't do your work for you or just give you the answers to questions, but they will teach you *how* to find the answers and how to become an expert library user.

Remember this – the process of research is not difficult, but it is detailed. It is important, therefore, to adhere to the steps involved in the research process:

1.  First, understand the topic about which you will be writing. Writing a research paper is not an opportunity to tell the reader what the topic is about. It is an opportunity to defend, refute, challenge, analyze, or suggest a new position on an opinion or topic. If you're not sure you really understand your topic, your library will have resources that can help you learn about and focus on topics. A big secret of success is selecting a topic that is right-sized: neither too broad nor too narrow.

2.  Second, identify databases and other library resources which will provide you with the evidence to support your thesis statement. Remember to take an interdisciplinary approach, because no topic exists without being influenced by other topics.

3.  Third, develop a search strategy, which includes discovering which words will be effective when you search. Open a new Word document and keep a list of the search terms you've

discovered to be effective, since the search may extend over several days or weeks, and it is unlikely you'll remember all the words or combinations you tried. As you find materials, be sure to collect the citation information for each work. And, for articles and other sources that are available in PDF form, save them in a folder on your desktop.

4.  Finally, critically evaluate the sources to ensure authenticity and objectivity. If possible, make sure that they are scholarly and are published in a peer-reviewed journal, rather than a for-profit publication. Your paper is only as strong as the evidence you find.

Hint: Avoid using Google or Google Scholar. These are search engines, not databases. The upside is that they are easy to use, but the downside is that not all articles you might need are available via Google, nor are they always the most recently published works. This is an important thing to understand – only your library's research databases will be able to provide you with full texts of recently-published and soon-to-be-published articles.

Libraries are prepared to assist you in other ways as well. Your library may have laptops and tablets you can take home overnight, study rooms where you can work undisturbed with your team, course reserves for items held specifically for your class, extended hours during final exams, and the option of scheduling a one-to-one consultation with a librarian.

Research is an important part of professional careers. And being an expert researcher is just another tool that you will need in order to be competitive in the job market, successful with what you do, and satisfied knowing that you are in control of your career. Your academic librarians are ready and delighted to help you learn to navigate the complex research landscape. But the responsibility of asking for help belongs to you – if you don't ask, you'll never find out. So, interrupt a librarian and ask for help. That's why we are here.

*Prof. Douglas Hasty*
*First Year Experience Librarian*
*Florida International University*

# HOW TO SURVIVE FRESHMAN ENGLISH

You are a college student! And with this new identity comes a rite of passage: freshman writing courses. Two semesters of college writing are generally required for graduation. Besides, future employers will want to make sure you are a decent writer in whatever career awaits.

If you're not an English or creative writing major, or are not already blogging away on Tumblr, you might not be thrilled about having to write in college. Almost every academic major requires some type of writing. It's true. I was the director of a university writing center and taught first-year writing courses at a health and science school, where many freshmen openly expressed their disdain for writing.

One day, while walking out of class with my students, one of them yelled in protest, "Why do we have to take f**king writing at a science school?" He didn't know I was within earshot. At the next class, I asked my students, "Who wrote your biology book? Your chemistry book? Your pharmacy book?" They looked perplexed... and then it hit them! Of course! Biologists, chemists, pharmacists and other health and science professionals wrote their books. They are writers, too! Writing is a necessary skill used in all types of professions and careers.

The good news is, that even if you don't like writing or feel you're not a good writer, freshman year is a good time to hone those skills with the help of your writing instructors and tutors from your college's writing center.

Writing is a process; don't rush it! Writing draft after draft is a good thing and is fully expected in freshman English. Get into the habit of reading your writing aloud. It's amazing how many errors, big and small, you'll capture.

Make sure you know when to use 'your/you're,' 'then/than,' 'its/it's,' 'affect/effect,' and other commonly confused words. Proofreading your drafts and final papers will also improve your submissions and your grades.

It's natural to feel overwhelmed by writing assignments. But don't panic. Meet your professors during office hours, or make appointments with your college writing center to go over your drafts, brainstorm, and get feedback on your thesis, overall organization, and grammar. The staff there can also advise you how to cite your sources and steer clear of plagiarism.

For style tips, the Purdue OWL// Purdue Writing Lab is one invaluable resource all can use, as is the Modern Language Association's online Style Center. MLA's handbook is considered the standard for many liberal arts programs.

Whatever you do, do not cut-and-paste from the Internet and plagiarize. Remember, you're not in high school anymore, and you will be caught.

Many colleges have sophisticated plagiarism detectors, ranging from the more familiar Turnitin to stealthier programs like Moss and Codio, which can detect subtle similarities in computer code. Sometimes, all a professor has to do is type a few sentences into Google to see if a paper has been lifted. I assure you, the consequences are not pleasant.

So be awesome in your freshman writing classes. Have high expectations for yourself as a writer, whether or not you are a natural. And who knows? One day, you might just write that thank-you note that lands you the job you've always wanted or that love letter that wins someone's heart, or even that textbook that earns you the respect of your entire profession – and some royalties too.

*Miriam Diaz-Gilbert directed a university writing center and has taught college students for more than 20 years.*

# COLLEGES THAT DOWNPLAY LETTER GRADES

- Reed College
- New College of Florida
- Evergreen State University
- Prescott College
- Alverno College
- Antioch University
- Hampshire College
- Brown University

*Jon Barr is an LA-based writer & comedian.*

**COLLEGE IS NOT HIGH SCHOOL;** it requires you to think in very different ways than one is used to. Find one place on campus where you can study without being interrupted and designate a portion of your time for that purpose. When reading, read for content, and know what you are reading (it makes skimming that much more effective). If you must cram, going to bed earlier and waking up at 6 A.M. to force a few more hours in is more effective, because at least you are awake for the test. But then again, that's just me.
> —*AMY*
> *PRINCETON UNIVERSITY, FRESHMAN*

• • • • • • • • •

**DON'T STUDY IN YOUR ROOM;** you won't ever get to it. Your phone and neighbors will be too enticing. I would suggest a quiet cube at the library, if you really need to get something done.
> —*J.S.*
> *UNIVERSITY OF GEORGIA, GRADUATE*

**DON'T EVEN THINK ABOUT CHEATING.** Cheating is one of the stupidest things one can do, especially if you do it in front of someone like me. In high school, I reported cheating at least three times and some of the culprits were valedictorians! In college, cheating has a finer line. Is looking up the question on an online quiz cheating? Is getting a copy of the test from someone who took it the previous semester cheating? It depends whom you ask.

During the final of my investments class, I heard two guys behind me whispering about the multiple-choice part!!!!! I was furious. I finished my final early and whispered to the professor about them. I left in a huff. I don't know what happened to those guys, probably nothing, but it really irks me!

—REBECCA
COLLEGE OF NEW JERSEY, SENIOR

## ASK A GRAD...OR MAYBE NOT

# 5 TOP EXCUSES FOR WHEN YOU'RE LATE FOR CLASS:

1. Your skateboard ran out of gas.
2. A protest for raising teachers' salaries blocked the path and you had to join.
3. You got lost in a corn maze.
4. There was free pizza on the quad.
5. You were grading papers and everyone gets an A. (This one only works if you are the professor.)

*Val Bodurtha is a Chicago-based writer and comedian.*

# NEW TOOLS THAT SNIFF OUT CHEATING

Computer science classes have grown in popularity in recent years as students see coding as an increasingly useful skillset. The intense interest in these courses, though, has coincided with another phenomenon: an outbreak of plagiarism cases related to computer code. Large numbers of students nationwide have been caught borrowing code from their friends or copying it from the Internet.

Advanced detection software has made it easy to flag plagiarism, and computer science courses have become a leading source of academic dishonesty complaints. At some schools, such as Brown and Princeton, more than half of all cases that now go up for disciplinary hearings involve computer code.

"People sometimes wonder why there are so many computer science cases," said Joyce Chen Shueh, Senior Associate Dean of Undergraduate Students at Princeton. She said that was partly a function of comp sci departments having routine detection methods that other departments don't. "But the other reason," she flagged, "is that when students are struggling with code that isn't working," and their programs won't run, "they feel like they can't turn it in."

"When they work on an English paper at the eleventh hour and it isn't their best work, it feels more okay to hand that in," she said. "With code, students can get desperate."

Students may also take on a collaborative mindset that is common among real-world programmers and engage in code-sharing in ways that aren't tolerated in classroom settings.

MOSS, one of the mainstay programs used by Princeton and other colleges, sniffs out similarities between a student's code and other students' submissions through time, in addition to code that is available online. Short for "Measure of Software Similarity," Moss looks for similar structure and identical bugs, among other commonalities. If a student's code shares enough similarities with an existing program, MOSS flags the assignment as a high-priority.

The program has now been rolled out at many campuses. Other programs, such as Codio, monitor students' keystrokes, and give colleges additional tools for detecting students who cut corners.

Since code might be similar for various reasons, including shared starter code or similar tips provided by the course instructor, or sheer coincidence, it ultimately falls to the department to decide whether or not to pursue a disciplinary case.

Dean Shueh explains that many students don't intend to copy but once they see someone else's code, they can't "unsee" it. "That's why we'll tell students in their first-year academic integrity workshop that you should start early enough on Computer Science assignments, so you can get your instructors' help," she said. "But if you find yourself stuck at the last minute, it's better to take the partial grade instead of taking the risk of looking at someone else's code."

*Sophia Cai is a freelance journalist studying International Affairs and Public Policy at Princeton University.*

I HEARD ABOUT A BUNCH OF PEOPLE CHEATING one time my sophomore year, during an economics exam, and the whole class got a zero. Another time, this kid sitting next to me in class was Googling answers during our exam and got caught by the TA. All she did was tell him to put his phone away and gave him a warning. So honestly, cheating definitely happens, and some TAs and professors are more adherent to the university policies regarding academic integrity than others are. Just don't do it; possible expulsion from the university is really not worth the one good grade.

—CHRISTINE
DREXEL UNIVERSITY, JUNIOR

COLLEGES ARE BECOMING MORE AWARE OF CHEATING and are paying more attention to what students are doing. At my school, like many other universities, there is a 'no tolerance' policy. If you are caught cheating, you have a very real chance of facing expulsion. Although it sounds cliché, the following holds true; cheating is never worth it, you only end up cheating yourself.

—AAVO
UNIVERSITY OF PENNSYLVANIA, JUNIOR

• • • • • • • •

THE BIGGEST THING I STRUGGLED WITH in regard to technology was that doing all of my problem sets, I could very easily Google the answer to them, but that's not necessarily in compliance with the honor code and I wouldn't learn much by doing that. So, I struggled a lot with the fact that, in theory, all the answers were at my fingertips, but I just couldn't get them. When you're actually in the workforce, you would be able to just Google the answer, whereas in class, you're not always able to use all the resources that would normally be available to you...That's where you have to talk to people. Talk out your problems, go to office hours, talk to your professors, use all the other resources available to you.

—ANONYMOUS
PRINCETON UNIVERSITY, SOPHOMORE

• • • • • • • •

NOT ALL PROFESSORS ARE SCARY OR STANDOFFISH OR SUPER PROFESSIONAL. They're honestly just humans too and most will understand if you need an extra day to complete an assignment. Just don't be that kid that shoots them a plea at 11:26 P.M. the night before the assignment in due.

—CHRISTINE
DREXEL UNIVERSITY, JUNIOR

**THE KEY TO SURVIVING** and having free time is to know what the teacher wants you to know and just study that. Skip everything else if it's not necessary to get a good grade in the course.
—*ANONYMOUS*
*UNITED STATES MILITARY ACADEMY AT WEST POINT, JUNIOR*

∘ ∘ ∘ ∘ ∘ ∘ ∘ ∘ ∘

**STUDYING IS ALL ABOUT KNOWING YOURSELF.** You don't want to end up in the library on the night before the final exam, crying. But you also don't want to be a shut-in bookworm. Something as simple as using a notebook to take notes instead of a computer will help. Studying in small bits will be easier, and you are more likely to remember what you wrote rather than what you typed. Show up to your class 5 minutes early, flip through your notes from the class before. Small things like that will leave you over-prepared, so that you won't be cramming last minute and you will have weekends free during the year!
—*MICHAEL CUMMO*
*BOSTON UNIVERSITY, SENIOR*

"It's an invite to our Kafka Society mixer."

# Extracurriculars: Making the Most of Your Free Time

So many clubs, so little time! Most college graduates will tell you they wish they'd done more extracurriculars during their four years. There's so much more to do in college than just looking for the next party. Campuses are brimming with people who are passionate about their causes and hobbies, everyone from the adventurers at Brown who go on 'donut safaris' to the traditionalists at Middlebury who bond over logrolling.

Clubs and associations reflect every interest under the sun, as the students in the next few pages can tell you, and there's little harm in testing the waters.. Who knows? You may discover new loves that stick with you for life and, along with them, a side of yourself you never knew you had.

**FIND A GROUP ON CAMPUS** that interests you, so you don't feel that the school is so huge.
—*STEPHANIE*
*UNIVERSITY OF PENNSYLVANIA, SENIOR*

**FREE TIME: USE IT. DON'T WASTE A DROP.**
—*ARIEL MELENDEZ*
*PRINCETON UNIVERSITY, FRESHMAN*

HEADLINES

- Clubs are a great way to network with other people . . .
- . . . and a good way to try out something new.
- Organizations in your area of academic interest may even offer scholarships.
- It's your free time, so make sure you're having fun.
- Exercise is great for relieving stress.

**BECAUSE COLLEGES OFFER SUCH** a breadth of extra-curriculars, it's important to learn about them before you decide which ones to devote yourself to. A lot of schools have activity fairs that allow you to sign up for any activity that interests you. After this, you will start receiving emails from the groups about meetings, events, and initiatives. With this information, you can decide if it is something you are passionate about or something you could eliminate from your résumé. And it's okay to back out!
—STEPHANIE DREIFUSS
DUKE UNIVERSITY, SENIOR

**GETTING INVOLVED IN CLUBS** that I felt would be interesting helped me network a lot and showed me things I enjoyed more than what I originally thought I'd be majoring in.
—LUKE YOUNT
MILLERSVILLE UNIVERSITY, SENIOR

**HOW DO YOU SURVIVE FRESHMAN YEAR?** Nap. Get up for class. Go to class. Then nap. That's how.
—MIKEY LEE
STANFORD UNIVERSITY, JUNIOR

**DON'T BE AFRAID TO BE YOURSELF,** and you'll find that many people are on the same wavelength as you. For example, I always loved basketball, but was pretty laid back all throughout high school. (I also was not very good). So, one of my roommates and I decided to be the "coaches" for our friends in the intramural league. We dressed up in buttoned-down shirts and ties, and brought clipboards, drew up plays, and called timeouts. We did nothing except for fake yelling at the refs. Every other team thought we were weird, but our teammates thought it was hilarious. It was a great way to bond with the people on our floor without playing.
        —*ANONYMOUS*
            *BOSTON COLLEGE, GRADUATE*

**ONE GREAT THING ABOUT JOINING** everything freshman year: I still get random emails from, say, the Korean Society or the Indian Students Organization, inviting me to their open houses. So I can go and have all sorts of wonderful free dinners. I have a friend who managed to spend only $14 on food for a whole week!
        —*DENALI*
            *PRINCETON UNIVERSITY, JUNIOR*

**MEREDITH COLLEGE HAD AN EVENT CALLED CORNHUSKIN.** People tell stories, sing songs and dance. When I first went, I was like, "I'm just going to see what this is like and watch." I didn't actually join in on the fun and when I graduated, I wish that I had actually contributed and joined in more because I saw that a lot of people who had been more involved in all the traditions came out with really good friends. The traditions bonded them and got them out of the classroom.
        —*PAISLEY*
            *MEREDITH COLLEGE, GRADUATE*

IF THERE WAS ONE THING THAT I WISH I HAD DONE IN MY FRESHMAN YEAR, IT WOULD BE TO GO OUT MORE. We were so close to the city that it was really easy, like a subway ride away. I wish that I'd taken advantage of the city a lot more, or just been outside of campus with my friends a lot more. I missed opportunities by not taking more advantage of the freedom of being a college student with friends and no supervision.
—IRIS CHIOU
UNIVERSITY OF CHICAGO, GRADUATE

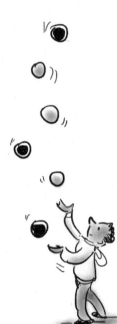

• • • • • • • •

THERE ARE BOUND TO BE COMMUNITIES OF PEOPLE WITH SIMILAR INTERESTS AS YOU, whatever they may be. College is such a cool time to be able to find things you are genuinely interested in and that other people are interested in too. There are so many different communities of people who share your varied interests. There's a snowboarding club at my school with like 400 people, and I didn't even know about it until my sophomore year. I met some of my best friends and went on so many great trips with them. I wish I would have known about that club instead of getting drunk and trying to find random house parties to crash.
—KEVIN
UNIVERSITY OF ARIZONA, GRADUATE

• • • • • • • •

TAKE FUN CLASSES. I took yoga and aerobics. I also joined the salsa-dancing club. These things break up the monotony of the usual classes.
—EMILY TUCK
CALIFORNIA STATE UNIVERSITY, GRADUATE

• • • • • • • •

JOIN DIFFERENT CLUBS FROM THE ONES that your roommate or friends are in. It's good to branch out of your comfort zone and connect with a variety of people.
—E.S.
DUKE UNIVERSITY, GRADUATE

I WISH SOMEONE HAD TOLD ME THAT MY ACADEMICS WOULD NOT SUFFER BY BECOMING INVOLVED. I was so concerned my first two years of college that joining an organization would take time away from doing work or seeing my friends. Fast forward to senior year, and I was the VP of a club, a peer educator, part of a sorority, volunteering, and a manager at my campus job – all while maintaining a 3.83 GPA my last semester. I found that joining all of these new things actually helped me academically – I knew that my time was limited, so I was more effective in the free time I did have.
—L.G.
BUCKNELL UNIVERSITY, GRADUATE

THE DUMBEST THING I've ever seen someone do at college is literally take advantage of nothing. I knew some people I was very good friends with, who would just watch Netflix all day. That's fine and it's a choice that people make but I just felt that with so many opportunities at college, you're missing out on a really expensive opportunity that you paid for.
—NICOLE ZELNIKER
GUILFORD COLLEGE, GRADUATE

I GREW UP DANCING TO TRADITIONAL MEXICAN MUSIC, and I loved it. But I always wanted to learn different styles. In my sophomore year, I tried out for a dancing team and I was accepted. I danced with the team for the rest of the time at UNC. That was, by far, sort of my 'Greek experience.' It was something I had to work for. And once I made it, going to competitions and travelling helped me find my closest friends, my community that didn't necessarily have to do with school, just something I loved and we all shared, which was the love of dance. That community really defined my whole experience.
—JOSE CISNEROS
UNIVERSITY OF NORTH CAROLINA AT CHAPEL HILL, GRADUATE

**GO FOR DEPTH AND NOT BREADTH WHEN CHOOSING CLUBS.**
Initially, I tried to do too much. I signed up for 20
different clubs and it ended up with my sitting
in my dorm room in tears on the phone with my
parents. They kind of simplified it and told me to
focus on *why* I want to do each of these things.
And if I couldn't come up with a reason, and it
was simply a line on my résumé that I didn't enjoy,
then I shouldn't be doing it. It's more important
to have a few things that are really meaningful,
and impactful, and informative than 16 things that
maybe you aren't that involved in.
>   —COLLEEN
>       UNIVERSITY OF VIRGINIA, JUNIOR

**CHECK THINGS OUT, PARTY-WISE,** when you first get to
college, because after a while it gets too crowded
with work. You get too busy, so it's important to
have fun at first.
>   —PATRICK
>       UNIVERSITY OF RHODE ISLAND, FRESHMAN

**I WAS IN A SEMI-PROFESSIONAL *A CAPPELLA* GROUP** that
travelled around the
country and the world
singing for thousands
of people every year. I
met my closest friends,
became a confident
public speaker, and
gained invaluable
leadership and time
management skills. It
was incredible, but it was
a huge time commitment

and did not give me much time to devote to other
extracurricular activities.
>   —MAYA NEWMAN
>       COLUMBIA UNIVERSITY AND THE JEWISH THEOLOGICAL
>       SEMINARY, GRADUATE

THE BEST CLUBS TO JOIN are the ones that incorporate your major. Many offer scholarships, field trips, invite guest speakers, and can give you a bit of background on what you need to do to succeed. They also provide community service, which is a great experience for anyone. Many of these clubs also connect you with professionals whom you can shadow and get internships with.
—WHITNEY
VALDOSTA STATE UNIVERSITY, JUNIOR

• • • • • • • • •

BECAUSE I'M JEWISH, I joined Hillel House. I love · the activities that they do, such as visiting soup kitchens and organizing meetings where they bring in a speaker. I am going to join them on their trip to New Orleans for Habitat for Humanities.
—CAROL
HUNTER COLLEGE, FRESHMAN

## ASK A GRAD...OR MAYBE NOT

# 5 CLUBS YOU CAN START TO MAKE A NAME FOR YOURSELF ON CAMPUS:

1. PDA: Porn Dramaturges Association
2. Penultimate Frisbee League
3. The Hufflepuffs: For Students with Harry Potter Obsessions Instead of Personalities
4. Virginity Losers Anonymous
5. Another terrible improv troupe

*Val Bodurtha is a Chicago-based writer and comedian.*

# VENTURING OUT OF THE BUBBLE

I WAS INVOLVED WITH THE CRISIS HOTLINE. The most common call we had by far was what we called the loneliness call. It would be a person on a huge campus who felt lonely – a person who doesn't know how to meet people, who's away from home the first time.

My college has more than 250 student organizations – fraternities and sororities, hang-gliding club, bungee-jumping club, weight-lifting club, all kinds of ethnic organizations, every religious group. There has to be a group out there that has your interest.
—*MICHAEL A. FEKULA*
*UNIVERSITY OF MARYLAND, GRADUATE*

THE BEST CLUBS AND ORGANIZATIONS to join on campus (outside of Greek life) are those that involve volunteering. It is a way to help others and to get to know your community at the same time. Sometimes it's easy to forget that your college/university does not exist in its own bubble. There are people, places and spaces that exist outside your classroom and dorm walls. Go out and explore. It will make you a more in-tune person in the end.
—*A.F.K.*
*DUKE UNIVERSITY, GRADUATE*

AT SCHOOL, I JOINED AN ORGANIZATION called p3, short for Paraprofessionals Promoting Peer*fection. We welcomed all the new freshmen in and were the first faces they saw at orientation. Along the way we pretty much gave them a heads-up on what to expect, and at the end we served as their mentors throughout the year if they chose to have one. You didn't get any compensation for being a p3; just the gratification and rewarding feeling when one of your mentees tells you that they don't think they could've made it through their freshman year without you.
—*BRITTANY*
*ALBANY STATE UNIVERSITY, GRADUATE*

**COMMUNITY SERVICE ORGANIZATIONS** such as the Red Cross and Project Giveback not only help the community but they make you feel good about yourself, knowing that you made a difference is someone else's life. If you have free time, and you need something to do, helping others is the perfect way.
—*HAYLEY MASON*
*HOWARD UNIVERSITY, SOPHOMORE*

**WE HAVE A VOLUNTEER PROGRAM** at the university called Madison House. They arrange all different kinds of activities to get involved in the community; helping out in classrooms, teaching English as a second language, and volunteering for hospital duties, among others. It's really heartening to see the school make an impact in the community and to know that the students truly care enough to wait in line just to volunteer.
—*Jo*
*UNIVERSITY OF VIRGINIA, SENIOR*

**COLLEGE IS DEFINITELY A TIME TO BECOME AN ACTIVIST.** There are many terrible things in this world that could and should be changed, but we can only do so much, so it's important to find a cause that is meaningful to you. For me, this cause is climate change.
—*DREW HILL*
*COLBY COLLEGE, JUNIOR*

**I WANT TO CHANGE THE WORLD** by learning self-defense techniques and teaching other students and people what the art of self-defense is all about. It's a great way of increasing one's energy and knowing how to act in certain situations.
—*MICHAEL CHOE*
*GEORGE WASHINGTON UNIVERSITY, GRADUATE*

**MY FRESHMAN YEAR** at George Washington was a lonely experience. I didn't really know anyone on my first floor. But the more I talked to other freshmen, the more I realized there was opportunity to network with other people. I got involved with a bible group on campus; it was an amazing time of sharing the bible, meeting people who cared, and singing songs. It was a beautiful experience.

—MICHAEL CHOE
GEORGE WASHINGTON UNIVERSITY, GRADUATE

" My freshman year I tried archery and karate for the first time. I wasn't good at either of them, but it was fun being bad at something new. "

—AMY FORBES
MISSISSIPPI STATE UNIVERSITY, GRADUATE

**EXTRACURRICULARS ARE WHAT COLLEGE IS ABOUT;** creating your own niche. If you're an academic, start a publication. If you're an actor, launch a theater. I started a debate team that competed against the Ivy League schools. Now I'm creating a theatre program located at Lincoln Center, with master teachers from Yale, Julliard, and NYU. At this great space, students and professional New York creatives will be working to produce plays together.

—RON Y. KAGAN
MACAULAY HONORS COLLEGE AT *CUNY HUNTER,* SENIOR

# SOME OFFBEAT EXTRA-CURRICULAR ACTIVITIES

- Kutztown University Medieval Renaissance Club. Gives you that opportunity to be a knight in shining armor and joust on that horse that you've always wanted! Pillaging not included.

- Students for an Orwellian Society (national society, founded at Columbia University). Attracts students from all over who want to live in a totalitarian society inspired by 1984, the George Orwell classic.

- Williams College's Beekeeping Club, where students learn how to manage hives and get to collect honey.

- For those who can't get Disney tunes out of their head, Disney A Cappella at the University of Pennsylvania is devoted to performing "any song featured on a soundtrack associated with a Disney movie, TV show or Broadway musical" and it takes its mission seriously. Miss a rehearsal and face a fine of $5; $1 for every five minutes you come late.

# EXPLORING DIFFERENCES

ONE OF MY BEST FRIENDS here is from Nepal. Conversations with him have opened my horizons. I learned a lot about different cultures and how women are treated in Nepal. I was talking about visiting and he was like, "These are things you can expect." It's refreshing. Be prepared to ask questions when you don't understand things and be open to new ideas and people.
—MEREDITH
BROWN UNIVERSITY, SOPHOMORE

. . . . . . . . .

I AM CAUCASIAN and am definitely a minority at my school. I have embraced this and been able to immerse myself in a vast array of cultures and people. I know that most of my friends went to homogenous, "white" schools and have not been able to face racial or discrimination issues up front. Here at Hunter College, I'm able to interact with people from all over the world. This diversity has kept me open-minded and aware of the issues surrounding race. I am thankful that I have been able to attend West African dance classes or tasted Islamic food during the Dean's Hours.
—GERALDINE SARAH COWPER
MACAULAY HONORS COLLEGE AT CUNY HUNTER, SENIOR

. . . . . . . . .

BE A PART OF SOMETHING that you sincerely enjoy because it's your free time. Upon my arrival on campus, I decided to dedicate my time and efforts to Duke Africa. It served as a space where I could celebrate my Nigerian culture, learn about other African cultures, and become informed about issues and causes affecting Africa socially, economically and politically.
—D.A.
DUKE UNIVERSITY, SENIOR

**IF THERE IS A STUDENT RETREAT FRESHMAN YEAR, GO.** I met my future wife on a secular retreat to Cape Cod called "48 hours," where you literally took one weekend in February freshman year and did self-reflection and team-bonding exercises. It challenged you to meet new people a few months into college life and gets you out of the rut of doing the same thing every weekend with the same group of people. It was refreshing. Literally. We did a polar plunge in the Cape in February at the end of the weekend. Physical and mental renewal.
—*ANONYMOUS,*
   *BOSTON COLLEGE, GRADUATE*

* * * * * * * *

**I'M GAY.** My college has a queer student union; their meetings take place every week, with typically 30 in attendance. Another organization, Queer Allied and Activism, discusses LGBT issues, and we try to implement actions to improve our community. This is definitely the more political organization, whereas the first is geared more towards social mixing, where hooking up is quite common.
—*ANONYMOUS*
   *UNIVERSITY OF VIRGINIA, JUNIOR*

* * * * * * * *

**THERE IS A HOWLING AT THE MOON CLUB** at Mt. Holyoke; when it is a full moon, you can hear them all over campus.
—*RUTHANN*
   *MOUNT HOLYOKE COLLEGE, GRADUATE*

* * * * * * * *

**CLUB SPORTS ARE FUN,** non-threatening ways to get your exercise in, as well as a way to meet a variety of people. Most people who join club sports are a grab bag of personalities.
—*STEPHANIE LEIGH DOCKERY*
   *WILLIAMS COLLEGE, GRADUATE*

# DONUT SAFARIS AND OTHER EXOTIC EXTRACURRIX

Debate Club and Model UN were fun in high school, but once you get to college you'll be exposed to dozens of new and exciting extracurricular clubs and activities. It's not just the newspaper or intramural sports leagues or the student government, either; from ballet to anime to Quidditch, there's something for everyone. Here are some you might not have thought existed that you can start at your own school:

**'Doctor Who' Club — Brigham Young University**
All Whovians are welcome to watch episodes of the BBC classic series, exchange theories and fight about which Doctor was *really* the best Doctor.

**Juggers of the Seven Regents — University of California, Berkeley**
This club is based on a "post-apocalyptic movie from Australia" directed by a Cal grad, that trades swords for foam rollers.

**Prometheus: Fire Arts and Performance — Wesleyan University**
This club features student fire spinners performing for their fellow Wesleyan classmates. Don't worry if you don't have the fire stick flips down just yet – the group will teach you how, safely.

**Carroll Adventure and Mountaineering Program — Carroll College**
This program, open to all students, takes advantage of Carroll's picturesque location in Helena, Montana to offer students hiking, biking, fly-fishing and sightseeing trips around the Missouri River, the Helena National Forest, Yellowstone and more.

**The Rebel MX Club — University of Nevada, Las Vegas**
This club introduces students to motocross and recreational dirt biking. So, if you enjoy supercross or motocross, this is the club for you.

## The Assassins' Guild — MIT

This club is a live-action roleplaying society that hosts several events throughout each semester for students to enjoy. The games last anywhere from a few hours to several days.

## The Donut Club — Brown

One of the newer clubs on this list, the Brown Donut Club has a rather simple, but noble mission: Find the most delicious donuts around Rhode Island. No small feat, but the club is getting it done.

## Logrolling — Middlebury

Looking for a cardio workout but sick of running? Then logrolling might be for you. This is one club you can join just for fun or compete against other schools like Loyola or the University of Maryland. Why not give it a roll?

## Yachting Club — Guilford College

No, it's not a boating club; Guilford's Yachting Club is designed for self-described geeks to indulge in whatever nerdy activities interest them. Each year the club hosts the "What The Hell?!" Con, where students and community members alike participate in board games, anime, cosplay and movie screenings.

## Fords Against Boredom (FAB) — Haverford

There are no fraternities or sororities at Haverford, but FAB organizes non-alcoholic parties and outings for students to enjoy throughout the year. FAB's activities range from trips to museums and concerts to an Iron Chef competition to Casino Night and more, and any student can send the club ideas for new events. The club's purpose is to help hard-working students unwind from studies with some "good, clean" fun.

*Alicia Adamczyk is a New York-based writer.*

**REJECTION CAN BE TRAUMATIC BUT IT MAKES YOU TOUGHER.** I loved theatre in high school. I had gotten leads all four years in my school musicals. So, at college, I skipped the chance to audition for plays and only auditioned for the musical "Godspell." Finally, I was gonna be back in my element with my theatre friends, I thought. Except, I auditioned…and didn't get cast. I didn't even get called back. I thought there must be some mistake, but nope. I applied to help with the crew but I wasn't accepted for that either. I was miserable. The group of people I clung to for support had rejected me.

Things didn't get any better until I got cast in a one-act play for the play club. It was student-written and only had four characters, and I was cast as the lead. I got into the spring show freshman year as well and made a lot of friendships from that. And then sophomore year, I got into the musical. And at the end of junior year, I was elected treasurer of the play club. During my college theatre career, I got rejected by more shows than the ones I got in. It made me more resilient and gave me tougher skin. All in all, a traumatic and frustrating experience but a good experience looking back.
     —*REBECCA*
       *COLLEGE OF NEW JERSEY, SENIOR*

• • • • • • • •

**WHEN I WAS A FRESHMAN,** I joined a Chinese club, because I was majoring in Chinese and it really helped me network. I still had that common network when I left Duke. I would advise freshmen to join an ethnic or religious club; I found that those were the clubs that kept people grounded.
     —*SHEVON*
       *DUKE UNIVERSITY, GRADUATE*

**WHEN YOU HAVE FREE TIME,** enjoy things that are non-school related and healthy: Join a really random club, be in a play, volunteer, run a marathon, become a film noir enthusiast. Your free time can really give you a chance to meet people of similar mind-set and interest, and can also expose you to interests and ideas you can't find in the lecture hall. Also, make sure you watch a little bit of TV now and then, to prevent college "bubble" syndrome.
—*AMY*
    *PRINCETON UNIVERSITY, FRESHMAN*

# BALANCING BOOKS & SPORTS

**IF YOU'RE INVOLVED IN AN EXTRACURRICULAR ACTIVITY,** you need to learn time management. Since I was a student-athlete in college, I found out first-hand what time management was. I had to keep up my grades and coursework in addition to practicing three hours a day, plus having games or meets to compete in. It was hard, but it was worth it in the long run. I can't tell you how good it looks on my résumé that I competed in an NCAA sport while keeping up my grades.
—*JAMESE JAMES*
    *UNIVERSITY OF TULSA, GRADUATE*

. . . . . . . .

**IT'S TOUGH TO BALANCE** doing a sport and being at school. You practice three hours a day, and you go to school all day. When you get home you're tired, and you have to find time to study. A lot of times you don't want to, but you have to learn how to do it. It took me all of first year to learn how. I mean, we're normal students in some ways, but in other ways we're not, because we're always doing something. We don't have the free time a lot of people do when they get out of class. When we get out of class, we have to go here and go there; we're traveling, we're on the road, we're in hotels. It's tough to make the grade when you play sports.
—*RUSTY BENNETT*
    *GEORGIA STATE UNIVERSITY, SOPHOMORE*

**TRY NEW THINGS.** I never acted in high school, but I tried out for a play and got one of the lead roles. It's a lot of fun. I'm going to do a lot more of that now.
—*CONOR MCNEIL*
*EMORY UNIVERSITY, SOPHOMORE*

. . . . . . . .

**CLUB SOCCER ROCKED!** We road-tripped all over the place. You get to know people pretty quickly when you have to spend hours with them in a car.
—*LINDSEY WILLIAMSON*
*VANDERBILT UNIVERSITY, GRADUATE*

. . . . . . . .

" Never underestimate the power of a Tuesday night game of cards. "
—*AMY FORBES*
*MISSISSIPPI STATE UNIVERSITY, GRADUATE*

. . . . . . . .

**SPORTS — I PLAYED A LITTLE BIT OF EVERYTHING** in college. I had never played water polo in my life and I played that in intramurals and it was great. I played flag football, softball, volleyball; all that stuff. Sports are a great release. I played competitive sports in high school but I wasn't good enough to play on the college level, so it was a good way for a frustrated athlete to get out there and keep alive and be active. Intramurals were a way to be competitive, but it wasn't so competitive that you had to deal with the pressures.
—*JOHN BENTLEY*
*TRINITY UNIVERSITY, GRADUATE*

# SLUTWALKS: A HIGHER PURPOSE FOR THOSE OLD FISHNET STOCKINGS

Every year, college students around the country shed their sweatpants in favor of bras, fishnet stockings and anything else they fancy. They scrawl messages on their bodies or grab a placard, and head straight for the nearest SlutWalk. It's not just women's sexual agency they're celebrating. These collective displays are powerful demonstrations against the ways victims of sexual violence are often blamed and shamed for their attackers' actions.

SlutWalks began in 2011 as an anti-rape and sexual violence movement in Toronto, after a police officer reportedly told women at Toronto's York University not to "dress like sluts" if they didn't want to be attacked. The movement that sprouted from that ill-advised comment means to draw attention to the way rape is often excused because of what the accuser was wearing, for example.

Reaction to the initial walk was, decidedly, mixed; many people took issue with the attempt to reclaim for women a commonly-used pejorative, while feminist supporters hailed the conversations it has ignited. "In just a few months, SlutWalks have become the most successful feminist action of the past 20 years," feminist writer Jessica Valenti wrote in 2011. "In a feminist movement that is often fighting simply to hold ground, SlutWalks stand out as a reminder of feminism's more grass-roots past and point to what the future could look like."

*Alicia Adamczyk*

# NEED OTHER IDEAS?

**DO STUPID STUFF.** One time our R.A. randomly said, "I'm going to the beach to go swimming, you want to go?" It was 2 A.M. in the fall and it was freezing cold. But we said, "okay." So we all went swimming in freezing water at 2 A.M. in the ocean – and I've never felt more alive. You'll never remember staying up and studying for a midterm. What you'll remember is staying up and doing something *instead* of studying.
    —MIKEY LEE
        STANFORD UNIVERSITY, JUNIOR

**DO THINGS YOU NEVER THOUGHT** you would do. Ride the mechanical bull in that bar, drink too much, and participate in karaoke. Do all these things while you can. Before you know it, these behaviors will be frowned upon, so you need to get it out of your system.
    —P.G.
        UNIVERSITY OF GEORGIA, GRADUATE

**COLD WEATHER FUN:** Take lunch trays and go sledding. Build giant snow sculptures; if you pour water over them, they won't melt until spring.
    —JACKIE
        STATE UNIVERSITY OF NEW YORK AT BINGHAMTON, GRADUATE

**IT'S FINE TO FEEL OUT CLUBS, BUT BE READY TO QUIT** if you feel like it's not a good fit. I joined the Asian American Student Association my freshman year because I thought it would help me meet more people. But it felt much more like a social organization than a political one, and I ended up quitting after a semester because I didn't feel like we were doing meaningful work.
    —ANONYMOUS
        PRINCETON UNIVERSITY, SENIOR

**EVERYONE HAS TO FIND SOMETHING:** it can be just watching a movie on a Tuesday night, hanging out in the hall with friends at 2 A.M., a weekly yoga class, or just reading a book for fun. But you need something outside of schoolwork and the party scene or else you just run out of steam before each semester ends.
—*SAMANTHA STACH*
*DUKE UNIVERSITY, JUNIOR*

. . . . . . . .

**IT'S NEVER TOO EARLY TO GET INVOLVED.** Don't think, "But I'm just a freshman." If you join as a freshman, you could have enough experience to be president of the club by junior or senior year. That will look great on your résumé. In my freshman year, I got involved with the campus radio station, the campus newspaper, and the campus magazine. Since I was a journalism major, I wanted to get as much experience in the field as possible. My junior year, I became the editor-in-chief of the campus magazine.
—*LAUREN TAYLOR*
*UNIVERSITY OF GEORGIA, GRADUATE*

. . . . . . . .

**USE THE GYM AS MUCH AS POSSIBLE,** because when you get out, it's not free anymore. It's in your tuition, so you're paying for it.
—*SANI G.*
*UNIVERSITY OF CALIFORNIA AT IRVINE, JUNIOR*

. . . . . . . .

**MY SOPHOMORE YEAR,** I joined the mountaineering club. Their weekend excursions and the boulder time at the rock wall helped me to counterbalance the burden of intense classes and blow off some steam. I met a lot of cool people in this club and strengthened my relationships with previous friends.
—*DREW HILL*
*COLBY COLLEGE, JUNIOR*

# PLANET COLLEGE

IT IS A COLLEGE STUDENT'S RESPONSIBILITY to educate himself or herself on the climate change issue. Saving the environment and taking on global warming isn't for everyone, but if a student feels passionate about the cause it is a worthwhile pursuit, just like any interest.
—PARISA BASTANI
UNIVERSITY OF PENNSYLVANIA, SENIOR

• • • • • • • •

BECAUSE OF A VARSITY SPORT AND A MUSIC GROUP, I personally have not had the time to commit to any environmental organizations. That being said, I have found I can still make a substantial difference just in my own dorm. A lot of kids on campus will leave windows cracked in the winter, leave lights on, and throw away recyclables. These things take very little effort to do but make a huge difference when hundreds of students are doing them together. You don't have to join an environmental group to avoid being wasteful.
—ANDREW
HARVARD UNIVERSITY, FRESHMAN

• • • • • • • •

I'M EXTREMELY CONCERNED WITH AMERICANS' SENSE OF SUSTAINABILITY. I fear that older generations have completely failed us by creating a society where a $10 gallon of gas will crush the economy. Living in Atlanta is a study on how not to plan a city with the future in mind. Americans need to reevaluate their desires to ensure that our society remains sustainable. Hopefully, my college education will not only enable me to live a sustainable lifestyle, but also allow me to influence others to do the same.
—ALEX
EMORY UNIVERSITY, SOPHOMORE

• • • • • • • •

LAMINATED CARDBOARD IS NOT RECYCLABLE. My roommate Kate was a kind of vegan hippie. She wouldn't allow us to use a trash bag liner because the world didn't need any more plastic in it. If we had something messy we needed to throw out, we would just walk to the trash room. She also inspected the recycling to make sure we were recycling the right things. I learned a lot from her.
—REBECCA
COLLEGE OF NEW JERSEY, SENIOR

**MY SCHOOL IS VERY ENVIRONMENTALLY CONSCIOUS,** with recycling bins everywhere and an emphasis on recycled goods. Take shorter showers, don't use styrofoam if at all possible, and be aware that your actions almost always affect the environment.

—*JACOB*
*UNIVERSITY OF MARYLAND, SOPHOMORE*

**I WAS PART OF MY SCHOOL'S** Sustainable Food Initiative, which was building an urban garden. During my second semester at school, I spent a lot of time hauling rocks out of dirt. Those less masochistically inclined will probably find that there are lots of easier ways to become involved in environmental issues on campus.

—*MOLLY*
*BROWN UNIVERSITY, SOPHOMORE*

**I DO NOT THINK THAT EVERY STUDENT HAS AN OBLIGATION** to become actively involved in an environmental organization. I do think that every student has an obligation to act responsibly towards the environment, from thinking about how many pages they print to how often they turn off the lights before exiting a room. Simple steps like this can create an environmentally conscious person.

—*JOSH*
*PRINCETON UNIVERSITY, SENIOR*

**THERE ARE TONS OF WAYS TO LEND SUPPORT.** One group here sponsored a meal where students were encouraged to bring their own bowls and utensils to cut down on wasted water needed to wash dishes. Even if you don't want to become a member of a group, I think it's important to listen to and cooperate with the environmental groups' programs. They are doing them to make the campus a better, cleaner place. It's so easy to take part in a program and give them the support they need. It's easy to try to change little things, like drink water out of the bubblers instead of bottled water, actually put your cans in the recycling, and turn out the lights in your room. Starting sustainable patterns of living at college will prepare you to continue them for the rest of your life. It's every student's responsibility to put in the effort.

—*TOBIAS*
*HARVARD UNIVERSITY, FRESHMAN*

# TIPS FOR LGBTQ+ STUDENTS

All students face a transitional experience as they enter their collegiate careers. Many LGBTQ+ (Lesbian, Gay, Bisexual, Transgender, Queer or Questioning) students may experience additional challenges as they develop their own identity and find new friends. Ultimately, it can be (and should be) a liberating experience. Here are some tips for LGBTQ+ students to help in this transition:

- Get to know new people. Do not make the mistake of limiting yourself only to the LGBTQ+ community, but also meet new friends who identify with other sexual orientations. College is a chance to expand your group of friends and get to know many new people with different perspectives and values.

- Some students find it helpful to join a Gay Straight Alliance organization on campus. Research your campus alliance online and communicate with the president of the organization. Determine if you feel comfortable with it and if it is aligned with your own personal values and goals.

- Be prepared to address questions that may be asked of you from other students. How open or private you want to be with your sexuality is your decision alone. But if you decide to talk about it, take these opportunities as a way to show an accurate picture of the LGBTQ+ community. If you do experience discrimination or harassment, be prepared to approach your resident assistant or hall director, as they are valuable resources and can help you address the inappropriate behaviors you are facing.

- Know that your resident assistants, hall directors, professors, the counseling center, university staff, and friends are there to talk to you, and that they want you to succeed.

*Justin Long*
*Associate Director for Residence Education & Student Relations*
*University of Southern Mississippi*

# HAVING A PET IN COLLEGE

Before you bring a dog, cat, hamster, lizard, goldfish (or other animal) to your house or dorm room, here are some things to consider:

- **If you live in the Residence Halls:** Odds are, that your university does NOT allow pets in the Residence Halls. Some residence halls may allow a small fish tank, but remember, even a fish needs daily care. Of course, service animals or emotional support pets are generally okay, but written permission from a medical professional is usually required. You should also make sure your roommates are okay with you having a pet - and that they don't have allergies.

- **If you live off-campus:** Landlords may ask for an extra 'pet deposit' or monthly pet rent to cover potential damage(s). There also might be breed restrictions. If you are planning to have multiple pets, check with your local animal control agency regarding certain regulations such as the maximum number of pets allowed per household.

- **Exercise:** Most pets such as dogs and cats need room to play and exercise. Younger dogs tend to have a lot of energy and need to go out for walks twice a day. If you are planning to let them out in the backyard unsupervised, make sure there is secure fencing around the yard and that your pet is not able to escape or possibly get hurt.

- **Also, pets get sick just like humans do,** and you will have to take care of your pet even when you have projects due or are in the midst of final exams. Pets need yearly check-ups and vaccinations, and you will also need to get your pets spayed or neutered for various health reasons.

There are so many loving animals in shelters looking for a home. Please 'Adopt don't Shop!'

*Peyvand M. Silverman, D.V.M., is the Veterinary Staff Manager at the Los Angeles office of the ASPCA.*

**IT'S VERY EASY TO OVER-COMMIT** to a lot of extracurriculars because they're all really wonderful and you want to try everything. I thought I wasn't over-committing since everything I was doing was arts related – dance and music and theater – but I had no idea what huge time commitments those three things would all be. Things take up much more time than they do in high school!
—*HALEY*
*HARVARD UNIVERSITY, SENIOR*

. . . . . . . . .

**TRAVELING FOR AWAY GAMES** is a lot more of a stresser than you'd expect. Just because, it's not as easy to do work on the bus or in the hotel as you'd expect because there's always some interesting conversation going on or you got to be prepared for warm-ups or you got to go see the trainer. You're rarely able to invest your full attention into your work. So, that was difficult to deal with on Fridays and Saturdays and having to get all my work done on Sunday, when we got back.

Don't pretend like you're going to have enough time to do it on the road. Basically, partition off that time as time you're not going to work, and find other time to do it. Or be better about shutting off the rest of the world during those away games and try to get it something done in the hour before going to sleep. At the same time, traveling to away games is a great opportunity to just get off campus and see another campus., I remember George Washington University as being a really good time, even though we were only there for Friday night and Saturday. Being in another gym in D.C. feels like you're part of something bigger.
—*CHARLIE BAGIN*
*PRINCETON UNIVERSITY, SOPHOMORE*

**DON'T STRETCH YOURSELF TOO THIN.** You'll get sick! My roommate was an athlete, in a sorority, woke up early, went out all the time and she had strep throat pretty much all year. Even when she wasn't coughing, she would be audibly moaning because she was so miserable.
    —MEGHAN WALLACE
        NORTHERN ARIZONA UNIVERSITY, SENIOR

• • • • • • • •

**HAVE FUN DOING ANYTHING,** and just smile and laugh at least once a day. You've got to find ways to have fun and relax every day, or else you'll go nuts. You can tell the kids that don't: they just suck at life and are no fun to be around.
    —ANONYMOUS
        UNITED STATES MILITARY ACADEMY AT WEST POINT, JUNIOR

Enjoy any good weather you get. Study outdoors, play some Wiffleball, anything to keep you busy.
—ARIEL MELENDEZ
  PRINCETON
  UNIVERSITY,
  FRESHMAN

*"Jose's gotten so popular since he started carrying his own power strip."*

# Technology: Social Media and the Online College Experience

Technology is advancing so rapidly that by the time you read this, Elon Musk may have implanted your phone straight into your brain, and pen-wielding robots may be gearing up to edit future editions of this book. Change is the only constant, so buckle up.

What's more, the rapid rise of social media and smartphones in every sphere of college life, along with the demise of paper and pen as the preferred mode of communication, have radically altered the way college feels and works on a day-to-day basis. So much is going on, and everyone is afraid of missing out on any of it. Here are some apps and (real) people, ready to light your way!

**MAKE YOUR FACEBOOK PASSWORD** difficult to type when drunk. Drunk Facebooking is horrendous and usually leads to stuff you don't want to deal with when you're hung over the next day.
—*J.V.*
*THE COLLEGE OF WILLIAM & MARY, GRADUATE*

**USE YOUR PRIVACY SETTINGS.**
—*MICHAEL*
*NORTHWESTERN UNIVERSITY, SOPHOMORE*

**HEADLINES**

■ Social media can be a great way to begin to meet people, but follow up soon with person-to-person encounters.

■ Don't post information about yourself that could be viewed negatively, even though you have some control over who will see your photos and details.

■ It's easy to misjudge people when all you have to go by are their profiles on social media.

Try to have a variety of pictures rather than one where you look exactly the same in 300 different poses.
—*Ron Y. Kagan*
*Macaulay Honors*
*College at CUNY*
*Hunter, Senior*

**On Twitter,** I always try to remember the point of a hashtag: it can either be ironic or useful. Nothing in between. For example, you can label your tweet with a hashtagged name of a movie you just saw, frat you just went to, or sports team you're following. But don't hashtag too much (#girl #cute #hair #party), and please, please, please don't hashtag long sentences. No one has the time or energy to read all of that.
—*Sophie Stone*
*Franklin and Marshall College, Junior*

• • • • • • • • •

**I was surprised to find myself using technology less** than I did at high school. While I still go on my laptop to look up homework assignments and study, one day I decided to start taking notes in my notebook only – which I never really did before. It's a bit weird switching to "older" methods of note-taking, but I like not having to look at a computer screen all day long. In fact, I feel like I learn better when I'm physically writing stuff down. It's important for people to find the learning and study methods that work best for them.
—*Summer*
*UCLA, Freshman*

**IF YOU'RE ALWAYS LOSING YOUR THINGS, GET THE TILES APP.**
This has literally been a lifesaver. The amount of
times I lose my phone when it's on silent because
I don't want it going off in class or misplace my
student ID is ridiculous. God forbid I misplace my
laptop, keys or wallet. Tiles are somewhat akin to
a patch or a key chain. You can stick them onto
important things like your phone and your keys, and
when you lose them, they serve as a GPS device.
—*ANONYMOUS*
    *NORTHWESTERN UNIVERSITY, GRADUATE*

**"** Putting your telephone number,
address, relationship status,
pics of yourself with cups in
your hand is way too much
information to put on Facebook.
Your friends know where they
can find you. **"**
—*DANIELLE*
    *DUKE UNIVERSITY, GRADUATE*

**SOMETIMES YOU MEET A PERSON,** talk with him online,
and become good friends; then you meet in
person and you wished you'd kept it online. The
awkwardness factor is pretty big when you meet
people through sites like Facebook. I don't usually
interact with people online unless they had some
other real-world connection to me already.
—*TERRY*
    *DUKE UNIVERSITY, SOPHOMORE*

# TOP FIVE THINGS NOT TO SHOWCASE IN YOUR PROFILE

1. Drugs

2. Alcohol, even if you're 21. (Some people go farther and avoid being caught on camera with any kind of cup in their hand because of the chance of that being misunderstood.)

3. Destroying or "improving" university property

4. Anything naked, sexual, or both

5. Yourself with half your face in light and the other half in darkness – it's not illegal or against school rules, but you'll just look like 10 million other people all doing the same thing.

**YES, YOUNG PEOPLE STILL DO USE FACEBOOK.** I'm really not sure why there's a big misconception that no one under the age of 30 goes on Facebook anymore. Sure, Instagram and Snapchat are extremely popular, but I would argue that Facebook and Facebook Messenger are used almost equally. In class, if someone's computer is out during a lecture, I guarantee you they're scrolling through Facebook. Plus, every college almost always has a class Facebook page. People use those pages to introduce themselves, find a roommate, share a funny meme, sell concert tickets or raise awareness about a club they're part of. The uses for Facebook in college are endless. If you don't have one already, I would definitely recommend making an account. It's not dead, it's very much alive and well and used by college students.

    —*ANONYMOUS*
    *FORDHAM UNIVERSITY, JUNIOR*

**SOMETHING A LOT OF STUDENTS DON'T KNOW** is that you can get Microsoft applications for free from the school. Also, don't overlook the tools available at the career center. Ours used a tool called Handshake and it was amazing! You create a profile, upload your résumé, maybe a cover letter, and you can apply to jobs. You can submit an application just by clicking a button. I applied to 20+ internships through it. The coolest thing was narrowing down the applications to ones interested in your major in places you want and are able to work in. I spent so many hours on this website just playing around. And yes, it got me my internship.

—*REBECCA*
*COLLEGE OF NEW JERSEY, SENIOR*

**HAVING ALL THIS TECH AT OUR FINGERTIPS** is terrible for both self-confidence and living in the moment. Every time I start an assignment, and I take a one-minute break to look at my phone, getting back into the assignment and orienting myself back into what I was working on takes time and mental energy. It would be so much easier to complete my work if I didn't have distractions, but with the phone – texting, social media, all that – there's just too much information coming at me at all times, and I can't resist!

As for self-confidence, it's terrible how people judge themselves based on other people's social media presence, based on physical looks and what other people are doing. It's really easy to feel like you're not living an interesting life if you see other people posting from another country or at fun event. That aspect of it, where like you feel like you're less than they are based on some fun experience that they share is really bad for people in general.

—*CHARLIE BAGIN*
*PRINCETON UNIVERSITY, SOPHOMORE*

**USE STORAGE WEBSITES FOR YOUR FILES!** There's nothing like the panic of your first midterms when your laptop dies, your friends are using all of theirs, and you can't get to any of the papers you may or may not have started. Not only that, but you have to find a way to figure out what the assignment was to begin with. Storage websites –Mediafire, Dropbox, etc. – help you access everything you've already done from any computer. Even the one you're using as a personal desktop/tissue holder in the public computer lab where everyone can see you panic. This way, you can relax. It's all there at your fingertips.

—*KATHARINE*
*BRYN MAWR COLLEGE, GRADUATE*

" Never pirate games or movies on the university's internet; they know what you're doing and will reprimand you. "

—*MAX*
*GEORGE WASHINGTON UNIVERSITY, GRADUATE*

**AVOID PUTTING UP ANY PICTURES** that you would not want your grandmother to see. Freshmen should do their best to untag pictures that portray possibly incriminating activities, such as underage drinking. You never know who can look at your profile.

> —KAMALI BENT
> CORNELL UNIVERSITY, GRADUATE

**IT'S GOOD TO AVOID HALF-NAKED PICTURES** and full body shots. Generally, a nice close-up of your beautiful face is best!

> —STEPHANIE LEIGH DOCKERY
> WILLIAMS COLLEGE, GRADUATE

**THE IDEA THAT A RELATIONSHIP IS "OFFICIAL"** when it's listed on Facebook is totally ridiculous. It's led to a fight with my last girlfriend and a confrontation with the friends of a girl before that. It's totally ridiculous but it's part of college life; it's unavoidable.

> —ANONYMOUS
> WASHINGTON AND LEE UNIVERSITY, JUNIOR

**STUPID DRINKING POSTS ON SOCIAL MEDIA MAY SCREW UP A LOT MORE THAN A FUTURE JOB.** I got rejected from my school's outdoors club because one of the leaders used my posts on Facebook to convince everyone else that I was a wild partier and wasn't right for the group. I also know sororities that hold it against potential pledges if they have pictures of themselves drinking on social media. It's totally hypocritical, since pretty much everyone in these groups drinks and parties. The outdoors club even runs through the library naked during finals. But I guess it's a public image thing.

> —ZOE
> JOHNS HOPKINS UNIVERSITY, GRADUATE

# NOTE TO OTHERS?
# LET THE ROBOT HELP!

You know that a handwritten note will probably go over better with your recipient – and might impress a potential employer or colleague – right? But, it's such a pain!!

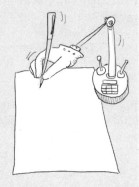

Well, you may want to check out a handy little website called Bond.co. For as little as $5 you can type out your note on the website, pick from a wide selection of stationery, select a handwriting style that mirrors your own, enter an address, and, boom! Your letter will be on its way, first-class stamp and all, courtesy of the robotic arm that will produce your "hand-written" note.

Two other companies offering similar robot-generated, "bespoke" services at about $3 each are Handwrytten and Felt. Felt lets you use your finger as a stylus to draft a note on your phone (iPhones only please) for mailing within one business day.

Handwrytten, meanwhile, boasts that its handwriting robots hold "real" pens when they write out notes "in the handwriting style of your choice." The company has lots of papers to choose from or it will use your stationery if you are particular, as long as it's not coated.

For a fee, Handwrytten will even create a custom font that it will reserve as your own personal machine-generated, "handwriting." The only thing Handwrytten won't do, according to its website, is hire humans to write its cards. "We get this a lot," the website apologizes. "We're sorry but we save that job for robots. They seem to like doing it."

Know, too, that none of the new services will seal your letter with a kiss. That you still have to do yourself.

*Liam Bodurtha is a college student who dreams of having his own army of robots someday.*

THE APP THAT LETS YOU ACCESS BLACKBOARD on your phone is pretty useful; your professor can post the readings as a PDF and you can access them on Blackboard. And you can email the other kids in your class if you need help with anything. It works pretty well.
—NINA
TEMPLE UNIVERSITY, JUNIOR

MY #1 PIECE OF ADVICE IS USE A CALENDAR TO ITS FULLEST. My personal favorite is an online calendar like iCal, which makes it super easy to change event times and days. Plan out the chunks of time during which you plan to study, eat, socialize, workout, etc. Use colors for different categories! Use your calendar every single day and make it a habit.
—MARISSA LICURSI
JOHNS HOPKINS UNIVERSITY, GRADUATE

IF YOU'RE TAKING A LANGUAGE, Duolingo is an amazing product that is free and will help with your grades in that class. And, setting Google Alarms for your calendar will also greatly help.
—MOLLY
COLLEGE OF SOUTHERN IDAHO, GRADUATE

WHENEVER SOMEONE TAGS ME in a picture or posts something on my wall, I ask myself, "Is it okay for my mom to see this?" I know a lot of people do not really use that rationale for Facebook. But it is definitely going to wake people up when they are trying to apply for jobs. I know for a fact that employers do look on Facebook to find out what their potential employees are up to.
—G.I.
GEORGE WASHINGTON UNIVERSITY, SENIOR

# GLUED TO YOUR DEVICE? TRY A BRIEF DETOX

**TAKE BREAKS FROM SOCIAL MEDIA.** On Instagram, you're always comparing yourself to someone else. I deleted the app for six weeks, and it was one of the best decisions I ever made. I was able to take a step back for a bit and actually live in the present with the people I was with rather than focusing on what everyone else was doing. You only see the parties and people hanging out with each other back home, and that gets hard. It's nice to keep up with your friends and it's an ego boost to get likes, but it gets to the point where you start thinking 'I can do this super cool thing but if I don't post about it and no one else knows about it, maybe it's not that cool.' When I start thinking, 'we should go here so we can take a picture!' I realize that maybe I should take a step back and just live in this moment instead of trying to capture it for the benefit of somebody else. Not having it for a while made me realize how much it affects me when I do have it.
　　—RHETTA
　　　UNIVERSITY OF NOTRE DAME, SOPHOMORE

• • • • • • • •

**STAY AWAY FROM YOUR PHONE AND COMPUTER DURING CLASS** if it's not required for class. Studies show that students who take notes on laptops score a whole letter-grade lower on average than students who take paper notes. There are way too many distractions from social media for phones or computers to be worth using in the classroom. I had a problem with using my phone during class, especially in large lecture halls where I thought no one would notice. Forcing myself to leave my phone in my pocket or my bag has shown a visible improvement in my subject knowledge and grades.
　　—SETH WILCOX
　　　PENN STATE UNIVERSITY, SOPHOMORE

• • • • • • • •

**DON'T ADD YOUR PROFESSORS OR ADVISORS TO YOUR SOCIAL MEDIA.** Clean up your social media or make yourself hard to find. Be wise with your choices: if you aren't old enough to buy liquor, you aren't old enough to take pictures with it, either. Develop a professional web presence!
　　—SAKIYA GALLON
　　　UNIVERSITY OF THE SCIENCES IN PHILADELPHIA, GRADUATE

**SOCIAL MEDIA CAN BE DESTRUCTIVE - FIND WAYS TO UNPLUG.** A lot of people who come here start to have issues like eating disorders or body dysmorphia. That type of thing is often due to seeing pictures of perfect people on the Internet. It's just too much comparison. You have to find ways to strip that away on occasion and get out of the college town or community and remind yourself that there's a world there beyond it. Taking a break and re-centering is important.
—*COLLEEN*
*UNIVERSITY OF VIRGINIA, JUNIOR*

. . . . . . . . .

**LIVE IN THE MOMENT, DON'T PREOCCUPY YOURSELF WITH SOMETHING THAT'S NOT REAL.** For too many of my classmates, it's all about the image. At parties and stuff, people will have their phones out the whole time, taking pictures and videos, editing them and posting them. It's unnecessary. They'll be standing in the middle of a dance floor surrounded by people just intently staring at their phone. They're so preoccupied by their self-image and they want to be in two places at once.

If someone took away your phone for a week, ask yourself: how would that feel? How would it affect you? It shouldn't be a big deal, you should able to go a week without social media, no problem. I've done it and it's really refreshing. You don't realize how much time you're wasting on it until it goes away. Just focus on the real people around you. Capturing those moments is great so you can remember them but that's all it should be used for. You're not gonna want to look back and realize you spent your time in college looking at a screen.
—*ANONYMOUS*
*UNIVERSITY OF ARIZONA, FRESHMAN*

. . . . . . . . .

**DON'T BE ATTACHED TO SOCIAL MEDIA.** It makes everyone look as though their transition into college life is smooth and fun, when in reality everyone struggles in their own way to adapt. Take what you see with a grain of salt. And, FaceTime is great for keeping in touch with people you are not physically near anymore.
—*CONOR MCGEEHAN*
*NORTHWESTERN UNIVERSITY, SENIOR*

**GET USED TO GOOGLE SUITE:** use Google Docs, Google Forms… you'll be able to access it on multiple computers, and you'll be good to go anywhere you are. So, in case your computer ever breaks down, you don't have to worry about losing all your work.

—*NAF*
*NEW YORK UNIVERSITY, GRADUATE*

• • • • • • • •

**THE ONLY APP I USED** other than GoogleDocs, was MyFitnessPal. At one point I came home and my mom had just bought a scale and I stepped on it and it was like, "You are 260 pounds" and I started crying. I was like, "I should lose some weight," so I got on MyFitnessPal and it really helped me manage. It helped me see what I was actually eating at the cafeteria instead of just wolfing down whatever I liked to eat. It made me more aware.

Other than that, I was a pen-and-paper kind of person and still am. I firmly believe that if you're looking at your agenda book and you're writing things down, you'll remember them a little better than when you just put a reminder on Google so you don't get, "10 minutes until exam 3. Oh shit, I forgot about that!"

—*PAISLEY*
*MEREDITH COLLEGE, GRADUATE*

# POWERING UP

Inevitably you're going to misplace a power charger – in class, at home, or at the coffee shop – which will quickly render your nice new laptop completely useless. Keep a spare one at your residence, plugged in.

**GOOGLE DOCS REALLY HELPS IF YOU ARE IN A GROUP PROJECT.** You don't necessarily need to meet up and type it up simultaneously in different dorms and turn it in.

—*J.G.M.*
GUILFORD COLLEGE, GRADUATE

**I FOUND THIS APP ON THE APP STORE CALLED MYHOMEWORK** the second semester of my freshman year, and it changed my life. It's basically an agenda and it allows you to plug in your schedule, due dates, exact times, and it gives you alerts when things are due. There was one week during March Madness – our team went all the way to the Final Four – where school was chaotic, and everyone was blowing off their assignments 'cause we were all so excited. The app definitely allowed me to be somewhat organized during that time and know what was due right away and what I could put off."

—*ANONYMOUS*
LOYOLA UNIVERSITY IN CHICAGO, SOPHOMORE

**BE AWARE OF YOUR PHONE AND COMPUTER USAGE.** I was shocked when I opened up the feature that tracks the daily hours spent on my iPhone. On average, I was spending 7½ hours on it every day. Seven hours! I sleep for less than that at night! And when I thought about how often I use my computer on top of that, I couldn't even imagine how much time I was wasting on technology. I needed to do something about this, so I stopped bringing my phone everywhere. I challenged myself to reduce my usage to 4½ hours a day or less. It was difficult at first, and the urge to check every notification was real. But reducing unnecessary screen time helped me be more productive and actually find time to do the things I like to do – time I used to complain "I didn't have."

—*ANONYMOUS*
FORDHAM UNIVERSITY, JUNIOR

# FACEBOOK: PRO AND CON

**THE BEST PART OF FACEBOOK** is how it allows you to stay in touch with friends from other schools. They can see what you're doing and vice versa. The one bad thing about Facebook is that you become more accountable for the one-night stand from the night before. You're going to hear about it the next day.
    —*ILAN GLUCK*
      *UNIVERSITY OF MARYLAND, JUNIOR*

**I UNDERSTAND THE APPEAL OF FLIPPING THROUGH GLAMOUR SHOTS** of friends and acquaintances, creeping on crushes and ex-boyfriends, and catching up on the latest from That Girl with the Constant Pregnancy Updates from high school. All I can say is that when you really stop to think about it, every minute spent on Facebook is a minute wasted. It is so easy to get sucked into the mindless pleasure of other people's (carefully edited) lives, but you only get so much time to spend in college, and trust me, you'll wish you could get it all back when it's over. Using that time to compare yourself to others – consciously or not, that's really what you're doing – is something you'll regret; spending time living in the real world is not.
    —*CAITLIN*
      *GEORGETOWN UNIVERSITY, GRADUATE*

**INSTAGRAM IS MY FAVORITE** social site because it acknowledges its pretentiousness and tackiness and then embraces it. Everyone knows that an Insta'd photo makes your eyes gleam, your skin glow, and your imperfections fade away; basically, you could not be more fake. But who cares? Just use this sparingly, and don't link it to your Facebook or Twitter. Your friends/followers didn't sign up to follow your Insta... they don't want to see every sunset, selfie, or cat pic that you post.
    —*SOPHIE STONE*
      *FRANKLIN AND MARSHALL COLLEGE, JUNIOR*

IN COLLEGE, THERE IS ALWAYS ANOTHER PARTY, another club meeting, another rehearsal. Facebook stalking can become a toxic habit which feeds jealousy and distracts you from your own needs and schedule. Seize the day and enjoy your life, but avoid feeling left out or like you're falling behind. The grass is always greener, so minimize Facebook stalking.
— *SARAH*
  *VANDERBILT UNIVERSITY, GRADUATE*

COLLEGE LENDS ITSELF VERY EASILY TO "PICTURES WITH BEER" and "beer bongs" and things like that. Just be careful. It's time to start thinking about privacy settings if you haven't already! I'm sure your mom has already told you this, but the summer internship or campus job you want to get will not want you if there are pictures of you getting super-drunk and high and whatnot every weekend.
— *ELIZABETH*
  *UNIVERSITY OF ILLINOIS AT URBANA-CHAMPAIGN, GRADUATE*

FACEBOOK AND THE ABILITY TO STREAM TV ON MY LAPTOP were the two biggest procrastination tools I had in college. They were the two things that most kept me from getting work done when I actually sat down to do it. I think I watched more TV freshman year than I ever had before; it was the first time I had a laptop so it was the first time I could watch episode, after episode, after episode... Be careful how much time you spend doing that!
— *NINA STOLLER-LINDSEY*
  *HARVARD COLLEGE, GRADUATE*

A LOT OF MY COLLEGE FRIENDS DEACTIVATED their social networks during midterms and finals week because it was too distracting. For myself, I'll work on a paper, take a quiz, or read, and all the while I'll go back and forth between Facebook and Twitter. Download the app, "Self Control." It helps you block certain websites, in order to help you avoid getting distracted when doing schoolwork.
— *CHARLINDA HAUDLEY*
  *UNIVERSITY OF ARIZONA, SENIOR*

**KHAN ACADEMY HELPED ME A LOT WITH MATH.** It's a great website. It helps teach you. It prompts questions. I'm using it right now to prep for calculus II.
—*CINDI CALVANESE*
*BLOOMFIELD COLLEGE, GRADUATE*

• • • • • • • •

**LESS IS MORE.** I still use Microsoft Word to take notes and use folders to organize them. No apps needed. I do use Google Drive to back up everything, Wolfram Alpha for math and Stack Exchange for computer science class.
—*LI*
*UNIVERSITY OF TORONTO, GRADUATE*

• • • • • • • •

**LEARNING HOW TO DO LABELS AND SORTING** in your inbox is one of the most important things because everything is so email-centric. I try to keep my inbox pretty empty so that I don't miss things. I filter out email lists for any clubs or organizations right into a folder and then I can read it when I have time. Like if I'm interested in the free food list, I can read that when I want, but then my inbox is just people emailing me directly, personally, like friends and professors.
—*CATIE*
*HARVARD COLLEGE, SENIOR*

• • • • • • • •

**YOU'D BE SURPRISED HOW MANY PEOPLE IN THE LIBRARY LOOK LIKE THEY'RE STUDYING** when in reality they're surfing the web or browsing social media. The best thing you can do to succeed in classes is to minimize your distractions. Let your time in the library be the time you focus, rather than goofing off with your friends. You'll feel accomplished and enjoy your weekend partying so much more because you've earned it!
—*P.B.*
*DARTMOUTH COLLEGE, GRADUATE*

**E**VERY SEMESTER, IT'S KIND OF HARD TO GET INTO THE ROUTINE OF YOUR CLASSES, so I have this app called Oohlala, and you literally put in your classes, what day they are, their times, and what buildings they're in. The first couple weeks of classes, I always check that, to make sure I'm in the right spot.
> —*JACOB SPIER*
> *UNIVERSITY OF SOUTH DAKOTA, JUNIOR*

**C**ONSIDER TAKING A SOCIAL MEDIA BREAK. I deleted my social media, Instagram and Snapchat accounts, freshman year during first semester. On social media, you see all of your friends posting pictures with their new roomies and best friends right away. The truth is, a lot of them aren't still friends with those people by second semester. Deleting social media really helped me, because I was more present and not comparing myself to my high school friends and other people I know.
> —*BRIANNA*
> *GEORGE WASHINGTON UNIVERSITY, JUNIOR*

# RICE TO THE RESCUE

Best remedy for a liquid spill on your computer? A bag of uncooked rice. Not instant rice; inexpensive, uncooked plain white rice. Should a spill occur, immediately cut power to the computer and remove the battery. If the battery can't be removed, shut the computer down. Put the device in a sealed container (typically a trash bag) with that uncooked bag of rice and wait 48 hours before trying to turn it on. The device may be okay after that. (Suggestion: you probably want to throw away the rice rather than adding it to your next meal.)

# STAYING ON TRACK: THERE'S AN APP FOR THAT

With all the activities available on campus, you may find it challenging to balance your personal and academic life while in college. To help manage your workload, consider going beyond standard "to-do lists," Post-Its, or reminder alerts on your phone. Here are a few apps that can help you keep important tasks in focus:

- **Pocket Schedule** – You can enter your course schedules and requirements into this application, and you can color-code courses, which helps when multiple assignments are due within a couple of days of each other. You have the option to separate assignment descriptions and titles from other tasks.

- **Evernote** – If you remember images more readily than lists, this taskmaster enables you to add images to your notes. Images may be saved on your phone or tablet, or taken while using the application. You also can record voice messages.

- **Remember the Milk (RTM)** – This app will send you text or instant message reminders. It's also accessible from a desktop computer and can sync with other calendars and social media feeds.

- **Awesome Note** – Consider the value of looking at a month's worth of activities on a calendar. You can color code activity types, and place activities into "folders." The travel folder, which logs daily activities for travelers, may appeal if you study abroad.

- **ClassTrack** – This app helps you keep track of pending assignments and upcoming exams, as well as completed credits towards graduation, and your GPA. You also can store grades on individual assignments.

*Tatum Thomas, Ph.D.*
*Senior Associate Dean of Student Affairs*
*Columbia University*
*School of Professional Studies*

**USE TECHNOLOGY, BUT DON'T FORGET TO UNPLUG.** My freshman year, I would think, "I'm going to go to the library," but I'd be listening to my music and could hear my notifications going off in the background, so every 15 minutes or so I'd be checking my notifications or looking at Snapchat or something, and suddenly I wasn't getting anything done in a three-hour study session.

Now, I have reminders on my phone of what time I need to leave for class so I'm not late, and I have reminders set to give me a three-hour warning that assignments are due, so I don't forget to get them done. I also have study times set aside, and my phone goes into nighttime mode during that time, and even if someone is texting or calling me, I won't get it until I'm done.
—*MORGAN KREIN*
*DAKOTA STATE UNIVERSITY, JUNIOR*

•  •  •  •  •  •  •  •

**I VIDEO CHAT WITH SOMEONE ALMOST EVERY DAY** – either one of my friends, family, or my long distance boyfriend. It makes the distance between you and your loved ones seem much shorter. Which, in turn, can almost make me homesick. Whenever I talk to my friends and family, it's always hard to say goodbye, to go back to my life in a new place. But I just have to remember I'll see them soon. I just have to remember all the great things I have with me in college and that semesters aren't very long. (Also, when you go home, you'll very quickly realize you miss college and want to go back.)
—*EVA DINES*
*UNIVERSITY OF MIAMI, JUNIOR*

*"Don't knock it, sweetie. It pays $33 an hour!"*

# Money Matters: Work, Finance & Beyond

T he cost of a college degree is soaring. But there are ways to stay afloat. You may be living comfortably on mom and dad's credit card or scraping by on loans, Ramen noodles, and double-shifts. But whatever your circumstances, having a cushion never hurts.

In this chapter, you'll see how other students keep their costs down and manage to make money on the side. They'll tell you which jobs are best, how to save money on your books, where to find the best freebies and student discounts, and how to make sure you get all the financial aid you are entitled to from your school. Can you really afford not to keep reading?

**TOSS EVERY CREDIT CARD OFFER.** Don't entertain the thought of new shoes, or that surround sound system. You don't need it right now; that's what Christmas and birthdays are for!
—AMANDA
UNIVERSITY OF COLORADO AT COLORADO SPRINGS, SOPHOMORE

**USE MEAL POINTS! YOU ALREADY PAID FOR THEM, AND SO THERE IS NO USE SAVING THEM.**
—HANNAH
UNIVERSITY OF CALIFORNIA AT BERKELEY, FRESHMAN

- Beware of credit card offers. But if you decide to get one, make sure you pay off the balance each month.

- A part-time job on or near campus is a good way to earn spending money and meet new people.

- There are easy budgeting programs for your computer – or just keep track of your expenses on paper. Whatever works best for you.

- Use your meal plan to its fullest potential – otherwise, it's wasted money.

My biggest worry when I was a freshman was that I would be broke all of the time... and I was.

—CECILIE
PARSONS SCHOOL OF DESIGN, JUNIOR

**LOOK INTO WORK-STUDY JOBS.** A lot of the time you can do homework for most of your shift, so it's a great way to make money without sacrificing study time. It's also a good opportunity to meet new people and add to your résumé. I ended up being a manager at an art studio for my campus job – and while the word "manager" looks great to employers, I basically did my homework while babysitting 20-year-olds using Sharpies.
—L.G.
BUCKNELL UNIVERSITY, GRADUATE

• • • • • • • • •

**IT'S BETTER NOT TO WORK** your freshman year, or at least the first quarter, because you're still adjusting. I was overwhelmed by the homework. And if you work your first year, you don't get to meet as many people. But later, working helps to keep you focused. You gain skills and it helps you learn to budget your time. It's good to work on campus because they're flexible, and they'll give you time off during finals.
—ABBY HERNANDEZ
UNIVERSITY OF CALIFORNIA AT SANTA BARBARA, JUNIOR

**GET A JOB ON-CAMPUS THAT RELATES TO YOUR INTERESTS.**
I ref intramural sports and I've made most of my
friends from work. It's been awesome, one of my
favorite things about college. All kinds of people
play intramurals and it's been great to meet a wide
variety of students.
—*PAT*
*GONZAGA UNIVERSITY, SOPHOMORE*

**IF YOU NEED TO WORK, GET AN ON-CAMPUS JOB.** On-
campus employers understand your situation
better and are used to working around student
schedules. Take advantage of the job boards
around school, and the job fairs, too. I went to a
job fair and it was the best thing I ever did. It was
so easy to get hired; I did my interview right there
and got a job at the student union.
—*JESSICA DOSHNA*
*UCLA, GRADUATE*

**I WORK AS A WAITRESS ON CAMPUS.** I work 11:30 A.M.
– 2:30 P.M. so it fits well into my work/study plan.
My nights are open, I'm paid in cash, and I get
tips. I keep a car at school, which is an expense,
so I enjoy working; it's empowering. My parents
are generous, but again, I enjoy having my own
income and have been able to save a lot, which is
important to me as I plan for my future.
—*VANESSA VALENZUELA*
*SONOMA STATE UNIVERSITY, SOPHOMORE*

**DON'T GET A JOB YOUR FRESHMAN YEAR.** You don't know
how involved in organizations you'll be or how
much time you'll have to dedicate to school. But
definitely work during Christmas and summer
vacations and save the money you earn.
—*SHEILA CRAWFORD*
*NORTH CAROLINA STATE UNIVERSITY, SOPHOMORE*

## HOW THEY PAID

Families with
someone in
college spend
an average of
$26,458 a year
on those ex-
penses, fund-
ed roughly as
follows:

- Scholarships
  or grants
  (28%)
- Student
  contributes
  (13%)
- Parents pay
  (34%)
- Parents bor-
  row (10%)
- Student
  loans (14%)
- Extended
  family or
  friends (2%)

**GET A JOB.** Even if your parents are supporting you. All my jobs during college, from barista to research intern, helped develop my people skills, build my résumé, introduce me to great contacts, and pad my wallet. Even though it's not a ton of money, a part-time job in college goes a long way in reducing stress. It's also important to remember to strike a balance between following your personal budget and feeling like you can treat yourself occasionally. Many of your friends at college will have more financial flexibility than you; don't feel pressure to keep up if they're spending money on dinners, shows, and trips that you don't feel financially comfortable partaking in.
—*CAITLIN*
    *GEORGETOWN UNIVERSITY, GRADUATE*

**EVERY TIME YOU GO OUT,** when all your friends are having that last drink, cut yourself off; don't have that last drink. Then, go home and put the money you saved in a piggy bank. You'll be surprised how quickly it adds up. And you can go out and buy a new outfit.
—*S.G.*
    *COLUMBIA UNIVERSITY, SENIOR*

# BUYING BOOKS

**YOU CAN BUY BOOKS ONLINE** but then you have to wait two days for the shipment. I bought mine like that, but then realized how long it would take them to get here, so I had to cancel the order. The problem with buying used books is that sometimes there will be pages missing. And don't get used books if there's a newer edition. I know people who did this; the page numbers don't match up and the problems don't match up. They're constantly coming to my dorm to ask me what's going on.
—*MORGAN*
    *COLUMBIA UNIVERSITY, FRESHMAN*

# SOME MONEY-MAKING (AND MONEY-SAVING) TIPS

1. **Start a free internship:** You won't make any money right away ... but if you do a good job and the department or company you intern for finds the resources, they may offer to pay you later.

2. **Sell stuff you don't need:** eBay is a great place to start. Classified ad websites like Craigslist.com can also be useful.

3. **Go to campus events:** A lot of them offer free food for attendees. You can probably find a few free meals every week!

4. **Search for more scholarships and apply, apply, apply:** A lot of scholarships are given out online with only a handful of candidates, so when you apply, you have pretty good odds.

5. **Take odd jobs:** Mow the lawn, babysit, housesit, etc. Maybe you're really good at fixing things (computers, anything around the house, etc.).

6. **Minimize how often you eat out or buy fancy coffee drinks:** At $5 each, fancy coffee drinks can drain any wallet. Fast-food and sit-down restaurants are great for socializing and going out. But if you eat out just to save time cooking, know this: You can probably feed yourself, at home, for $2 to $3 per meal.

*Scott C. Silverman*

**If I were writing a book** about the things they don't tell you when you enter college, the first chapter would cover the hidden costs of living away from home – travel and school supplies, for example. However, the most shocking expense is food: the midnight pizzas, the birthday dinners, the celebration dinners, and the random exoduses from campus when you just can't take it anymore, add up in a hurry.

—*Adam*
*Elon University, Sophomore*

" Get a desk job. If there was nothing happening, I would work on school work. "

—*Paisley*
*Meredith College, Graduate*

**There is a lot of hidden grant and scholarship money** waiting to be used by deserving and struggling students! I almost transferred from my school due to adjustment and financial issues, but after speaking with the dean of my college, I was offered additional grant money and ultimately decided to stay. So it pays to seek out your resources!

—*Sakiya Gallon*
*University of the Sciences in Philadelphia, Graduate*

**There are tons of cheap opportunities** for students, you just have to search for them. For instance, students should take advantage of that free condom service they have around the dorms.

—*Ben Miller*
*University of North Carolina at Chapel Hill, Senior*

# GET THE FLOOD INSURANCE!

**IN JANUARY OF MY FRESHMAN YEAR,** I was woken up one cold morning at three o'clock by the fire alarm going off in the hall of my dorm. I ran outside as fast as I could in my pajama shorts and T-shirt. They turned off the fire alarm, but something in the sprinkler system had malfunctioned, setting off the sprinkler in our hall, so we had a good five inches of disgusting, rusty water on the floors of our rooms. I had stored all of my schoolbooks under my bed, and they were now completely submerged in water, along with a good deal of dirty clothes strewn about, my printer, and all the electronics. The school informed me that because I hadn't bought insurance through them, they wouldn't cover any of the damage.

So, keep your room neat, because you never know when you'll have gallons of rusty water flooding your room. And if the school offers insurance for a reasonable price, it's worth getting.
— *MOLLY DONAHUE*
  *SYRACUSE UNIVERSITY, SOPHOMORE*

**INTERNSHIPS ARE GREAT FOR YOUR DEVELOPMENT BUT** they can require you to go out of your shell a little bit. I almost didn't get my degree because I didn't find internships fast enough. I was too scared to send emails out to people I had never met, and wasn't sure where to start.

You need to get over that fear. Get comfortable emailing strangers. If you need work or an internship, email whomever you can think of to ask about it. Be polite. No one will be offended that you asked, and no matter how many no's you get, all you need is one person who knows someone, who knows someone who has what you need.
— *R.S.*
  *GUILFORD COLLEGE, GRADUATE*

# FEDERAL WORK-STUDY PROGRAMS

Federal Work-Study (FWS) is a campus need-based program that is administered by the Financial Aid Office at participating colleges. The amount of work-study funds you are awarded depends on financial need, the amount of other aid you receive, and/or the availability of funds at your college. FWS provides each participating school a specific amount of funds that can be administered each year from July 1 through June 30. Therefore, it is essential to apply for federal student aid early, by completing your Free Application for Federal Student Aid (FAFSA) form. **It is best to complete your FAFSA as early as January 1st of each academic year.**

Upon securing FWS, you will be paid by the hour; the rate of pay will equal at least the current federal minimum wage. Students are also required to carry a minimum course load, usually 12 credits or 36 units. FWS jobs are usually located on campus in various student support and services offices and departments. However, in some instances you may be assigned to work for a nonprofit organization or a public agency affiliated with your college. There is usually an office on campus that maintains a current list of FWS positions; check with the Financial Aid or Career Services Offices on your campus.

Lastly, there is an added perk for FWS positions. While the money you earn is considered taxable income, your earnings will not be used in determining your financial need when filing the FAFSA form the following year.

*Pamela M. Golubski, Ph.D., has many years of experience in student academic and career advising, mentoring, and teaching in higher education.*

**LOOK FOR STUDENT ADVANTAGE CARDS.** Craigslist is great for furniture. Buy in bulk at large grocery stores to get the best value.
—*MANNY*
*GEORGE WASHINGTON UNIVERSITY, SENIOR*

. . . . . . . .

**WHEN I FIRST GOT TO CAMPUS, I WAS REALLY SELF-CONSCIOUS ABOUT MY SPENDING ABILITIES.** Unlike a lot of my peers, who came from super-wealthy families and whose parents paid for all of their experiences, I was responsible for everything from rent and my meal plan to other discretionary expenses. While it was really tempting to go out for dinner with my new friends every night or to get some clutch concert tickets at the last minute, I constantly had to remind myself that I can't be spending money left and right. I definitely felt jealous of my peers at first because I felt like I was missing out, but eventually I became more savvy with my spending and started to hustle outside of class to earn money for discretionary expenses.

Also, by researching all of my spending habits and tracking them in apps like Mint, I'm able to cut expenses where I can and have money left over for fun things. I always check my local grocery stores for the best deals before buying and take advantage of free memberships when I can. I tend not to eat out, which is not only healthier for you (no Freshman 15 for me), but it's also a lot cheaper. I also only order water, unless it's a special occasion. When I want to splurge on things like clothes or excursions, I always check Groupon to see if there are any cool deals. I've done everything from boat rentals, to kayaking, to Swedish massages to wine and paint nights through Groupon, and I've never spent more than $20 dollars on one thing.
—*ANONYMOUS*
*NORTHWESTERN UNIVERSITY, GRADUATE*

# THINGS YOU COULD BUY WITH THE MONEY YOU'LL SPEND ON TEXTBOOKS...

- A small waterpark
- A movie ticket for every child in America
- A struggling European country out of debt
- Renaming your college after you
- A 9th Harry Potter book
- Love, probably

# ...AND THINGS YOU COULD BUY WITH THE MONEY YOU'LL MAKE FROM YOUR SCHOOL'S USED TEXTBOOK BUYBACK PROGRAM:

- Actual peanuts
- Travel-size shampoo
- Any one item from a dollar store
- A free trial of a website
- A blade of grass
- 1/1000 of a textbook

*Val Bodurtha is a Chicago-based writer and comedian.*

**I COMPETED IN THE MS. VIRGINIA PAGEANT** at the end of my freshman year. Those competitions provided a good amount of scholarships. Unfortunately, the way the scholarships were processed, I had some of my other financial aid taken away because I was considered less in need once I won. So, it ultimately evened out and I ended up paying the exact same amount as if I had not gotten those scholarships at all. Which was really frustrating because you work hard for that sort of thing.
—*SHELBY SMITH*
*GUILFORD COLLEGE, GRADUATE*

• • • • • • • •

**REDUCE YOUR STUDENT LOAN DEBT WHILE YOU'RE STILL IN SCHOOL.** I didn't like the party scene, so while my friends were going to parties and to the bars, I either went home and farmed or I was focusing on building my direct-sales business with Thirty-One Gifts or working at a local daycare.

I knew my degree would make me money in two years, but Thirty-One was making me money right now. I wasn't going to be one that let the college force me to do a four-and-a-half- or five-year-or-longer degree, because I didn't have the money to pay for that. Because of Thirty-One, I paid the interest on my federal loans as I was going to school, and I only ended up financing about one-fifth of the cost of my education.
—*MCKAYLA MOE*
*SOUTH DAKOTA STATE UNIVERSITY, GRADUATE*

• • • • • • • •

**WORK THE NIGHT SHIFT.** Instead of partying, I was a hotel receptionist. That was the best job I could have had, because I did all of my homework there. I didn't go to the library, because I worked the night shift, and no one came in but a few stragglers.
—*ANONYMOUS*
*UNIVERSITY OF SOUTH DAKOTA, GRADUATE*

It's a good experience to have a job.
—*M.B.*
*SAN JOSE STATE UNIVERSITY, GRADUATE*

# HOW YOUR STUDENT ID CAN SAVE YOU MONEY EVERYWHERE

College is a notoriously trying time financially. Luckily, vendors across America are sympathetic to this fact, and despite your potentially pathetical buying power, they still want your business. The best advice? Always, always ask, because student discounts are everywhere!

Everyone is familiar with student ticket prices at the movies, but that's just the tip of the iceberg. Significant discounts are widely available on almost anything: fast food, clothing, travel, insurance, technology, cell phone plans and nearly any kind of membership or ticket.

To list all of them would be a book in and of itself, and these things are always changing. But just to give you some idea of the possibilities, here are a few that stuck out at press time:

**Spotify + Hulu + Showtime**
Get all three of these services for one combined price: $4.99 per month – one-fifth what the rest of us pay.

**Amazon Prime**
Try it free for 6 months. Then pay just $6.49 a month after that.

**Krispy Kreme**
These are better than the dining hall donuts, and ultra-affordable (financially if not calorically) with a 20% student discount.

**McDonalds**
As if it wasn't already cheap enough. Show your ID and you may get a free cheeseburger, hamburger, or McFlurry with any large value meal purchase.

### Microsoft
Get Word, PowerPoint, Excel, OneNote, and Microsoft Teams for free. Yes, for free.

### New York Times
Get unlimited online access to articles anytime, anywhere with the NYT app as well as access to the paper's full archives dating back to 1851 for just $1 a week. If that's too steep, you may be in luck, as many schools cover this cost for their students. Google "New York Times Edupass" and put in your school email address to find out. Also, the paper allows home subscribers to award free gift subscriptions to people in their lives. So, ask your folks if they have a spare gift subscription they can send your way. If you crave the crinkle of paper in your hands, check dining halls and student centers! Many stock free copies of newspapers for students.

### Squarespace
Have a passion? Promote it with a website. Use Squarespace's super easy software and enjoy 50% off your first year.

### Urban Outfitters, Levi's, H&M, Banana Republic, Forever 21
Be stylish for less. Enjoy a 10-20% discount from these and so many other clothing retailers.

### Student Advantage Card
This card costs $22.50 a year and comes with a plethora of perks. Use the one free $20 Lyft ride, and you've nearly recouped your initial investment already. You'll get discounts on hotels, restaurants, rental cars, magazines, and so much more.

*Anthony Wallace is a Phoenix-based writer and thinker.*

# POSERS WANTED: THE BEST-PAYING CAMPUS JOB EVER?

While waiting tables and babysitting are tried-and-true money-making staples, there are plenty of other side hustles to explore. Here's one you may have not considered...

Shed your clothes and free your inhibitions as a figure-drawing art model. Check your student newspaper or ads. Fees run the gamut, but at many schools, you could make up to $25 per hour just for posing naked in front of budding artists. (Princeton was recently offering $33 an hour. "Diversity is appreciated," its ad noted, "and models of color and varying body type" were encouraged to apply.) Here, Susan Hanway, a former art model at Duke, looks back fondly on her experience:

"There was no interview. I just showed up and the art teacher gave me some instructions about being natural and not posing stiffly, which I found hard to do as I was self-conscious.

At first, of course, I felt shy about taking my clothes off in front of strangers! I remember sitting very still while they drew sketches of me and entertaining myself with a question about how doing this job was different from prostitution. (Of course, it's very different, but it was fun to argue internally.) After a few sessions it became second nature to sit still nude, and I didn't even mind when I had to – ahem – spread my legs slightly. Honestly, the best part was the pay, as I didn't interact with the class or the teacher and didn't even get to see many drawings. They took them home after class and by the time I was dressed, they were gone!

After about 4 months I got a full-time job with the Dance Festival and stopped modeling. I didn't miss it, as I didn't like sitting still (still don't!) and didn't like being cold. Also, it wasn't a job that used any skills I was proud of or wanted to develop. So, it was purely a relatively easy way to make money until I could get a job I liked. Unlike waitressing, it wasn't enough money to pay the rent, but it was more money per hour than waitressing, and an adventure!"

*Louise Connelly is a writer based in New York City*

I SPENT WAY TOO MUCH MONEY my freshman year on ridiculous things. Did I need the giant flag which eventually became home to three-week-old Easy Mac? No. Did I need the knockoff GameCube controllers that eventually broke? No. Just don't spend money that you don't have.
—*BARRY LANGER*
   *OGLETHORPE UNIVERSITY, JUNIOR*

" When you're broke, you can still go hiking, sit on the main quad with your friends, play Frisbee, and catch a student production, whether it be a play, a dance show or an *a cappella* show. "
—*P.B.*
   *DARTMOUTH COLLEGE, GRADUATE*

YOU NEED TO FIND A JOB that allows you to work around your schedule. Living at the shore, I was able to work during the summer and save up some cash. Don't skimp on your classes, they are just as important as your job.
—*MICHAEL*
   *RUTGERS UNIVERSITY, JUNIOR*

AVOID CREDIT CARDS unless they belong to your parents. I spent over $1,000 my first semester, over half of it on booze.
—*J.V.*
   *THE COLLEGE OF WILLIAM & MARY, GRADUATE*

# USING THE CAREER CENTER

(EVEN THOUGH YOU JUST STARTED COLLEGE!)

You might think that the career center is only a place to visit when you're a senior looking for a full-time job. Here are some ways career services can help you now:

1. Collaborate with you to develop your résumé. They likely have résumé templates on their website, as well as helpful tips on making your résumé stand out. Once you've created a résumé, visit your career center to get it reviewed. (If that's too intimidating, send it to your folks, or find an English major who has some extra time.) Either way, make sure that your résumé is free of errors so that you make the best first impression on an employer.

2. Resources to help you find a work-study position or a part-time job on campus. Many career centers offer an online job posting service, where employers can post jobs and internships. Be sure to sign up for this important resource, and ask career services for tips on applying.

3. Self-assessment tools to help you discover possible career paths. Most institutions offer career tools such as the Myers-Briggs Type Indicator or CliftonStrengths to assist with discovering what appeals to you and how you can best use your skills and talents in your life, not just your career.

In addition to these resources, it's worth mentioning that freshman year is a process of self-exploration and assessment: discovering your interests and strengths. Career exploration means trying anything – a new club, an internship, or volunteering – to gain experience and find out what suits you. And if you end up hating what you signed up for – change it, but first ask yourself what was so bad about it. Was it the tasks, duties, people, environment, or something else? And if it's awesome, why did you love it so much? It's not so much what you decide to sign up for; it's what you learn from the experience that will help you get to the next step.

*Lee Desser*
*Career Coach, University of California San Diego*

**DON'T SIGN UP FOR CREDIT CARDS** just for the possibility of discounted prices. I faced a near disaster with a credit card company, because I signed up for a card that would give me points and discounts at various stores. Little did I know that there was a minimum fee required to keep the card, and it would accrue fees every month. I didn't read the fine print. I eventually canceled the card.
　　　—*MICHELLE*
　　　　*EMORY UNIVERSITY, SENIOR*

**GETTING A JOB IN A HOTEL** is a great idea, especially if you go to school in a city with a good-sized tourism industry. Jobs at larger hotel chains like Marriott or Hyatt offer decent pay and don't require a lot of hours per week. If you work in a bar, restaurant, or banquet within the hotel you get hourly pay plus a share of the tips – and things are quite expensive inside hotels, which means higher gratuities. It's more versatile than you think, too. You might start off as a server, but if you're a business major, you can try to transfer to the business side, or if you're a marketing major, you can try to move to that department. There's a lot of room for growth and they like to hire from within. It's an untapped resource.
　　　—*COREY*
　　　　*SAN DIEGO STATE UNIVERSITY, JUNIOR*

**MAKE SURE YOU KEEP YOUR FINANCES** in order in terms of how much you're spending. I usually give myself a monthly allotment of money I can spend on miscellaneous items such as going out to eat, going to the movies, ordering in, and any other random expenses. If you can successfully map out a good spending plan, you will find it much easier to keep track of money.
　　　—*ANDREW OSTROWSKY*
　　　　*PENNSYLVANIA STATE UNIVERSITY, JUNIOR*

# WORK-SCHOOL BALANCE

If you get a part-time job during school, it requires effective time management. Here are a few tips to help you manage your hectic schedule:

- Determine a strict limit on the number of hours you can work each week, based on the time you need for reading, attending classes, homework, joining organizations, sports, and having fun. As a guide, you should not be working more than 15 hours a week.

- As soon as you begin a job, provide your supervisor with a copy of your class schedule as well as a list of other weekly commitments. Your employer should NEVER require you to be at work during a class. You should also let your supervisor know the maximum hours you can work each week.

- If an academic or personal emergency arises, notify your supervisor as soon as possible if you will be late or unable to work. Ask him/her for the preferred method of contact (email, telephone, text, etc.).

- Opt to turn your cell phone off during work hours, and inform your friends of your schedule. This will make you appear more professional and will ensure you're not interrupted or tempted to answer incoming e-mails and text messages or Facebook posts.

*Pamela M. Golubski, Ph.D.*

**MONEY GOES FAST AS A FRESHMAN.** Dining hall meals only go so far. Let's be real, most of your spare money goes to alcohol. And it's a worthy expense, but money goes quickly. My advice to students who don't have jobs right away is to be smart about what you buy. Alcohol is a good use of college money. McDonald's is not.
—*MICHAEL CUMMO*
   *BOSTON UNIVERSITY, SENIOR*

* * * * * * * *

**I USUALLY HAD LITTLE MONEY** because I ate dinners at restaurants all the time. It is so easy to just stop at Jimmy John's between classes, but that money really adds up. Get things to make lunch with. Wait until you get home to eat lunch. Bring a snack. Make a sandwich. All of these will save you more money than you even realize!

That being said, since I tended to make the financially irresponsible decision to eat lunch in restaurants and found myself with little money, I got a job! There are hundreds of campus jobs that are lucrative and that work around student schedules. With those, you (usually) don't need a car, either! You don't have to work 40 hours a week, just work enough to not overwhelm yourself and to make up for the money you're spending!
—*ELIZABETH*
   *UNIVERSITY OF ILLINOIS AT URBANA-CHAMPAIGN, GRADUATE*

* * * * * * * *

**IF YOU RELY ON YOUR PARENTS FOR FAFSA,** the Free Application for Federal Student Aid, and they don't file their taxes, you will be screwed. Grill your parents and make sure they do their taxes because in my junior year, my parents didn't file their taxes in time for the school year to start and I was unable to sign my FAFSA. So that whole year was full cost. If you have to rely on your parents for it, then pressure them.
—*PAISLEY*
   *MEREDITH COLLEGE, GRADUATE*

> Only 4 in 10 college students felt very or extremely prepared for their future careers, as of 2018. And that ratio represents a jump from 2017, when fewer than 1 in 3 reported feeling prepared.

# HOW TO FUND YOUR FRESHMAN YEAR (AND BEYOND)

Sometimes, freshmen find that the hardest part of adjusting to college life is *affording* college life. Whether you find yourself looking for ways to finance your entire college career, or just need a little spending money, the Internet Age has made job searches easier than ever. Check these sites out:

### QuadJobs.com

This website helps students find odd jobs in their area. QuadJobs. com is perfect for students who don't have enough time for a traditional part-time or full-time job, but want to make a few extra bucks. The service is especially popular among babysitters, bartenders, and tutors, but nearly any job can be found there, too, including opportunities to work for companies like **Hundreds of Heads!** Students pay nothing to participate and can apply to jobs from the website or app, using a simple profile they create. Employers have profiles, too, and students are notified whenever new jobs pop up that meet their criteria.

### Babysitting

Especially in or near large urban centers, Urbansitter.com and Sittercity.com offer two popular ways of locating families that might need babysitters or nannies near you. Another outfit that specializes in the childcare industry, with a following across all 50 states, is Care.com. Its app makes the job-searching process easy, and, like Quadjobs, it expects employers, not students, to pay the freight; the service is free to prospective hires.

### Tutoring

If you made it into college, chances are you're pretty smart! So, why wait until you graduate to cash in on your intellect? If you were good at math, science, or English in high school, you may be able to earn $30, $40, or even $50 an hour tutoring students locally or even far away using one of these websites:

### Wyzant.com

Many tutoring companies require tutors to have at least a Bachelor's degree. However, Wyzant considers applicants based on experience, written applications, and online assessments. Qualifying tutors can get paid well -- they set their own rate -- and can schedule tutoring sessions based on their own schedule. Additionally, all tutoring sessions are online, meaning you could tutor students from around the world at any time of day! The commission you pay starts high – up to 40% – but gets lower the longer a tutor works for Wyzant. You can also ask for a background check of yourself to make yourself seem more appealing to prospective students.

### Verbling.com

If you are fluent or near-fluent in another language, you can tutor students on Verbling.com. All tutoring happens over video-chat, and applicants undergo interviews and competence tests. Verbling takes a 15% commission on courses, however tutors can set their own rates. Verbling does not currently offer a background check option.

*Victor Bernabei is a Connecticut-based passport agent and travel blogger.*

OWNING A CREDIT CARD led to dreaded experiences for me. Before college, I had no account and no financial responsibility. Once I got my first credit card, I would spend money occasionally on food and clothes. I came to think that spending a small amount of money every time meant that my expenses would be kept at a minimum. I didn't take into account that the expenses could add up to uncomfortable amounts. Eventually, I had to control how much I would eat, what I would eat, where I would eat, how often I would shop for clothes, where I would shop for clothes, etc.

—RAJ MATHEW
MACAULAY HONORS COLLEGE AT CUNY HUNTER, JUNIOR

**TAKE AS LITTLE FINANCIAL ASSISTANCE** as possible; debts stink. Work hard and try to pay as much upfront as you can. I worked in the summers and at night leading up to college, and that helped pay bills during my first year of school.
—*MICHAEL ALBERT PAOLI*
*UNIVERSITY OF TORONTO, GRADUATE*

**INTERNSHIPS ARE A GREAT WAY TO KNOW** what type of career path you want to go on. Start looking for one of those immediately.
—*MICHAEL*
*RUTGERS UNIVERSITY, JUNIOR*

**I THINK IT'S GOOD TO WORK A FEW HOURS** a week at least, and that can be your weekend spending money. I worked at a restaurant and I used my tips as my spending money. It's also a good way to meet people in your school's town, so you get away from college, so you can vent, so you can be well-rounded.
—*MEGHAN*
*UNIVERSITY OF NOTRE DAME, JUNIOR*

# UNDERGRADS' WORKLOAD

Percentage of respondents who said they work...

| | |
|---|---|
| 0 hours a week for pay: | 44% |
| 1 to 9 hours a week for pay: | 19% |
| 10 to 19 hours a week for pay: | 19% |
| 20 to 29 hours a week for pay: | 10% |
| 30 to 39 hours a week for pay: | 4% |
| 40 or more hours a week for pay: | 4% |

*Studies have shown that your risk of dropping out increases significantly if you work more than 20 hours a week.*

**COLLEGE IS NOT CHEAP.** If you need to apply for financial aid, just do it. Make college affordable for yourself. Even if you end up having loans to repay when you come out, it is definitely worth it. Invest in your future.
—*MICHAEL*
*RUTGERS UNIVERSITY, JUNIOR*

• • • • • • • • •

**WHEN YOU'RE WORKING IN A HOSTILE WORK ENVIRONMENT,** there's always someone you can confide in who will care. I was a waitress at a restaurant and my general manager would tug my hair and say things like "your voice is erotic" or "your body looks really tight." I put up with it because I needed the money, I didn't want it to be a big deal, and I thought if I told, I would get in trouble somehow.

Looking back, I would tell myself that just because this isn't an extreme example of harassment doesn't mean you can't be upset about it. There were so many people I could have talked to: other managers, or the owner. Especially with the #MeToo movement, it's been reassuring to see that there are so many people in every industry who won't stand for people in positions of power creating a hostile work environment, regardless of the degree of harassment.
—*MARY*
*UNIVERSITY OF ARIZONA, GRADUATE*

# THE GIFT OF EDUCATION?

The more college money parents provide, the more likely their children will graduate, but also, the more likely that grades will suffer, according to a national study conducted by a University of California professor: students who get a blank check from their parents may not take their education as seriously as those who don't.

# NEED IT FREE? TRY THE LIBRARY

Libraries are not just stacks of dusty old books anymore; they've transformed in order to stay relevant. Many libraries have taken to sponsoring student events, guest speakers, technology workshops and makerspaces.

Sure, the library is still a good place to go for peace and quiet – or for collaborative study, or even just for unwinding and watching Netflix. But, since some of your tuition money helps fund the library, why not take advantage of all the events and freebies it has to offer?

### College Librarians

Need help with an essay or research project? It may seem old-fashioned, but you may want to consider asking a school reference librarian for a hand. Certain librarians at your college may have a background in the subjects you're studying and may be familiar with the course requirements. For instance, Haverford College in Pennsylvania takes pride in having librarians assigned to each of its courses, who can guide students to resources that may be useful for that course. That can take some of the fear out of taking a course such as "Topics in Enlightenment History: The Self Before the Selfie."

### Local libraries

At many colleges, the libraries are a major hub where lots of students congregate. If that's too distracting for the work you have in mind, finding the nearest public library may provide a short break from on-campus life and its temptations. Not to mention that joining another library gives you access to all of the resources and freebies that library offers. You should be eligible to join the local library for free with just your campus address, cell number, and email. While off-campus libraries may feel less academic, some resources, such as current fiction, also tend to be more popular in public libraries and thus they tend to supply a wider selection.

### Libraries in the Internet Age

As libraries adapt to an era where students learn more from online resources than books, research databases have exploded, with many colleges providing free access to millions of online articles, movies, and books through databases like the Wall Street Journal, JSTOR, and ProQuest, whose subscriptions are normally expensive. Some universities are now extending this privilege to their alumni. So, signing up for the free digital access can help you later, too.

### *Swag*

Colleges have begun lending more than books. At many libraries, you can now check out DVDs, music CDs, audiobooks, film and video equipment – even laptops. At M.I.T., Oberlin and the University of Chicago, students can borrow art they can hang on their dorm walls, though be warned: if you have your heart set on a Picasso, you may have to line up the night before the doors open.

Collections run the gamut, from cake pans to Halloween costumes, and everything in between. The Dallas Public Library lends out prom dresses, while the Bolivar County Library in Mississippi lets patrons check out Santa suits. The New York Public Library's Riverside branch in midtown Manhattan has a collection of handbags, briefcases and striped ties it lends out that are ideal for job interviews. Yale's law library lends out sleds and snow shovels in the winter as well as board games,

tool kits, air mattresses and soccer balls year-round, not to mention, "happy lights" and "slankets," whatever those are.

And both Yale Law and New Orleans' Loyola University, offer what may be the ultimate perk for patrons: therapy dogs for checkout. At Yale, a border terrier named Monty – short for General Montgomery – is listed in the law library catalogue and is available for 30-minute sessions of puppy stress relief.

*Victor Bernabei is a Connecticut-based*
*passport agent and travel blogger.*

# MONEY MANAGEMENT

Complete the chart below and see if you've still got a positive balance at the end. If you come up short, figure out which cash outflows can be cut back or eliminated.

| CASH INFLOWS | Amount | Tips | Your Notes |
|---|---|---|---|
| Employment income | | | |
| Parental support | | Thank your family for their ongoing financial support. | |
| Financial aid/ scholarships | | Keep your grades up. Most Financial Aid packages and scholarships require a minimum GPA, and if your grades don't make the cut, neither does the check. | |
| Other sources: | | | |
| **TOTAL INFLOWS** | | | |
| | | | |
| **CASH OUTFLOWS** | | | |
| **Fixed Expenses** | | | |
| Tuition | | Pay on time. If you don't, your college may not let you enroll in classes and it may impose late fees. | |
| Rent or room/board costs | | | |
| Car payment | | This, and a number of other expenses, may very well be paid for by your parents. | |
| Car insurance | | | |
| Health/dental insurance | | Your college may also provide this for you. | |
| Cell phone bill | | Watch your minutes and usage to minimize overages. | |
| Personal computer | | Most colleges have computer labs you can use for free, with limited printing, and many have, or are getting, free wireless Internet access, in case you have a laptop. | |

| Laundry | | Unless you live close enough to do laundry at home. | |
|---|---|---|---|
| **Variable Expenses** | | | |
| Books | | | |
| School supplies | | | |
| Eating out & entertainment | | | |
| Gas | | Carpool, use public transportation when possible. | |
| Luxuries/spontaneous shopping | | | |
| Groceries | | | |
| Utilities | | Whether it's built into your room/board or not, turn appliances/lights/water off when not in use to help the environment and reduce costs. | |
| **Periodic Expenses** | | | |
| Clothing | | You can always ask family for gift cards to your favorite stores. | |
| Gifts (Holidays, birthdays) | | You don't have to spend a lot to give something meaningful to friends and family. It is the thought that counts! | |
| Car repairs/maintenance | | | |
| Toiletries | | | |
| Doctor visits/medicine | | | |
| Other: | | | |
| **TOTAL OUTFLOWS** | | | |
| **CASH BALANCE** | | | |

Tips:
1. Create a budget based off of this table, and as cash flows in and out, track it.
2. If you have a checking account, keep track of transactions using your ledger.
3. When you have a positive cash balance, put it into a savings account to earn interest.
4. Watch out for credit cards…the ability to buy things you otherwise couldn't afford is very tempting, but you'll suffer for it in the long run, until you're ready to handle it.
5. Many banks and college Financial Aid Offices offer workshops and suggestions on how to manage your money effectively.

*Scott C. Silverman*

*"And that's what happens on a diet of Dominos and Red Bull."*

# Food for Thought: Pop-Tarts, Beer & Other Essential Nutrients

I s it humanly possible to eat pizza every day for a whole semester, and if so, why doesn't this activity have its own time slot on ESPN? Is the "Freshman 15" a myth – or an unhappy reality? Will your 10 A.M. history professor mind if you bring your breakfast to class?

Does that maraschino cherry on top of your sundae count as one of those daily fruit and vegetable servings you heard about growing up? Pop-Tarts and M&M's for dinner? Hey, no one's stopping you. For the first time in your life, you can eat when, where and whatever you please. Let our friendly guides help you use that freedom wisely.

THE FIRST INCLINATION when you get to college is to eat anything you want. Mom isn't there making sure you eat your vegetables. But three months and 15 pounds later, you find out why a mom is a good thing when it comes to food.
—D.R.
UNIVERSITY OF NORTH CAROLINA, GRADUATE

THE MICROWAVE IS DEFINITELY YOUR BEST FRIEND.
—REBECCA
HUNTER COLLEGE, SENIOR

**HEADLINES**

- Food is an adventure at school. Treat it that way and you'll seldom be disappointed.

- If you eat the pizza, you will gain the weight.

- Cheap college food: Mac 'n' cheese, ramen noodles, yogurt, fruit, trail mix.

- Try to eat healthy at least half the time.

- Take advantage of your meal plan. Otherwise, it's wasted money.

---

**GET A GEORGE FOREMAN GRILL,** or even just a toaster oven. You'd be surprised at how much you can make with those, from bagel pizzas to steak.
—*JESSIE*
*VILLA JULIE COLLEGE, JUNIOR*

• • • • • • • •

**PEOPLE NEVER EAT BEFORE PARTIES** because they think there's going to be food at the party. Not in college! Eat a lot. Pizza is always a fun option.
—*CATLEYA*
*UNIVERSITY OF MIAMI, JUNIOR*

• • • • • • • •

**DON'T BUY THE FULL MEAL TICKET,** unless you're sure you can eat breakfast every day. I made it to breakfast once the whole year. When I got up, I didn't have time to go downstairs and eat; I had to go to class.
—*JAKE MALAWAY*
*UNIVERSITY OF ILLINOIS, GRADUATE*

• • • • • • • •

**THE HOT-DOG** vendor will become your new best friend.
—*J.G.*
*FLORIDA STATE UNIVERSITY, GRADUATE*

If you drink the beer, you're gonna gain the weight.

—*BRIAN ROSEN*
*PRINCETON UNIVERSITY, GRADUATE*

I RECOMMEND THAT ONE ACQUIRE a taste for hummus. Hummus can really be put onto anything, it comes in all sorts of flavors, it's healthy, and it's relatively cheap if bought in bulk. Seriously, try and think of something that hummus wouldn't be good on; you can't!

— *STEVEN COY*
*SAN DIEGO STATE UNIVERSITY, SOPHOMORE*

" Buy lots of Tupperware containers to take to the cafeteria and sneak food out, so you don't have to buy it. You're paying for a meal plan anyway. "

— *MEG*
*UNIVERSITY OF NORTH CAROLINA, GRADUATE*

IT'S EASY TO OVEREAT AT A DINING HALL because there's no cap on how much you can get. Just bear that in mind and work out.

— *G.B.*
*PRINCETON UNIVERSITY, JUNIOR*

TAKE EVERY FREE MEAL YOU CAN GET. Generally, the dining hall is not bad. But when you eat it seven days a week, it gets pretty old, no matter how good the food is. Every time someone wants to take you out, take them up on it. If nothing else, it's a good way to make friends or meet people.

— *JONATHAN COHEN*
*EMORY UNIVERSITY, SENIOR*

I MAY SOUND LIKE AN ANNOYING PARENT when I say this, but please, for the love of God, do not spend all of your money on alcohol. There are so many ways to still be able to enjoy yourself (and drink) for less. Have your friends pitch in when you buy it (legally) at the store. Share it! Buy just one drink if you're at a club or pub because that stuff's expensive. Steal it from home. I don't care. It can just turn into a huge money-eater.
—SHANNON KELLEY
KENYON COLLEGE, JUNIOR

The "Freshman 15" happens to everyone – and don't believe anyone who tells you otherwise.

—AMY
PRINCETON
UNIVERSITY,
FRESHMAN

• • • • • • • • •

DON'T EAT THE EGGS IN THE DINING COMMONS. They're fake. Anything you can eat from a bowl, like cereal and salad, is good. Don't eat a lot of fast food just because it's there and it's cheap. Jamba Juice is the way to go: it won't make you fat, it's kind of healthy, and it doesn't smell bad so you can take it to class and no one will yell at you. You get these people who go to class with a burger and onion rings and sit there for an hour in class and it's gross.
—KYM
SAN JOSE STATE UNIVERSITY, SOPHOMORE

# QUALITY CONTROL

I often see first-year students get really excited about the "all you can eat" dining options. I would encourage students to pick a few options that look tasty and manage the portions of those options. You don't need to try every dining option to get your money's worth. You can eat a few great items and avoid gaining weight during your first year of college. Quality over Quantity!

*Jen Miller*
*Dean of Students*
*California State University, Los Angeles*

# COOKING NO-NOS

**BE CAREFUL WHAT YOU COOK IN YOUR TOASTER.** My friend bought some frozen hot dogs – like, six of them – and then one day she was hungry so she tried to cook them in the toaster in her dorm room, and smoke came out of it and she set off the fire alarm. So, she had to go to peer review, which was funny because most of the cases they get in peer review are people using excessive bandwidth from downloading too much, and then they get this interesting case. For punishment they said she had to make a few posters saying, "Be safe – don't put hot dogs in toasters."

    *—J.R. MCKINNEY*
      *UNIVERSITY OF CALIFORNIA AT BERKELEY, SOPHOMORE*

**DO NOT MICROWAVE CHICKEN NUGGETS!** I loved dinosaur-shaped chicken nuggets growing up and they reminded me of home. But when I put them in my dorm microwave, they were soggy and wet and it didn't matter how much ketchup I put on them. Just give them up or bite the bullet and use the oven in the gross communal kitchen.
    *—MEGHAN WALLACE*
      *NORTHERN ARIZONA UNIVERSITY, SENIOR*

**MOST IMPORTANT PIECE OF ADVICE** I ever received about college food: If you find a hair in your food in the dining hall, just assume it's yours and move on.
    *—MATT LACKNER*
      *PRINCETON UNIVERSITY, GRADUATE*

**EAT LIKE MOM IS THERE.** I was in pretty good shape going into college. I used to work out a lot. But then I started drinking a lot and got real lazy and school got hard. I got complacent and I got a real beer gut.
    *—TOM*
      *ARIZONA STATE UNIVERSITY, GRADUATE*

# CLEVER CAMOUFLAGE

**YOU'RE GOING TO GAIN WEIGHT** and you're going to take it off the next summer. Don't worry about it. Buy some fat pants. Everybody I know gained a lot of weight.
> —HANNAH
> EMORY UNIVERSITY, JUNIOR

**IF YOU START TO GET FAT AND FIND YOURSELF WEARING JUST DRESSES,** pay attention to that. Try your jeans on every once in a while. That's how I figured it out. I didn't realize I was getting fat because I kept wearing skirts and dresses and they were just so accommodating.
> —PAISLEY
> MEREDITH COLLEGE, GRADUATE

**HOW TO DECIDE IF YOU WANT THE MEAL PLAN:** If you like to eat lots of food and you're not picky about quality, then eat at school. But if you care about things like taste, plan on buying your meals elsewhere. I bought the meal plan and was happy with it. You could eat tons of food cheap. Was it good? No. But as long as I was full, I didn't care.
> —DON WAZZENEGER
> YOUNGSTOWN STATE UNIVERSITY, SENIOR

**I WASN'T TRYING TO EAT HEALTHY,** but I think I managed to by eating a lot of different foods. My cafeteria had a bunch of options. They had international food: gyros some weeks, stir-fry stations on others. I like to try something new every day and the cafeteria really gave me that option. I actually lost weight the first 6 months that I was away at school. They talk about the "Freshman 15," but I was the "Freshman Negative 15."
> —BEN LEACH
> JOHNS HOPKINS UNIVERSITY, SOPHOMORE

I HATED COLLEGE FOOD! College food is a hard adjustment on the body. I stopped going to the cafeteria and started bringing food that I could make in my room. Microwavable meals are great and cheap.
—*DAVID*
*KEAN UNIVERSITY, JUNIOR*

· · · · · · · ·

THE FOOD YOU'LL FIND IN YOUR DINING HALL is either going to be really expensive or really greasy. A great way to save money is to limit how much you eat in the cafeterias and start eating more in your dorm. If you buy $1 yogurts at the grocery store instead of a $5 breakfast sandwich on your walk to class, that will really start to add up, and you'll have more control over your diet. Cooking is also a great way to bond with your roommate!
—*L.G.*
*BUCKNELL UNIVERSITY, GRADUATE*

# TOP THREE ZERO-EFFORT HEALTHY SNACKS

1. **Bananas:** Requiring no preparation and no utensils, these wonders of nature are also easy to carry in a backpack.

2. **Natural yogurt:** Try to avoid the brands full of artificial sweeteners and other chemicals, and you're all set.

3. **Frozen orange juice:** No, not the concentrate that comes in a can. Instead, buy the smallest cartons you can get at the campus store, wedge them in the freezer section of your mini fridge, and pry them out the next day for frosty deliciousness.

# JON'S BEST POST-PARTY FOODS

- Mac 'n Cheese cups
- Pizza
- Nutella, straight from the jar
- Pop Tarts
- French Fries
- Chinese Food
- Feta Bread
- Cereal

*Jon Barr is an LA-based writer & comedian.*

**I HAVE A LOT OF SNACKS IN MY ROOM** – macaroni and cheese, and peanut butter and jelly. You might want to bring that kind of stuff, in case you can't make it to the cafeteria or don't want to go, for whatever reason.
—*ANONYMOUS*
*UNIVERSITY OF MARYLAND, FRESHMAN*

• • • • • • • • •

**DON'T ASSUME YOU WON'T GAIN WEIGHT** just because as a teen in high school you ate a lot. In my first year of college, I didn't understand the concept of self-control with food. The all-you-can-eat buffet seemed like a good idea at the time, especially where the cookies and brownies were concerned. I used to stash as many as I could carry under a folded napkin and was so proud of myself for being able to sneak out with it – as if it were an accomplishment! I didn't realize that all I accomplished was a good 15 pounds. I was convinced that I couldn't fit into my clothes anymore because the dry air in the dorm room shrunk them all.
—*VERONICA*
*QUEENS UNIVERSITY, GRADUATE*

**GET YOUR OWN MINI-FRIDGE** and buy your own food. Buy Easy Mac – it's microwaveable macaroni and cheese. So, you don't need a stove.
—*SIERRA*
*CALIFORNIA POLYTECHNIC STATE UNIVERSITY, JUNIOR*

. . . . . . . .

**AFTER I COULD NO LONGER AFFORD A MEAL PLAN,** my friend and I would scour the campus paper and fliers for events with free food. Then, we would fill in our own "Free Food Calendar" with all the times and places of those events. We would end up at academic speeches, random barbecues, or various group meetings, none of which we belonged to or knew anything about. But they put out free food at these events. We wound up eating for free at least three to four times every week. You can't beat that!
—*CHAVON MITCHELL*
*XAVIER UNIVERSITY, GRADUATE*

. . . . . . . .

**DON'T BE FOOLED** by the "Freshman 15." Real men go for the "Freshman 30." At least that's how I cope with it.
—*ADAM*
*ELON UNIVERSITY, SOPHOMORE*

. . . . . . . .

**THINK FOOD. THINK AMAZON PRIME.** The free two-day delivery is great for ordering clothes and other stuff. But I didn't expect how much I'd use it for food and drinks. I drink a lot of Gatorade and Vitamin water after exercising and the vending machine charges $2.75 per bottle. Amazon Prime delivers it right to my door for $6 or $7 per case. They also have lots of microwaveable foods, like Barilla pasta dishes, which is really helpful when I'm in the middle of studying, super hungry and I don't want to go out in the cold to Syracuse's dining hall.
—*ANONYMOUS*
*SYRACUSE UNIVERSITY, SOPHOMORE*

# SIX WAYS TO BEAT THE DINING HALL BLUES

Meal kit services are all the rage in America. People don't know how to cook, but they want to cook. So, capitalism has provided them with impossible-to-screw-up, Lego-like kits of pre-portioned ingredients with big laminated cards featuring nice pictures and simple steps that make users feel like Rachel Ray. It's fantastic! Almost magic! Plus, everyone's on a diet now and VERY proud of it. Whether it is Gluten Free, Dairy Free, Sugar Free, Soy Free, Paleo, Ketogenic, or good ol' Vegetarian, there's a meal kit for type of food snob out there.

Let's face it. Dining hall fare can get old. And maybe food shopping is just a chore you'd rather live without. Meal kits can solve all of these very common college dilemmas. The thing is, not all of these services are conducive to a college budget, fridge size or eating habits. To find the ones best suited for dorm room dwellers like you, we waded through a horde of services and brought you the best below. If none of these catch your eye, feel free to browse around yourself. This is a shockingly crowded market, and new services are popping up all the time.

**Home Chef**                          **about $10 per serving**
Like the better-known Blue Apron and Sun Basket, Home Chef follows the standard, general meal-kit formula. That is, sign up for a weekly plan of 2 to 8 meals per week providing 2, 4, or 6 servings per meal. Select your meals a few days ahead of delivery and await the arrival of your big, heavy, tasty box of ingredients and instructions. There are plenty of options for those avoiding gluten, dairy, or meat, but very few vegan options, and strangely, Home Chef doesn't include sugar content in the nutrition facts for its meals.

The box is full of ice packs that keep its contents cool (an issue that could land you in hot water with environmentally-conscious dormmates) and you do need to transfer everything quickly to a fridge. That brings us to one showstopper for most students: fridge space – these things demand a lot of it, more than what mini-fridges will generally allow. Assuming you have somewhere to put the stuff that comes in the box, the other thing you kinda need to make this work is a partner to go in halfsies with you. If you're doing this alone, you are gonna be eating a lot of leftovers, and, again, you may not have the fridge space to store them. Home Chef also assumes you have some basic cooking tools and spices, such as pots, pans, spatulas, salt, and pepper, to get going. The meals are indeed "homey," and easy enough for the worst chefs among us.

## HelloFresh                               about $10 per serving
HelloFresh operates on a similar model, and offers recipes that are simple to make and a little more adventurous than Home Chef. The ingredients are healthful, and the menu is very upfront about the nutritional contents and allergens in each dish. As with Home Chef, the smallest portion size is for two, and you need to order at least two meals a week. There are at least fifteen meals from which to choose each week, and there is even a vegetarian plan, as long as you don't mind accepting the vegetarian meals that have been preselected for you. Another drawback: nearly every ingredient – sauce, seasoning, meat, or starch – comes in its own little plastic bag, and the waste piles up fast.

## Freshly                               about $10-12.50 per meal
Now, this is a meal service a collegian can get behind and come to love. Unlike the classic meal-kit services, Freshly's meals are pre-cooked and designed for one person only. The cheapest plan costs $50 for four meals a week. The little boxes each one comes in are easier on the dorm-room fridge than the ingredients bags of other meal-kits and the only kitchen instrument the service expects you to have is the almighty microwave. This is truly as easy as it gets.

As for taste, Freshly shatters microwavable-meal stereotypes. We're not talking corn dogs and mac n' cheese either. These dishes are ultra-healthy and culturally diverse. The entire menu is free of gluten and refined sugars, and there are plenty of vegan, low carb, soy-free, and dairy-free options. With dishes like cod cakes, chicken tikka masala, Moroccan style root veggie tagine, and spaghetti squash with meatballs, Freshly will expand your horizons, save you time, and keep you feeling trim and energized. The best part? You can do it all without leaving your room. The downside: portions can be unsatisfyingly small (especially for the price) and if you wait any longer than the recommended 3 to 5 days to heat the dishes, things can get soggy.

**Daily Harvest**                                    **$7 to $8 per cup**
Unlike the other guys, Daily Harvest doesn't offer kits or meals, but rather 'cups.' The cups come frozen, and this is something they're quite proud of. According to their website, all of their ingredients are organic, gluten-free, and vegan, and are frozen almost the instant they are plucked from the wild, preserving all of the glorious micronutrients that might otherwise decay as food sits.

The cups open to reveal everything from soups, lattes and smoothies to chia parfaits, 'harvest bowls,' and sundaes, and some of the ingredients are mind-boggling. I'm talking cauliflower, sweet potatoes, and avocado in ice cream, dragon fruit in parfaits, and spinach and coffee mixed in the same smoothie. The dishes are packed full of super-foods that purportedly "relieve stress, support the immune system, keep skin looking glow-y, improve energy and focus, and keep you at your best." The matcha lemongrass latte I tried tasted like a fresh cut lawn in drink form...in a good way. The smoothies and sundaes require a blender, so be forewarned, but the rest of the 'cups' require no preparation beyond a microwave or time to defrost.

Plans range from 6 to 24 cups a week. So, yes, at first glance, this plan seems cheaper than the others per serving. But each cup is more like a snack than a meal. Some of the smoothies and parfaits are pretty substantial, but most of the lattes, soups, and harvest bowls are between just 100 to 300 calories. That's great if you have a light appetite or are seriously trying to lose weight – but they aren't gonna fill you up.

## SuperCook.com                                      FREE

This is not a meal delivery service, so much as a survival tool. It's kind of like WebMD without the hypochondria. Enter the contents of your fridge into the website and SuperCook scours its library of recipes looking for the best ones that make use of what you already have in front of you. Pop in "banana, peanut butter and cereal," and out pop five suggestions, including "oven-baked banana chips." Genius! It doesn't save you a trip to grocery store but it can certainly spark your creativity.

## From Home With Love                    $30 for a reusable kit

Love is that elusive ingredient that makes a famous family recipe taste like home, and no restaurant or commercial meal service can replicate that. Wisely, From Home With Love doesn't try. It simply provides the specialized packaging needed to send home-cooked meals from anywhere in the United States. Their number-one customer? Parents of college kids. The company's containers are insulated, microwave-safe, and small enough to fit in the dorm fridge. So, if you're lucky enough to have loved ones back home who cook, now you're lucky enough to have their cooking safely shipped to your dorm room door. What could be yummier than that?

**SNEAKY PRO TIP:** This market is flooded with players, desperate to win your business, and nearly all of them offer steep discounts for first-time users, usually about half off! There are so frickin' many of them out there that you can literally try a new one every week for your entire freshman year. It's fun, interesting, cheap, and kind of cheating. Just don't forget to cancel!

*Anthony Wallace is a Phoenix-based writer and thinker.*
*His favorite part of every day is eating.*

# ONLY 1 IN 25 STUDENTS GET RECOMMENDED DAILY FRUIT & VEGGIES

Percentage of undergraduates who reported eating...

| | |
|---|---|
| 5 or more servings of fruits and vegetables per day: | 4% |
| 3 to 4 servings of fruits and vegetables per day: | 23% |
| 1 to 2 servings of fruits and vegetables per day: | 64% |
| No servings of fruits and vegetables per day: | 9% |

**YOU SHOULD ALWAYS HAVE CHIPS** in the dorm room when you're up at four in the morning writing a paper.
> —DAN AMERMAN
> YALE UNIVERSITY, SOPHOMORE

. . . . . . . . .

**DORM ROOM SNACKS SHOULD BE BORING.** I came up to school with this insane amount of junk food for my room – Gushers, Doritos, Pop Tarts, candy. It was cool to have the freedom to eat whatever I wanted. But after about a week, that all got pretty tired. Now, my go-to's are pretzel sticks, a big bag of dried apricots, dried chick peas, some trail mix and peanuts. They're not as fun as the junk food, but they really tide me over between meals at the dining hall.
> —OLIVER MENKEN
> TUFTS UNIVERSITY, SOPHOMORE

. . . . . . . . .

**IF YOU FIND A DINING HALL FOOD YOU LOVE, DO NOT EAT IT EVERY DAY.** My first week, I discovered I really liked the baked ziti. So, I ate it all the time. After about a week I never wanted to see it again.
> —ANONYMOUS
> SYRACUSE UNIVERSITY, SOPHOMORE

**LIVING IN MIAMI,** I've learned a lot about Cuban food. I'd say a necessity in any college student's home is a rice cooker. I like to fry up two over easy eggs and break them on top of some garlic rice. Apparently, it's a traditional Cuban comfort food. It's also nice to keep slice-and-bake cookie dough in the fridge. Easy to make, and they make your house smell so yummy. Your friends will think you're quite the baker.

—*EVA DINES*
*UNIVERSITY OF MIAMI, JUNIOR*

• • • • • • • •

**THINK ABOUT WHAT YOU'RE EATING!** When I first got to college, every day I would drink an extra-large Caramel Macchiato – which was probably 600 calories in and of itself – and then every night, I would have an iced tea and entire bag of Peach-O's. They're just gummy candies with sugar all over them that kind of taste like peaches. I gained 20 pounds, and I was sick all the time! And now I'm studying to be a dietician. So, all's well that ends well.

—*MARY*
*UNIVERSITY OF ARIZONA, GRADUATE*

# FRESHMAN 15: FACT OR FICTION?

According to one study, the so-called "Freshman 15" – the weight gain phenomenon said to go along with starting college – is little more than myth. It showed that while new college students do tend to gain between 2.5 to 3.5 pounds on average, the weight gain has little to do with college and much more to do with natural body change as students enter adulthood. In fact, even 18- to 19-year-olds who didn't attend college were shown to gain weight at an almost identical rate.

RAMEN. I KNOW IT'S WILDLY UNHEALTHY, but I lived on it freshman year. It's fast and it's filling. What more do you need? I had two big staples when I decided to make my own meals. First: I would always get large bags of frozen chicken breasts and keep them in my freezer. I'd thaw them, throw them in the oven with BBQ sauce, and then I'd steam or microwave a frozen vegetable. When I wanted to be really balanced, I'd add some rice, but I had to really plan ahead for that. My other big staple was stir-fry, which exclusively happened within three days of grocery shopping. I'd get some vegetables and then I'd cut up chicken and throw the vegetables together with some teriyaki sauce, creating a stir-fried miracle!
—*ELIZABETH*
*UNIVERSITY OF ILLINOIS AT URBANA-CHAMPAIGN, GRADUATE*

•  •  •  •  •  •  •  •

I HAVE WEIRD EATING HABITS. I eat rice cakes and dried pineapple. I don't know why. Also, chocolate helps.
—*ANONYMOUS*
*YALE UNIVERSITY, SOPHOMORE*

•  •  •  •  •  •  •  •

HEALTH IS THE MOST IMPORTANT ASPECT OF WELL-BEING and it is often forgotten. Perhaps the most difficult aspect of freshman year for me was my lifestyle. I ate each meal at the cafeteria (often high-fat, high-calorie meals), lived in the dorms, went out for ice cream at night with friends, and seldom worked out at the gym. The "Freshman 15," which is often referenced, is very real. I found myself struggling to maintain my ideal weight – which became an added frustration. I highly, highly recommend setting a workout regimen during the summer before freshman year and sticking to it.
—*ANONYMOUS*
*COLLEGE ON THE EAST COAST, GRADUATE*

**FIND A FEW THINGS** in the dining hall that you like. Oftentimes, the dorms are far from the city, so you don't have the option of going out to eat. My friends and I ate at the dorm dining hall pretty much all the time. I found the meat especially disappointing; I missed the steaks we made back at home. I ate a lot of chicken that year, and cereal.
—*ANDREW*
   *UCLA, SENIOR*

· · · · · · · · ·

**COOKING MOST DEFINITELY TAKES SOME GETTING USED TO,** especially as you move from dorms to off-campus homes and apartments. Long live the days when mom's cooking was waiting for you after class or a swipe into the dining hall was at your fingertips. Let's face it, cooking is not necessarily an easy feat. The Yummly app can help you meal prep based on your preferences and the ingredients in your fridge. You can set meal preferences, search different cuisine types, and enter various ingredients you have in your fridge, and voila! Recipes pop up that fit your preferences. Other filters include dietary restrictions and cook time. Chances are you'll find some new foods you never would have thought to try!
—*DANIELLE FOWLER*
   *ELON UNIVERSITY, GRADUATE*

"You can always spot the freshmen from the West Coast."

# Ready to Wear: Fashion & (at Some Point) Laundry

*I*f you wish to avoid the universal nightmare of having nothing to wear, you're going to need to pack wisely when you first set out for college and use home visits to ditch what's not working. Ideally, your college wardrobe will be stocked with sensible items that make you feel good and require minimal effort to put on or take off. (There's a reason why so many students now sleep in their sweatpants; it makes getting ready the next morning that much easier.)

And if you want to avoid being the person the rest of the class can smell, now might be a good time to educate yourself on how that whole laundry thing works.

**AS LONG AS YOUR WARDROBE DOESN'T CONSIST** of only leather pants and tiger print shirts, fashion isn't a big deal.
—Jo
*UNIVERSITY OF VIRGINIA, SENIOR*

**WEAR YOUR PAJAMAS AROUND CAMPUS; YOU WON'T BE THE ONLY ONE.**
—AMY FORBES
*MISSISSIPPI STATE UNIVERSITY, GRADUATE*

**HEADLINES**

- College is casual these days. T-shirts are standard.
- Don't be the one who waits too long to do laundry or take a shower.
- Freshmen are known for wearing school-themed apparel. We're just letting you know.
- There's a "best" time to do laundry in your dorm. Figure it out.

**BIG FASHION FAUX PAS** – the lanyard with the ID in it. We have what is called a "one-card." It gets you into the dorms and some other buildings. The sure sign of a first-year is the lanyard with the one-card, especially the "Wellesley College" lanyard in your class color. Some first years don't catch on and the poor dears wander around with them all year.
> —SARAH
> WELLESLEY COLLEGE, SOPHOMORE

• • • • • • • • •

**AT STANFORD, THE MAJORITY OF STUDENTS RIDE BIKES** around campus. I attempted to wear a miniskirt and ride a bike. I immediately realized the awkwardness of it. I tried to push my skirt down and cover my underwear with my hand, but I don't think it really worked.
> —TIFFANY
> STANFORD UNIVERSITY, SENIOR

# HISTORY CORNER

Oberlin College, long known for its progressive ideals, became the first coeducational college in the United States back when it admitted women in 1833. But all was not equal, even at Oberlin. For many years, female students were responsible for doing their male classmates' laundry.

**IF YOU LIVE IN A DORM AND YOUR BATHROOM** is down the hall, get good shower shoes. If you go barefoot, by mid-October they'll be studying the stuff on your feet in biology class.
>  —*J.T.*
>  *UNIVERSITY OF FLORIDA, GRADUATE*

* * * * * * * *

" No one will really notice if you wear the same two or three (or one) pair of jeans or khakis – it's the shirt that people notice. So, get plenty of shirts and one or two pairs of jeans and you can cut laundry efforts in half. "
>  —*DAN*
>  *MIAMI UNIVERSITY, FRESHMAN*

* * * * * * * *

**DON'T TURN COLLEGE** into an uncomfortable place to be. There is no sense in wearing high heels to school!
>  —*ERICA LANGE-HENNESEY*
>  *TEXAS STATE UNIVERSITY, SENIOR*

* * * * * * * *

**USE MOM'S LAUNDRY** detergent and fabric softener to make your dorm room smell a little bit more like home!
>  —*LAURA WOLTER*
>  *UNIVERSITY OF TEXAS AT AUSTIN, GRADUATE*

Just get lots
of underwear
and only do
laundry when
you run out.

—*MEREDITH*
*BROWN UNIVERSITY,*
*SOPHOMORE*

**LAUNDRY IS EXPENSIVE,** and you have to be careful because people will steal your stuff. I had a problem with that. I had to take my homework down there and do it while doing laundry.
—*B.M.*
*UNIVERSITY OF MARYLAND, JUNIOR*

• • • • • • • •

**IF YOU WANT TO BE COOL,** don't wear anything with your school name or colors on it. It's called Freshman Fashion Wear for a reason.
—*J.G.*
*FLORIDA STATE UNIVERSITY, GRADUATE*

• • • • • • • •

**DURING CRUNCH TIME, YOU ONLY NEED** a few pieces of clothing: Sweatpants in school color of choice, comfy tank top or ratty T-shirt, and a hoodie.
—*AMY*
*PRINCETON UNIVERSITY, FRESHMAN*

# NOT-SO HOT TREND AT COLD SCHOOLS

At Cornell's mid-winter Rush Week, flocks of aspiring sorority sisters braved the cold this year in puffy Canada Goose down coats as far as the eye could see.

Sure, it's only natural to want to blend in. But here's a reason – besides price – to resist bringing one of these high-fashion pieces to school: you may not have it for long.

In Chicago, armed robbers have been targeting people clad in Canada Goose and demanding their coats. Coat-inspired thefts occurred at least three times in one week in and around the University of Chicago. In one instance, hapless thieves did not even get the real deal: they made off with a knock-off.

# SPECIAL HYGIENE SECTION

*Thanks to all those imperfectly socialized freshmen who made this page possible – and necessary.*

**IF POSSIBLE, TRY TO FIND THE SHOWER IN YOUR DORM** with the best pressure and the most considerate bathroom users and ask politely to share it with them. A nice hot shower under a showerhead with good pressure is a great way to unwind. Be considerate of other bathroom users! Don't leave a mess for your janitors; they are there to maintain a standard of hygiene, not to clean up your messes.
>—ARIEL MELENDEZ
>PRINCETON UNIVERSITY, FRESHMAN

**EVEN IF IT DOESN'T BOTHER YOU** to walk around for a few days without a shower – please, oh God, before you forgo the morning cleaning, please think of the person sitting next to you in class.
>—ADAM
>ELON UNIVERSITY, SOPHOMORE

**IF YOU HAVE A LIMITED CLOTHES BUDGET,** spend it on jeans. Jeans never go out of style. If you have some extra cash, buy socks and underwear. They seem to disappear between the dorm rooms and the Laundromat.
>—DON WAZZENEGER
>YOUNGSTOWN STATE UNIVERSITY, SENIOR

**GUYS, BRING KHAKIS** in the fall and then cut them off in the spring.
>—STEVE DAVIS
>FLORIDA STATE UNIVERSITY, GRADUATE

**I**F YOU GO TO A SCHOOL WHERE IT GETS COLD, get a somewhat fashionable jacket that can stand the wear and tear of a party. You'll want a jacket that's cheap, that will stand up to dirt, spit, beer, the weather, and your friend's drool.
—*Joseph S. Smith*
*Pennsylvania State University, Graduate*

* * * * * * * *

66 Do not bring clothes that require ironing or dry cleaning or special handling. And do not loan your favorite shirt to a party-happy friend if you want it back in the same condition. If you are female, leave your handbag at home. No one brings a purse to a party, and during the day your backpack is your bag. 99
—*J.*
*University of Georgia, Graduate*

* * * * * * * *

**W**ARNING: **D**ON'T WASH DOWN COMFORTERS. You'll flood the laundry room and ruin your blanket.
—*Ethan Wasserman*
*Boston University, Junior*

# LAUNDRY TIPS FOR THE HELPLESS

Just about the last thing I ever feel like doing in college is my laundry. Either I don't have quarters, don't have soap, or just don't care that my clothes are wrinkled and dank. If this sounds like you, try sticking to the following strategies for avoiding the laundry room:

For shirts, pants and the like, divide your clothes into two categories. Category One is the stuff you wear every day. Keep these items as clean as possible and when you're done wearing them, fold them neatly, put them in your drawer, and pretend they're clean. A squirt of Febreze might help as well.

Category Two is your "going-out-to-parties clothes." This should be only one or two shirts and a pair of pants, which will stink of beer and smoke after a night out. Keep these in a trash bag on

your closet floor. Wear them on Friday nights. No one will know the difference.

Tempting as it may be, you're not allowed to wear underwear twice. It's just wrong. You'll need to go to Wal-Mart and get 30 pairs of tightie-whities and 30 pairs of white tube socks. Wear each pair one day, and then once a month, throw all of them in the wash. It's all white, so you can do one load, and because it's just socks and underwear, you don't have to fold or sort anything. Just put them in another trash bag, next to your Friday night clothes. Keep two pairs of clean boxers on hand for dates.

—A.F.
GEORGE WASHINGTON UNIVERSITY, GRADUATE

# STRANGE BUT TRUE UNDERWEAR TALES

I WAS ON THE WAY TO THE LAUNDRY ROOM and I dropped my underwear on the dorm stairs. I didn't realize until someone came up to me and said, "You dropped your underwear on the stairs." I was so embarrassed.
> —CONSTANCE A. LINDSAY
> DUKE UNIVERSITY, GRADUATE

I HAD THIS GIRL WHO DID MY LAUNDRY and I would notice that I was losing underwear. I rummaged through her stuff one day and found six pairs of my Fruit of the Looms! I haven't trusted anyone with my clothing since.
> —RYAN BOWEN
> UNIVERSITY OF GEORGIA, SENIOR

ONE TIME, THE WASHERS WERE BROKEN at the dorms. So, I asked my new guy friend, who was six years older, if I could wash some clothes at his place. I finished washing and left but had forgotten a load at his place. His friends came over that night and saw my yellow thongs and pink granny panties. Needless to say, we stopped hanging out.
> —M.T.
> GEORGIA STATE UNIVERSITY, SENIOR

I HAD GIRL'S UNDERWEAR in my laundry one time; she must have left it in the dryer. They had her name in them, so I went to her room to give them back. It was kind of awkward, at least for me.
> —ALEX
> EMORY UNIVERSITY, SOPHOMORE

KEEP TRACK OF THE TIME when you are doing your laundry. During my freshman year I was late to take my clothes out of the dryer and someone stole my Victoria's Secret underwear and left my granny panties. I was so mad!
> —DANIELLE
> DUKE UNIVERSITY, GRADUATE

**FIND SOMEONE WHO REALLY KNOWS** how to do laundry. You get here and you realize that you don't understand how not to dye all your clothes pink.
—*LUCY LINDSEY*
*HARVARD UNIVERSITY, FRESHMAN*

**FOR LAUNDRY, I WAIT** until I have no clothes left, and then I do two big loads all at once and I'm done with it in a couple of hours.
—*ANONYMOUS*
*UNIVERSITY OF PENNSYLVANIA, SOPHOMORE*

> " Never wear anything from high school. I mean, we all went to high school, but you don't have to advertise it. "
> —*J.T.*
> *UNIVERSITY OF FLORIDA, GRADUATE*

**I LIKED THRIFTING FOR A WHILE,** and Depop was an online way to thrift. It started off as an app to sell secondhand goods or clothes you didn't want anymore, but now some people have gotten really good at making a living from the app. When I started, I didn't think anyone would buy my worn clothes, but people did!

I spend a lot of time writing product descriptions, doing photo shoots, providing good service – all to elevate the worth of my products. I learned about product packaging, how to ship at the cheapest cost – the list goes on. What's amazing is I figured it out on my own, so I'm proud of that.
—*GINA XIAO*
*UNIVERSITY OF PITTSBURGH, GRADUATE*

Pajamas are okay for 8 A.M. class but not for 4 P.M. class.
—*DANIELLE*
*DUKE UNIVERSITY, GRADUATE*

# HEADING NORTH? REMEMBER TO PACK YOUR "FRACKET"

Because it's so cold at Dartmouth, most people have a pretty expensive winter coat they use for day-to-day activities, including skiing and walking from class to class.

However, at night, when people go out to frats, they wear their "frackets." Frackets are usually old jackets that students wear when going out or cheap coats bought at places like Walmart or a thrift shop. They are usually oversized and a crazy color, so when drunk, students can tell their fracket from someone else's. The point of a fracket is to keep your good coat from getting ruined; frat basements are covered in "miscellaneous liquids," but people don't mind if a fracket gets wet, dirty, or stolen.

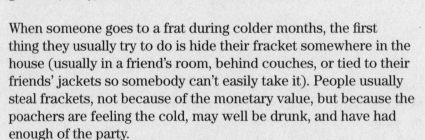

When someone goes to a frat during colder months, the first thing they usually try to do is hide their fracket somewhere in the house (usually in a friend's room, behind couches, or tied to their friends' jackets so somebody can't easily take it). People usually steal frackets, not because of the monetary value, but because the poachers are feeling the cold, may well be drunk, and have had enough of the party.

The unspoken rule is simple: if your fracket is stolen, tough luck. It stinks but you knew the risk of leaving your jacket in a frat, so it's fair game.

*Paulomi Rao is a student at Dartmouth College in New Hampshire. Her freshman year, someone grabbed her coat on a 3 degree Fahrenheit night so she had to walk back to her dorm across campus wrapped in a blanket to stay warm!*

**I FIND MYSELF BUYING UNDERWEAR** instead of actually doing laundry. My advice is to wait until after the holidays and get the holiday packs of boxers for $1.99 at the Gap. I do that a lot. I have a lot of boxers with holly on them. And you can get a lot of free T-shirts from clubs.
　　　—MARTIN
　　　　GEORGETOWN UNIVERSITY, SOPHOMORE

**❝ If at all possible, go to a school in a state where your grandmother lives an hour away and just take your laundry there. You need to visit her every once in a while, anyway. So take your laundry there; she'll cook you dinner. ❞**
　　　—ANONYMOUS
　　　　UNIVERSITY OF VIRGINIA, SOPHOMORE

**DON'T OVERSTUFF THE INCREDIBLY SMALL DORM WASHERS.** Your clothes won't get washed and you'll end up with detergent stains all over your white tank tops. Just pay the extra dollar and do another load.
　　　—SAMANTHA STACH
　　　　DUKE UNIVERSITY, JUNIOR

**IF YOU FIND YOURSELF IN THE LAUNDRY ROOM** and don't know how to wash your own clothes, do not push the "help" button. This button is for security purposes only; for example, if you are attacked. No little helper will come and help you wash your clothes. Instead, you will sound the alarm and call the police.
—*ANONYMOUS*
*UNIVERSITY OF PENNSYLVANIA, SENIOR*

. . . . . . . .

**I'VE BEEN DOING MY OWN LAUNDRY SINCE I WAS 12,** but in college, I got a really big laundry bag and saved it and took it home, an hour and a half away.
—*MELISSA K. BYRNES*
*AMHERST COLLEGE, GRADUATE*

. . . . . . . .

**COLLEGE IS A GREAT PLACE TO MEET** all kinds of new people. But sometimes you can get into a rut – your daily routine becomes so regimented that you don't encounter as many new people as you did in the beginning. That's when it's time to try something new or go someplace different. In my case, this was the laundry room. I found that on the rare occasions I went to the laundry room, I would make friends with one or two of the people waiting for their clothes to dry.
—*BRANDON W.*
*JAMES MADISON UNIVERSITY, SOPHOMORE*

. . . . . . . .

**THE TIME I GET UP DETERMINES WHAT I WEAR** to class. Sweats, sneakers, and slip-on shoes make it easy to hop out of bed and head to class. Unless I am going out with friends, I want to be comfortable when I am sitting at a desk.
—*DAVID*
*KEAN UNIVERSITY, JUNIOR*

**MAKE FRIENDS WITH KIDS** whose parents live close by and do laundry at their parents' house. I lugged laundry home on a two-hour train ride just so I didn't have to do it. It was a real pain. And do the essentials so that you don't run out of underwear and towels.
—*J.P.G.*
    *UNIVERSITY OF PENNSYLVANIA, SOPHOMORE*

* * * * * * * *

**IF YOU HAVE NO IDEA HOW TO DO LAUNDRY,** see it as an opportunity to meet your neighbors. Maybe three weeks into the year, a couple of girls I lived next to were going downstairs to do laundry, when some of the boys in our hall came up to us and confessed that they hadn't done their laundry yet because they didn't know how. So, we ended up going down the halls, asking boys if they knew how to do their laundry and we gathered a huge group of them and had a laundry class. They were helpless, like little puppies! We told them all about the washers and dryers and how to separate your whites from your colors. It was so frickin' cute!
—*MARY*
    *UNIVERSITY OF ARIZONA, GRADUATE*

* * * * * * * *

**ALLOT MORE TIME THAN YOU THINK IS NECESSARY TO DO LAUNDRY.** Sometimes you'll go back to the washer and find out it never actually started. Sometimes you'll have to run things through the dryer twice. One time I overfilled the washer, and ended up flooding the laundry room, so having manageable sized loads is a MUST. I think it's nice to wait five minutes after the timer expires before taking out someone's clothes, but after that, the machine is fair game. You shouldn't have to rearrange your schedule because someone else can't find the time to remove their clothes.
—*EMMA*
    *UNIVERSITY OF PENNSYLVANIA, GRADUATE*

**LITERALLY, JUST GOOGLE IT. EXAMPLE: "SIRI, GOOGLE HOW TO DO LAUNDRY."** It is not rocket science. I have faith that if you can understand special relativity in physics or Game Theory in Econ or how to hand sew an entire outfit in 2 days for fashion design, you can figure out how to do laundry.
　　—CHRISTINE
　　　DREXEL UNIVERSITY, JUNIOR

• • • • • • • •

**HAVING TO SHARE WASHERS/DRYERS WITH OTHER PEOPLE** is one of the things I hated most about college. Make sure, if you're leaving your laundry unattended in the machines, that you set a timer to get back BEFORE it's finished. The last thing you want is to walk into the room and someone has tossed all of your clothes onto the counter, or worse.
　　—ELISE
　　　WESTERN CAROLINA UNIVERSITY, GRADUATE

• • • • • • • •

**BEWARE OF WHAT YOU PUT** in the communal washing machines. When I was a freshman, I decided to wash my orange rug. There was so much lint on it that it got on everyone else's clothes in that washing machine. Everybody knew it came from me.
　　—GLENDA L. RICHARDSON
　　　DUKE UNIVERSITY, GRADUATE

• • • • • • • •

**I'M THE GIRL IN JEANS, A UNIVERSITY T-SHIRT, AND FLIP-FLOPS.** At the beginning of every fall semester I would see freshman girls walking around campus in high heels, and I would always smile and nod because I knew by the end of the day their feet would be in so much pain. The only advice I can give about fashion is to be comfortable in whatever you are wearing.
　　—QUONIAS
　　　UNIVERSITY OF WEST GEORGIA, SENIOR

# DO IT OFF-PEAK

**DO YOUR LAUNDRY IN THE MIDDLE OF THE WEEK,** not on the weekends.
—*KELLI*
*UNIVERSITY OF DELAWARE, SOPHOMORE*

. . . . . . . . .

**DO LAUNDRY IN THE MIDDLE OF THE NIGHT** or early in the morning – no one's there.
—*CASEY*
*GEORGETOWN UNIVERSITY, SENIOR*

. . . . . . . . .

**DO NOT DO LAUNDRY ON FRIDAY, SATURDAY, OR SUNDAY.**
Wait until Monday, midday, when most people are at class. The maintenance staff has already fixed the machines from the weekend, and you don't have to worry about people taking your laundry out.
—*H.D. BALLARD*
*UNIVERSITY OF VIRGINIA, FRESHMAN*

. . . . . . . . .

**I DO MY LAUNDRY SUNDAY MORNING.** I set my alarm clock early. By the end of the week, all my clothes are dirty, and during the week I don't have time.
—*AMY HOFFBERG*
*UNIVERSITY OF DELAWARE, FRESHMAN*

. . . . . . . . .

**IT WAS AN EXCITING ACCOMPLISHMENT** that I was able to take care of things like laundry by myself. I would wash my clothes at two in the morning. It was a relaxation thing. After I spent the whole night studying, I could just put my laundry in and watch it spin. I also realized I didn't have time to separate my clothes, so I just did everything in one cold batch.
—*ELIZABETH ROTH*
*UNIVERSITY OF PENNSYLVANIA, SENIOR*

**RESIST CONFORMITY.** We have too many Gap kids and Abercrombie look-alikes running around campus.
—*KHALIL SULLIVAN*
*PRINCETON UNIVERSITY, JUNIOR*

**EMBRACE YOUR ROOTS** and incorporate that into what you wear and how you go about your day. I'll wear my state's sports teams gear all the time and people will stop me and say, "I'm from Arizona!" or "I have a friend from Arizona and I'll introduce you!" Usually several questions come up immediately: Why did you go so far from home? What high school did you go to? Did our teams play each other in high school? How are you dealing with the winter? It's just really comforting to talk to someone from your home state, and it's a great way to meet people.
—*ANONYMOUS*
*LOYOLA UNIVERSITY IN CHICAGO, SOPHOMORE*

**I DO LAUNDRY A LOT, BETWEEN CLASSES** in the morning or afternoon, during the week, and on the weekend. I do it whenever I can, to get it out of the way.
—*JENNIFER A. SICKLICK*
*GEORGE WASHINGTON UNIVERSITY, FRESHMAN*

**YOU KNOW IT'S TIME** to do laundry when you run out of underwear. I know guys who said it was time to do laundry when you've worn your underwear inside out. That's pretty gross.
—*NAT*
*UNIVERSITY OF RHODE ISLAND, SOPHOMORE*

**BUY A LOT OF UNDERWEAR** before you go. You can wear jeans until they walk. But you have to wash your underwear.
—*CHRISTINE*
*UNIVERSITY OF RHODE ISLAND, SOPHOMORE*

**READ THE LABELS!** Whenever I did laundry, I made it a point to read the directions on the detergent boxes and the labels on the clothes. I also read the directions on the washing machines. I didn't want anything going wrong; clothes are too expensive!
—*JOSH*
*MISSOURI STATE UNIVERSITY, GRADUATE*

**NEVER, EVER MOVE SOMEONE'S LAUNDRY** from the dryer. I did this once. When I came to pick up my clothes, I found a girl sitting in a chair she'd dragged into the laundry room, waiting for me to come back so she could give me a piece of her mind.
—*ALLISON GRECO*
*MONTCLAIR STATE UNIVERSITY, GRADUATE*

**CONTRARY TO THE LAUNDRY INDUSTRY'S CLAIMS,** all clothes can be washed and dried in one load. Over time, this will amount to a considerable saving, as well as create more time for partying.
—*BRIAN TURNER*
*UNIVERSITY OF GEORGIA, GRADUATE*

**GET BACK TO THE LAUNDRY ROOM** on time! Time your cycles and don't be late. There were way too many times when people took my clean clothes out of the washing machine or dryer and put them on the dirty folding table.
—*RENE*
*DUKE UNIVERSITY, GRADUATE*

**MY WORST LAUNDRY EXPERIENCE** happened during my freshman year; someone stole all but four pairs of my jeans out of the laundry in my dorm. I was pissed off, but my parents gave me money for new clothes, so that was a plus.
—*M.G.*
*VALDOSTA STATE UNIVERSITY, SENIOR*

**LEARN ABOUT YOUR CAMPUS** before you decide to wear high heels! I've seen a girl fall down a hill in her stilettos – not a good look!
—*JANELLE*
*UNIVERSITY OF GEORGIA, JUNIOR*

• • • • • • • •

**SOME FRESHMEN TRY TOO HARD.** They try to be too radical, or too preppy. I mean, fashion is part of who you are. But don't try too hard.
—*THEODORE SCHIMENTI*
*COLUMBIA UNIVERSITY, FRESHMAN*

• • • • • • • •

**HOW TO MANIPULATE YOUR PARENTS** into doing your laundry: When my mom was scheduled to visit, I'd throw practically all my clothes – clean or dirty – around the room. I knew that she wouldn't be able to take the sight of it. She'd take my stuff, clean it, fold it, and bring it back. That's a service you just can't beat!
—*JENNY PRISUTA*
*YOUNGSTOWN STATE UNIVERSITY, SENIOR*

# LIZZIE'S 3 LAUNDRY TIPS

1. Don't let laundry (especially damp/sweaty clothes) sit around for weeks on end. It smells and your roommates will be angry.
2. When using a dorm laundry room, you have to be patient because everyone tends to leave their clothes in the washers and dryers until it's convenient to get them out, even though it's extremely inconvenient for everyone else. (Flip side of this: Time your laundry and get it out immediately. It's just common courtesy.)
3. Don't bring anything to school that's "hand-wash only" or "dry clean only." Unless you're a diehard fashionista and will go out of your way to find a dry-cleaner AND pay the extra money for it, you'll never get it washed and thus never wear it.

—*LIZZIE*
*BOWDOIN COLLEGE, FRESHMAN*

**AFTER LIVING IN THE DORM** for a week my friends and I decided that we needed to do laundry. Being the freshman that we were, we didn't want to leave the laundry room while our clothes were in the washer and dryer, so we stayed down there for the whole time. One of our friends brought down his iPod and speakers and we ended up having a dance party in the laundry room. It is one of my fondest college memories and we still talk about it today.

—ANNIE THOMAS
UNIVERSITY OF MICHIGAN, SENIOR

* * * * * * * *

> ## If it doesn't smell bad or have stains on it, it's not dirty.
>
> —HASSAN
> UNIVERSITY OF TULSA, GRADUATE

* * * * * * * *

**THE LAUNDRY ROOM IS A PRETTY COMPETITIVE SPOT.** Stay with your clothes while they are in the washer and dryer. Bring homework with you, your phone, your laptop, whatever. Don't leave! If you do, there is a significant chance you will come back to find your underwear strewn all over the room because someone wanted your machine. This will probably happen as you enter the laundry room with a member of the opposite sex.

—LAURA
HAMILTON COLLEGE, JUNIOR

* * * * * * * *

**IF YOU SEE A FREE LAUNDRY MACHINE,** grab it. I have a little card I keep with me that says, "Dibs on these machines – Molly." If I see a free machine, I put the card on it, run upstairs and get my clothes.

—MOLLY
BROWN UNIVERSITY, SOPHOMORE

Always dress a cut above the rest. College has a lot to do with image.

—*Sean Cameron*
*Princeton University, Sophomore*

I HEARD SOME HORROR STORIES about people's roommates forgetting to wash their sheets. That will keep people out of your room.
> —*Mike Parker*
> *Georgetown University, Sophomore*

• • • • • • • •

HANG UP CLOTHES IF THEY'RE NOT REALLY, really dirty. It keeps them from getting wrinkled.
> —*Joel*
> *Princeton University, Graduate*

• • • • • • • •

I NEVER DID MY OWN LAUNDRY before college, so I had no idea what to do. I felt embarrassed because I thought that I should know how to do this and I was the only one at college who didn't. But that isn't true; most people don't do their laundry at home. My roommates were more than happy to help me. My roommate and I pooled our laundry into one big laundry bin. The first couple of times, he did it. Then I took over.
> —*Dan Amerman*
> *Yale University, Sophomore*

• • • • • • • •

TIP: BLUE JEANS DON'T GET DIRTY FOR ROUGHLY SEVEN DAYS of consecutive use unless you spill something visible on them.
> —*Barry Langer*
> *Oglethorpe University, Junior*

# HOW TO MAKE YOUR OWN DETERGENT IF YOU'RE OUT

Melt a grated bar of soap in a saucepan over medium heat. Stir in a cup of water. Pour mixture into two gallons of hot water and mix well. Add 2 cups of baking soda (not baking powder). Now see if it works: Do a load of laundry with a cup of it.

# THE 'ROOM SERVICE' LIFE . . .

It's the end of a long week. You just finished a full day of class, there's hours of homework ahead, a club meeting to attend, plus your friends want to hang out. Exhausted, you go back to your messy dorm and find a huge pile of dirty clothes waiting for you.

As a new college student, you already have a lot on your plate. Fortunately, there are valet-like laundry services that can give you a hand. Used regularly, they will set you back, but for some, the convenience may be worth the price.

At the University of Pennsylvania, FirstServices offers once-a-week pickup for $600 per semester; $850 if you want the "executive" plan that picks up twice weekly. At other campuses, there are outside companies that do the job, including MyLazyBones.com and DormMom.com. With most of these services, you can pay a la carte or sign up online for a prepaid program and time that works best for you.

In most cases, laundry is returned, neatly packaged, within 24 to 48 hours, so you shouldn't be without your favorite jeans for long. UniversityLaundry.com, another service that covers multiple campuses, actually promises to return everything "impeccably folded," suitable for display.

Many of the services also affix barcodes that allow you to track your clothes.

Bear in mind that habitual use of these services could add up to $1,600 or so, over the course of a 32-week school year. Far more than you'd spend if you went to the laundromat yourself with your own suds to do the same two loads every week.

Of course, the services would much rather you focused on all the time you'll be saving rather than the dent in your or your parents' pocketbook. "With this service," DormMom crows, "you will never worry about laundry day again while you are in school and can focus on what matters most – getting a 4.0 GPA." Likewise,

UniversityLaundry.com reassures customers that they can regain many of the 96 hours a year they would otherwise be stuck in laundry rooms: "That's four complete 24-hour days doing laundry ... washing, waiting for a dryer, and folding your clothes."

Granted, there are better things to be doing in college than waiting for the dry cycle to finish up. But you might just bring a book with you to the laundry room, while you wait. Just think of all the money you'll save.

*Catherine Oriel is a student journalist at George Washington University, who does some of her best thinking in campus laundry rooms while waiting for her towels to dry.*

# ... VS. THE SELF-SERVICE LIFE

**DOING YOUR OWN LAUNDRY IS AN IMPORTANT LIFE SKILL.** Doing laundry as a freshman at Penn isn't difficult. The washing machines and dryers are completely free, so you can separate your clothes into as many different loads as you need. I've heard of some schools charging almost $2 per wash and dry. In my dorm, it's a two-minute walk to the laundry room, so convenience and wasting time isn't an issue. There's even an app you can use that will let you know when your cycle is completed.

I understand that not everyone knew how to do laundry coming into college; I didn't start doing my own until high school! However, it wasn't hard to learn and the machines were easy to figure out. If you use Tide Pods, you don't have to worry about measuring detergent or any of that fuss. All you have to do is learn what temperature water to wash your clothes in and how to separate them! It blows my mind that 18- and 19-year-olds are having their parents pay for a laundry service. In my opinion, that's completely unnecessary.
—SYDNEY
UNIVERSITY OF PENNSYLVANIA, FRESHMAN

"I told her she needs to make new friends in college, but she's having trouble letting go of high school."

# Getting Along: Making Friends & Talking to Strangers

*I*f you're like many prospective frosh, you may be nervous about making new friends and maintaining the high school friendships that matter. It may be comforting to know that everyone else feels the same way, too. Apps such as FaceTime have made it easier (and cheaper) than ever to stay in touch with close friends from home.

And the good news is, there's no easier place to meet people than colleges that are filled with other people your age, all trying to make friends. What's more, there's no buddy like a college buddy. Going through college together is one of the most powerful bonding experiences two humans could ever hope to share. So go ahead and introduce yourself! Chances are, that person over there is shyer than you are.

**SURROUND YOURSELF WITH GOOD PEOPLE.** It's more about quality than quantity when it comes to friends.
—JESSICA
BARNARD COLLEGE, JUNIOR

**IT TAKES TIME TO MEET GOOD FRIENDS.**
—ZAK AMCHISLAVSKY
GEORGETOWN
UNIVERSITY, SENIOR

- Reuniting with your old friends can be strange when you realize you all have new lives.

- Be open to meeting new people, but remember it's the quality – not quantity – of people around you that matters.

- It can take some time to make new friends at college; be patient.

You are going to meet so many different people every day. Just stay open.

—*LINA J.*
*GEORGIA STATE UNIVERSITY, SOPHOMORE*

**SIT WITH STRANGERS IN THE DINING HALL.** It's the best way to meet new people! Just remember to put yourself out there; almost everyone else is in the same situation as you when it comes to trying to make new friends!

—*NATHALIE*
*RUTGERS UNIVERSITY, GRADUATE*

. . . . . . . . .

**I MADE A BUNCH OF FRIENDS** that, coming out of high school, I wouldn't have expected to be my friends. And that was great. You gotta go to clubs, take risks, talk to people. Really anyone can be your best friend but you gotta say hi.

—*MATT*
*TUFTS UNIVERSITY, SOPHOMORE*

. . . . . . . . .

**FRESHMAN YEAR OF COLLEGE WAS A BIG STEP IN MY LIFE.** It was the first time I was on my own, the first time I was in a different state, and the first time I depended on myself. Surrounding yourself with a couple of friends to help you alleviate stress is a good idea, and talking to people who went through the same things I was, made me believe in myself. They helped me see that everything is achievable.

—*BRYANT FOSTON*
*UNIVERSITY OF BRIDGEPORT, GRADUATE*

**ICE-BREAKER GAMES WORK.** I met some of my really good friends doing those games where I was thinking: 'Is this dumb?' I was playing one where you try to find something in common with the person standing across from you and this girl goes, "I'm from Phoenix." Immediately I was like 'Okay, we're friends!' It was so cool to find someone who knew everything about where I'm from being so far away. She's one of my best friends now.
　　　　—RHETTA
　　　　UNIVERSITY OF NOTRE DAME, SOPHOMORE

   • • • • • • • •

" Sometimes, if you're confused, just look for other confused people. You can just ask them a question and be like 'I totally don't know what I'm doing,' and then you just bond because you're both confused. "
　　　　—DANIELLE
　　　　SUSQUEHANNA UNIVERSITY, SOPHOMORE

   • • • • • • • •

**IT'S FAR TOO EASY TO MAKE FRIENDS** in college. What is difficult is weeding through the self-serving jerks and spending as much time as possible with your true crew. But make it your first priority. These select people are the key to eternal happiness and enlightenment.
　　　　—JOHN
　　　　UNIVERSITY OF WISCONSIN AT MADISON, GRADUATE

**REMEMBER THAT YOU'RE NOT THE ONLY ONE** who's starting from scratch with few or no friends. Most of the people there are in the same situation. And most colleges have events for freshmen, especially if you live in a dorm. They will usually involve free food or a movie. Go, even if you don't like the food or the movie. At least you'll have the opportunity to meet people. That's the whole point! It'll give you something to talk about with the person later ("Wasn't the food last night horrible?").
　　　　—*LAUREN TAYLOR*
　　　　　*UNIVERSITY OF GEORGIA, GRADUATE*

. . . . . . . .

**THE BEST THING ABOUT COLLEGE** is that your friends are there. If you think that you're weird because you love Judy Garland, or superheroes, or the smell of books or whatever, your friends are still there. Your friends were probably there in high school as well, but this time there's more of them. And these friends are great, great people who are going to support you through everything, but are also going to sit you down if you're completely and utterly wrong.
　　　　—*SHANNON KELLEY*
　　　　　*KENYON COLLEGE, JUNIOR*

. . . . . . . .

**TRY AND FIND A FEW UPPERCLASSMEN FRIENDS,** who can help you find new classes, meet new people, and broaden your perspective from the typical freshman experience. I had one guy on my hall who would talk to me every night when we would brush our teeth, and he would always invite me to things, or just ask me about school and stuff. It was good to have someone like that. Some people use RAs, bible study leaders, group presidents – whatever it is, it's important to realize that you're here with 3 other classes of awesome and successful Tar Heels, not just your own year.
　　　　—*BEN MILLER*
　　　　　*UNIVERSITY OF NORTH CAROLINA AT CHAPEL HILL, SENIOR*

IT's VERY EASY FOR A GIRL to find guy friends. My freshman year all my friends at first were guys. I loved the attention and they were cool to hang out with. But while other girls were making friendships with girls that were solid, I was not. So, when I hit a rough time and needed a female shoulder to cry on, it was not there. This was a big mistake I paid for dearly.

—K.E.
CARNEGIE MELLON UNIVERSITY, JUNIOR

WALK TO CLASSES WHEN YOU CAN. It's good for you and it will give you a chance to get to know the campus. Notice the people around you. Take time out of your day to sit on a bench and look at your surroundings. Be friendly; make the effort to say hello, even if the other person looks grumpy.

—J.S.
UNIVERSITY OF GEORGIA, GRADUATE

## ASK A GRAD... OR MAYBE NOT

# 5 GOOD CONVERSATION STARTERS FOR MEETING NEW FRIENDS IN CLASS:

1. "My name is Artie. It's short for Artichoke."
2. "If Fifty Shades of Grey isn't on the reading list, then why are we even here?"
3. "Want some gum? It's from Vietnam and it's banned everywhere else."
4. "This is Advanced Dianetics, right? I need some science courses for my minor."
5. "I got to take classes from prison, too, but these are much better. I bet the warden hasn't even noticed I'm gone."

*Val Bodurtha is a Chicago-based writer and comedian.*

# FRIENDS FROM 'BEFORE'

GOING HOME FOR THE FIRST TIME is a combination of the best and worst feelings you will ever have. Although it is fabulous to hook back up with the old crowd, party where you used to, and possibly rediscover that old flame, it is also very hard to realize that every one of your friends now has a life that is completely separate from your experience. Sometimes reuniting is not the celebration you thought it would be. Acknowledge your differences and enjoy your friends for who they are. Look at photos, hear crazy stories, and go out and have fun together, but always remember that things have changed (which is not necessarily a bad thing.) And never go back to the old ex; it only ends in trouble.
> —*A.*
>     *PRINCETON UNIVERSITY, FRESHMAN*

• • • • • • • • •

IT'S UNFAIR TO COMPARE YOUR NEW FRIENDS TO YOUR OLD ONES. There are a lot of people where if I see them around campus I can say, "Oh, hey, what's up?" We know each other but it's nothing super-personal. My new friends at college feel more superficial. But a lot of my friends from high school I've known for four years or even longer, and the ones I've met in college I've only known for one year.
> —*PAT*
>     *GONZAGA UNIVERSITY, SOPHOMORE*

• • • • • • • • •

IF I COULD GO BACK AND CHANGE ONE THING, I would not try as hard to keep in touch with everyone from my small high school graduating class. I would have focused more on securing more meaningful relationships in college and on my studies.
> —*DAVID*
>     *ANDERSON UNIVERSITY, SENIOR*

• • • • • • • • •

SAVE HIGH SCHOOL FRIENDS FOR DRUNK-DIALING. Or for face-to-face contact on breaks.
> —*J.V.*
>     *THE COLLEGE OF WILLIAM & MARY, GRADUATE*

I HAVE ONE LIFE BACK HOME, and now I'm starting up a new life. In the beginning it's hard; you want to maintain your old life. But you also have to realize that you're maturing and changing.
—MATT MONACO
GEORGE WASHINGTON UNIVERSITY, FRESHMAN

INVITE YOUR HIGH SCHOOL FRIENDS over for a couple of days. The ones who stay in touch are the ones worth keeping for a lifetime.
—KHALIL SULLIVAN
PRINCETON UNIVERSITY, JUNIOR

I WENT TO COLLEGE PLANNING ON STAYING IN CLOSE CONTACT with all my "friends" in high school – all 200 of them. I had to learn that being a social person did not mean I had to talk to everyone I was friends with in high school on a regular basis. With my true friends, I found the best thing to do was send an encouraging or "just saying hi" text message or email to those I really cared about when I didn't have time to have a long conversation.
—MERELISE HARTE ROUZER
GEORGIA INSTITUTE OF TECHNOLOGY, SOPHOMORE

WHEN I MET MY BEST FRIEND, she was crying in her bed in our freshman dorm. She had a long-distance boyfriend. She was from the mountains of Georgia. I'm from St. Louis. I went to a private Catholic girls' school. She went to a public school with people with gun racks on their cars. We couldn't be more different. But we had a class together and one day, after I found her crying, she overslept. So I was like, "Oh, I'll call you in the morning," and we started walking to class together, and we got breakfast after class. We became friends.
—J. DEVEREUX
GEORGETOWN UNIVERSITY, GRADUATE

**YOU MEET THE RIGHT PEOPLE WHEN YOU NEED THEM THE MOST.** I hope that the friends you make from the start are there at the end of your four years and beyond, but sometimes they won't be. Some of my very best friends came during my junior year, while my Day 1 friendships dwindled in the distance.
—*DANIELLE FOWLER*
*ELON UNIVERSITY, GRADUATE*

. . . . . . . .

**MAKE REAL EFFORTS TO BE WITH YOUR FRIENDS,** even if you're just doing dumb stuff like watching a movie or painting your nails. This is the only time in life where you'll be living with all your friends, and you'll miss it when it's gone.
—*JULIE*
*PRINCETON UNIVERSITY, SOPHOMORE*

. . . . . . . .

**RATHER THAN LOOKING FOR COOL KIDS** to be friends with, find people you just really get along with. I ended up being friends with people across the hall – they were nice, and really into music. They didn't go out every night but that was better. I haven't heard of a lot of people who go out every night who have a good academic standing!
—*MATTHEW GUTSHALL*
*ST. JOSEPH'S, JUNIOR*

. . . . . . . .

**WHOM YOU HANG OUT WITH IS IMPORTANT.** You have to look at it as an extension of high school: there are still going to be different groups and cliques, and you have to make sure you don't hang out with the partyers too much. It's good once in a while, but I suggest having a core group of friends that are motivators and that really help you stay on track and go to class. The freedom in college can be great, but it can also get you in trouble. You need to stay motivated.
—*JESSICA DOSHNA*
*UCLA, GRADUATE*

**YOU DON'T HAVE TO BE BEST FRIENDS WITH THE FIRST PEOPLE YOU MEET.** During the first few days and weeks of school, everyone is desperately trying to make friends and no one wants to be alone. The first person I met was a girl whom I became good friends with at the beginning of freshman year, but I realized we had too many differences and it became too hard to be friends with her. I never made the effort to branch out because I didn't really feel like making new friends. So I decided to cling to her and be best friends, but I regret doing that. I'm glad I finally I branched out and became more social since I found my true best friends eventually. It's okay if you feel a bit lonely along the way.
—*ANONYMOUS*
*FORDHAM UNIVERSITY, JUNIOR*

**BEING FRIENDS WITH UPPERCLASSMEN** can help you prepare for tougher assignments.
—*MORGAN KREIN*
*DAKOTA STATE UNIVERSITY, JUNIOR*

**PRACTICE YOUR HANDSHAKE AND GO INTRODUCE YOURSELF** to people. When I got up to school, this kid stuck out his hand and I instinctively tried to dap him up – which is this NJ thing that kids do, kind of like a high-five. It was pretty awkward. I quickly realized that everyone was going around shaking hands and introducing themselves. It didn't make sense to stand there acting too cool to meet anyone. I decided to just go for it. It was the first time I'd ever stuck out my hand and introduced myself to someone who wasn't my parents' age or older. When I saw my friends back home at Thanksgiving, they all said they'd noticed the handshake thing, too.
—*OLIVER MENKEN*
*TUFTS UNIVERSITY, SOPHOMORE*

**MAKE FRIENDS WITH PEOPLE WHO ARE NOT FRESHMEN.**
Doing organizations on campus helps you meet older students. Now that I'm a senior, I have a big network of friends outside of college, that I can ask for advice about things I'm about to do.
　　—CATIE
　　　　HARVARD COLLEGE, SENIOR

• • • • • • • •

" Introduce yourself to everyone; it makes a difference. If you continue to say hi to people, you'll get to know people. Not everyone will be your best friend, but you'll get there. You'll have new friends. "
　—J. DEVEREUX
　　GEORGETOWN UNIVERSITY, GRADUATE

• • • • • • • •

**DON'T LET THINGS THAT BOTHER YOU LINGER TOO LONG.**
My friend went out with a guy that I had been seeing. That hurt my feelings. Instead of resolving the problem immediately, I waited until I was too angry to discuss it like a rational adult. I learned later that she honestly never intended to hurt me. But since I waited until I was furious, her feelings got hurt and she never got over it. Our friendship never fully recovered.
　　—ERIN
　　　　CENTRAL BIBLE COLLEGE, GRADUATE

**MAKING FRIENDS WAS MY NUMBER-ONE** worry before going to college. I'm incredibly shy; during orientation week, I didn't go to half the planned activities for my dorm. Before I knew it, everyone had settled into their own groups. One day I was talking to my mom about a bench-painting event going on at my dorm; she encouraged me to just go outside. So, I did; by the end of the day, I had a dinner date with the girl who is now my closest friend. Talk to random people because you'll find something you have in common to bond over. With my friend Carrie it was a love for Cosmic Cantina chicken burritos.

— *SAMANTHA STACH*
 *DUKE UNIVERSITY, JUNIOR*

* * * * * * * *

**THE BEST WAY TO MAKE FRIENDS IN COLLEGE** is to cling to them and never, ever let them out of your sight. You might think I'm kidding, but I'm not. The first time I hung out with my closest friend in college, we just ate ice cream and watched "Doogie Howser." Neither of us particularly enjoyed the show, and we didn't seem to have much in common, except that we were both nervous and desperate. Bam! Friendship. Before long, we texted each other before every meal and hung out in each other's room every night. Obviously, we needed to make more friends, but we were both at a loss as to how to find them. Fortunately, we figured out the eating schedule of a group of kids we liked and stalked them mercilessly, pretending that we just happened to run into them every day. (My school is really small, so that's not too unbelievable.) And to everyone's surprise, it didn't end in a restraining order but in real friendship. I still consider my friends in college to be the coolest people I've ever met.

— *SHANNON KELLEY*
 *KENYON COLLEGE, JUNIOR*

Go meet new people; they won't bite!

—*JANELLE*
 *UNIVERSITY OF GEORGIA, JUNIOR*

# TELLTALE SIGNS OF A PATHOLOGICAL LIAR

- HE looks healthy, but suffers mysterious, highly-contagious, but blessedly brief, illnesses that render him (sadly) unavailable to attend certain events with you.
- He calls out "Baby," "Honey," "Gorgeous" or "Sugar" – never your first name – when things start to get steamy.
- He is fond of quoting entire scenes from "The Talented Mr. Ripley."
- When you express interest in meeting his family, he all but claims they're in witness protection.
- A never-mentioned female "cousin" suddenly visits campus, bunks with him for an entire weekend and is inexplicably "too busy to meet you."

---

- SHE begs off the weekend's light-cleaning session because of debilitating Lyme Disease pain, but, later, you find beastly pics of her navigating Tough Mudder obstacles.
- Multiple Instagram profiles feature endless selfies with celebrities, annual Habitat for Humanity builds and videos of puppies learning to swim.
- During your visit to her family home, elementary-school albums go missing and parents seem nervous when asked about having raised kids in Tanzania and summited Kilimanjaro.
- When confronted about her habit of sending raunchy texts to *your* bae, she claims she was merely testing his faithfulness, then reminds you she's your dearest friend.
- In the dorm room you two share, you accidentally uncover transcript showing she aced "Photoshop for Dummies" the previous semester. (Under piles of restraining orders filed by former friends, lovers, and even some celebrities.)

*Rebecca R. Ayars is a Connecticut-based writer who enjoys exploring stories about the arts, wildlife, and sometimes, fellow humans.*

I HANG OUT WITH ABOUT FIVE PERCENT of the people that I hung out with freshman year. You hung out with them because you had to spend time with them; they were on your floor. But then you figure out whom you like.

—ZAK AMCHISLAVSKY
GEORGETOWN UNIVERSITY, SENIOR

I'VE LEARNED THAT PEOPLE CARE if you spare enough time in your day to think about them and send them something, even if it's just a stupid meme. I think that's enough to even get a little bit of a conversation going, get people to remember you, and get talking again, even if it's only for a little bit – as long as you are still putting in the time and effort, even if it's just occasionally, to make someone a part of your life. I have definitely blown up a friendship if someone didn't choose to make time for me anymore. I think you need to be willing to do a little bit of a give-and-take.

—IRIS CHIOU
UNIVERSITY OF CHICAGO, GRADUATE

BE YOURSELF! A lot of people change themselves to impress others, and that's pretty stupid in my opinion. There are people out there who will like you for you!

—MELANIE
UNIVERSITY OF THE SCIENCES IN PHILADELPHIA, GRADUATE

PICK A DAY – FOR ME IT WAS SUNDAY AFTERNOONS – where you sit down and text or call all the people you haven't spoken to in a while. Maybe a friend you had in class last semester.

—R.S.
GUILFORD COLLEGE, GRADUATE

**IF YOU'RE THE KIND OF PERSON** who studies alone, you're not going to be finding a support system by focusing on classes. You need to make sure you're finding a support system in your new environment.
> —EMILY
> HARVARD COLLEGE, SENIOR

• • • • • • • •

**BE PREPARED TO BE A FRIEND TO SOMEONE IN NEED.** College is hard, and we all need someone to study, eat dinner, laugh, and cry with.
> —SAKIYA GALLON
> UNIVERSITY OF THE SCIENCES IN PHILADELPHIA, GRADUATE

# FREE SPEECH ON CAMPUS

*College campuses in the United States have long been a hotbed of protest and passionate politics. Recently, though, the rhetoric has become so heated that the very idea of universities serving as places that encourage the free-wheeling exchange of ideas has come under fire. Fights break out on some campuses if you choose the wrong hummus in the dining hall, wear the wrong costume at Halloween, or attend a lecture that others feel should not be taking place. Look no further than what happened at the College of William & Mary, where a representative of The American Civil Liberties Union, there to discuss "Students and the First Amendment," was drowned out by protestors and denied the chance to address students, from the podium or one-on-one.*

*What can you do if you find yourself in the silenced minority? Will friends and professors stand by you if you voice opinions outside the mainstream? Does it matter if the speech under attack took place in a classroom, versus, say, the Internet? Are some topics just too hot to broach? Some schools now try to keep the peace by imposing gag orders on students they deem to be "disruptive." But what exactly constitutes "disruptive" – and who decides? Do students have any recourse, or should they just bite their tongues for four years? Read on to hear how other students grappled with these pressing issues.*

**SAY WHAT YOU WANT, BUT KNOW THAT YOUR WORDS HAVE CONSEQUENCES.** Sure, freedom of speech is an American right, but if you're living in a dorm or on campus, your school likely has rules that would override that right at times. Freedom of speech in college doesn't give you the right to be rude and say racial slurs whenever you want. Or to make a sly comment about that bombshell in room 1205. If you think you have that right to freedom of speech, you will quickly find yourself facing Student Conduct. Just be mindful of what you say, and try to use inclusive language. No one can stop you from saying anything, but you can – and likely will – face consequences for inappropriate comments.

—*CHRISTINE*
*DREXEL UNIVERSITY, JUNIOR*

**MY FIRST DAY OF CLASS,** a department chair said something that stuck with me. He said, "It's possible to go through four years of college unscathed by education. It's a tragedy if that happens." He went on to say that college is about challenging all of your preconceived notions; from your personal values to your religious values to your social values to your political values. If you have a real college experience, it should all be challenged. If you don't have the courage to face that, you're not getting as much out of college as you could. Be prepared to be challenged.
—*MICHAEL A. FEKULA*
*UNIVERSITY OF MARYLAND, GRADUATE*

. . . . . . . .

**HAVE AN OPEN MIND ABOUT ABSOLUTELY EVERYTHING** and question authority the good ol' fashioned way. Of course, always be respectful. Your friends, your professors, and your school administrators don't have any more of a claim on what is true than you do. If they're pushing a line you don't agree with, that's okay. And if they're pushing a line you do agree with, that's okay too, but never forget that the world is a lot bigger than your college campus and even if everyone agrees inside its gates, you're going to need to convince people outside the gates as well. Practice doing that.
—*MAX*
*DARTMOUTH COLLEGE, GRADUATE*

. . . . . . . .

**I TOOK A BREAK FROM THE PAGAN MYSTICISM GROUP** in my junior and senior year because everybody was very opinionated to the point where that was the only correct opinion and there was only a certain way to go about being pagan, when, in actuality, it varies, depending on the individual. If you get into environments like that, it can feel really isolated if you don't completely conform or agree with a lot of the more popular opinions.
—*SHELBY SMITH*
*GUILFORD COLLEGE, GRADUATE*

**TAKE THE OPPORTUNITY TO PARTICIPATE IN CLASS.** Never again in your life will you be confronted with such an open forum for sharing ideas; this is the time to develop your skills to make a persuasive point.
—*SCOTT WOELFEL*
*UNIVERSITY OF MISSOURI, GRADUATE*

* * * * * * * *

**SOME PROFESSORS WILL HUMILIATE YOU.** For my university writing course, I had to write a paper based on some personal experience. I spoke about a friend whose dad happened to be a truck driver, and stated in my paper, "...my friend's dad who was a truck driver," which apparently offended my professor to the point where she berated me in front of my entire class, calling me a spoiled, rich, white boy. Needless to say, I did not enjoy that class anymore.
—*MAX*
*GEORGE WASHINGTON UNIVERSITY, GRADUATE*

* * * * * * * *

**I HAVE ONE REALLY GOOD FRIEND WHO IS REALLY PRO-LIFE AND ANOTHER WHO IS VERY PRO-CHOICE.** They wrote editorials in the student newspaper back and forth at each other for about 3 weeks. I respect both of these people a lot. I think they're both smart and both very good people. Being so close with both of them, I found it interesting to see that they were both making very valid points and both really believed in what they were saying. But I also realized that they were never going to agree because they just see things in a different way. Neither of them was wrong, I thought, but neither of them was completely right. I talked to both of them individually because I felt that it was important to understand where both of them were coming from. It made me realize that it's not about being right. It's about understanding the other person and seeing both sides.
—*RHETTA*
*UNIVERSITY OF NOTRE DAME, SOPHOMORE*

# THE POWER OF LISTENING

It's easy to come from a small town, a fishbowl of harmony, where the biggest controversy concerned who got cast as the lead in the musical, and think that freedom of speech always benefits the community and advances interests. But, unfortunately, that can be an ignorant opinion.

Something I've learned from my time in higher education is that a lot of kids are born and raised behind a shiny window of privilege. Everyone inside the room looks and thinks a lot like them, with similar backgrounds and ideals, and it's not until someone who doesn't look like them, think like them, or, at the very least, was raised behind a different window enters the room that they realize that different norms exist. It's not until something cracks the pane that they even see the glass in the first place.

It's easy to speak your mind when everyone around you was raised the same way. It's easy to make fun of a culture you know nothing about when everyone in the room knows nothing about them, too.

College is the first time that a lot of kids are exposed to so many passionate people from all over, and this allows for a melting pot of ideologies and cultures. A racial slang word that may have flown under the radar in your hometown could be met with resentment on your campus, and the uncensored rantings from a classmate about their religion may upset you. America is founded on people being able to voice these things and not face consequences, but America was founded by a bunch of old white men, and, in 2018, we know these aren't the only people who can speak and be heard.

Freedom of all kinds of speech can ruffle feathers, cause divisions and allow the seeds of intolerance to be sown. My advice is to listen closely to the community that surrounds you, think about what you say, and understand that whatever privilege you may know from a life before this may not be treated with the same care here. Fully unadulterated freedom of speech is a nice thought, but the basic human rights of others is even nicer. Try not to cross the line there.

—HANNAH BENSON
ELON UNIVERSITY, SENIOR

**YOU HAVE TO PUT YOURSELF IN POSITIONS WHERE YOUR BELIEFS ARE QUESTIONED** and you feel uncomfortable. Before taking this particular U.S. History class, I had a strong sense of nationalist pride in America. The class tried that pride almost to a breaking point. There was a focus on civil rights and women's rights and I remember feeling kind of attacked as a man in the class, and never once raised my hand to ask a question. I felt trapped in a kind of perpetual roast. It was an uncomfortable experience, but the fact is that horrendous things were done to women and minorities in our country and that was something I had to face as a white male.

It wasn't offensive to me but it certainly tried my beliefs. You don't have a right to not be offended. If that existed, you'd have to acknowledge that others don't have the right to free speech. To be shaped, you need to be exposed to fire. It's only through uncomfortable experiences that you can test the foundations of your own beliefs.

—*MICHAEL*
*NORTHERN ARIZONA UNIVERSITY, GRADUATE*

• • • • • • • •

**IT IS VERY IMPORTANT TO BE ABLE TO SPEAK YOUR MIND, BUT A PERSON WHO JUST TALKS AND DOESN'T LISTEN IS JUST LIKE A RADIO.** While college can be a bedrock for growth, this can only come when you listen to others. Take what people believe seriously, and take what you believe seriously.

—*ANONYMOUS*
*GEORGETOWN UNIVERSITY, JUNIOR*

• • • • • • • •

**FREE SPEECH IS GREAT, BUT DON'T GET SO CARRIED AWAY** exercising free speech rights that you forget what you're on campus for, i.e. to study.

—*LI*
*UNIVERSITY OF TORONTO, GRADUATE*

**KNOW THE DIFFERENCE** between an idea you don't agree with and a comment that is offensive in a malicious way. You can complain about the latter, but you should embrace the former.

I was in a very small ethnic studies class during my freshman year. We were discussing religion and the professor made an off-hand comment about how, although Catholics find the Eucharist to be so special, it is really just 'a piece of bread.' He chuckled and everyone else in the class kind of laughed, but as a Catholic myself, I was pretty shocked. No teacher would make an equivalently disparaging comment about a race or gender issue. He wasn't presenting an idea or philosophy that I disagreed with. It was just a side joke at the expense of something that was sacred to others. Different perspectives are so important to learn but hurtful and belittling comments are unnecessary.
—*MEGHAN WALLACE*
*NORTHERN ARIZONA UNIVERSITY, SENIOR*

• • • • • • • •

**IF YOU'RE PUT IN AN UNCOMFORTABLE SITUATION** where sensitive topics are brought up, be considerate of what other people have to say and be sure that you're including other people's opinions. I'm part of a theater group at school. We were trying to narrow down a list of plays to put on and one of the plays proposed had an all-female cast. When we were discussing it I said, "Maybe we shouldn't do a play with only women." Immediately, I was laughed at and mocked for bringing that up. They were agreeing with me, but they were very condescending in their tone. The way they responded shut me down and made me afraid to speak my mind in the future. I was a new member of the group and I wanted to be accepted and I felt like I needed to shut up. People should be comfortable with sharing what they believe and other people should be comfortable hearing it.
—*BEN LEACH*
*JOHNS HOPKINS UNIVERSITY, SOPHOMORE*

IT'S IMPORTANT TO FEEL COMFORTABLE with your own opinions, but you should also be willing to hear out others, which may even lead to your own opinions changing. College was the place where I met more people of different backgrounds, race, religion, and nationality than I ever had before. As a result, my worldview expanded dramatically, and I began to see many issues in a different light. But there's a difference between the right to express your opinion and the right to say anything that pops into your head, especially when it's hurtful toward a disadvantaged group, or is factually incorrect. This past year, a hate group has been on campus, singling out sections of society as well as individuals, and saying nasty things about them. While it's questionable at best that they're protected by a right to free speech, it's not questionable that what they say is hurtful and cruel. This type of speech should be ignored or at the very least approached with caution, since the speakers' goal is to incite a reaction.

—EMMA
UNIVERSITY OF PENNSYLVANIA, GRADUATE

"Can I stay in your room tonight? Looks like Jacob finally got a date."

# 15

# Going Out, Getting Serious: Dating & Sex

Tinder, Title IX, the long-distance bae back home versus the cutie in your chem class. There's a lot to sort out when it comes to dating on campus, now more than ever. The natural urges of hormonal youth are intense and if you're healthy, you're no exception – that's just how it should be.

College is a wonderful time to explore the glorious terrain of love and lust, but things don't always go so smoothly, and, as headlines keep illustrating, not everyone wants to be revisiting the wild and crazy things they did at 18 when they are 50. Fortunately, many have come before you. Take their wisdom to heart and proceed with caution.

WHEN YOU'RE NOT PAYING ATTENTION, that's when someone will be looking at you.
—SARAH
GEORGIA INSTITUTE OF TECHNOLOGY, GRADUATE

IF YOU'RE LOOKING FOR LOVE, BE PATIENT.
—K.
PRINCETON UNIVERSITY, JUNIOR

**HEADLINES**

- ■ Don't leave a high school sweetheart waiting at home – you'll miss out on a lot of dating.
- ■ Frat parties are not the best places to look for long-term relationships.
- ■ Avoid dating someone in your dorm – breakups can be very messy.

**YOUR FIRST SEMESTER, DON'T DATE.** You're still trying to get settled in college, you're making some new friends, you're dealing with all the anxiety of being away from your family and high-school friends, you're trying to get into classes that are much harder than you've had before. There's a lot of stress that first semester. Whether you're a guy or girl, you've got four or five years, and maybe after college, to meet the right person. Enjoy the freedom and you'll have a lot more fun that way.
—*C.W.*
*RHODES COLLEGE, SENIOR*

. . . . . . . .

**DON'T DATE PEOPLE ON YOUR FLOOR.** Don't date people in your clubs. Do date their friends. One degree of separation is perfect.
—*VALERIE BODURTHA*
*UNIVERSITY OF CHICAGO, GRADUATE*

. . . . . . . .

**DON'T TRUST PEOPLE** as quickly as you might want to. As a freshman girl, you could get in a lot of trouble if you don't watch yourself. Listen to your friends when they say you shouldn't do something. They probably know something more than you. You probably won't listen to them; but you should.
—*LAUREN*
*GEORGETOWN UNIVERSITY, SOPHOMORE*

**YOU COME TO COLLEGE** and there are women everywhere; that's probably the best thing about it. But you have to have your act together. If you don't have your obligations in order, you're never going to make it. I've seen people fail out of college in the first year. But if you have your time managed right, there's nothing you can't do.
—*CHRIS M.*
*UNIVERSITY OF DELAWARE, JUNIOR*

**SOME GUYS ARE GREAT;** some guys are not so great. Coming to school, no one has a past; people are going to be pushing the image they want you to see. So many people put up a front. They are who they're not. You can't possibly trust someone if you've just met them, so take time to get to know people. And don't have a relationship your first semester.
—*KERRY*
*GEORGETOWN UNIVERSITY, GRADUATE*

**A GREAT PLACE TO MEET GIRLS** is at the bookstore. Upon receiving the class syllabus, you have to buy books. If you're in the bookstore and you see a girl buying books, it's an easy entrance: "Oh, are you taking history?"
—*J.R.*
*COLUMBIA UNIVERSITY, GRADUATE*

# MIND THE (GENDER) GAP

According to government statistics, there are 9.5 million women in college, and only 7.5 million men! Put another way, 56 percent of all undergrads are women, and 44 percent are men. At Hampshire College, the ratio is even more lopsided: 62 percent of the student body are female.

I WASN'T A VERY PROMISCUOUS GUY in high school so the thought of going to a frat party with two kegs, tons of 21-year-old frat guys who knew what they were doing and a bunch of scantily-clad women was terrifying. I went, though, and eventually got used to it. You have to be proactive or else you won't get what you want. Do anything – talk to girls, talk to guys, dance, or have a drink. I swallowed my pride and accepted that there is nothing wrong with someone saying to you, "I'm not interested." If you can't accept that, you might as well not even bother.

—MICHAEL
NORTHWESTERN UNIVERSITY, SOPHOMORE

# ADVICE FOR THE DATELORN

IT'S A MISTAKE TO START DATING the first few weeks of college. I mean, compared to high school, college is paradise for dating: you're surrounded by people with your interests, you can stay up late, go to parties whenever you want, you can sleep together and not worry about parents – it's amazing. But be patient. There's this huge rush to date someone, but it's important to make friends first. That way, when you break up with someone, you still have your friends. If you start dating someone right away, you may miss out on making real friends, and that's more important.

Date someone who is also a freshman. In the first few months of school, it's hard to really relate to someone who's older. Plus, if you date someone who's older, it takes you away from your dorm and first-year activities; it almost makes you skip your first year. If you date someone who is also a freshman, you can go through freshman year together.

—SUMMER J.
UNIVERSITY OF VIRGINIA, SENIOR

**DON'T BELIEVE THAT AN UPPERCLASSMAN** is going to call you for a date, like he says he's going to. Don't wait by the phone. He gets drunk at frat parties and hooks up with the first thing he sees; that's how guys "date" in college.

—*K.E.R.*
*FLORIDA STATE UNIVERSITY, GRADUATE*

• • • • • • • •

**USE REQUIRED P.E. CREDITS** to your advantage in meeting potential dates. Women might want to try bowling or weightlifting. Men might want to go with ballroom dancing or walking.

—*WENDY W.*
*UNIVERSITY OF GEORGIA, GRADUATE*

• • • • • • • •

**BE PREPARED TO MEET NO WOMEN** your freshman year who want to date you. They are just not available. Either they have boyfriends, or hang-ups, or they like girls. Whatever the reason, as a freshman you will have no girlfriend. If I knew why, I would not be alone.

—*JOE MAYAN*
*CARNEGIE MELLON UNIVERSITY, SOPHOMORE*

• • • • • • • •

**DON'T DATE SOMEONE IN YOUR HALLWAY;** I did. Not only are you living together, but you also have shared counselors and shared activities; you can't escape them. Anytime I went anywhere, or anytime he went anywhere, we would know about it. We'd have fights over IM, and sometimes we'd have to run down the hallway to go yell at each other. And even if we were to break up, there was no chance of having our own lives without the other person knowing about it. So, I basically continued to date him for the whole year, regardless of how happy I was, in order to not deal with the issues involved with having him around.

—*CATE*
*BROWN UNIVERSITY, JUNIOR*

**DON'T COME WITH A GIRLFRIEND FROM HOME.** There are several reasons. First, this is the first time you will really taste freedom and you do not want to be limited and restrained by someone from home. Second, there are booze and parties everywhere. You will feel like you are in a candy store. And you will see girls who are not the girl you grew up with. Everyone is insecure and looking for a connection.
—*DEREK LI*
*CARNEGIE MELLON UNIVERSITY, JUNIOR*

**DON'T EVER LISTEN TO WHAT ANY COLLEGE GUY SAYS.** They all lie – about everything. Especially if they say, "Let's go for a walk." That's the worst: Run screaming.
—*JENNIFER SPICER*
*FOOTHILL COLLEGE, GRADUATE*

**ROLLER-SKATING, BOWLING, AND GETTING ICE CREAM CONES** are still great dates in college. In fact, you get major points for being bold enough to do them with gusto.
—*BRIAN TURNER*
*UNIVERSITY OF GEORGIA, GRADUATE*

**YOU WANT TO KNOW HOW TO GET GIRLS?** Respect them. Be nice to them; it's that simple. Forget pickup lines or getting them drunk. In fact, warn them about guys like that. It sounds silly, but be their hero by being nice and thinking of them.

Also, never, ever, ever try a pickup line, unless you're just kidding around. They never work. The only pickup line that works is, "Hi. How are you?" It's a legitimate start to a conversation.
—*R.B.*
*MASSACHUSETTS INSTITUTE OF TECHNOLOGY, JUNIOR*

I LEFT A SERIOUS RELATIONSHIP hanging when I left high school, so I didn't date anyone seriously my whole freshman year. I just hooked up and had one-night stands. I enjoyed being single in college. True love will come eventually, and until then, you should have some fun.
—P.
PRINCETON UNIVERSITY, SOPHOMORE

" Be friends until you know you really want to take it to the next level. I see so many girls having sex right away because they need reassurance. They later regret it. "
—SARAH LOLA PALODICHUK
RIVERSIDE COMMUNITY COLLEGE, GRADUATE

DON'T DATE SOMEONE you're good friends with. If you go to a small school, it becomes a thing where everyone knows about your business, everyone knows everything about your relationship.
—CONOR MCNEIL
EMORY UNIVERSITY, SOPHOMORE

THE BIGGEST THING I TOLD MYSELF was to put the whole boyfriend thing on hold. I figured it would be too much of a distraction to have a significant other. That helped.
—JERI D. HILT
HOWARD UNIVERSITY, SENIOR

# SADDER BUT WISER

I met my girlfriend in my freshman year. All year long I had been active with my dorm. It was coed and very community-oriented. Then my girlfriend moved into my dorm, and things changed. We started dating and did the whole isolation thing, and it was especially dumb because of the community feeling on our floor. As it turned out, I dated her until spring of senior year, and in the process, I stopped really doing the whole college scene thing; this is something one should definitely not do. Breaking up with my girlfriend was the hardest thing I have ever done: Basically, you grow up with the person in college, and you go through your whole college experience with just them. I found myself almost at the beginning of the cycle; having to develop friends and cultivate relationships and trying to bring back friendships with people I had deserted over the years.

—*D.*
*AMERICAN UNIVERSITY, GRADUATE*

**MY SISTER IS A FRESHMAN.** I told her not to hook up with a lot of guys, not to get a bad reputation, because you can't shake it; it follows you everywhere. I'm a senior now, and some of the people that in my opinion have had bad reputations for whatever reason, when I look at them now, that's what I think of. Some people have been away for a year, studying abroad; some people, I haven't seen them since freshman year. But the reputation sticks.

—*TIM JOYCE*
*GEORGETOWN UNIVERSITY, SENIOR*

* * * * * * * *

**THE SINGLE-ROOM BATHROOMS** in the college library are the best place to have quickie sex on campus.

— *J.*
*UNIVERSITY OF GEORGIA, GRADUATE*

**IT MAY LOOK LIKE THE GIRLS** who are out partying, and doing who knows what with who knows who, are the girls getting the guys. But they're not, really. Also, the nice boys are not on sports teams. I don't know where they are, but they're not on sports teams.

> —*EBELE ONYEMA*
> *GEORGETOWN UNIVERSITY, SENIOR*

● ● ● ● ● ● ● ●

**I'VE SEEN THE MISTAKE OF PEOPLE** staying with their high-school boyfriend or girlfriend, then breaking up with them senior year. That's a terrible experience. You lose the entire novelty of being in college. I would recommend meeting new people and going out with different types of people, whether they're from other states or countries, or whatever.

> —*MIKE*
> *UNIVERSITY OF TEXAS AT AUSTIN, GRADUATE*

● ● ● ● ● ● ● ●

**HOOKING UP – DON'T DO IT** on Halloween unless you really know who is behind that costume. I had a lot to drink and ended up with a very big surprise once we got comfortable. I ran out of there quickly.

> —*J.*
> *CARNEGIE MELLON UNIVERSITY, SENIOR*

● ● ● ● ● ● ● ●

**IN THE FIRST TWO WEEKS OF MY FRESHMAN YEAR,** I met a senior. We started dating and were soon an official couple. It was good while it lasted, but a year later, after he graduated, we broke up. All of the friends I had before going out with him had already moved on to hang out with other friends. They all had their own groups, and I wasn't included because I thought that I was so cool going out with a senior. Yeah, right! I was left in the dust.

> —*L.W.*
> *KUTZTOWN UNIVERSITY, JUNIOR*

Be careful about dating too many older men when you're 18. Make sure they're actually going to your school.

> —*ANONYMOUS*
> *CALVIN COLLEGE, GRADUATE*

**Two rules:** Don't date three guys at the same time who are all on the soccer team together. And don't date anyone on your dorm floor.
—*Heather Pollock*
*California State University at Fullerton, Graduate*

* * * * * * * *

" Always go to parties with a buddy. At one point my freshman spring, my friend had left the party and there was this guy who wouldn't leave me alone and was being really aggressive – but luckily the fire alarm went off and the whole building had to evacuate so I got out of that situation! Just try not to let yourself get isolated. "
—*Catie*
*Harvard College, Senior*

* * * * * * * *

**Advice to guys: know that she's just waiting for you** to come up to her and say hi. I'm now in grad school; it took me seven years to figure that out.
—*Kamal Freiha*
*University of Oregon, Graduate*

# TIS THE SEASON . . . FOR LOVE

Take full advantage of all of the social opportunities that college offers a freshman, and avoid any serious relationships that may hamper or deter you from enjoying all of the rites of passage of being a college freshman. There is no better time than fall on a college campus, with fraternity/sorority rush, parties, and football games to enjoy and revel in.

I learned this lesson the hard way; I had a serious girlfriend who attended Auburn while I was attending Georgia Tech. Not only did I put many unnecessary miles on my car, I also missed the opportunity to meet many other interesting coeds with a lot to offer. While my fraternity and college experience was certainly not without its share of fun, a serious long-distance girlfriend did not enhance it. And to make matters worse, I actually dropped a Naval ROTC scholarship (and an opportunity to become a pilot) after my freshman year because I thought I would rather marry the Auburn coed than cruise the Mediterranean on an aircraft carrier. Needless to say, we broke up less than a year after this very forward-looking decision. That's another reason to stall those seriously entangling relationships early in college; they hamper logical decision-making.

—*S.A.H.*
*GEORGIA INSTITUTE OF TECHNOLOGY, GRADUATE*

**"TURKEY DROP":** This is the time around Thanksgiving when freshmen break up with their significant others they "promised" to date for life. This is typical. Expect it.
—*RAE LYNN RUCKER*
*BIOLA UNIVERSITY, GRADUATE*

# MORE LONG-DISTANCE ROMANCE

**THE SUMMER AFTER MY FRESHMAN YEAR,** I met this guy who lived hundreds of miles from my school. We dated for a year and a half: I drove to his town, five hours away, almost every single weekend of my sophomore year; it really got old. Long-distance relationships suck. Don't try it.
> —KATHERINE
> AUBURN UNIVERSITY, GRADUATE

**IF YOU'RE IN A LONG-DISTANCE RELATIONSHIP,** be disciplined about it and don't cheat on him or her. If you really love that person, then actually do it. That's noble. But if you're not into it, don't do it, it's so stupid.

I hated being with my girlfriend long-distance, so I broke up with her. Then, I'd get lonely and I'd call her and we'd get back together and we'd be on and off and on and off and that started hell. I wish I would've broken up with her earlier. I let her talk me into not breaking up. Playing these games and only sometimes being emotionally available and always looking for someone better who lives closer is a pointless thing to do to yourself. I treated that girl so bad because I didn't want to be with her and she wanted to be with me. So, I thought the best thing to do was to be with her sometimes.
> —ANONYMOUS
> UNIVERSITY OF COLORADO, GRADUATE

**IT'S HARD DOING LONG-DISTANCE,** but my long-distance girlfriend and I FaceTime a lot and text all the time and that helps. I feel like it may be a generational thing because I've met a lot of people here who are in long-distance relationships, but my dad hasn't been as supportive of it.
> —ANONYMOUS
> LOYOLA UNIVERSITY IN CHICAGO, SOPHOMORE

**IF YOU KEEP YOUR BOYFRIEND BACK HOME,** you must learn to trust each other. My boyfriend lives in Maryland and I'm at school in North Carolina. My freshman year, we talked on the phone every night, and he would always tell me how much he missed me and how hard it was to be that far away. We visited each other, but he would complain that it wasn't enough. It was also hard to see the other girls go to parties and dance and kiss other boys. But I didn't want to break up; I love my boyfriend. Over the past year, he has learned to trust me. I have told him a million times that I would never do anything to hurt him; he finally believes me.
—*ALLISON*
*UNIVERSITY OF NORTH CAROLINA AT GREENSBORO, SOPHOMORE*

• • • • • • • • •

**IF YOU GENUINELY WANT TO BE SINGLE** so you can party hard your freshman year, that's great. However, if you're in a serious relationship that you don't want to lose just because you're going to college, don't let anyone pressure you into ending it. Yes, many high school relationships fail during the freshman year of college, but the good ones can stand the test of time and distance. I have two friends who are now married to their high school sweethearts, and two more who are engaged.
—*ANONYMOUS*
*ILLINOIS WESLEYAN UNIVERSITY, JUNIOR*

• • • • • • • • •

**SOME THINGS NEED TO STAY IN HIGH SCHOOL.** I started dating a guy in 11th grade who followed me to college. I was sort of done with the relationship anyway, but it was comfortable. So, I stuck with it for another two years. Staying with him stopped me from making new friends, going to events, or doing any of the things I originally wanted to do in my first year of college. I was too comfortable just staying in my dorm room hanging out with him to go anywhere and I really missed out on a lot of potential friendships because of that.
—*ELISE*
*WESTERN CAROLINA UNIVERSITY, GRADUATE*

**ASK PEOPLE OUT.** It takes guts but you'll never know unless you try. And everyone appreciates a little more courtship and a little less of the senseless hook-up culture.
—*SEAN CAMERON*
*PRINCETON UNIVERSITY, SOPHOMORE*

- - - - - - - -

**ADVICE ON DATING: DON'T. IT COSTS TOO MUCH.** Go out with friends and meet new people. If you do date, don't date one person exclusively. It only leads to trouble.
—*JIMMY LYNCH*
*AUBURN UNIVERSITY, GRADUATE*

- - - - - - - -

**IF YOU HAVE BEEN QUESTIONING YOUR SEXUALITY OR YOUR GENDER** or anything like that, moving away from home and being in a new place is a good time to explore those things.
—*ALISON*
*GRADUATE*

- - - - - - - -

**AS A FRESHMAN,** a male friend of mine invited me to his room to "watch a movie." I had a boyfriend back home and was not promiscuous at all, so I honestly thought this guy was a friend. Halfway through the movie, I turned around to realize he had pulled out his penis and was sitting there looking at me. After a few confused and startled words, I got my stuff and left. He later apologized and said he thought we were on the same page when he invited me to his room. He thought I knew what the words "watch a movie" meant in college, especially at 10 P.M. on a Friday night. I did not!
—*CHAVON*
*XAVIER UNIVERSITY, GRADUATE*

# UNIVERSITY HEALTH CENTER

It's not just for treatment of minor cuts and sprains. Your college's health center may provide some or all of the following services:

- Advice nurse
- Alcohol and drug treatment, counseling, prevention
- Allergy injections
- Birth control
- Emergency contraception (Plan B)
- Ergonomic evaluations (especially for computer setup)
- Flu shots
- Health classes
- HIV testing/prevention/care
- Nutritional counseling
- Physical exams
- Physical therapy
- Rape/sexual assault prevention/response
- Referral to medical services in the community
- Sexual health education
- Smoking cessation assistance
- TB testing
- Vaccines and immunization, such as:
  - Gardasil (for HPV)
  - Hepatitis A & B
  - Meningitis
  - Travel shots
- Weight management

Services are confidential and are typically offered at no or low cost to you (other than the health fee typically built into the cost of college).

*The Editors*

**BE SMART,** be safe, and remember that the university health centers are a great place to go in situations of need.
—*ERIN*
*SUFFOLK UNIVERSITY, GRADUATE*

• • • • • • • •

**KEEP CONDOMS READILY AVAILABLE.** Your RA should also have condoms, if it comes down to it. Ultimately, it's up to the couple to use them. If the thought of sex is out there, it is important to talk about condoms. The last thing you want to happen is there to be a "miscommunication" mid-hookup.

After hooking up, stay awhile. Spend some time after, talking. Don't zip and run.
—*E.F.*
*CLAREMONT MCKENNA COLLEGE, SOPHOMORE*

• • • • • • • •

**I DIDN'T REALLY DATE.** I went to clubs a lot; danced and partied, but all for fun. I gave guys fake phone numbers (*that* was fun). Just remember, dancing with a guy and going home with a guy are two different things. Kissing a guy at a club and going home with a guy are two different things. One thing does not always need to lead to the other. Be patient. And no, boys will not die if you don't "help them out."
—*LESLIE M.*
*UNIVERSITY OF FLORIDA, GRADUATE*

• • • • • • • •

**STAY AWAY FROM THE BOYS ON THE ATHLETIC TEAMS;** they're players in the dating scene. They think they're really cool, and they take advantage of the freshman girls. The freshman girls come in and they're in awe, and the athletes hit on them and take advantage of them. Beware.
—*A.*
*GEORGETOWN UNIVERSITY, SOPHOMORE*

Don't give in to pressure. I'm glad that I didn't and stayed true to myself.
—*ALLISON*
*UNIVERSITY OF NORTH CAROLINA AT GREENSBORO, SOPHOMORE*

**SCHOOL FIRST.** That's my biggest thing. Don't force yourself into anything. Just let it happen naturally and make sure they're as involved with their grades as you are. You don't want to be involved with a slacker because it gets very frustrating. They're not so focused on homework and then you hound them to get their stuff done and they are like, 'Why are you nagging me?' kind of thing.
—*CINDI CALVANESE*
 *BLOOMFIELD COLLEGE, GRADUATE*

**DURING MY ORIENTATION,** I met a girl who ended up on the same floor in the dorms. We became best friends and a month later we started dating. We're about to celebrate our fourth year of that. I strongly advise incoming freshmen to look for friends, not dates. You'll want them as you make the transition into and eventually out of college. Also, the connection that comes from being intimate with someone you're friends with makes being in a relationship worthwhile and takes away what might otherwise be awkward or even dangerous.
—*RON Y. KAGAN*
 *MACAULAY HONORS COLLEGE AT CUNY HUNTER, SENIOR*

# THE FACEBOOK BREAK-UP

**ONE THING THAT** I would totally steer clear of (and I think many of my friends would agree) would be putting your relationship status on Facebook. When my boyfriend and I broke up, we decided I would be the one to take it off Facebook first. It was really upsetting. It is so weird to go from looking at that on your Facebook page to it suddenly not being there. Not to mention the fact that if you haven't set your privacy settings, everyone on your newsfeed will find out about it and suddenly you are explaining your situation to people who didn't even know you were in a relationship in the first place!
—*ANNIE THOMAS*
 *UNIVERSITY OF MICHIGAN, SENIOR*

# HAUNTED BY THE NIGHT IN QUESTION

It was one of those Halloween parties, and I had dressed as a skeleton. Waking up the next morning to go to work, I didn't feel hungover or anything. I was just kind of tired.

But my roommate was visibly worried. Asking me how I felt, she said, "Have you seen your face in the mirror?" I was like, 'No why?' She said, 'Take a look.'

I did, and there were bruises all down my neck.

I had run into her walking home the night before. A guy was walking me home because I couldn't really walk by myself, but beforehand, we had all been drinking.

She told me that when she was helping me get ready for bed that night, she noticed that my underwear was inside-out and backwards. She also said there were red marks on my face. At first, she thought I was breaking out really badly from the Halloween make-up, so she started taking it off. But then she saw that there were bruises and stuff, so she called one of our other friends to help her out and they stayed with me until I fell asleep.

I was fine for a week. I thought, 'Oh, I'll just let it go.' But after a week, I started struggling, just being able to sleep and go to class and stuff like that.

We did five hours of bystander training as freshmen, but the university's reporting process was still really difficult to figure out. If I made a formal report, would the University open up an investigation, or would I just be providing the University with information? That was really confusing. I wasn't sure, so I emailed this secure sexual assault response program and ended up meeting up with a confidential counselor at Health Education Services, who also focuses on sexual assault and domestic violence.

That led to two meetings with the university's Title IX Coordinator. First meeting, she walked me through the steps of how I could report the incident without triggering an investigation – the university would just have the person's name in its files. Then, she outlined the other option of making a report that might result in disciplinary charges. I took the first option and told her what had happened that night. She wrote it all down.

Second semester, I circled back and asked her more about having the Title IX office conduct an investigation, but I decided not to go that route; it just didn't seem like something I'd benefit from. So few of these disciplinary hearings have been done, and so few of them have had consequences. Besides, the Title IX coordinator I originally spoke to isn't even here anymore. She left over the summer.

It's really important to take care of yourself and make sure you're doing things that you need. And getting the support you need. Even though the Title IX office wasn't super helpful in my case, my professors and my dean were super understanding.

Even if it's not something you're comfortable going into detail about, if you talk about it generally, it's such a common topic with the Me-Too movement, people will understand, and I think people are being a lot kinder about it.

> —ANONYMOUS
> GEORGETOWN UNIVERSITY, SOPHOMORE

**DON'T DATE PEOPLE IN YOUR DORM,** especially if you're just hooking up after a party, because there will be a break-up and, therefore, awkwardness in the dorm. It's impossible to avoid someone in your building. You'll step into the elevator and they'll be there and everything gets silent.
> —REID ATTAWAY
> JAMES MADISON UNIVERSITY, FRESHMAN

I advise against dating anyone exclusively as a freshman.

—*J.V.*
THE COLLEGE OF
WILLIAM & MARY,
GRADUATE

**DATING IN COLLEGE** can be one of the most fun and confusing experiences. I had a boyfriend for a year, and I loved every minute of it. Getting to know someone outside of their high school "label" allows you to make your own refreshing decisions about them. You get to know them on a deeper level and you get to experience really fun, new and challenging things together. However, college is the one time in your life when you're surrounded by a million different people your age. Meet as many boys or girls as you can. It's really fun! It's so important to also experience being single. It can be painful at first, but college helps to form, create and shape independence. More importantly, you try more things when you are single. It is just a fact of life.

You are out more, meeting more people and having different experiences.
—*A.T.*
UNIVERSITY OF MICHIGAN, SENIOR

" Take everything a guy says to you at parties with a grain of salt, especially, "you're so beautiful." Know that there are probably ulterior motives. As a freshman, it's easy to be fresh meat. Keep that in the back of your head. "
—*ZOE*
JOHNS HOPKINS UNIVERSITY, GRADUATE

**DON'T SERIOUSLY DATE ANYONE** your first semester. Or even your second semester, honestly. Use this time to seriously think about what you want in a romantic partner and what you need to be happy in a relationship. This is the perfect time to mess around and be trashy, so take advantage of it. You're too young to be looking for your soul mate.
—*SETH*
    *OGLETHORPE UNIVERSITY, FRESHMAN*

* * * * * * * *

**LATE-NIGHT HANGOUT:** top of the parking deck at the medical center. Great views, quiet, good for making out. For the thrill factor: the 50-yard line in the football stadium.
—*MARGOT CARMICHAEL LESTER*
    *UNIVERSITY OF NORTH CAROLINA AT CHAPEL HILL, GRADUATE*

* * * * * * * *

**AS FAR AS CONSENT GOES,** if somebody is pushing you, and you don't want it, leave. Just leave if you can. If you can't, punch them in their dick and leave.
—*PAISLEY*
    *MEREDITH COLLEGE, GRADUATE*

# COLLEGE MATING HABITS

The incidence of casual sex on college campuses is no more common with this generation than it was 20 years ago, according to a study published in the Journal of Sex Research by professors at the University of Portland. Likewise, the American College Health Association in a recent survey of 26,000 undergraduates found fewer than one-quarter reported having more than one sexual partner in the prior 12 months.

# RULES OF CONSENT

**READ YOUR TITLE IX RIGHTS!** For women and minorities on campus, Title IX changed what college life was like. We have so many more rights than we know.
—*REBECCA*
*COLLEGE OF NEW JERSEY, SENIOR*

**I REALLY WISH PEOPLE DID A BETTER JOB** in emphasizing how important consent is before entering college as an exuberant freshman.

Also, if you break up with someone at a small college, it is very likely you will run into this person a lot, which is awkward.
—*ELI CLOONAN*
*GUILFORD COLLEGE, GRADUATE*

**GET EDUCATED ON ISSUES OF SEXUAL ASSAULT AND CONSENT.** We tapped into the resources of the university to find someone to give an educational talk to our fraternity about consent. The person was engaging and it was really informative. Their message was basically that "no" means "no" and you need to get consent at every step of the process. The key take away from it was that it needs to be made clear that there is consent before any sexual activity takes place.
—*KEVIN*
*UNIVERSITY OF ARIZONA, GRADUATE*

**A WOMAN IS GONNA BE INTERESTED IN YOU OR NOT.** If you try to push beyond that, you're gonna get in trouble. There was one event where one guy was accused of reaching up under a girl's dress at a party and he got expelled and we kicked him out of our fraternity. There was a culture of it, but within my group of friends, you didn't get away that kinda stuff.
—*TOM*
*ARIZONA STATE UNIVERSITY, GRADUATE*

**DON'T LET ANYONE BE A #METOO.** Unfortunately, sexual assault and date rape are becoming all too common in today's society. If you are ever in any situation where you see something happening, step in and stop it. Even if you don't know the person, find a subtle way to interrupt the situation to break them away from it.

Validate their feelings and let them know you support them and want the best for them. Try and get them to a safe place or with a person that they feel safe with. If you can't find either of those, you be that person for them. Don't just assume since they know the person, that they will be okay. So many instances today happen with people that the person knows.
—*TAYLOR ELLINGSON*
*NORTHERN STATE UNIVERSITY (S. DAKOTA), SENIOR*

**AT ALL COSTS, AVOID BEING ALONE IN A ROOM WITH A DRUNK GIRL YOU DON'T KNOW.** I stopped in at the dining hall for a late snack one Friday night and ran into two girls who were in a class of mine. One was incredibly drunk and the girl who was with her asked if I could help get the drunk girl to her dorm. The drunk girl was so wasted, I literally carried her like a baby in my arms across campus and into her dorm. The other girl – I don't know if they were good friends or not, but she wasn't being particularly helpful – started heading back out and asked me if I could take the drunk girl up to her room and put her to bed without her help. I was basically, like, "No way, you need to come with me."

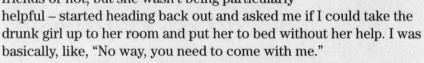

She was annoyed and made it seem like I was being a jerk. But from a guy's perspective, if I had been alone with the drunk woman, she could have said I did anything and there wouldn't have been anyone else around to corroborate what actually happened. It sounds paranoid. But sometimes being paranoid helps protect everyone.
—*ANONYMOUS*
*DARTMOUTH COLLEGE*

**I** LOVE MEETING NEW PEOPLE, so I went with my best friend to a party at a wrestler's house. I don't drink, so I was perfectly sober when I gave a guy my phone number that night. I started hearing things about this guy, that he had attended three different high schools and had been kicked out of his last college. But he was absolutely phenomenal at wrestling; he was even a national champion. But he was super-aggressive around me and I kept hearing things. After doing a little research, I found out that he had been kicked out of those three high schools for sexually assaulting girls and he was kicked out of Virginia Tech for sexually assaulting someone! I'm so glad I trusted my gut instinct and checked him out, because I could've been his next victim.
   —ANONYMOUS
     IOWA CENTRAL COMMUNITY COLLEGE, GRADUATE

**HONESTY AND OPEN COMMUNICATION** are what's going to help you resolve your differences. Don't say you're okay or don't say you're fine, when you're not actually fine, because if you say that, the other person's going to take your word for it and it's going to come back and bite them and they'll have no idea why. So always keep talking. Keep communication open.
   —KEVIN
     JOHNS HOPKINS UNIVERSITY, GRADUATE

**DON'T DO ANYTHING WITH A GIRL** who's not making rational decisions; that's a good way to get thrown in jail. It's better to be extremely modest in that situation. If a girl wants to do something with you, you can do it the next time or three times down the road.
   —NICHOLAS BONAWITZ
     UNIVERSITY OF ROCHESTER, GRADUATE

**MOST PEOPLE GO ON TINDER.** So, if you want options, go on Tinder. Bumble is also really helpful, but I am not particularly loquacious. I don't like to talk to people first, and Bumble is like "hey, if you want to use this, you have to talk first!" I think those two are the best. Coffee Meets Bagel is the WORST. Don't let anyone tell you that's a good app. It is garbage. It takes, like, 30 minutes to fill in your profile, you have to tell them your whole goddamn life story… absolutely not.

—*TESSA*
*NEW YORK UNIVERSITY, GRADUATE*

. . . . . . . .

" If you are too drunk to be writing a coherent text to your mom, you're too drunk to hook-up with anyone. "

—*ANONYMOUS*
*DARTMOUTH COLLEGE*

. . . . . . . .

**ON THE FIRST DAY OF SCHOOL, SCOUT OUT THE PEOPLE** and sit by whom you think you could like. It's best to meet people you might end up dating in class. You already have something in common and you see each other regularly. It's not a party or some other weird social context. You see how they really are on a day-to-day basis. In college, there are so many different ways to meet people that you don't really need Tinder.

—*MEGHAN WALLACE*
*NORTHERN ARIZONA UNIVERSITY, SENIOR*

# #METOO & ME

THE #MeToo THING has made me think about this more: You're a freshman and you don't know how much you should be drinking, So, you drink too much. My experience is, that I blackout, wake up the next day with a guy next to me in bed, and I don't know what happened. At the time, I may not feel violated and wouldn't want to consider that sexual assault, but legally speaking, if you black out, you cannot consent. So, I've been thinking about what that means.

I have a litany of bad drinking experiences. Back in the spring, there was one of those themed nights at one of the eating clubs. I don't know how I got that drunk or how my friends lost me. Apparently, I was super into this guy, which I don't have any recollection of, and we went back to my room and stuff happened. I don't remember much of it except that it hurt.

When I woke up, I just remember being on my bed in my room. He was really happy and satisfied and I just kind of played along because I didn't want to make it awkward. We ended up going to CVS because he was, like, "Oh yeah, I don't think I kept it on the whole time." So, we had to go buy Plan B. He paid for that at least and friended me on Facebook.

After I took the Plan B, I remember feeling really ill for two days. I don't know if it was because of the experience or just my body not handling the hormones well.

Later, he followed up and asked if I wanted to hang out more. I met him in person to tell him, "No, thank you. We're not doing this again."

It was a really blurry situation because, by all accounts, I was really into him when I was drunk and it wasn't immediately obvious that I was really, really drunk. If it seems by your behavior that you're consenting but wake up the next day and you don't remember making any decisions at all, then, what is the situation there?

The only way I could see myself changing my outcome is, if I drank less. I think that's good advice but at the same time I'm wary of saying girls need to take it upon themselves, that you are responsible for not being assaulted. I don't think that victim-blaming is okay. So, be wary of what you're drinking, but if you are assaulted, it's not your fault.

I do wish I knew where my limit was. I think I know how many drinks I should be having now, but I wasn't super well-connected when I was freshman. So, whenever there was a pre-game, I would go hard and that led to a lot of problems. That's another thing. There are going to be a lot of pre-games. Don't drink like it's the last time you'll ever go out because you're not going to feel great and there are going to be way more opportunities in the future.

—ANONYMOUS
PRINCETON UNIVERSITY, SENIOR

# INCIDENCE OF SEXUAL ASSAULT ON COLLEGE CAMPUSES

| *Percentage of Respondents who Reported "Yes" to question* | *Male* | *Female* |
|---|---|---|
| In the last 12 months, were you sexually touched without your consent? | 4% | 13% |
| In the last 12 months, were you sexually penetrated without your consent? | 1% | 6% |
| In the last 12 months, were you a victim of stalking? | 3% | 8% |
| In the last 12 months, has sexual assault affected your academic performance? | 0% | 2% |

# LIGHTNING STRIKES... SOMETIMES

**I MET MY NOW WIFE ON THE FIRST DAY OF COLLEGE!** First "don't:" don't expect that to happen; that's way too much pressure.

Second "don't:" don't buy the hype about all your friends and peers having all the sex. They aren't. If you want to, great. But don't do it because you feel that's what everyone is doing.

Third "don't:" don't put off being exclusive with someone you really like just because that seems antiquated or out of date. It isn't, and by the way, it will make you happy.
—*MAX*
    *DARTMOUTH COLLEGE, GRADUATE*

**FOR SOME REASON,** I thought that I was going to find my husband in the first month of college. I was wrong. This belief was my biggest misconception about college because in terms of dating, it gave me tunnel vision. College is about experience and experimenting. Work on building friendships; relationships will come later.
—*E.S.*
    *DUKE UNIVERSITY, GRADUATE*

**YOU DON'T EVER WANT TO MOVE IN** with a girlfriend. If you do, your lifestyle becomes limited; you always have to come home with her and you always have to deal with her. I had roommates who were a couple living together in my house and I saw them fighting all the time. The reason was that they were together too much, and the expectations grow and grow and if they don't meet those expectations for one moment, they get in a fight.
—*STEPHAN*
    *UNIVERSITY OF CALIFORNIA AT SANTA BARBARA, GRADUATE*

**AT THE BEGINNING OF COLLEGE,** everyone is a stranger (which means random hook-ups aplenty). Get to know people and learn how the social scene works before even thinking of "doing anything." I saw two of my roommates get involved with guys they barely knew during the first month of school.
    —LIZZIE
        BOWDOIN COLLEGE, FRESHMAN

"I guess you're right. There <u>was</u> a party last night."

# 16 Parties: How to Have Fun & Be Safe

Y*ou don't see them featured on college websites or in the glossy brochures, but you and your friends know that parties, drugs, and alcohol are a crucial part of the college experience. In college, you can do things like down a bottle of whiskey with a dorm-mate on a Wednesday and no one will call you an alcoholic – but you're not invincible.*

*Sometimes, managing fun and preserving your own survival can be a delicate balancing act. Some of the most remarkable feats in human history have come from those who have just uttered, "Hold my beer." The swirling world of intoxicating substances and loud, sweaty crowds is a heady one, ripe with epic, life-changing experiences. But it can go very, very wrong. So, it can't hurt to be prepared and plan a little before stepping out in that toga or heading off to that "pre-game."*

**WHEN YOU'RE AT A PARTY, TRY TO THINK ABOUT THE NEXT MORNING.** Ask yourself the question: Will I be able to look at myself in the mirror?
—*G.*
UNIVERSITY OF NORTH CAROLINA AT CHAPEL HILL, SOPHOMORE

**DON'T PARTY BEFORE TESTS.**
—*H.K.S.*
OXFORD COLLEGE, JUNIOR

**HEADLINES**

- In college, the words "party" and "beer" go hand in hand.
- If you set your drink down and walk away, don't go back for it – it's too risky.
- Never drink and drive – DUIs go on your permanent record.
- If you're having trouble keeping on top of your work, you may be partying too hard.

**IF A MAN APPROACHES YOU** and your friends at a garden party offering strange-looking mushrooms in a baggie, tell him you're not hungry.
—*D.D.*
*UNIVERSITY OF PENNSYLVANIA, GRADUATE*

. . . . . . . .

Don't drink the punch. There's a lot more alcohol in there than you think.

—*ANONYMOUS*
*YALE UNIVERSITY, SOPHOMORE*

**WHEN YOU FIRST START COLLEGE,** the phrase "three-day weekend" takes on a whole new meaning. The more social students tend to go out on Thursday night for the sole purpose of drinking themselves into a stupor. Friday night is a rest-and-recuperation night, and then the partying résumés Saturday night. By the time you wake up on Sunday it's already mid-afternoon. This trend fades by the time you start sophomore year. If it doesn't, you are officially an alcoholic and/or a stoner.
—*JOSHUA BERKOV*
*BROWN UNIVERSITY, JUNIOR*

. . . . . . . .

**IF YOU GO TO SCHOOL IN A BIG CITY,** you have to be more careful. Watch out for your surroundings. If you have to take a route where you might have trouble, stay away from it. Take the long way. There's nothing more important than your life.
—*B.L.*
*JOHN JAY COLLEGE OF CRIMINAL JUSTICE, GRADUATE*

**A LOT OF PEOPLE COME IN HERE** and they don't have experience drinking, and they just sort of explode. My friend had a freshman roommate who failed out the first semester because he had spent all his time drinking. Don't get in over your head.
   —*LEE ROBERTS*
      *UNIVERSITY OF NORTH CAROLINA AT CHAPEL HILL, SENIOR*

• • • • • • • •

**DON'T DRINK HARD LIQUOR** – stick to beer. You have better control with beer. I had bad experiences with liquor. If you wake up the next morning and you don't remember what you did, you've had too much to drink.
   —*REID ATTAWAY*
      *JAMES MADISON UNIVERSITY, FRESHMAN*

• • • • • • • •

**KNOW THAT IF YOU CHOOSE NOT TO DRINK,** there are tons of other people who don't either. But don't lecture other people – if they wanted you to be their mom, they would've asked. Exceptions: your close friends, people who are being offensive to you, people you are close to, and girls who are about to be taken advantage of because of their state.
   —*JULIE*
      *PRINCETON UNIVERSITY, SOPHOMORE*

• • • • • • • •

**DON'T TRY TO DRINK ALL THE BEER ON CAMPUS.** You can't, trust me. And, not having a car your freshman year is a good safety measure.
   —*STEVE DAVIS*
      *FLORIDA STATE UNIVERSITY, GRADUATE*

• • • • • • • •

**HOW CAN YOU TELL IF YOU'RE PARTYING TOO MUCH?** If you're doing fine in classes, you're not partying too much. If you don't do well in classes, you're partying too much.
   —*NOURA BAKKOUR*
      *GEORGETOWN UNIVERSITY, SENIOR*

# ASK THE ADVISER

*Everyone knows that college students drink. Am I really going to get into trouble for having a couple of beers in the dorm?*

You're half right – all college administrators know that *some* college students drink. Plenty of students don't drink at all, or drink very moderately. But your question is about getting into trouble. The answer depends on your college. Some colleges have almost supernatural powers when it comes to sniffing out that kind of rule-breaking, whereas others operate on a purely human skill level. The second half of the story is what happens to students who are caught drinking. There will always be consequences, but they may vary in type and severity. Read your dorm handbook to find out your college's policy, and don't be fooled by other students who tell you that "they don't really mean it;" if it's on the books, it could happen to you.

*Frances Northcutt*

JUST BEING ANYWHERE WHERE THERE IS TROUBLE, YOU'RE IN TROUBLE. If you're at a party or at a gathering of people in a dorm room and some people are underage and drinking – then, you're already in trouble.
—*J.G.M.*
GUILFORD COLLEGE, GRADUATE

• • • • • • • •

As MUCH FUN AS IT MIGHT SEEM, do your best not to get black-out drunk to the point where you cannot find your way home. First of all, no one likes to take care of the person who can't stand up or find his or her way home. People will help, but they don't like to. Recognize when enough is enough.
—*ELIZABETH*
UNIVERSITY OF ILLINOIS AT URBANA-CHAMPAIGN, GRADUATE

**Football games are so much fun here** – everyone is drunk in the stands. On game day, the whole campus is up by 9 A.M. You can't get students up at 9 A.M. for school, but they'll get up early to start partying before a game.
   —*M.M.*
      *Boston College, Junior*

. . . . . . . .

**If you are nervous about your ability to imbibe** at the start of college, and worried about peer pressure, just have a red Solo cup in your hand at parties. Those are the drinking cups. Pour in cranberry juice or Sprite. No one is the wiser if you don't have vodka in there.
   —*P.B.*
      *Dartmouth College, Graduate*

. . . . . . . .

" Alcohol makes some people seem more attractive than they will look the next morning. "
   —*H.K.S.*
      *Oxford College, Junior*

. . . . . . . .

**You have to learn** that the week is for studying and the weekend is for partying. You can't think that you just party every day. That's what I thought: I thought that college was a never-ending party, without work. I thought it was going to be easier than high school, without busy work. But it's overwhelming.
   —*Amy Hoffberg*
      *University of Delaware, Freshman*

**I DON'T DRINK.** It's not hard to socialize if you don't drink, because everyone needs a designated driver. If I go, they usually buy my dinner. So, it works for me.
—*B.M.*
    *UNIVERSITY OF MARYLAND, JUNIOR*

⟨⟨ Drinking: I got written up by the police multiple times for stupid reasons. It caused me some problems with housing for my sophomore year. And I lost housing for my senior year. I'm pretty liberal about drinking, but you've got to watch yourself. Blackouts are never good. ⟩⟩

—*M.M.*
    *BOSTON COLLEGE, JUNIOR*

**IF YOU WANT TO DRINK FOR FREE,** head to a bar and pretend you don't want to drink alcohol. You'll suddenly be everyone's pet project. As the efforts to convert you mount, give in slowly; not only will everyone have a good time, but you'll have a good buzz to match.
—*BRIAN TURNER*
    *UNIVERSITY OF GEORGIA, GRADUATE*

# WOMAN TO WOMAN

**WHEN YOU GO OUT, GO WITH A FRIEND** who knows when to take you home. I have a friend and we do that for each other; we don't let each other out of sight. Sometimes I'll get pissed off and get in a full-on fist fight, saying, "No, I can handle this!" and she's like, "No, I'm taking you home right now." We have to be strict with each other, but it's good to have someone looking out for you.

—*MOLLY SELMER*
*SONOMA STATE UNIVERSITY, GRADUATE*

. . . . . . . . .

**DON'T PUT DOWN YOUR DRINK.** I think I went to a great school, but you don't know who is around. I had a friend who was drugged her sophomore year. She had two beers and all of a sudden she's out of her head and can't stand. And we thought she must have done shots we didn't know about it. But the next day, she was in bed and couldn't get up. And she'd had hardly anything to drink.

—*J. DEVEREUX*
*GEORGETOWN UNIVERSITY, GRADUATE*

. . . . . . . . .

**GO TO FRAT PARTIES** with a bunch of girlfriends, and make sure you all go home together. Don't listen to any of the crap the guys try to hand you. They're looking for freshmen; they're waiting for them. Freshmen are so naïve and gullible and they think everything the guys say is true, and it's not. The guy will say anything: he'll say all these nice things and make a girl feel special, but it doesn't matter. He won't know your name the next day. He probably doesn't know your name right then.

—*KRISTIN THOMAS*
*JAMES MADISON UNIVERSITY, JUNIOR*

# WHAT TO DO (AND NOT DO) IF ARRESTED WHILE AT SCHOOL

Don't smirk in your mugshot. And never, ever hit the horse.

When a Penn State University pre-football tailgate started getting out of hand, university and state police, including a team of mounted officers, were called in to help tame the unruly crowd. One allegedly inebriated tailgater smacked a police horse as he tried to dodge the cops.

Bad idea, defense lawyers say. The tailgater was arrested, and was in even more trouble for resisting. And on top of the usual disorderly conduct and public drunkenness charges, he was also charged with taunting a police animal. Don't be that guy.

But if you find yourself on the wrong side of the handcuffs, our defense team offers a few guidelines:

> **Rule #1: "Don't be an asshole,"** says Willie Dow, who for decades has been the go-to lawyer for many a Yale University student in legal trouble. Police officers appreciate courtesy as much as anyone else.

> **Rule #2: Don't try to talk your way out of it.** In fact, talk as little as possible. "You can do a lot of damage to your defense," if you start rambling to police officers, said Eugene Riccio, a Connecticut defense lawyer, who has also seen it all.

The vast majority of college arrests are typically alcohol- or drug-related, and they usually constitute less-serious misdemeanor crimes such as trespassing, underage drinking, public drunkenness, bar fights, vandalism.

Sabrina Puglisi, a Florida attorney, has represented students from nearby University of Miami as well as Spring Breakers from out of town who have a little too much fun while visiting. Puglisi advises students to make the hardest call – the one to your parents – first. "As scary as it is, parents love you no matter what, even when you do stupid things," Puglisi said. Parents will help you find a lawyer who, ideally, will try to get the charges dismissed. In some cases, your lawyer can stand in for you in court – especially helpful for Spring Breakers who need to leave Miami and head back to school, pronto.

Your main goal when you've been arrested is getting yourself out of jail as quickly as possible, Riccio says.

Other tips for the first few hours you're in police custody:

- Ask to call your family so they can help you find a lawyer. A good lawyer.
- Answer only basic questions. When police are booking you after your arrest, they will need your name, date of birth, address and other information. Once the booking is done, you can ask for a lawyer and decline further questions.
- Politely decline to talk about the incident until you have a lawyer with you. Once you ask for a lawyer, police are supposed to stop asking you questions.
- Do not consent to let the police search your backpack, phone, car, or dorm room.
- Decline an alcohol or drug test, if possible.
- Do not smile, smirk or do anything that could call attention to your mugshot. Straight-faced is the way to go.
- Remain polite and respectful when speaking with authorities. (Don't be an asshole, remember?) Don't ask for someone's badge number. (It should all be in the police report you can ask for later.)
- If you know you're a target of an investigation, remember that the police are not there to help you. They are there to investigate.

Dow also recommends planning ahead, just in case you ever stumble. "Every town has a lawyer who handles college kids' cases," he said. Get that number, and hold onto it.

Of course, your best-case scenario is to avoid getting arrested in the first place. One last suggestion: Make 'not getting arrested' one of your college goals. And when your tailgate goes sour, don't hit the police horse. "That's a rule to live by," Puglisi says.

*Kristin Hussey is a Connecticut-based writer*
*who keeps several lawyers' numbers on speed dial.*

NEVER, EVER DRIVE AFTER DRINKING any amount of alcohol at all. A DUI will give you a police record and cost you thousands in legal fees and fines; don't even chance it.
—*WENDY W.*
*UNIVERSITY OF GEORGIA, GRADUATE*

• • • • • • • •

YOU'RE AHEAD OF THE CURVE once you accept that the upperclassmen get all the hot girls at parties. The football players do, too. Instead of worrying about this, work on building friendships.
—*MICHAEL*
*GRADUATE*

• • • • • • • •

TO PREVENT SERIOUS TROUBLE, you must follow some simple rules. First, you need to do the stand-up test: The first time you drink a lot of liquor, don't do it all sitting down. You won't feel what it's doing to you. But the first time you stand up, hit the floor, and eat some carpet, you will suddenly feel what it is doing to you. So, stand up often while drinking liquor, to better measure the effect.
—*R.S.*
*GEORGETOWN UNIVERSITY, GRADUATE*

• • • • • • • •

BE HONEST ABOUT WHAT IS COMFORTABLE AND WHAT IS NOT A GOOD IDEA. I had a professor who lived nearby who was like, "Oh, why don't you just come in and chat with me and have a drink and stuff." I was like, "Uh, okay." You feel like you have to do what they say. Then you get in there, and you think, "Well, this is weird and this isn't the right boundary to set."

I had another professor my freshman year who invited me to a wine event and I wasn't 21 yet and I was like, "No. I can't go to that. I'm not 21."
—*J.G.M.*
*GUILFORD COLLEGE, GRADUATE*

ONE OF MY CLOSEST FRIENDS KNEW THIS PERSON who was out drinking one night. He wasn't super drunk but obviously had a lot of alcohol in his system, and drove back home. He accidently ran over someone, and the person passed away. That was a huge, huge thing that happened. Of course that meant he was no longer going to be at school and he had to go through the judicial system for what he had done.

Putting yourself in safe situations is a must. If you do go out, try to go out with people you trust so you can help each other stay safe, and make yourself aware of any local restrictions or laws.
—JOSE CISNEROS
UNIVERSITY OF NORTH CAROLINA AT CHAPEL HILL, GRADUATE

• • • • • • • • •

IF YOU DO DECIDE TO EXPERIMENT WITH ALCOHOL and drugs in college, be prepared to accept the consequences of your actions; what you're doing may be illegal and, as such, a poor decision. Alcohol and drugs are only a temporary escape from the dullness of life. If you find yourself consumed by these substances, you may need to reevaluate the directions your life is going in and realign yourself. If you're drinking to be more social, then maybe you're too self-conscious. If you're smoking marijuana to relax and be happy, then maybe you need a hobby. There are plenty of people and activities on campus to keep you busy without having to resort to drugs and alcohol on too regular a basis.
—ARIEL MELENDEZ
PRINCETON UNIVERSITY, FRESHMAN

• • • • • • • • •

THE BEST WAY TO GET OVER A HANGOVER is water and bread. Bread is your best friend: It helps take care of your stomach, and it fills you and soaks up anything. The water makes you not dehydrated anymore.
—BETH
DIABLO VALLEY COLLEGE, FRESHMAN

# CALLS FOR RESTRAINT

**TRY TO LIMIT THE DRINKING** to three times a week. Work hard Monday through Thursday, and party Thursday, Friday, and Saturday nights; that's what worked for me.
—NICK DOMANICO
UNIVERSITY OF CALIFORNIA AT SANTA BARBARA, SENIOR

**YOU'RE GOING TOO FAR** with the drinking when you have to drink every time you want to go out. When you "pregame" for everything: "Let's go to the diner, let's pregame first!" – that kind of thing. Some people have an obsession with it.
—DANIEL RUSK
UNIVERSITY OF MARYLAND, SOPHOMORE

**DON'T DRINK TOO MUCH;** at this school, it can cost you a lot of money. My freshman year, my roommate got alcohol poisoning. She came home early one morning and passed out. We couldn't wake her up so we called campus security and an ambulance came and took her to the hospital. She was fine afterwards, but the school fined her $2,000; plus, she had to pay her hospital bill.
—LIANA HIYANE
SANTA CLARA UNIVERSITY, JUNIOR

**SOMETIMES, IT'S BEST JUST TO WALK AWAY.** One time at college, one of my friends who was a little inebriated, got a door slammed in his face trying to get into a party. Instead of knocking on the window of the house to get the attention of someone inside, he actually broke the window with his clenched fist. There was a foot pursuit, bloody clothes, and lots of confusion involved.
—ANONYMOUS
BOSTON COLLEGE, GRADUATE

**IF YOU'RE GOING TO DRINK,** drink *before* you go out. It saves tons of money.
>—*JIMMY LYNCH*
>*AUBURN UNIVERSITY, GRADUATE*

• • • • • • • •

**IF YOU GET DRUNK,** don't throw chairs at your dorm neighbor. My neighbor had the same major as me, and I saw her for the next four years. She remembered that.
>—*CASEY*
>*GEORGETOWN UNIVERSITY, SENIOR*

• • • • • • • •

**BE EXTRA CAREFUL ABOUT DRINKING OFF-CAMPUS.** Cops in the small town in Maine where Colby is located seem to go out of their way to catch underage drinkers. People say cops literally listen in on cab radios to hear where they're taking kids to off-campus parties. One time, I was on a bus that was taking 30 kids to an event. The police stopped the bus and gave everyone on board Breathalyzer tests. I was one of many who got a warning. They took our pictures. I had to do an alcohol education course. It was a huge drag.
>—*ANONYMOUS*
>*COLBY COLLEGE, GRADUATE*

• • • • • • • •

**HERE'S SOME ADVICE** that my brother left me on my answering machine the first week I was in college: "If you smoke pot in your room, make sure to put a towel under the door."
>—*B.K.*
>*CORNELL UNIVERSITY, GRADUATE*

• • • • • • • •

**THE FIRST WEEK OF SCHOOL,** I went out partying with my friends and next thing I remember, I was locked outside my room with no key, naked and soaking wet at five in the morning.
>—*S.*
>*HARVARD COLLEGE, SOPHOMORE*

**DON'T BE SO DRUNK** that you can't enjoy sex. Bad things happen. Just make sure you know your limits and that you're not afraid to say no. You have to know what kind of person you are and what works for you.
—*MATT*
*TUFTS UNIVERSITY, SOPHOMORE*

· · · · · · · ·

" Everyone does stupid things, but don't get caught doing something illegal. You pick up habits in your freshman year where you say, "Oh, I didn't get caught then, so I might as well do it now." Then you get caught, and you're like, "Oh, that's how the real world works." "
—*JOSH H.*
*PURDUE UNIVERSITY, GRADUATE*

· · · · · · · ·

**MY FRIENDS AND I HAVE A BUDDY SYSTEM.** When we go to a party, the first thing we do is tie all the sleeves of our jackets together. Why? Because people sometimes steal or accidentally take jackets at parties! I lost my North Face that way!
—*TAYLOR WHITNEY PETTIS*
*BLOOMSBURG UNIVERSITY, JUNIOR*

**IF YOU'RE BEING STALKED,** make sure you give a photo to campus security, and let all your friends know so they can be aware and not just "Oh, I saw your boyfriend" or "I saw so-and-so." Get the word out.
—*PAISLEY*
   *MEREDITH COLLEGE, GRADUATE*

• • • • • • • •

**DON'T MAKE DRINKING A COMPETITIVE ACTIVITY.** If you find yourself trying to prove how much you can drink to impress others, then it's going to end badly. You'll get alcohol poisoning, whether you believe you're immune or not. Or, you'll end up puking your guts out in front of your friends and people you don't even know. Also, drinking should not be the main activity of your night. If you go out just to drink, you're going to get drunk. If you go out to meet people at a party, or to dance, play a game, or bowl, focus on the main activity first, and then just let the drinking be an additive; it should never be the focus of your night. The funny thing is, the people who make it the focus of their night can't understand why everyone else might not want to do the same thing. But watch those people; they're cool when they're making jokes and doing shots, but they'll end up puking or acting like idiots.
—*ANONYMOUS*
   *VILLANOVA UNIVERSITY, GRADUATE*

## BOOZE OVER BOOKS?

Freshmen who said they had at least one drink in the past 14 days spent an average 10.2 hours a week drinking ... and only 8.4 hours a week studying.

# SEATBELTS, CHECK. HELMETS, SUNSCREEN – UMM ...

Percentage of college students who report using seat belts all the time over the last 12 months: ...................................................80%

Percentage of college students who have always worn a helmet when riding a bike over the last 12 months:......................12%

Percentage of college students who report using sunscreen regularly with sun exposure:............................................................55%

# APPS 4 THE SAFETY-CONSCIOUS

College means freedom: to date whomever you want, attend the parties you want, study as late as you want, without checking in with parents, and so on. And while you should enjoy yourself as much as you can, you also want to have fun safely and responsibly.

Whether you need your hand-held device to track your walk home from the library late at night, or to check up on you during a Bumble date, there are plenty of apps that can help you stay safer at school:

### bSafe
The bSafe app, available for free on both Apple iOS and Android, lets you connect with a friend who can track you on a map as you walk home for extra peace of mind. You can also set 'Guardians' who can view a livestream of your walk if you're in danger; hit a voice-activated alarm should you not be able to reach your phone; and send a friend or family member your exact location if they need to come get you. The app is free, but you'll need to give it access to your contacts to complete the installation.

### Circle of 6
This popular free app is similar to bSafe, but lets you select up to six people to share your location with at any time with just two taps of your phone. It will pin your exact location or send a notification to a friend to call you, in case you need an out in a potentially dangerous situation. The app also requires you to let them access your contacts to "complete your circle."

### Kitestring
Kitestring is a free text service that checks in with you in pre-set time increments to make sure you're okay. If you don't respond, the service will send a designated emergency contact a text message stating something like, "Hey, this is Madison. I'm going out for a walk. If you get this, I might not have made it back safely. Give me a call at 123-456-7890." Light users should be okay with the free service. It accepts one emergency contact from you that you can enter by hand – no need to share all your contacts – for use up to three trips a month. For heavier users, $3 a month provides unlimited monitoring and as many emergency contacts as you want.

## Uber

The app's safety center lets riders designate up to five friends to share their location with during each ride, and there's a new emergency button that will call 911 if you're in danger.

## uSafeUS

This app will not only text your friends to let them know your ETA and remind them to check in with you if you don't show up at the expected time, but you can also use it to send a fake call to help extricate you from an uncomfortable situation. If you or a friend are assaulted, it will also walk you through how to report the incident and access your school's Title IX policy. Another cool feature: it allows you to send a discrete message to a bartender asking for help in the guise of ordering an "Angel Drink." The app is free, but you will need to allow it access to your contacts to enable all of the features, including alerting friends to your location and arrival time.

## Watch Over Me

Watch Over Me is similar to Kitestring, except it's a standalone app with a few more features: You can add notes (say, a picture of where you're going or details of your running route) and pause the timer. Just check in with it before time runs out or it will text your emergency contacts. The app can also warn you when you enter high-crime areas in case you wish to activate monitoring. And you can shake the phone to enable an alarm and live video recording, even when the phone is locked. This app is slightly costlier than some others: there's a one-time $4.99 download fee.

## Your school's app

For years, schools posted blue-light phones around campus for emergency calls. But with the proliferation of mobile phones, many schools are instead focused on customizing their own apps to make students feel safer. Some of these apps contain useful info like bus and shuttle times and routes. Or, they may able to connect you quickly with campus security or other safety or medical resources.

*Alicia Adamczyk is a New York-based writer.*

# THIS WORKED FOR THEM

**HAVE SOME SAFETY NETS SET UP** with your personal network of friends and family. I have a few people that if I text my "safe word" to them, they know something is wrong. I carried pepper spray my first two years of college, and, thankfully, I never had to use it. Now I pay more attention to what time I walk home and always let someone know where I am or where I'm headed. I have a close network of college friends and some family that I am always in touch with.

There are also a lot of safety apps. You can set someone as your emergency contact, and, in an emergency, it will send that person an emergency message. There are multiple Blue Lights with emergency call boxes on campus at SDSU as well, which give some peace of mind.
　　—*ABBY*
　　　*SOUTH DAKOTA STATE UNIVERSITY, SENIOR*

. . . . . . . . .

**BSAFE IS A REALLY GOOD FREE SAFETY APP** for your phone. You can have a community of people, and all they have to do is also have the app – so my parents have it, my roommates have it, a couple really good friends of mine, and like, one of my bodybuilder friends. So they can always know where you are… I can say, "I am here, and I'm gonna be heading home." So, then the app says "how long do you think it's gonna take for you to get home?" And I'll say "about 45 minutes," and if I'm not there in 45 minutes, everyone gets an alert…I would recommend it if you're going to a place that's kinda scary, or really different, or if you have parents like mine, who get worried all the time. It kind of appeases everyone.
　　—*TESSA*
　　　*NEW YORK UNIVERSITY, GRADUATE*

# ALL-TIME WORST DAY OF COLLEGE

**YOU'RE GONNA MAKE BAD DECISIONS,** and that's okay. Just forgive yourself and learn from them. One night, me and my buddy drank a whole bottle of vodka together, and then we go to our other buddy's room and we start taking shots. We were drinking just to drink.

I blacked out and next thing I know I'm woken up and every single RA in my building is in my room telling me my roommate called them because I threw up in our trash can. I said, 'Sorry write me up, whatever.' Then, they leave and come back with two cops and they wake me up again and do these sobriety tests and they're like 'Well, you're drunk.' I was asleep in my bed and they wake me up to give me a ticket.

This is all happening at like 3 A.M. and I have work at the dining hall at 5:30 A.M. I go to work and every 30 minutes I throw up. Finally, after the eighth time I throw up, the supervisor comes up to me and thankfully says, 'If you do this again, you're fired – but you need to go home.'

So, I go back to my room, and I get a call from my aunt and uncle who tell me they're in Boulder and want to surprise me with lunch. I love Italian food and it was like a "Congratulations for being in college" thing, but I couldn't stand the thought of eating. I went and threw up in the bathroom at one point and only managed two bites of pasta. Everyone knew what was going on. It was one of the worst days of my life. It was a great learning experience, though, and it made me never want to do drink like that again. And I haven't.

> —*ANONYMOUS*
> *UNIVERSITY OF COLORADO, GRADUATE*

HAVE A STORY TO SHARE ABOUT YOUR WORST DAY OF COLLEGE EVER? TELL US ABOUT IT! SEND YOUR STORY TO EDITOR@HOWISURVIVED.COM

Just because the beer is being served in Dixie cups doesn't mean you can drink 40 cups and still drive home.

—*Scott Woelfel*
*University of Missouri,*
*Graduate*

**IF YOU'RE DRINKING UNDERAGE AND YOU ENCOUNTER THE COPS, DENY.** Always deny! Police do not have the right to Breathalyze you, especially if you're not behind the wheel.

My fraternity had a party bus to and from a big golf tournament. I packed a flask, and we were drinking on the bus on the way there. We get to the event and I realize my girlfriend is stumbling and slurring her words. We go up this hill to sit down and catch our breath and she slumps over and literally rolls down the hill! I get down there, her dress is around her waist, her boobs are hanging out. Two bike cops ask for my ID while firefighters start putting my girlfriend on a stretcher. This cop asked me if I'd been drinking; I said, 'no.' He told me to do a Breathalyzer. I said, "No, I'm not driving. I'll do a blood test." He said he couldn't do that if I wasn't under arrest and I wasn't under arrest.

So, the cops let me go and I was able to ride with my girlfriend in the ambulance to the hospital. After a half-hour, she was released, and we got some In-N-Out. My girlfriend got a citation for underage drinking and an ambulance bill, and I got a burger.
—*Tom*
*Arizona State University, Graduate*

# FRESHMAN DRINKING PRIMER

1. Every college student needs to know the old mantra, "Liquor before beer, never fear. Beer before liquor, never sicker."

2. It helps to have a glass of water with, or in between, drinks. And don't drink on an empty stomach.

3. If you close your eyes and you can't keep your balance, it's probably time to stop drinking for the night.

—*D.R.*
*University of North Carolina at Chapel Hill, Graduate*

**HAVE YOUR GUARD UP** and know that people are looking for things in other people. One time I was at a party having a good conversation with this guy. In my mind we weren't flirting, just having a friendly interaction, and eventually, he offered to walk me back to my dorm. The party was a little way off campus and it was sketchy to walk alone, so I was happy to take him up on it. But about halfway there, I naturally mentioned my boyfriend, and he totally stopped in his tracks and was, like, 'Oh, wait – you have a boyfriend? Why didn't you tell me that earlier?' He totally switched off his charm and his whole demeanor changed. He actually abandoned me mid-walk and I had to go the rest of the way home alone. That was a wake-up call for me that even what feels like the most innocent, surface level conversation can be taken as an invitation for sex.
> —MEGHAN WALLACE
> NORTHERN ARIZONA UNIVERSITY, SENIOR

• • • • • • • •

**DON'T FEEL THAT YOU NEED** to be at every party all the time. It's perfectly okay to be at home sleeping on a Saturday night; there's nothing wrong with that. More people do it than you think. If you get too caught up in the social scene, you lose sight of other things.
> —HANNAH SMITH
> HARVARD UNIVERSITY, JUNIOR

• • • • • • • •

**IF YOU DON'T WANT TO DRINK,** then it's all about the people you find. If you surround yourself with people who drink and who will pressure you, it will be a difficult situation. If you surround yourself with people who are hesitant to drink or who are responsible, it won't be such a problem.
> —ANONYMOUS
> UNIVERSITY OF VIRGINIA, SENIOR

## BINGE-DRINKING

More than a quarter of college students reported having at least 5 drinks the last time they partied or socialized, according to a national study. For men, binge-drinking is defined as having 5 or more drinks in a row. Women qualify after only 4 drinks.

# VAPING

WHEN IT COMES TO VAPING, AVOID GIVING IN TO PEER PRESSURE. Vape culture is prevalent, I believe, on every college campus. They want to seem cool around their friends. Once at a party, I saw my friend, who had never smoked before and was very much against smoking, start Juuling. When I asked her about it, she told me she wanted to impress this boy she liked. You're going to be around people who are hitting their Juul every single second, but if they're really your friends, they won't force you to do something you don't want to do. Don't feel like you need a nicotine addiction just to fit in.
—*ANONYMOUS*
*CHAPMAN UNIVERSITY, FRESHMAN*

STUDENTS AT STANFORD ARE GENERALLY HEALTH-CONSCIOUS and aware of the negative impacts of vaping, which serves as a deterrent. But there's a minority that does vape and does so fairly regularly. They see nicotine as a coping mechanism and stress reliever. It's not uncommon to find people panicking when unable to find their Juul.
—*ANONYMOUS*
*STANFORD UNIVERSITY, FRESHMAN*

KEEP IN MIND THAT VAPING WILL COST YOU BOTH MONEY AND HEALTH. I vaped a lot throughout high school. Everyone did. It was a very normal thing. I even knew one kid who would hit two Juuls at the same time. Honestly, I probably would still be doing it, but it got expensive. I was going through a pack of pods a week, and those cost about $25. I just couldn't afford it anymore. But I'm glad I basically quit because my health has gotten a lot better, and I've saved a lot of money. I'll admit that I still hit my friend's Juuls when I'm with them, though.
—*ANONYMOUS*
*SYRACUSE UNIVERSITY, FRESHMAN*

ONE TIME, I WAS AT A PARTY IN A DORM AND SO MANY PEOPLE WERE VAPING that it set off the fire alarm! The entire party had to leave and once they kick you out you can't come back in, so vaping killed the party.
—*RHETTA*
*UNIVERSITY OF NOTRE DAME, SOPHOMORE*

**IF YOU HAVE A FAKE ID,** be careful and make sure you know where you can and can't go – ask around.

There's this bar, Cubby Bar in Wrigleyville and it's the only Arizona State University bar in all of Chicago. I had just gotten my fake ID, and I was feeling pretty confident. There was a big football game I was dying to watch with fellow ASU fans. So, I walk up to Cubby Bar with my ASU gear and the guy knows right away. First of all, I show up with a fake ID from Ohio, I go to school in Chicago, and I'm wearing ASU gear... So, it's kind of hard to sell that one. Immediately, he bent it and realized it was fake. He let me buy it back from him for 60 bucks, and he takes my money and gives me the ID and tells me to scram. He had already bent it enough to where it will never work again, so I spent that money for nothing. He got me.
—*ANONYMOUS*
*LOYOLA UNIVERSITY IN CHICAGO, SOPHOMORE*

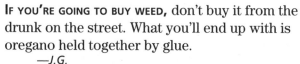

**IF YOU'RE GOING TO BUY WEED,** don't buy it from the drunk on the street. What you'll end up with is oregano held together by glue.
—*J.G.*
*FLORIDA STATE UNIVERSITY, GRADUATE*

# ABSTINENCE IN THE MINORITY...

Percentage of respondents who said "zero" when asked how many alcoholic drinks they had the last time they partied or socialized: 35%.

# ...AND VAPING ON THE RISE

Percentage of respondents who said they had used e-cigarettes in the last 30 days: 19%

"I was thinking about rushing a frat, but now I'm not so sure."

# Animal House: Fraternities & Sororities

**M**aybe you've seen *"Legally Blonde," "Animal House,"* or the more recent romp, *"Neighbors,"* and wondered, *"Are sororities and frats really like that?"* Naturally, Hollywood does exaggerate. But the answer to that question is: yes....kind of. Much as Greek organizations prefer to dwell on the camaraderie they promote, their many hours of community service, and the career opportunities that come from having octopus-like alumni networks, the wild partying and debauchery (and, yes, hazing) they sometimes unleash do dominate the social life at many campuses.

In an effort to curb some of the worst excesses, some fraternal organizations have banned alcohol altogether or held off courting freshman to give them time to learn their limits. But as long as frat houses continue to be the life of the party at your college, maybe you need to read on.

**BE A PART OF THE GREEK SYSTEM.** It is a great place for networking down the road. People get hired because they were in the same sorority as the boss.
—HEATHER POLLOCK
CALIFORNIA STATE UNIVERSITY AT FULLERTON, GRADUATE

**EVEN IF YOU DON'T WANT TO BE IN A FRAT, YOU SHOULD DO RUSH; YOU'LL GET FREE DRINKS AND HAVE FUN.**
—J.D.
EMORY UNIVERSITY, SENIOR

**HEADLINES**

- The majority of people involved in Greek life generally love it.

- When deciding whether to "go Greek," first figure out what you want from college; then check which organizations offer this.

- Got free time? Greek life will fill most of it with socials, volunteer events, sports and more. Consider taking fewer courses the semester you pledge so you'll be better able to deal with all the added demands.

- Fact: People who don't take part in Greek life also enjoy college.

**AT LEAST TRY RUSH.** You don't have to pledge but going through Rush is a really good time to meet other girls who are going through what you're going through. It's a really great bonding time.
—*DENISE O.*
*UNION COLLEGE, JUNIOR*

• • • • • • • •

**DO NOT BELIEVE THE HYPE** that Greek organizations feed you during your first semester in college. You will not find friends who 'will be there for you' if you join a fraternity or sorority just as you get into college. These organizations try to get freshmen to join by saying that this is the best way to find friends. On the contrary, it's the best way to exclude yourself from people who can become your best friends, and to get a narrow view of college life. Before joining a Greek organization, find an organization that shares your interests, perhaps something where you can have a wide variety of friends.
—*D.*
*MOORHEAD STATE UNIVERSITY, JUNIOR*

I **DIDN'T JOIN A FRAT** because I didn't want to do chores. I did chores at home and left that behind; who needs it? But to meet girls, the frat guys do have an advantage.
—*INSU CHANG*
*CARNEGIE MELLON UNIVERSITY, JUNIOR*

" The first frat party I went to as a pledge, they told us not to wear anything nice. First thing that happens when I walk in, a girl throws an entire beer on me. It was called Beer Splash. I was like, "This is where I want to be." "
—*A.G.S.*
*UNIVERSITY OF TENNESSEE, DID NOT GRADUATE*

**"I HAVE TO PAY TO BE YOUR SISTER?"** That was the first question that popped into my head after accepting an invitation to join my dream sorority house. My whole family had been Greek in college, but I couldn't get past the fact that I was paying to have friends. Now I understand that the friends I made in my sorority are forever, and even when I no longer pay for room and board and T-shirts, my sisters will still be there. I never bought my friends – I just put down a deposit.
—*AMANDA SOUKUP*
*UNIVERSITY OF NEBRASKA, SOPHOMORE*

# DON'T BE IN A RUSH TO RUSH...

I'M IN A SORORITY, and it's the best thing I've ever done in my life. I'm such a better person for being in a sorority. But it's way too early to pledge freshman year; I pledged sophomore year. You need to establish yourself at your college first. You meet your freshman group of friends; then you can pledge sophomore year. I did, and I didn't feel like I was pledging too late. The year I pledged, there were 450 sophomores, versus 50 freshmen. It's just too much for freshmen.
—*KRISTIN THOMAS*
*JAMES MADISON UNIVERSITY, JUNIOR*

I JOINED A FRAT SPRING SEMESTER of my freshman year. It was a great experience; the best thing I ever did. I was against fraternities completely, I got dragged into it, and now the brothers are my best friends. I was that guy who said, "Frat guys suck!" But things change.
—*CHRIS MCANDREW*
*UNIVERSITY OF DELAWARE, JUNIOR*

I WENT TO A LARGE SCHOOL where you didn't have to be Greek to have a life. But I wanted both, so during my sophomore year I decided to pledge. This gave me time to make other friendships with people who weren't necessarily going Greek. And as it turned out, not all of my closest friends from freshman year decided to go Greek. My advice: Don't jump into pledging. Get to know the campus, get to know friends outside of Greek life, and get used to what life is like without it. That way you can decide if it's right for you. At my school, sororities were very competitive, and many women never got invited to join any sorority. So, this was tough for some people.
—*ANONYMOUS*
*INDIANA UNIVERSITY, GRADUATE*

DON'T PLEDGE YOUR FIRST YEAR. You will limit your experiences as a freshman. And it takes up a lot of time. I pledged my sophomore year, and I know people who did it their junior year. Don't be in a hurry: Greek life isn't going anywhere!
—*NIROSHAN RAJARATNAM*
*UNIVERSITY OF MARYLAND, GRADUATE*

# ...AND ONE REASON TO QUIT EARLY

**IF YOU'RE GOING TO JOIN A SORORITY,** bail after the first year – two years at most. The whole sorority fraternity thing inhibits having a rich and diverse college experience. You're lumped together with a small percentage of the campus population, and you cheat yourself of the opportunity to meet interesting people who wouldn't be caught dead on Greek Row. At first, a sorority or fraternity can be comforting. You just left home for the first time, and being around people who are like you can put you at ease; that's okay. But after the first year or two, it's not doing you any favors. Get out. Find the best in the bunch, keep them as friends, then bail. You may catch flak, and you won't be a lifetime member of your frat or sorority. But you will be better off, finding your own way on your own terms.

> —*B.P.*
> *FLORIDA STATE UNIVERSITY, GRADUATE*

**BASE YOUR CHOICE ON THE PEOPLE YOU MEET,** and not the perspective or stereotype that other people assign it. Looking back on the Greek process now, I think I was obsessed with superficial things... The girls that I'm with now have truly shaped my college experience, and really helped me learn about who I am, and how to be independent. I can't even believe that I was obsessed with who had the best parties, or who mixed with the hottest frat, or had the coolest apparel. That's stuff that doesn't really matter, and I would be so unhappy if I had ended up in the sorority that I thought I wanted, versus the sorority that I actually got.

> —*SARAH*
> *UNIVERSITY OF MICHIGAN, JUNIOR*

If you're in a frat or sorority, be prepared for people to put you down for being Greek.

> —*SHEILA CRAWFORD*
> *NORTH CAROLINA STATE UNIVERSITY, SOPHOMORE*

# GREEK LIFE: BOTH SIDES NOW

## PRO

**I JOINED MY SORORITY ON A WHIM** – I was in a suite of eight girls my freshman year, and a lot of them were rushing. They encouraged me to come along for the fun experience. They said it's a great way to meet people, etc. And I went, but I didn't think I would join. But I found one sorority where I met a bunch of girls and had a lot of great conversations, so I figured I'd try it. I don't think it's right for everyone, or that everyone would feel that it's worth the time commitment. But I've had a great experience.
    —COLLEEN
      PRINCETON UNIVERSITY, JUNIOR

**REGARDLESS OF WHAT YOU'VE HEARD** about it prior to college or what your stance is on Greek life, don't hate on it unless you've tried it. Sure, there's always going to be talk about dying of excessive alcohol consumption, hazing, and the like, but most chapters are just like normal, social organizations of college kids.

I came into college not even knowing what sororities were. When I heard you had to pay dues, I thought: that's dumb to pay for your friendships. But the reality is, you're paying for opportunities. Opportunities to meet and make new friends, opportunities to have leadership skills, opportunities to engage in community service and campus activities as part of a larger organization, etc.

Most importantly, joining a sorority offered me the opportunity to grow into a better version of myself. Of course, Greek life isn't for everyone. But everyone should have the opportunity to determine that for themselves. If anything, you'll get a t-shirt and some free food out of the recruitment/rush process.
    —CHRISTINE
      DREXEL UNIVERSITY, JUNIOR

MY FRIENDS GOT ME TO ATTEND MY FIRST GREEK THING by claiming I was a hermit, who didn't do anything. It was a way to get me out of my dorm, and it ended up totally making my college experience.

After the four-day formal recruitment process, I decided to join because I didn't have very many friends when I came to South Dakota State. So I needed an outlet to meet people. Ceres, a sorority, was one of the ways that I did that, because I ended up with 50 new friends there. I stayed in it because there are a lot of leadership opportunities I was able to take on through the sorority itself. We were always doing community service events and holding sorority meetings. I think I would have found some of those opportunities without Ceres, but it made them easier to find.
—MERCEDES LEMKE
    SOUTH DAKOTA STATE UNIVERSITY, GRADUATE

## CON

DON'T LET OTHER PEOPLE TELL YOU WHAT YOU SHOULD DO OR WHERE YOU SHOULD RUSH. At my school, starting on the first day of move-in, Greek life seems to be all that anyone is able to talk about. Many conversations start the same way: "Where did you guys go last night?" and, in the early spring, "Where are you rushing?"

Because Greek life has such a hold over freshmen, it's very easy to forget that you don't have to join a frat or sorority to have friends or enjoy college. During my freshman year, I was one of the kids who was completely blinded by the romanticization of Greek life; I was so caught up in going to frat parties every weekend, and debating with my friends about which frat is the best, or where we should rush, that I never gave myself the opportunity to take a step back and really reflect on joining a frat and if it would be the right move for me. It wasn't until the tail end of freshman year that I ultimately realized that joining a frat was not the path I wanted to go down. My message is this; joining a frat or a sorority is your choice. Don't listen to the bullshit rankings that freshmen are so concerned with. Just listen to yourself and do what feels right.
—AAVO
    UNIVERSITY OF PENNSYLVANIA, JUNIOR

**FRATS ARE FOR IDIOTS.** But if you really feel like you have to pay dues to make friends, or spend a month scrubbing toilets and performing idiotic stunts so people will like you, then I guess frats are for you. If you don't care about individuality, or respect for yourself or for women, sign up. If you want to bypass all opportunity for meaningful relationships and skip right to drinking buddies and one-night stands, go for it. Don't get me wrong: I was good friends with some frat boys and sorority girls in college, just like I'm friends with some Republicans now. But it was *despite* their affiliations, not *because of* them.
—E.S.
STATE UNIVERSITY OF NEW YORK AT BINGHAMTON, GRADUATE

. . . . . . . . .

**I'VE MET A BUNCH OF DIFFERENT PEOPLE** through work and social life who participated in Greek life and I don't feel like their life was better because of it. I think my college experience was just as beneficial and just as enjoyable without it. We had parties in the woods.
—LILLIE REITER
GUILFORD COLLEGE, GRADUATE

**HAZING HAPPENS EVERYWHERE, NO MATTER WHAT COLLEGES TELL PARENTS.** Sometimes it's just about drinking. But there's some pretty terrible stuff pledges are forced to do. I knew a kid who had to bob for onions in a bucket of vomit. One frat made their pledges stick toothpicks under their toenails and then go around kicking doors. Do your research. Spend time with frat brothers when they aren't partying. Ask around about the reputation of a frat. If people say that hazing there is crazy or that the basement is too scary to go into, believe it. And think about pledging somewhere else.
—ANONYMOUS
DARTMOUTH COLLEGE

# SCIENCE EXPERIMENT?

In my fraternity house, we had a very old iron stove in the kitchen, original to the house. The stove was huge, and completely useless – it hadn't worked in decades. But nobody could move it because it was so heavy, and no trash disposal company or dumping ground would accept it. It seemed as though our house was stuck with this old relic for another 80 years. Then one night we had a brainstorm. In the middle of the night, about 10 of us hoisted this piece of useless iron onto a dolly and rolled it across campus to the Science Center. Now, in the lobby of the college's Science Center was a small museum of scientific artifacts (you know, like a 200-year-old microscope, or a skeleton of a million-year-old small rodent). So, we found a nice little nook for the stove (right in between some relics) and placed a professional-looking sign on the stove which said: "Random Kinetic Energy Enhancer, circa 1842." Only a science geek would know that that is another way of saying: "This is an old stove."

The relic stayed for about a week, then was hauled off by the university. We didn't pay a dime.

—I.L.S.
WESLEYAN UNIVERSITY, GRADUATE

# FILE UNDER "H," FOR "HELL, YES!"

College deans like to joke that they can usually tell when students pledged just by looking at their transcripts. Their advice, then, is to consider taking fewer courses the semester you pledge to give yourself some extra bandwidth to deal with the added demands you'll be juggling.

# THE GREEK ALPHABET

KEEP THIS CHEAT SHEET HANDY IF YOU ARE THINKING OF RUSHING. KNOWLEDGE OF THIS ALPHABET MAY SPARE YOU FROM HAVING TO DO MORE PUSHUPS OR DRINKS THAN YOU MIGHT OTHERWISE ENJOY.

*The Editors*

# SURVIVING RUSH...
# WITH YOUR DIGNITY INTACT

THE ONLY WAY TO GET INTO THE RIGHT HOUSE FOR YOU is to be yourself during Rush. Rush is awful. You wake up before 7 A.M. every morning and you go out all day, running around to different houses in the 100-degree heat in heels, talking to girls in, like, 30-minute increments. It's like speed-dating, but with chicks. If you're quiet and simply answer their questions and don't enthusiastically respond with questions of your own, chances are you won't get asked back to that house. It's all very superficial. You have to be bubbly and energetic all day long and that is just not how you feel after doing this for six days. I noticed that when I was at the houses I wasn't interested in, I had much better interactions with them because I wasn't worried about how I was coming across. That's how I should have approached all of them.
   —ANONYMOUS
      UNIVERSITY OF ARIZONA, FRESHMAN

RUSH WITH NO EXPECTATIONS OR PRECONCEPTIONS: YOU'LL BE THANKFUL YOU DID LATER. In a weird way, things worked out for me because of my lack of knowledge of sororities. I really didn't do any research about the individual chapters beforehand, so I was basically flying blind. I didn't know anything about which house was the top house or which house had cool vibes. I was able to talk to girls in each chapter with no preconceptions and just had to worry about enjoying my conversations. My decision was quick and painless because it was purely based off of which chapter I had the most positive experience in. By contrast, some of my friends brushed off houses that they now – years later – have very good friends in and regret not considering more heavily because they were so focused on getting into whatever the top house was our freshman year.
   —ANONYMOUS
      NORTHWESTERN UNIVERSITY, GRADUATE

**Y**OU'RE GONNA MAKE CHOICES AND SOMETIMES YOU'RE GONNA FIND YOURSELF IN A PIT and you gotta find a way to be resilient, especially during hazing. Lo and behold, it's the night before my first two exams in college and we have our Monday pledge event and they tell us we're going to get our Big Brother. You go up to your prospective brother and you take a shot, if they take it with you that's your Big Bro. If they don't, you have to go to someone else. I knew exactly who mine was, but he wanted me to drink more, so I went up to four or five different people and finally came back to my Big Bro. Then, strippers came, it was a party and it was debaucherous to say the least. I blacked out pretty hard.

I woke up on the couch in my friend's apartment in just my underwear one hour before my first midterm. He gave me a giant Lakers baseball-jersey, bright red Atlanta Hawks shorts, and UGGs slippers. I looked like a Ronald McDonald caricature.

We stopped and got coffee on the way to class and I fell asleep in the Dunkin Donuts, still drunk. I got a pen from the lady at Dunkin and I went to class. Luckily, I was able to wing it through the multiple-choice parts, but then there was an essay question and I hardly got any points for it because the teacher couldn't read my handwriting. I got a B- on one test and a C+ on the other, and after that, because I didn't have my phone, my wallet, or my keys to my dorm, I went back to this girl's room from my class to take a nap and we ended up making out. That morning, I woke up in a pit of clothes, very drunk, but I found a way to get up and solve my problems.

 —*T*OM
  *A*RIZONA *S*TATE *U*NIVERSITY, *G*RADUATE

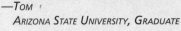

**THE WHOLE PROCESS TRULY IS SUPERFICIAL.** Sorority members judge Rushies based slightly on appearance and primarily on a 5- to 10-minute conversation that takes place within the most fake and uncomfortable environment. With all this in mind, if you want to join a sorority, you take it for what it is. Don't go into Rush believing that the girls you meet have the final say (or any say, for that matter) on who you are, or how "cool" or desirable you are. They're judging you based on a glimpse of who they think you are.

    —D.
        *DUKE UNIVERSITY, SENIOR*

**IF YOU'RE LOOKING FOR SOMETHING OTHER THAN THE STEREOTYPICAL 'FRAT' EXPERIENCE,** there are other options that provide a close-knit community with personal and professional development that can really be fulfilling. I went through the traditional Rush week process and I didn't find a fraternity with what I was looking for. I was a little discouraged but kinda like, "this is not for me. I'm not looking to party all the time anyway."

The next year, I was recruited to start a new SigEp chapter on my campus without pledging or hazing and with a personal development curriculum that included classes on personal finance and vehicle maintenance. We were college students and we still partied, but our focus was not on partying – it was on these other things. I made some amazing friends that I'll have for life. Looking back on it, it was a great decision.

    —*KEVIN*
        *UNIVERSITY OF ARIZONA, GRADUATE*

## A POPULAR OPTION

Some 800,000 undergrad-uates par-ticipate in fraternities and sororities on 800 col-lege campus-es, joining a social network that encom-passes rough-ly 9 million alumni around the world, according to a recent report in CNN.

**THE FIRST FEW PARTIES OF THE YEAR,** they'll let pretty much anyone in just to get themselves known for killer parties. After a few weeks, though, they start patrolling their parties by placing a few brothers in the driveway to tell the masses that "the house occupancy is full, but try back later." If you drop the name of a brother, though, they'll let you in. So, at the first party of the year, I randomly met a guy named Steve and found out he was from Louisiana. So every time I went back, I told the guys in the driveway I knew "Steve from Louisiana," and it worked like a charm. I passed Steve from Louisiana's name on to whoever wanted to hang out at that frat.
  —*ASHLEY LEAVELL*
   *BOSTON UNIVERSITY, SENIOR*

• • • • • • • •

**CHOOSE THE FRAT HOUSE THAT FITS YOUR LIFESTYLE.** Ours is a dry house, so we can't drink in the house, which is nice, because you have a place to come back to where you know people won't be partying late at night. So you have a quiet place where you can go back and do your homework. If you party where you live, you wake up the next morning and your house is trashed, because the rest of the people at the party don't really care what happens, because it's not their house. This way, I could just go home at night and didn't have to worry about a bunch of people partying.
  —*JACOB SPIER*
   *UNIVERSITY OF SOUTH DAKOTA, JUNIOR*

• • • • • • • •

**FRESHMAN GIRLS SHOULD GO THROUGH SORORITY RUSH,** but don't take it too seriously. If you take it to heart, people can tell. You run the risk of getting really hurt. It's just a group of girls; there are other things in life.
  —*ANONYMOUS*
   *UNIVERSITY OF VIRGINIA, SOPHOMORE*

WHEN I WAS MEETING THE GUYS, I was expecting the typical fraternity stereotypes to come out – like using very specific words like Dude, Bro, 'that's so frat, Bro,' Bruh – especially Bruh.

If you enjoy that kind of lifestyle, go for it. But people need to understand that not all fraternities are like that. My fraternity, especially – we were just a bunch of nerds all put together and we specialized in different areas of nerdiness. We didn't use the stereotypical language. We didn't dress the same way as what people might think of a fraternity brother. We didn't *behave* like that. A lot of people were very surprised by how we behaved compared to other fraternities. So, at the end of the day, what I expected was definitely not what I received.

Keep an open mind when meeting these fraternities. There are fraternities out there that might fit your personality style.

When I was in high school, I was a very quiet kid. I didn't talk much, didn't participate in class as much. I just didn't really speak to a lot of people other than my small group of friends. So, when I finally joined this fraternity, I really enjoyed the social aspect. I jumped out of my comfort zone from high school and learned how to speak with other people; that's one of the biggest things I got from this fraternity.
—A.C.
UNIVERSITY OF PITTSBURGH, GRADUATE

# THE CAT IN THE FRAT?

Theodore Geisel went on to write children's books under the pen name, Dr. Seuss, after he graduated from Dartmouth. But the budding writer left a piece of himself at rival Cornell, too. On a visit to Ithaca, he took the liberty of leaving some penciled illustrations on the walls of a speakeasy that eventually became Cornell's Delta Upsilon fraternity.

# SORORITY SISTER LOOKS BACK

**I** JUST REMEMBER NOT KNOWING A SINGLE THING ABOUT **RUSH.** All my dresses were from Target, and I didn't own a pair of heels. There are a lot of girls who consider Bid Day as important as their wedding day, and they had prepared since birth. They have their résumés professionally done. I just made mine on Word in Calibri, the default typeface.

At first, not knowing anything benefited me because I was able to go in with an open mind. But then there were red flags: not liking the rules, not feeling like I fit in. Most people think "hazing," and they think alcohol, being forced to party, and being forced to do drugs. In my experience, that is not the most common form of hazing or the way that hazing actually manifests itself through more implicit, less overt means. A lot of hazing goes unreported, 'cause people don't realize it's hazing or realize they have a right to stand up to it, or they consider it a bonding experience.

The worst hazing I experienced was related to my involvement against "The Machine," a political coalition that controls local, campus, state, and national politics in Alabama. I lived at the sorority and the girls just kind of did everything they could to make me feel unsafe and unwanted in what was supposed to be my home. Dissenting opinions weren't allowed. I ended up moving out, and tried contacting the higher-ups, who implied that the hazing I experienced didn't matter because I was the only one speaking out. Nothing got done. It was just a really excruciating and isolating experience, because your sorority is supposed to be your home. Sometimes, I talk about my experiences and I get Alabama Sorority Trolls in my mentions saying, "We don't get hazed. We don't haze," and I say, "That's great. But there are definitely girls in your sorority who have been hazed who are just too scared to talk about it."

Looking back, I was just kind of a naive freshman, following these rules blindly. And plenty of people are like that. I wish I had been a little more vocal.
> —*HELMI HENKIN*
> *UNIVERSITY OF ALABAMA, GRADUATE*

BEFORE COLLEGE, I WAS VERY ANTI-SORORITY; I thought they were evil. But now, even though I'm not in a sorority, I live with sorority girls, and they're all my good friends. I go to lots of their functions and have a great time. It's not a big deal if you're not in a sorority. It's only a big deal the first few weeks of the year and then the five days of Rush. During Rush, I just remind myself that I do have friends; they're just all busy this week. If you're not sure whether you want to join a fraternity or sorority, remember that you can still join and it doesn't have to be the top priority in your life. Join; just don't become president. Sororities and fraternities are a great way to make a big school seem smaller.
—SUMMER J.
UNIVERSITY OF VIRGINIA, SENIOR

• • • • • • • •

BE SWEET AS PIE during your sorority pledge period and wait until after you're active to tell off the snots who were mean to you. Better yet, just steal their boyfriends.
—LYNN LAMOUSIN
LOUISIANA STATE UNIVERSITY, GRADUATE

# HISTORY CORNER

1776 – Phi Beta Kappa, the first Greek letter organization, was founded at the College of William & Mary, according to CNN. Envisioned initially as a secret society whose members would be free to discuss any topic they chose, the society had its first meeting at the Apollo Room of the Raleigh Tavern in Williamsburg, VA. Its name originated from the motto, "Love of learning is the guide of life."

1870 – The First Greek letter organization for women, Kappa Alpha Theta, did not begin for nearly another century.

# THE 411 ON HAZING FROM 3 FAMILIES WHO WOULD KNOW

*By the families of Marquise Braham, Max Gruver, and Timothy Piazza*

As you begin your college career, it's important to fully understand the social activities available on campus, including fraternities and sororities. Greek letter organizations promote brotherhood and sisterhood and promise a home away from home. Many people have fond memories of their Greek life experience. But Greek organizations are also secret societies, and there is a dark side – with potentially serious risks – that school officials will not readily share with you. Tragically, each of us has had a child die as a result of fraternity hazing. We want to share with you what we wish we and our children had known so that you return home safely to your own family.

## NEW TO CAMPUS: WHAT TO DO?

As a freshman, you may find yourself in a completely new environment, making important decisions on your own for the first time. Knowing few, if any, people on campus, you might be lonely and struggling to fit in. This can be a daunting and overwhelming experience. Resident advisers, counselors and others on campus will encourage you to get involved and join organizations as a way to make new friends. As a new student, you may naturally be drawn to fraternities and sororities. These groups often offer a party scene and access to alcohol that is not readily available at other organizations. While Greek letter groups can be worthwhile and perform community service, due to a lack of meaningful management and oversight, Greek members can foster, encourage and engage in potentially deadly traditions and rituals that involve hazing, binge drinking, sexual violence and illegal substance abuse (including the toxic use of prescription drugs).

The consequences of participating in these high-risk activities, or having them inflicted on you, can be life-shattering. You might think we're being overly dramatic, but we assure you, we're not. Not only might you rack up expensive legal bills for your family, you might be criminally charged as an accomplice to sexual abuse or some other crime because of the actions – and inactions – of your so-called brothers or sisters. Most kids aren't thinking about things like that when they go to college. As a young person, you probably feel invincible. But, please – take it from us. It's really important for you to rein in any feelings of invincibility. Those thoughts don't mesh well with the heavy alcohol and drug use or the forced activities that characterize many aspects of Greek life.

All of our kids were in their teens when they died as a result of hazing. We, like they, never saw it coming. We miss our kids more than life itself, just like your parents, family and friends would miss you. Horrible – and preventable – tragedies like ours, are real and do happen.

## WHAT IS HAZING?

Hazing is generally seen as any activity expected of someone seeking to join or participate in a group that intentionally or recklessly causes them physical or emotional harm, exposes them to danger, humiliation or ridicule, regardless of their willingness to participate. Be aware that while hazing is most identifiable in Greek life, it also occurs in other organizations like bands, sports teams, the military and other campus groups.

## ASK QUESTIONS ABOUT GREEK LIFE VIOLATIONS

Finding information about Greek life violations isn't easy. Universities, national fraternities and sororities, and their insurance companies closely guard incidences of injury and death. Most schools prefer to dwell on the positive aspects of fraternities and sororities: lifelong friendships, job connections, better GPAs. Administrators often insist they "have zero tolerance for hazing" even when their rebukes amount to mere slaps on the wrist.

Ask school officials at your college whether they keep records of Greek life violations. If not, how do they track criminal and code-of-conduct violations? Which frats or sororities have been sanctioned in the past five years? For what and for how long? Have any students been suspended or expelled due to hazing activities or other serious misconduct tied to Greek life? Have any been investigated by authorities or charged with a crime? How could someone new to the community know which Greek organizations have questionable records? If the university can't or won't answer these questions, that should be a red flag to you about a lack of seriousness in its oversight of Greek life.

You are also within your rights to demand a similar accounting from the fraternities and sororities themselves. Request specific details about any hazing-related incidents they've investigated for the last five years. If the local chapters are reluctant to share that information, or you think it might harm your admission as a pledge, consider contacting the national umbrella organizations.

Upperclassmen are another valuable resource when inquiring about the reputation of any fraternity or sorority you're keen on joining. They may be able to tell you a lot about an organization's true character. Waiting one semester to rush would also give you time to look further into organizations and their members before putting yourself on the line.

## WHAT ARE THE RISKS FROM HAZING AND HOW TO AVOID THEM?

On any given weekend at universities across America, it's not uncommon for students to end up in the emergency room due to injuries they've suffered while participating in Greek life. The public seldom hears about these incidents unless someone dies or is injured seriously enough to attract media attention. In 2017, there were at least five hazing-related deaths on college campuses, and over the past 10 years, there have been more than 40 hazing-related deaths at Greek letter organizations, of which our families are but three.

The grim details can all be read at hanknuwer.com/hazing-deaths, the website maintained by Hank Nuwer, a national expert who has been tracking hazing-related deaths stretching back two centuries.

If you do join a fraternity or sorority, one of the most important things we urge you to do is call 911 if your Brother or Sister needs help. You need to call 911 even if you're worried that doing so might get you or other members in trouble. If it's a situation where you'd call 911 for a family member, then do it for your fellow student. Peer pressure can be a big part of Greek life. But making that call could literally save a life! We wish someone had the good conscience to call 911 when our kids were in danger. We don't want you, your Greek Brothers or Sisters, your family and friends, to be in the position we're in now, wishing that someone had stepped up so that our kids might still be alive.

## HAZING SIGNS AND HELPFUL RESOURCES

For students and the people who love them, here are some telltale signs of hazing to watch out for, courtesy of HazingPrevention.Org:

- Sudden change in behavior or attitude after joining an organization
- Decreased opportunities for family and friends to communicate with the student
- Unexplained injuries or illnesses
- Physical or psychological exhaustion
- Expressions of sadness and worthlessness
- Changes in sleeping and eating habits
- An increase in secrecy and evasiveness in sharing details

The parents who've co-authored this piece are working with national fraternity and sorority leaders in an anti-hazing coalition to strengthen laws and raise awareness of the risks, dangers and unimaginable loss that result from hazing. By bolstering anti-hazing laws and increasing the penalties, we aim to deter dangerous and reckless hazing activities, and hold those who still choose to haze their brothers and sisters criminally accountable for their actions to the fullest extent of the law. No one should have to experience hazing to be part of an organization at college.

Finally, please take a moment to view this educational video, "Love, Mom and Dad," where we tell the stories of our beautiful boys and how their unnecessary deaths from hazing have devastated our lives and the lives of our families, forever, at https://therecordonline.net/featured/love-mom-dad-educational-version

# WHAT I KNOW NOW

**AT FIRST, I WAS OPPOSED TO JOINING A FRAT.** It was only because of a pre-game I attended, where the frat brothers were deceptively welcoming to the point where I thought this was a cool group of people I could learn a lot from. Maybe, it'd be worth checking this out more.

They said, "Oh yeah, this is going to be super fun. You'll get out of your comfort zone," and I thought, "Ah, right up my alley. I love getting out of my comfort zone."

Bid night came, and they dropped a note in my room that said, "Be in your room next week with an orange, a tie, and this invitation card."

The weekend comes, they knock on the door. I have the orange and tie in my hand, and open the door. I'm like "Hey, what's up?" and the dynamic changed all of the sudden. They were no longer friendly. They were, like, "You're a pledge now. You listen to our orders. We're not friends. That's it. This is a process." They took me to a car that was waiting outside. They said put the blindfold on. I put it on and they pushed me into the car. There were two other kids in the back seat with me, and one more student to pick up. So, there were four of us pledging. They handed us 2 forty-ounce bottles of beer each, and we had to finish them in the car. That was the start of the night.

At one point, they saw cops and decided not to do the stuff they were planning. Instead, they took us back to campus, led us up some stairs, still blindfolded, and forced us to squat on our knees. They told us we couldn't move or talk or we'd get punished. Finally, they led us into a dark room, lined us up, and started asking us about the pledge class. Any question we got wrong, we had to chug beer. "How many people are in the pledge class?" they asked. We answered 'four.' All of us kept guessing and kept getting it wrong. They said there was only one in the pledge class since "you guys are all one." They gave us a handle of vodka and asked, "Who is going to lead this pledge class? You guys have to finish this handle in two minutes." One guy who was really passionate said he'd do it. As this was going on, we were all taking handle pulls from the handle. But a minute and a half went by, and we still had a quarter of the handle left. People were on the verge of puking. I decided to finish of the bottle because no one wanted to do that. After that, they took us back in the room, and we showed them the finished handle and they gave us each a nickname and said you guys are officially part of the pledge class. After that, I don't remember because I blacked out.

I ended up in the hospital. That's how intoxicated I was. After that, I quit.

Don't succumb to peer pressure. I had some bad feeling from the beginning when I started interacting with them more. If you have bad feelings, you should communicate that. In the long run, it's not going to matter whether you did this or not. Don't be afraid of missing out because it's not worth it. It's just dangerous and irresponsible.

—ANONYMOUS
PRINCETON UNIVERSITY, JUNIOR

DON'T LET THE PEER PRESSURE AND EXPECTATIONS OF BEING IN A FRATERNITY force you to drink so much. Right at the end of the first quarter of college we had a party and one of my buddies got so messed up that he was unconscious, and we had to call an ambulance. Not only was it scary for all of us, but he had to pay a huge ambulance bill. Nothing good came of it. Also, you can get in a bubble in a frat. It can shelter you from the cooler things there are to do.

—RILEY HOFFMAN
UNIVERSITY OF CALIFORNIA AT SANTA BARBARA, GRADUATE

"Don't mind Brad. His junior year abroad just got approved."

# 18 Road Trip! Everything from Quick Getaways to Study Abroad

A s awesome as college may be, there may come a time when you feel like hitting the pause button and getting away for a while. Whether you crave a week-long, spring fling in Miami or a languid semester in Cuba – stepping outside of your day-to-day existence can bring a welcome break and a shift in perspective.

Or maybe the tropics aren't for you, and you see yourself sipping coffee in a Paris sidewalk café, flipping through some Sartre or Camus before your afternoon class at the Sorbonne, or signing up for a year of tutorials in English lit with the dons – at Oxford. With so many guided trips and academic programs to pick from, you may never have a better chance to see the world. Too good to be true? Be inspired by the true tales of those who have gone before you. Adventure awaits!

DECIDEDLY COLLEGIATE AND BROTASTIC, first-year road trips are an absolute must. Bring at least one responsible guy/girl with you to make sure that everyone gets back alive.
—J.V.
THE COLLEGE OF WILLIAM & MARY, GRADUATE

BRING FRIENDS HOME FOR THE HOLIDAYS.
—D.D.
UNIVERSITY OF PENNSYLVANIA, GRADUATE

- Your school most likely has one, if not several, study abroad programs. Check them out.
- A random road trip can be an important part of your time in college. Just bring everyone back alive and out of legal trouble.
- Many students use Spring Break to travel to third-world countries and volunteer – it's better for the résumé than partying!

**WHEN YOU SEE THE WORLD FROM A DIFFERENT PERSPECTIVE,** you realize what you can be.
—*M.A.*
*FLORIDA STATE UNIVERSITY, GRADUATE*

* * * * * * * *

**ONE OF THE BEST PARTS** about college is visiting your friends who go to other schools. Visit when your football teams play each other. It's a whole new batch of girls, and it'll spice up your party life.
—*ILAN GLUCK*
*UNIVERSITY OF MARYLAND, JUNIOR*

* * * * * * * *

**THE LESS OFTEN YOU GO HOME** your freshman year, the better. The more you're at school your freshman year, the more you're going to make friends and have people to hang out with after that. Your ties from home are going to break anyway. The sooner you do it, the better off you are.
—*BETHANY*
*JAMES MADISON UNIVERSITY, SENIOR*

* * * * * * * *

**ADVICE TO GUYS:** Go on a cruise for spring break. The odds are unbelievable! You will be amazed at the ratio.
—*JIMMY LYNCH*
*AUBURN UNIVERSITY, GRADUATE*

**IF SOMEONE YOU KNOW OFFERS TO HAVE YOU STAY WITH HER** over a break, take her up on it. One of the most interesting experiences I had was staying with the parents of a roommate or friend and discovering what her life was like before I met her. It is really mind-expanding and allows you to get to know someone in your life even better. You also have the added bonus of a personal tour guide to show you around. Nothing is more fun than rediscovering where you have lived for your whole life by showing your college friends all of the tourist destinations.
—*AMY*
*PRINCETON UNIVERSITY, FRESHMAN*

- - - - - - - -

**I WENT HOME FOR THE HOLIDAYS** my freshman year, and I think it was a good thing, because it can just get really crazy. Everything is so new and so exciting and there are so many people that you feel like you're at camp for an extended period of time.
—*SHANNON*
*STANFORD UNIVERSITY, SENIOR*

# DOESN'T FEEL LIKE SCHOOL

**Getting that vacation feeling - without leaving campus!**

- Beach house – The Citadel (South Carolina)
- Ski cabin on Mount Hood - Reed College (Oregon)
- Research boat – Hawaii Pacific University
- 2 private beaches and a private dock with a fleet of sailboats – Mitchell College (Connecticut)
- 20-foot boat "for marine studies" – Muhlenberg College (Pennsylvania)
- 28,000-acre experimental forest – University of Montana

# WHERE SPRING IS IN THE AIR

Most people imagine Orlando, Las Vegas and Cancun as the most sought-after destinations for anyone planning a spring break getaway. But based on Google searches, TravelMag determined that the most popular destinations were actually Panama City Beach in Florida and South Padre Island in Texas. Cancun came in fourth, behind Lake Havasu City, Arizona.

I WOULD RECOMMEND DRIVING your parents' van, with a nice bed in back, coast to coast, 3,000 miles. It doesn't take too long. I did that with my girlfriend. I learned to surf once I got to California. My parents didn't know I had taken the van until I was in another state. But when I called them, they said, "We've been waiting for you to do something like that." It was great.
—STEVE BAKER
COLUMBIA UNIVERSITY, SENIOR

• • • • • • • • •

PART OF COLLEGE IS SCULPTING YOUR BELIEFS and attitudes about the world. I'm a huge advocate for getting out there and seeing the real world; it's easy to stay caught up in the drama of classes, classmates, bad teachers, good or bad grades. My favorite so far is car-tripping around the East Coast with my buddy, who is a history major. We did the Freedom Trail in Boston, took a train into New York City and stayed overnight in a hostel where only a minority of the kids were speaking a language we could understand. We stopped in Salem, Massachusetts, saw the Flume in New Hampshire, and our base was in Vermont. We learned a lot about ourselves, and the areas we needed to focus on in order to excel in the basics of getting along in life.
—AMANDA
UNIVERSITY OF COLORADO AT COLORADO SPRINGS, SOPHOMORE

# A ROAD TRIP TO REMEMBER

One of the most memorable times I had in college was a road trip to New York City with about five pals, an idea hatched at 10 P.M., executed immediately, and celebrated in Central Park in the wee hours. We all flopped on the floor at a friend's place at Columbia University, partied some more with him, and woke up in a stupor.

The highlight was a morning visit to the home of one of the pals, the only son of a working-class couple in Queens. In that cramped apartment, during the time it took to eat a carefully prepared breakfast, we observed in utter awe the incredible, unfettered love of a mother and father for their son. They were so proud of their boy. It wasn't so much in what they said, but the ambience, the pictures on the mantle, the beam in dad's eye, the doting by the mother. There was nothing overpowering or unbalanced or pushy about it; it was a natural pride and confidence in their son. For me, there have been few times when I was inspired by the human condition; this was one of them.

—R.S.
GEORGETOWN UNIVERSITY, GRADUATE

CALL YOUR FRIENDS before you go on a road trip to see them. My friends and I went up to Providence. We were having a good time, and then we decided we wanted to go to Newport. When we were driving, it was pretty late at night, so my friend in Newport wouldn't pick up his phone. So, we had to keep on driving. When we got to Connecticut, we tried to call my friend there, and he didn't pick up either. Then we passed New York City and none of our friends would pick up the phone. They were all asleep. We ended up down at the Jersey Shore at four in the morning, after five hours of driving from Providence.

—THEODORE SCHIMENTI
COLUMBIA UNIVERSITY, FRESHMAN

#  SPRING BREAKS

**FOR SPRING BREAK, I WENT TO EUROPE** with my good friend Dave. We went to Switzerland and France with backpacks and thoroughly enjoyed getting to know the cities and each other. I think this was valuable because we are now greatly connected and also learned so much about the cities we explored. In particular, it was nice to be with a fellow student because this attracted other student travelers over the break.
  —*GERALDINE SARAH COWPER*
  *MACAULAY HONORS COLLEGE AT CUNY HUNTER, SENIOR*

**I TOOK AN ALTERNATIVE SPRING BREAK** to Honduras with a bunch of friends. We helped build latrines. It was a great experience. At college there are amazing volunteer opportunities.
  —*ELIZABETH ROTH*
  *UNIVERSITY OF PENNSYLVANIA, SENIOR*

**IF IT'S NOT YOUR THING TO DRINK A LOT** and do all that stuff, you probably won't enjoy spring break. You only get four spring breaks while you're in college. If you don't enjoy partying all the time, you're not going to enjoy it in Mexico after you spent $1,000.
  —*JONATHAN COHEN*
  *EMORY UNIVERSITY, SENIOR*

**MANY OF MY FRIENDS HAVE BEEN TO CANCUN** or did the "crazy" Spring Break thing. They've inevitably been disappointed. I found that leaving those weeks unplanned has been a big blessing. I've gotten in shape, and caught up on work and (what I miss most in college) sleep. That said, I've also gone to Liverpool, London, and Oxford for Spring Break when I was studying abroad. My girlfriend went with me. We're huge Beatles fans and we loved staying in hostels and visiting all the haunts and museums dedicated to that awesome band.
  —*RON Y. KAGAN*
  *MACAULAY HONORS COLLEGE AT CUNY HUNTER, SENIOR*

**I GOT INVOLVED IN SERVICE WORK,** traveling to other countries. I've been to Mexico and down south to North Carolina for Habitat for Humanity. That's defined my college career, my transformation. It gave me a better appreciation for my position in the world and at the same time for others in the world who don't have as much as I do. It's been an enlightening experience. But I've still had plenty of time to party.
— *JONATHAN GIFTOS*
*BOSTON COLLEGE, SENIOR*

**IF YOUR FRIENDS GO TO BIG SCHOOLS** that have huge annual weeks (Indiana's Little 500, Wisconsin's Halloween, Penn's Spring Fling, etc.), these provide good excuses for road trips to see them and have a great time at a different school. Music festivals are also fun.
— *MANNY*
*GEORGE WASHINGTON UNIVERSITY, SENIOR*

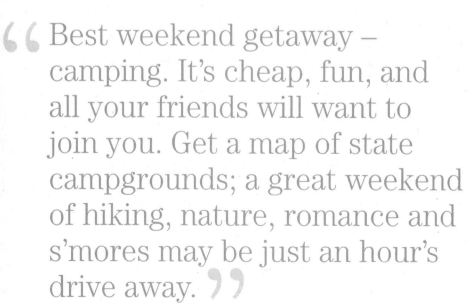

" Best weekend getaway – camping. It's cheap, fun, and all your friends will want to join you. Get a map of state campgrounds; a great weekend of hiking, nature, romance and s'mores may be just an hour's drive away. "
— *WENDY W.*
*UNIVERSITY OF GEORGIA, GRADUATE*

# TAKING YOUR EDUCATION ON THE ROAD

EVERY SINGLE STUDENT SHOULD STUDY ABROAD AT SOME POINT – it changes your perspective about everything. As a sophomore I went to South Korea for a month. It was essentially free, and we could sign up for anything, for credit. So, I took yacht-sailing. In the mornings, we'd go out and sail for three hours, and in the afternoon, we would come back for a Korean culture class. We'd go to shrines and temples and Korean baseball games, and we made Korean food and all these different things every day. It was amazing. We still talk to each other every day in a group chat, and we're hopefully planning a reunion trip to Europe in a few years. It's absolutely the best experience of my entire life. I wasn't just getting Asian culture – I was exposed to every culture around the world, because of everyone else on the trip.
—*TAYLOR ELLINGSON*
*NORTHERN STATE UNIVERSITY (S. DAKOTA), SENIOR*

IF YOU'RE GOING TO STUDY ABROAD, PLAN FOR THAT EARLY. I was abroad for a whole year studying Japanese and Japanese-related courses. Some of them couldn't really count for anything towards graduation, because I already had all those classes accounted for. They were just extra. So, I almost couldn't graduate on time with all the general education requirements I needed.
—*JESSICA SHILLING*
*UNIVERSITY OF PITTSBURGH, GRADUATE*

I STUDIED ABROAD FOR A SEMESTER IN SANTIAGO, CHILE. It was a fantastic experience, breaking out of the Princeton bubble. Going out and meeting new people, seeing a new culture, and learning from a different perspective was absolutely integral to my collegiate experience. We went on weekend trips, and one weekend we went to the south of Chile to Patagonia. We climbed a volcano and went camping. It was awesome.
—*JOSH*
*PRINCETON UNIVERSITY, SENIOR*

**THE ONE TIME I HAD REAL ISSUES WITH FINANCIAL AID** was when I was studying abroad. The company that was going abroad charged quite a bit and the college could only cover a certain amount. That involved a lot of headaches bouncing between the study abroad office and the financial aid office. But I did get to study abroad at Oxford University, which was absolutely incredible. Study abroad was literally some of the best months of my life.
—*ABE KENMORE*
*GUILFORD COLLEGE, GRADUATE*

**MY JUNIOR YEAR, I TOOK ADVANTAGE OF THE "TERMS ABROAD" PROGRAM** and lived in Ecuador for a year. It was a phenomenal opportunity to study abroad. Life had seemed sort of small before that experience.
—*CALE GARAMANDI*
*UNIVERSITY OF CALIFORNIA AT BERKELEY, JUNIOR*

**I WENT ON A SEMESTER-LONG TRIP ON A CRUISE SHIP.** It's a program where professors from around the country come and teach everything from anthropology to music to economics. We went to 10 countries around the world. It's the most amazing opportunity ever. You get to learn about countries from a very non-Western point of view. I went to a wild game reserve in South Africa and visited the sand people who live on the outskirts. We learned about them and they sold us their wares. We went skydiving. We went to Carnival in Rio. When you're a freshman you should plan to do something like that; it had such an impact on me.
—*MAYTAL AHARONY*
*GEORGE WASHINGTON UNIVERSITY, SENIOR*

**GO TO ITALY.** Spend a semester there. I did, and it completely changed my outlook on life. Before I went, I was only interested in the American college existence: partying, getting by, attending football games. After I got back, I wanted to learn more, to be more.
—*M.A.*
*FLORIDA STATE UNIVERSITY, GRADUATE*

# GETTING YOUR SCHOOL'S HELP TO MOUNT THAT EXPEDITION

Internships, Study Abroad programs and Alternative Spring Breaks are three amazing opportunities that are only available while you're in college. Explore them now. After you graduate and move on to graduate school or full-time employment, you probably won't have time to go on any form of Spring Break or Study Abroad programs, and internships are what helps you discover possible career fields.

**General tips to help you to discover these opportunities:**

1.  Check out what your campus offers, starting with the Campus Activities office, the Career Center, and the International Education departments. If there are workshops on how to select a program, or how to make your application stand out – attend them.
2.  Review your options and decide on a few to apply for.
3.  If letters of recommendation are necessary, ask for them early on.

**Internships:** Are you interested in a specific career field, inside or outside your areas of study? An internship in this field is a great way to learn more about it, and do something that looks good on your (future) résumé. Some tips:

*   Research the company or department for which you want to intern. Spend some time thinking about what job experiences and skills you want to gain from the internship. That will help you during the interview.
*   Don't expect to get paid for every internship; in fact, most of them are volunteer positions.

**Study Abroad:** This is a fun way to meet students from other colleges and spend an entire term, or even a year, with them in another country, while earning class credit. Many colleges offer them – even to students who don't attend the college. The University of California, for instance, currently offers over 400 program options in over 40 countries. (http://www.eap.ucop.edu).

To get started:

- Select two or three similar programs that you may want to apply to. It will increase your odds over just applying to one foreign college, and you may only need to do minor tweaks on your application answers for each.
- These programs are competitive because spaces are limited. Also, check out opportunities your college may have for you to gain comparable experience in Washington, D.C., a growing trend.
- Your cost for your term studying abroad will likely be the same (in terms of tuition.) Living expenses may be higher, and you have to pay for your airfare. There are companies that run Study Abroad programs outside of the college realm. These are more expensive, and your credits may not always transfer.

**Alternative Spring Break:** This is exactly what it sounds like – something different from the usual partying. Instead, you can spend Spring Break helping feed the homeless in Los Angeles, rebuilding New Orleans post-Hurricane Katrina, planting trees in South America, etc.

You may also look into sites like these for other possibilities:
http://www.semesteratsea.org/
http://www.studyabroad.com/

*Scott C. Silverman*

# SEEING THE WORLD

More than 300,000 American college students pursued their studies abroad in 2015-2016, according to the U.S. Department of State. Cuba had the highest rate of growth among leading destinations, while the Czech Republic and South Africa also grew. Diversity has also increased among those who go: racial and ethnic minorities increased from 17 percent to 29 percent in ten years' time, and the number of students who report having a disability has also tripled from roughly 3 percent to 9 percent. Roughly 1 in 10 U.S. students study abroad during their undergraduate career.

# THE NOT-TOO-EARLY STUDY-ABROAD LIST

Even though you're only a freshman, it's not too early to start planning to study abroad. Follow these steps, and you'll be (almost) on your way.

**Find out:**
- Where is your college's study abroad office?
- What programs are offered?
- How much do they cost, and is financial aid available?
- Is there a GPA requirement? Will you need recommendations from professors to go?

**Think about:**
- Why you want to study abroad and where you want to go.
- What kinds of classes you want to take.
- When you should go. (Fall semester of junior year is a popular choice.)
- Whether there are older students who can share their study abroad wisdom with you.
- Whether you will need to sublet the place where you are living for the months you will be away.

**Sketch out:**
- A rough, four-year plan to cover all your course requirements.
- How you'll earn/save/beg/borrow the funds you'll need.

And while you're thinking about it, check your passport – it should be valid until one year *after* you plan to get back from your adventures abroad.

*The Editors*

# GET AWAY – AND BOND

**MY SCHOOL GIVES EVERYONE A "FALL BREAK" DURING OCTOBER,** something I wasn't used to in high school. At first it sounded like a long weekend. But as it drew nearer, it seemed like people were treating it more like a mini-spring break. I started to panic because, while I had friends, I didn't have any I considered close enough to travel with. Fortunately, one of my friends in a similar position took a chance and invited me and three other girls to drive to St. Simons Island, Georgia for a short beach trip. Nervously, we all accepted and packed up the car one Friday afternoon. The awkwardness quickly faded away as we all sang songs at the top of our lungs the entire six hours to the beach. That trip turned into the most memorable experience of my freshman year and those four other girls are now my best friends. If you have a chance to take a trip with people you think might turn out to be good friends, take it! Trips are one of the best ways to bond and you'll share memories for the rest of your life.
—*MERELISE HARTE ROUZER*
*GEORGIA INSTITUTE OF TECHNOLOGY, SOPHOMORE*

**WHEN YOU GO TO SCHOOL OVERSEAS,** you get a better perspective on the world. You don't see the world from an American point of view. It will help anybody.
—*MICHAEL LANDIS GOGEL*
*NEW YORK UNIVERSITY, SOPHOMORE*

• • • • • • • • •

**TAKE A FUN JOB IN THE SUMMER** after your freshman year; you deserve the break. I couldn't stand the thought of being at home all summer, living with a curfew, so a friend and I went to Orlando for the summer and got a job at Disney World. We didn't make any money, after paying our apartment and expenses, but we met lots of people and had a good time.
—*K.E.R.*
*FLORIDA STATE UNIVERSITY, GRADUATE*

# 3/2 PROGRAMS: A HIDDEN GEM THAT CAN TAKE YOU PLACES

If you're interested in pursuing a degree in engineering but don't want to miss out on a traditional liberal arts college experience, a 3/2 dual-degree program offers the best of both worlds. Students spend three years at their chosen liberal arts school, obtaining a degree in a field like chemistry, math or physics before transferring to an engineering school for two final years of study, after which they'll earn a second bachelor's degree in engineering.

Participants not only gain the technical skills they need to land a top-tier engineering job, but they'll learn other valuable skills from their liberal arts school that will help them stick out in a sea of like-minded engineering grads – like writing analytically and concisely, giving presentations and thinking outside the box.

So you can attend a small-town college like Benoit, Middlebury or Vassar and get a bachelor's degree, and then transfer to another university like Columbia, Dartmouth, Georgia Tech or Washington University for an engineering degree – depending on each school's program requirements – before you venture into the workplace.

*Alicia Adamczyk is a New York-based writer.*

# NICE, UM, ~~WORK~~ IF YOU CAN GET IT

Make sure to browse the listings of travel grants at your school. Some have only the lightest of strings attached. For instance, female undergraduates at Cornell can qualify for up to $2500 in travel assistance from a memorial travel fund established to honor Ruth Bierman Linnick, a math major from the Class of 1960. The main restriction is that the money can only be used by "students who wish to travel for pleasure, adventure and exploration over the summer break. The fund is not to be used to support students' traveling as part of a study abroad program, internships, research projects, conferences or any other academic or career-focused endeavor." Got that? No work allowed!

# THINGS TO BRING ON A RANDOM ROAD TRIP

Look, we realize that part of the joy of a road trip is the lack of planning. One moment, you're sitting around with your friends at 3 A.M., and the stress of college is the topic of discussion. The next moment, you suddenly know just the way to rid yourself of stress: Road trip, right now, destination TBD.

We don't want to interfere with the spontaneity. But after you pocket your wallet and keys, if you happen to see any of the following items on your way out the door, grab them. Most of all, be careful and have fun in TBD!

1. **Sleeping bag and pillow.** Depending on how cold it is, the pillow might be the most important item here. Have you ever slept in a car without a pillow? In place of the sleeping bag, you can use a long-sleeved shirt or a friend's shoulder.

2. **Cooler for drinks,** medication and perishables.

3. **Hat.** Not many people know this, but the hat was originally invented as a way to hide the fact that the wearer hadn't showered in days.

4. **Small flashlight.** Worth every penny if you break down or need to use the woods at night.

5. **Phone charger.** Plug-ins for the car are a lifesaver. But if you pack one of those cheap hand-cranked flashlights that also charges phones, you'll never be without juice, even if you run out of gas.

6. **Water purification tablets.** Helpful if you have to drink water you find.

7. **A map.** Trust us, you'll be glad you have one on you when your phone is out of range or out of juice.

*The Editors*

"Oh, it's not a study group. We're just posting on Facebook
so our parents will think we're happy."

# 19

# Family Ties: Keeping in Touch & Setting Boundaries

Y ou may be leaving your family home, but you aren't leaving your family. (Wait, you say, so now you actually have to try and stay in touch with parents and siblings? Yes: welcome to the rest of your life.) Maybe your family is one of those blessed to have a free-flowing group chat full of LOL-worthy memes to keep you connected – or maybe your Dad has already converted your childhood room into the man-cave he always wanted.

Either way, it's nice to have some communication with the people who love you back home, and who still have your back. How much is too much? How much not enough? Hard to say, but here's how others have handled this issue before you.

IN THESE TIMES OF TECHNOLOGY, when people text faster than they walk, I would say a phone call or text every day back home should not be too difficult.
—KANU
HUNTER COLLEGE, SOPHOMORE

WHEN YOUR PARENTS VISIT, JUST LET THEM BABY YOU.
—M.A.
FLORIDA STATE UNIVERSITY, GRADUATE

- Surprise visits from the family are off-limits.
- Scheduling a weekly phone call with your parents will help with homesickness.
- Don't tell your folks everything that goes on.
- Staying connected to your family can help get you through the stressful times.

**Become easy to reach.**

—*Reyner*
*Olin College,*
*Freshman*

**By mid-semester I was** extremely homesick. I suddenly realized that my life was never going to be the same. I called home a lot and talked to my parents all the time. My dad emailed me every single day, and he always said, "p.s., Take your vitamins, go to church, and pray." Talking to them really helped.
　　　—*A.G.H.*
　　　　*University of Virginia, Senior*

• • • • • • • •

**I'm close to my parents.** We talk on the phone every other night and my mom IM's me. In college it's important to have your parents in your life, because we may think that we're really mature and know everything, but a lot of times they give you really good advice. They've been there before. In college, your parents are finally honest with you. In high school, they're like, "I never drank." Then in college, they're like, "This one time, I did this. You never want to do that." They become more human and less authoritarian. They help you.
　　　—*Alyssa*
　　　　*James Madison University, Sophomore*

**DO A LOT OF THINGS YOUR MOTHER WOULD DISAPPROVE OF:** tattoos, body piercing, spring break trips. As long as you can act like an adult, the sky's the limit.
—*ANONYMOUS*
*MISSISSIPPI STATE UNIVERSITY*

. . . . . . . . .

" Make it clear to parents and grandparents that surprise visits are not a good idea, given how often you will be at the library. "
—*D.D.*
*UNIVERSITY OF PENNSYLVANIA, GRADUATE*

. . . . . . . . .

**I HATE TO ADMIT IT,** but freshman year I learned that when my parents tell me something, they may actually be right, and I realized that I should start to listen to what they say, especially since they have much more life experience than I do.
—*STEPHANIE KLEINER*
*UNIVERSITY OF DELAWARE, SENIOR*

. . . . . . . .

**MY MOTHER, WHOM I LOVE DEARLY, IS A BIT OF A HELICOPTER PARENT.** I think it was really hard for her that I was in North Carolina and she was in New York. I think what helped my mom and me was when she started to feel like she knew more about my life at college. She started to get to know my friends and knew that I was comfortable. Ironically, the more I was able to step in, the more she was able to step back.
—*NICOLE ZELNIKER*
*GUILFORD COLLEGE, GRADUATE*

✔

Only tell your parents a fourth of what's really going on. They're on a need-to-know basis.
—*J.G.*
*FLORIDA STATE UNIVERSITY, GRADUATE*

**I CALL MY GRANDPARENTS A LOT AND TELL THEM ABOUT MY WEEK.** Sometimes they'll make comments like, 'It sounds like you're being really productive, but what did you do this week to have fun?' Or, 'What did you do with your friends today?' And so, it's interesting to talk to someone who is outside that environment, who isn't worried about your grades or how you did on that test or any of that. My grandparents don't care. I mean they do, but that's not what they want to be talking to me on the phone about.
— *Colleen*
*University of Virginia, Junior*

· · · · · · · · ·

**IF YOU GO OUT OF STATE, TRUST THE DECISION YOU MADE** and remember why you made that decision. It gets tough sometimes, but just know that it'll be okay. I twisted my knee playing pick-up basketball, and I had to go to the doctor and handle that all on my own without my parents. I was walking into the dining hall and I got a call from the doctor and he told me I tore my ACL. I blacked out for a couple seconds. I was shocked. The next day I started figuring it all out. I just took it one step at a time and tried not to freak out. A big reason I went out of state was to be independent and on my own for a while, and that was a huge growing experience.
— *Pat*
*Gonzaga University, Sophomore*

Never let your parents track you.

—*Anonymous*
*Dartmouth College*

· · · · · · · · ·

**SKYPE IS A REALLY AMAZING THING.** You shouldn't Skype every night because you need to be spending time socially, but especially if you have little siblings – like my friend with a 5-year-old brother – it can really help you feel in touch to be using Skype regularly.
— *Emily*
*Harvard College, Senior*

**YOUR PARENTS ARE GREAT WELLS OF KNOWLEDGE** and you can certainly go to them for information, but at a certain point you don't learn anything unless you try it for yourself. I think that if you're struggling with homesickness, a little bit of a detox from your parents helps with that. Obviously, you don't have to completely avoid them, but maybe some people are a little too attached to their parents.

I broke my phone screen and I had to figure out how I would fix it. I found where the Apple store was and hopped on the public bus to go take care of it. While I was at the store, I thought "You know what, this is an older iPhone, why don't I just get a new one?" So, I didn't ask my parents – I just bought a new iPhone. It was a huge learning experience for me. I made a really big decision without consulting my parents and I came out of it none the worse for wear.
—*BEN LEACH*
*JOHNS HOPKINS UNIVERSITY, SOPHOMORE*

. . . . . . . .

**GO TO SCHOOL AWAY FROM HOME AND AWAY FROM YOUR PARENTS.** But let them into your life. Be friends with them.
—*GINGER M. BRODTMAN*
*SPRING HILL COLLEGE, GRADUATE*

. . . . . . . .

**JUST MAKE SURE TO KEEP IN TOUCH WITH YOUR PARENTS.** It makes it easier when problems arise or you make drastic changes in your plans for the future.
—*MANNY*
*GEORGE WASHINGTON UNIVERSITY, SENIOR*

. . . . . . . .

**YOUR PARENTS WILL LET GO OF A LOT** once you leave for college but swearing (especially f-bombs) when you're home on visits won't be well received.
—*D.D.*
*UNIVERSITY OF PENNSYLVANIA, GRADUATE*

# DO I HAVE TO CALL? DON'T TEXTS COUNT?

**KIDS SHOULDN'T FEEL PRESSURED TO CALL THEIR PARENTS** (or not call them at all). They should call them when they want to talk to them, even if that's five times in a day because it's a really exciting day. I was ready to move out of the house when I came to college, but that doesn't mean you can't talk to your parents just because you don't live with them.
> —*TOBIAS*
> *HARVARD COLLEGE, FRESHMAN*

• • • • • • • •

**I HAVE REALLY CLOSE TIES WITH MY FAMILY.** I get along well with my parents and my little brother is my best friend. It was hard to say goodbye. I talk with them a lot. I call them every other day and talk for 45 minutes to an hour. And I email my little brother.
> —*CESAR*
> *YALE UNIVERSITY, FRESHMAN*

• • • • • • • •

**I AM REALLY CLOSE WITH MY PARENTS,** so I talk to them at least once a day. A good time to make these calls is walking to and from class. This way, you have enough time to fill your parents in – but if you don't want to get into a long conversation you have an easy out.
> —*ANNIE THOMAS*
> *UNIVERSITY OF MICHIGAN, SENIOR*

• • • • • • • •

**ONCE I GOT TO COLLEGE, I CURTAILED ALL CONTACT WITH HOME.** I didn't call home as often as we agreed; sometimes I just wouldn't call home at all. My parents really worried. In retrospect, I really regret that, because I put them through a lot of shit doing that. That's definitely a resolution for next year – to be more up on it when it comes to communication with back home.
> —*F.S.*
> *STANFORD UNIVERSITY, SOPHOMORE*

**ONE THING I TRY TO DO** in terms of talking with my parents is to keep a set "talk schedule." I tend to talk to my parents over the phone about three times per week. I'll call my dad every Sunday to rehash the weekend in sports. I'll call my mom on Monday when I have a free hour between classes. If you can set up an informal schedule, that makes it much easier to keep in contact. Your parents will know when you're calling and will be eager to speak to you. This also avoids any calls at unwanted times.
— *ANDREW OSTROWSKY*
*PENNSYLVANIA STATE UNIVERSITY, JUNIOR*

**I TALK TO MY PARENTS A LOT AT NIGHT.** Last night was the season premier of a show I used to watch with my dad a lot. So, I called him before and after. And besides that, I talk to them twice a week just to catch up and see how it's going. It was my little brother's birthday and I wished him a happy birthday.
— *MATT MONACO*
*GEORGE WASHINGTON UNIVERSITY, FRESHMAN*

**I'M FROM L.A.** and I have no family up here, so the transition from having a lot of family to not having anybody was tough. My mom used to call me twice a day – once at noon and once around 9 or 10 at night, just to check in on me, and say, "Where are you?" And I'd say, "I'm out." She'd be okay as long as I wasn't doing anything bad. When I think about it, it was a good thing that she gave me a call every day, even though sometimes it was an invasion.
— *EDUARDO CHOZA*
*SAN FRANCISCO STATE UNIVERSITY, SOPHOMORE*

**MY PARENTS GET THEIR TWO CALLS A WEEK** and that's about all they're going to get right now. It's the best way to do it.
— *WALTER*
*UNIVERSITY OF MARYLAND–COLLEGE PARK, SOPHOMORE*

**FACETIME, ONCE A WEEK.** I recommend you have a usual time where you always call and have other times where you can call when things happen.
—*LI*
*UNIVERSITY OF TORONTO, GRADUATE*

• • • • • • • • •

**IF YOU DON'T CALL HOME AT LEAST ONCE A WEEK,** parents will get antsy. And for good reason. If you don't call home at least once a week, you have done something in that time frame that you know would make them uncomfortable. Parents are smarter than you will give them credit for, mainly because they've smothered you for 18 years.
—*J.V.*
*THE COLLEGE OF WILLIAM & MARY, GRADUATE*

• • • • • • • • •

**IT'S GOOD TO SHARE YOUR EXPERIENCES** with your parents, but not all your experiences. Part of becoming your own person is having your own secrets and your own personal business. But if you share with your parents the things that fascinate you about growing up and being an adult, then that strengthens your bond. And they remember that they were kids once, too; they remember how it was.
—*SHELBY NOEL HARRINGTON*
*UNIVERSITY OF CALIFORNIA AT SANTA BARBARA, FRESHMAN*

• • • • • • • • •

**FRESHMAN YEAR, WHEN I GOT IN TROUBLE,** when I was feeling stressed out, I wish I'd talked to the folks back home more. I owed it to them. They were paying. I was having a blast. I just forgot. I regret that. I would say if you can't do every Sunday night, do every other Sunday night and text throughout the week. It's healthy to call home. Parents are so removed from that atmosphere. My school was very competitive. Calling home was a nice step away from that, a chance to check in with reality. If I had called home more, I would have gotten more therapy from my parents.
—*ANONYMOUS*
*COLBY COLLEGE, GRADUATE*

**YOU'VE GOT TO BE HONEST WITH YOUR PARENTS.** You've got to break them in. If you do bad stuff, you've got to let them know. They're going to find out anyway. So, you might as well be honest about it. If you tell them the way it is, they'll get used to it.

—*BETH*
    *DIABLO VALLEY COLLEGE, FRESHMAN*

• • • • • • • • •

**IF YOU GO HOME FOR THE SUMMER,** make sure you go on vacation. I had to take trips by myself because I cannot be around my parents all the time. I realize they are real people and not all their habits are ones I want to live with.

—*S.*
    *UNIVERSITY OF CALIFORNIA AT SANTA BARBARA, FRESHMAN*

# GRANDMA KNOWS BEST

It was the second half of my freshman year and I had my first hangover. My friends and I were at a concert and we were all drinking. I couldn't tell exactly what I drank and how much, but I tried anything and everything. It's all about discovering what you like and what you don't like, right? The next morning when I woke up, before I even opened my eyes, my head was throbbing. I hadn't eaten anything and my stomach and I were definitely not on speaking terms. I called my grandmother and asked her if she had ever experienced a hangover. She said, "Yes." I then told her I was having one. She laughed and came over to my apartment to comfort me. It's funny; I was 18 and thought I knew it all, but once I got my first hangover, whom did I go running to? My grandmother! Keep close ties with your family as you may need them at any time.

—*STEPHANIE M.*
    *FROSTBURG STATE UNIVERSITY, SENIOR*

**I REALLY ENJOYED MY MOM'S CARE PACKAGES.** She always made them specifically for me. It wasn't just the traditional, "Here's some snacks, here's some candy, here's a condom." My mom would send the Sunday comic section 'cause that was a thing I loved about being at home. I would wake up on Sundays, read the comics. So, she would send me those. She'd take them, put them all in a pile, and mail them to me. One time, she put a bunch of condoms in the middle of them and I opened the comics and said, "Oh my god!"

　　　　　　—LILLIE REITER
　　　　　　　GUILFORD COLLEGE, GRADUATE

• • • • • • • •

My relationship with my parents has improved a lot over the phone versus in person.

—C.W.
　BARNARD COLLEGE,
　SOPHOMORE

**THE CRAZIEST THING THAT HAPPENED TO ME** was when my family, with their dogs, had to move in with me and my roommates during my junior year of college. It was certainly unexpected, and a lot of the stories that you imagine when you go to college and that you see in movies are about you going off and separating from your family and having this time of self-exploration. That's a 100 percent wonderful part of college, but something that's not talked about a lot is that things may come up that mean your family is way more involved in your life than it would be in a traditional college narrative. Those can also be opportunities for growth, even if they're frustrating and difficult to deal with at the time because a lot of other people in college aren't having to worry about family.

If you have a family yourself or if you have to deal with illness or money problems with your family, that's something you might not hear people talking about. But you're never the only person who's going through that. So don't feel alone.

　　　　　　—ALISON
　　　　　　　COLLEGE GRADUATE

# SOCIAL MEDIA AND YOUR FOLKS

**FACEBOOK IS A VERY IMPORTANT TOOL IN COLLEGE** – even if your mom has signed up. However, if you are concerned with your mom checking your wall posts and other information, you can easily block her from viewing your profile in its entirety by changing the privacy settings. That way, you can continue flirting with that hot person in your psychology class without worrying about your parents.

    *—KANU*
      *HUNTER COLLEGE, SOPHOMORE*

**WHEN I GET OUT OF AN EXAM,** I sometimes post online from my phone about how "rough" it was or how I never want to go back to school again, to vent from stress. By the time I check my Facebook page later that day, I find all kinds of responses from my dad, mom, stepmom, brothers, sisters, cousins etc., reassuring me that all is not lost, or making sassy comments. It's a different way of doing things. It's made me want to keep a lot more under wraps regarding school and schoolwork, but at the same time it is good to get some encouragement when you know that the next economics exam is going to kick your butt.

    *—AMANDA*
      *UNIVERSITY OF COLORADO AT COLORADO SPRINGS, SOPHOMORE*

**NEVER BE FACEBOOK FRIENDS WITH YOUR PARENTS. NEVER.** It's just not a good idea, because, without fail, at some point in time, there will be something posted on your Facebook, be it a comment or a picture of a status or whatever, that you will NOT WANT YOUR PARENTS TO SEE. And if you're friends with them, they'll see it. And then ask you about it. And then you're screwed.

    *—SETH*
      *OGLETHORPE UNIVERSITY, FRESHMAN*

# HOMESICKNESS

Homesickness is the number-one stressor for college students because of the temporary loss many people experience when they leave home. Adapting to this temporary loss involves four basic tasks: accepting the reality that you are away from family, friends, pets, etc.; experiencing the pain (crying, sadness, and loneliness); adjusting to a new environment, and withdrawing and reinvesting emotional energy.

Participating as fully as possible in the activities sponsored by the First Year Experience, Living/Learning Floors and other college organizations, can help with the anxiety, fear, and discomfort that may result from the transition to college. And don't overlook the power of friends helping friends; this requires trust and willingness to really listen to your friend and then allowing the friend to listen to you. Many times we try to "cheer up" our friend – but this has the effect of minimizing, or discounting, the importance of the person's feelings. It's not helpful to say, "Next week, month, or year, you'll forget about all this."

If we are miserable we can move through it in a healthy manner if we are allowed to express our misery and sit for a while and reflect. We soon get tired and figure out a way to do something different to improve our own situation. Before you even think about it, you will call home less frequently, stay on campus on the weekends instead of going home, attend sporting events to meet new friends, and invite friends from home to visit your campus. Remember, there are people on campus who can help you through the homesickness process: your resident adviser, professor, staff, and counseling center, to name just a few. You will be welcomed by all no matter how you feel, while at the same time finding your "niche" at your college/university.

*Dr. Clarice Ford*
*Vice Chancellor for Student Affairs*
*University of Illinois Springfield*

I NEVER GOT HOMESICK, but staying close to my parents and siblings definitely kept me sane over the course of freshman year.
—*PETE*
*PRINCETON UNIVERSITY, SOPHOMORE*

• • • • • • • •

I'M A FIRST-GENERATION COLLEGE STUDENT. My parents didn't really know what college was going to be like for me or for them. When I left, they were depressed for the whole first semester. For me, I was excited. I was pumped. I already had friends at UNC and made friends over the summer. I was raring to go. Freshman year, I never felt homesick because I was so excited. My house was only 2 hours from UNC, and I would go home every two weeks. This way, I could have my independence but also felt supported by my parents if I ever felt like I needed to go home and get away from UNC.

I started feeling homesick the summer before my sophomore year, when I was doing an internship and I had to be there all summer. I could barely go home and I got sick in the middle of it. That was the first time I had been sick away from home. That's when it hit me. I was really homesick during that entire time. My mom couldn't come because she was working. That was when I realized I actually did miss home.
—*JOSE CISNEROS*
*UNIVERSITY OF NORTH CAROLINA AT CHAPEL HILL, GRADUATE*

# IF YOU'RE FEELING BRAVE...

Thanks to the Family Educational Rights and Privacy Act, or FERPA, and Stanford University students who pressed the issue, students at many colleges now have the right to view their own admission files upon request. Harvard recently reported that it has been receiving 200 such requests per month.

# KEEPING PARENTS IN THE LOOP, A LITTLE OR A LOT

When you get to college, or maybe before you even set foot on campus, you might hear buzz about something called FERPA. Even if this funky-sounding term never comes up, FERPA is something you and your parents absolutely must take time to discuss. It may seem dry, but hang in there. It's super important.

**What is FERPA?** FERPA stands for the Family Educational Rights and Privacy Act of 1974. It was created to protect the privacy of students' educational records. Once you turn 18 or begin attending college, control over these records essentially transfers from your parents over to you. This means that your parents may no longer be privy to information about your grades, attendance, behavior or financial standing.

**There are exceptions.** For instance, your FERPA rights can be overridden:

- **If you are considered a financial dependent of your parents, based on tax law.** Even so, intel about you will not automatically flow to mom and dad. Parents must furnish proof to the school that you are a dependent and then submit a written request for information to the administration. This is not an iron-clad mandate that colleges must obey. But by providing proof, parents simply give the school the *legal ability* to skirt FERPA's restrictions and share information about you as it deems necessary.
- **If you violate university policies or engage in unlawful conduct.** For instance, some disciplinary information can be released. Nor will FERPA shield your privacy rights off-campus. If you have a run-in with the law in town and local police tattle to your school, administrators are free to share *that* information with the 'rents.'
- **If you sign a waiver** that expressly gives parents access to information about you in your records (more on those opt-out procedures below.)

- **If the school determines that your health or safety is at risk.** Technically, schools are permitted to alert parents in certain emergencies. But that can be a judgment call. And wrong decisions are sometimes made with tragic results. For instance, there have been situations where suicidal students have exhibited signs of distress such as cutting class, failing courses or complaining to advisors. And yet schools failed to share that vital information with parents, ostensibly to avoid running afoul of FERPA. A law that was initially intended to protect student privacy may thus be making it harder for parents of college-age students to step in when things go seriously wrong by leaving them too much in the dark.

**Waiving confidentiality rights under FERPA:**
Some moms and dads may not be so thrilled about the whole FERPA thing. In their eyes, you're still their baby, and if they are footing the bill, they may also feel they have a right to know what you're doing with their dollars. You may also want them to have access to financial records kept by the bursar, so they can pay your bill!

**That's where FERPA/confidentiality waivers come in.**
Unfortunately, there's no universal "FERPA waiver" that signs over all FERPA privacy rights to your parents. Each institution has its own procedures. Some may give you the opportunity to sign a master document when you get to campus. Others may advise you to sign separate waivers for different departments. Many now give you the option to sign an online "proxy" at registration that various departments can then access electronically. Some schools may not even mention waivers at all. It will be up to you to inquire about opting out and supply your own forms. (Not to worry. Print a sample waiver out here at https://www2.ed.gov/policy/gen/guid/fpco/ferpa/safeschools/modelform2.html.)

In general, though, most colleges will allow you to pick and choose which aspects of your college record you want parents to access. For example, a school might put information about grades and classes in one bucket; financial aid and student accounts in another, and records relating to student life and discipline in yet a third.

**Health Records:** Health privacy in academic settings is generally covered under FERPA and/or the 2002 privacy rule of the Health Insurance Portability and Accountability Act (HIPAA.) If you want parents to have access to your health records, call your college health services center and ask how best to arrange that, because this generally requires its own set of forms. Plus, rules vary state to state.

If you must supply your own forms, you can find a generic HIPAA release form here at https://www.athenaeum.edu/pdf/free-hipaa-release-form.pdf. Keep a hard copy with you, hand one to your parents, and store scans on your phone and computer. This can make things far less complicated if you are hospitalized with a concussion or aren't otherwise in position to be making complicated medical decisions for yourself. To play it safe, you may also find that you need to sign and stash away an advance directive that outlines your medical preferences should you become incapacitated and a medical power of attorney that allows others to make health care decisions for you.

**So, should you grant mom and dad access?**
If you have a fraught or abusive relationship with your folks, you may not want them having any access to your records. On the other hand, if you have a history of mental health issues or are feeling extremely anxious about how you will handle school emotionally, you may want to waive your privacy rights so your folks can speak more freely with your deans and advisors. Signing such a form won't make the school come running to your parents with every last tidbit about your experience at school. But with this kind of document on file, schools will be less fearful of violating FERPA and more likely to reach out if they are worried about your well-being. That, alone, could be a lifesaver.

Best of all, most schools let you adjust your preferences as needed. So, decisions aren't permanent!

*Peg Rosen writes about education and health*
*and is based in Montclair, N.J.*

**WHENEVER YOU THINK ABOUT OLD FRIENDS OR FAMILY,** call them or write them right then. If you put it off, you'll get preoccupied with a million other things and never get to it.
—*AUBREY WALKER*
*SANTA BARBARA CITY COLLEGE, SOPHOMORE*

• • • • • • • •

**I WENT THROUGH TIMES OF HOMESICKNESS,** and I texted my parents constantly. Being busy helped combat the sadness. Get involved. Explore your surroundings. Meet new people.

My freshman year was pretty rough, but I got my bearings and sophomore year was totally awesome. I consider the people who lived on my floor my family now. Once I got over the fact that high school is behind me, and it's okay to move on, but never to forget where you came from, it got easier.
—*ABBY*
*SOUTH DAKOTA STATE UNIVERSITY, SENIOR*

• • • • • • • •

**SCHEDULE TIME.** Be like, "Sundays at 6 P.M., I'm going to call my parents." When I first came here, I was so overwhelmed with work that I forgot to talk to them. I just never thought to make the time because I never had to do that before. So, the first semester, I didn't talk to them at all. I realized that I really missed talking to them and there was so much my mom didn't know about my life.

Winter break, I was so happy to be home. Then, I came back to school, and that first week back, I was the most homesick I'd ever felt. I realized I wouldn't see my parents again until June. So, the second semester I made sure to call them once a week, and my communication skills with my parents gradually improved.
—*ANONYMOUS*
*PRINCETON UNIVERSITY, SOPHOMORE*

MY PARENTS UNDERSTAND that this is my college experience and that I am legitimately doing my own thing. Some parents that I know of are not quite as understanding, and some students seem unable to tell their parents, "This is my time. Let me have it. They're my mistakes to make, not yours. It's my turn." Whether or not you're actually making mistakes, parents need to understand that you can be on your own without them.
—*BARRY LANGER*
*OGLETHORPE UNIVERSITY, JUNIOR*

• • • • • • • •

IT'S OKAY IF YOUR DISTANT FAMILY RELATIONSHIPS DON'T GET BETTER. I'm originally from the West Coast, so I moved all the way across the country from my dad. He and his girlfriend have a newborn baby at home and he began a new job, so he's got a lot going on. We never really had a close, dependent relationship anyway, so moving away has made us more distant.

When I went home for break, I felt just as distant from home as I do in Boston. He is bad at texting, sometimes accidentally deleting my unread messages, and hates when I call him on the phone. I noticed I started to get into a lot of fights with my boyfriend because I would become defensive about my dad to compensate for us not talking as much. The truth of life is that not everyone has a great relationship with their parents, and not everyone's bad relationship with their parents magically gets better after going away to college. I've tried to talk to him about it, and it's gotten slightly better, but I've learned that it's okay that our relationship might not completely change.
—*PORTIA*
*NORTHEASTERN UNIVERSITY, FRESHMAN*

**IF YOU'RE GOING TO GO HOME ONE WEEKEND,** you probably shouldn't go home the next weekend, because they'll ask you on the third weekend, "Where are you? Why aren't you here?" Then you set a precedent for "I'll be home every weekend."
—*J.G.M.*
   *GUILFORD COLLEGE, GRADUATE*

"It's only my opinion, but he doesn't look like the best choice for an emotional support animal."

# Coping: Keeping Your Head – and Options – Open

**20**

Despite the endless stream of pure bliss and jubilation you're getting from Snapchat stories and Instagram posts, not everyone in college is perfectly happy all the time. In fact, studies suggest that depression and anxiety among college students may be at all-time highs.

The good news is that universities are well aware of the stress weighing on students and are often willing to help. Think of it this way: there's no better time to try therapy than when it's being offered for free. Also, it's never been more socially acceptable than now to admit that you're struggling. So, don't bottle it all up! Asking for help, as many of these students did, is wise, admirable, and may be the best decision you've ever made.

**SOMETIMES, YOU NEED TO PAT YOURSELF ON THE BACK** for the small stuff you do right. Even getting out of bed, even eating a real meal, putting on real clothes – doing anything in college is an accomplishment.
—JESSICA SHILLING
UNIVERSITY OF PITTSBURGH, GRADUATE

**IT'S VERY IMPORTANT TO DO SOMETHING PHYSICAL. THAT'S HOW I RELEASE ALL MY STRESS.**
—B.M.
UNIVERSITY OF MARYLAND, JUNIOR

**HEADLINES**

- Find time to be alone to reflect and recharge.
- There will be hurdles but you can navigate them.
- Don't be afraid to ask for help, especially when your college offers free counseling.

**MY TRICK IS TO JUST CHANT, "IT'S FINE, EVERYTHING'S FINE"** when I'm stressed, and to have a motto of "fake it 'til I make it." Honestly, a lot of stress in college is temporary. You may have a mini-breakdown in the library at 3 A.M. but in two days, that exam is over with. You may spend days wondering if this boy is ghosting you, but then you'll find a new guy to set your sights on and you move on.

Don't take life so seriously, because life for sure isn't going to take you seriously half the time. Obviously set goals and be motivated to reach your dreams, but also learn to just accept things for the way they are. Some things in life just happen and you can't control them, so it's much more productive to just move on and not dwell on them. As for staying out of trouble – just don't be dumb enough to get caught. You may think you're clever and sly, but trust me, your RA's probably did the same exact thing their freshman year that you're trying to get away with now.
    —CHRISTINE
    DREXEL UNIVERSITY, JUNIOR

**DON'T BE EMBARRASSED ABOUT GETTING HELP, BECAUSE EVERYBODY NEEDS HELP.** When I got to college, my friends just picked me up and dragged me to the facility to go get help. In my head, I thought, "This is something that I need to be able fix on my own. If I can't fix it by myself, then what kind of person am I?" But once they helped me, it made me feel a lot better thinking I'm not alone in this because there are people supporting me.

I think it was the academics, but I was thinking way too far into my future. The person who prescribed me Prozac said she wished she could give all the freshman class Prozac because the academics *are* the stressful part of college. It's a big jump from high school to college 'cause your classes get a lot harder and then eventually they get a lot more specific, so they get a lot more difficult. In your head you're thinking like 'wait, I used to be able to do this in high school, why is it so difficult now?'
—A.B.
*RUTGERS UNIVERSITY, GRADUATE*

# ASK THE ADVISER

*I'm having a few problems, and not just with my classes. It's not like I can't handle it, but it would be nice to just talk to someone and not have them tell me all the things I should be doing differently.*

The staff at the counseling center are trained to listen, and not to tell you what to do. You are an adult, and can make your own decisions, but sometimes it helps to talk through your experiences with someone objective. Counseling sessions are generally confidential (you can ask if you want to make sure,) so you can be upfront and honest about whatever's on your mind without worrying about it getting back to your professors, your friends, or your family.

*Frances Northcutt*

**TWO APPS POSITIVELY IMPACTED MY YEAR.** The first is Calm, an anxiety and stress-reducing application. When my therapist recommended it, I thought it was going to be the most useless application I'd ever download. However, a year later, I still use it quite often. It helps lower my stress, anxiety, and improve my sleep patterns.

The second and perhaps surprisingly more influential app is 1 Second a Day. You take a one-second video every day of the year. It might sound irrelevant, but I found this extremely helpful when I was feeling hopeless and like nothing was going right at college. In times like this, I would look back to all my videos from the previous weeks and it would remind me that I had a lot of amazing times and that more good times were to come. It's easy to get lost in your thoughts when you're away from home and feeling alone, so these videos were a good reminder that things were and would continue to be all right.
   —ANONYMOUS
      UNIVERSITY OF RICHMOND, JUNIOR

• • • • • • • •

**THERE WILL BE HURDLES, BUT YOU HAVE TO NAVIGATE THROUGH THEM.** I had just started spring semester of my freshman year when I found out that my grandmother had passed away. I was only 18 and I had lost my uncle a year earlier. Death was truly knocking on my door. Prior to my grandmother's death, she and I were not seeing eye-to-eye due to family issues. But, I released the hurt and anger I had towards her. I realized life is too short to hold grudges and I said 'so long' to my grandmother gracefully.

I used the same ammunition to complete that semester of school. I knew my grandmother wouldn't want me to sink and flunk school. I knew there was so much more in me; Life doesn't go the way we plan but we have to keep living.
   —DOMINIQUE M. CARSON
      BROOKLYN COLLEGE, GRADUATE

I WAS EXPOSED TO A LOT OF THE SCARY SIDES of people that I hadn't come so close to before. Like the time some guys beat up and killed a raccoon outside my dorm. Or the time a dorm mate expressed to me that she often felt like committing suicide, and I felt like there was nothing I could do to help her, except let her know that a lot of people around her really cared about her.

  —K. HARMA
   WESTERN WASHINGTON UNIVERSITY, GRADUATE

• • • • • • • •

> " Don't be afraid to use the health center, for both medical and mental problems. It's cheap, it's confidential, and it really can help if you get the blues. "

  —ANONYMOUS
   UNIVERSITY OF GEORGIA, GRADUATE

• • • • • • • •

MENTAL HEALTH IN COLLEGE, LIKE, YIKES! And that's part of the reason I've done so much mental health college campus work.

I have experienced symptoms of mental health conditions since I was about 3 years old. But I hadn't gone to a psychiatrist at the University until August of my senior year. Partly because it took me forever to get to a point where I felt like I should and could, and partly because it took forever to get an appointment. But it 100 percent changed my life, and that's one of the things that make me wish I had prioritized my mental health more.

  —HELMI HENKIN
   UNIVERSITY OF ALABAMA, GRADUATE

# REFLECTIONS FROM AN UNDOCUMENTED STUDENT

**A** LOT OF PEOPLE HAVE NO IDEA WHAT IT MEANS TO BE UNDOCUMENTED. With me, it was very complicated because I'm undocumented and first-generation. That was a really hard process to go through. For a lot of things, I was on my own because my parents had never gone to college. They don't really read English. They can kind of speak it. That was really hard. When I was doing all of this, I didn't feel too much stress. I've always been good at dealing with stress but now that I'm older, it's a really tough process in so many ways.

For undocumented students especially, you've got to be really good at school, excelling as best as you can in the circumstances you are in.

Your story is powerful. Whatever you've been through, it defines your experience in life and of course who you are. Yes, it is risky and you have to take that into consideration...but you can try to find ways to make an impact on people through your story and the fact that you want to go to the school.

Also, make connections with other people. A lot of people want to help but don't know how to. Being very open like, "This is what I need and if you can help me, I would really appreciate it." It's putting so much pressure on an individual who is going through so much already to expect them to put themselves out there so much. I hate that it's like that. But I think that's a powerful thing, if you can elevate yourself and do that in whatever situation you find yourself in.

—*Jose Cisneros*
*University of North Carolina at Chapel Hill, Graduate*

**I**T'S REALLY HARD TO FIND TIME TO BE ALONE IN COLLEGE.
You're always surrounded by people: your
roommates, your friends, your classmates. In
high school you have your own room; in college I
always shared a room. It's important to find time
to be alone so that you can reflect on everything
you're going through. Go on walks and write in
a journal. If you go through your routine every
day, the days pass so fast; if you don't think back
on your day, it doesn't seem as meaningful. You
don't treasure the memories that you make if you
don't record them in a journal. In the future you'll
be able to look back and see how your freshman
year was. Try to find yourself and think about your
experiences.
> —*MEGHAN*
> *UNIVERSITY OF NOTRE DAME, JUNIOR*

• • • • • • • •

**I** FOUND THE COUNSELING CENTER HELPFUL because it's
one thing to have a friend to talk to but it's another
thing to have somebody who is trained to make
you be reflective and make you think about what's
going on in your life and make you aware of
whatever triggers you have or what the stress is
doing to you.

Also, it's cool to have somebody who is solely
there to listen. Not offer any advice if you don't
want it, not tell you how to fix things, 'cause
sometimes friends will do that or judge you. So
it was really nice to have a safe spot for that. It's
really nice to be able to go and get rid of that
stress without having somebody say, "Okay, but
you just need to relax" or "You just need to let go
of it." They aren't going to say that to you. They
are going to help you explore and help you find
tools to deal with it. Certainly, better tools than
alcohol.
> —*PAISLEY*
> *MEREDITH COLLEGE, GRADUATE*

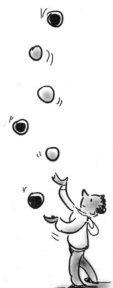

**IT'S HARD TO FIND PLACES TO DE-STRESS ON CAMPUS.**
I would go out in nature, but people would get
really mad at me because they say it's dangerous
out there and you can't go alone. Another way
to de-stress is to do something that really takes
your attention. Something sort of difficult, like
playing an instrument or juggling or even a sport.
For a couple of hours, that's really healthy. You
could take detox days from technology by saying
to your friends, "I'm not going to answer my
phone tomorrow" and just turn it off. That helps
recalibrate if you're stressed. For me, when I was
really stressed and couldn't go into the woods,
I would wait until about 10 P.M. when most people
were in their dorms, and go out and juggle for a
couple hours. I had light-up juggling balls so it
didn't matter that it was dark.
　　　　—J.G.M.
　　　　GUILFORD COLLEGE, GRADUATE

· · · · · · · · ·

**DON'T BE AFRAID TO GO TO THERAPY.** My school had
free therapy and it really changed my life. Not
enough people take advantage of it. There were
times when my faith in humanity would be
through the roof because the waiting room would
be completely full. I would think, "It sucks that
people are struggling but, man, I feel normal"
because you see all kinds of people there: the
hot girls, the bros. So many people on campus
are medicating with drugs and alcohol instead of
talking to someone about their problems, whether
it's a friend or a therapist. Therapy made me
realize that I was normal and everyone is suffering
and it's something you can learn from. Be upfront
about struggling sometimes. It's okay to suffer,
to be depressed or anxious or sick. Just talk to
someone. It's incredibly important.
　　　　—ANONYMOUS
　　　　UNIVERSITY OF COLORADO, GRADUATE

# FINDING MY VOICE

Cursed with an annoying stammer, I always scrupulously avoided doing anything at all in front of an audience. But in my first week as a freshman I was forced to come face-to-face with "the stammer."

In a business management course, we were asked to debate issues given to us by our lecturers. My group was given the ridiculous proposition that "welfare benefits assist unemployment" and told to argue against it. Maintaining my treasured high school stance of protected anonymity, I offered a few ideas to my group while steadfastly refusing to be the spokesperson for the group. However, our dear teachers were not to be fobbed off with such an approach. They started firing questions at *all* the participants.

I waited for my turn to come. When it did, I opened my mouth to answer and . . . nothing. Zilch. I writhed and wriggled, and still nothing.

I prayed hard that the earth would open and swallow me up. I knew that I'd blown it for the rest of my college life, and all in the first week.

And then, suddenly, it came: "This form of intolerance and preconceived notions is the same that the proposers of this motion are suggesting for the unemployed."

There was total silence, then applause. I had bowled them over with an outrageous display of demagoguery. Within the month, I was a candidate for the Student Representative Council. Within the year, I was conducting workshops and making speeches before thousands. Lots of screaming, plenty of demagoguery and no end of guilt-tripping. A political career was born; I had survived my freshman year.

—*Phil*
*University College–Salford (England), Graduate*

I ATTENDED COLLEGE VERY FAR AWAY FROM HOME. It was a new state and a new country. Because of how independent I was in high school, I thought I was completely set. As it turned out, there were things I missed about home that I never anticipated. My roommates' parents would swing by and buy them groceries or they'd go home for the weekend and I'd be all alone in the apartment. I would get to a point where I felt disconnected from everyone and that built up. I felt like I didn't know anyone well enough to talk about my feelings and I didn't want to burden my friends and family at home.

Eventually, I FaceTimed with my best friend from home. I cried for over an hour and she realized that I needed to be reaching out to people. She let me get all my feelings out, then told me to not wait so long the next time I had stuff going on. I then began to frequently keep in contact with my loved ones back home and I maintain a good relationship with friends when I come back for the summer.

It's hard adjusting to a new school and a new routine surrounded by new people. To cope with the loneliness that some students feel at college, I had to find something to occupy my time. I became more invested in my home hockey team and looked forward to watching games. You're busy at school but you also have enough free time that if you don't find the things that make you happy to fill those times, you'll find yourself engaged in harmful routines. It is also okay to not be okay and to reach out to people closest to you. They are very proud of you and have your back more than you could ever imagine.

—*PAIGE SIEWERT*
*UNIVERSITY OF SAINT MARY, SENIOR*

**PRIORITIZE YOUR MENTAL AND PHYSICAL HEALTH OVER YOUR GRADES.** There are so many people who get straight A's in high school, but that's not really how it works in college. You're good at some things, and you're not as good at others, and that's okay. There's no need to have a breakdown because you didn't get an A+ in every class. You're probably going to get a C at some point, and that's okay too. If you're struggling with mental health, seek your school's mental health services or drop a class if you have to. I had to do that for my health last year, and I had to drop two classes. It was worth it, and I get to retake those classes this year. Make sure to look into your school's policies and talk to your academic advisor before you start spiraling, in order to get the help you need to succeed.

    —*KATHERINE*
      *GEORGE WASHINGTON UNIVERSITY, SOPHOMORE*

• • • • • • • •

**TAKE TIME FOR YOU.** Everything in college seems like the end of the world, but you have to take a step back and take a deep breath, because it's going to be okay. I wasn't the most athletic person in high school, but when I got to college, I joined a yoga class, and that really helped with stress. It's important to find a stress-reliever, because when I get really stressed, I get scatterbrained and just can't focus. Sometimes you just need to leave to get a coffee.

    —*SARA*
      *SOUTH DAKOTA STATE UNIVERSITY, GRADUATE*

• • • • • • • •

**WE HAD THE THERAPY DOG DAYS,** which I looked forward to because it was just wonderful to go and play with the dogs. If you go to those events, you definitely want to go early because a lot of people go, and one person can hog the dog.

    —*LILLIE REITER*
      *GUILFORD COLLEGE, GRADUATE*

# SNAPSHOT OF THE HEALTH AND HABITS OF UNDERGRADUATES

Twice as many undergraduates have sought the help of their colleges' counseling or mental health services than play varsity sports or belong to Greek organizations, according to surveys collected by the American College Health Association from 26,139 undergraduates at 52 institutions in the United States in Fall 2017.

| MENTAL HEALTH | % of respondents who said "yes" |
|---|---|
| Have you ever felt so depressed it was difficult to function? | 16% |
| Are you interested in receiving information from your college on depression or anxiety? | 61% |
| Are you interested in receiving information from your college on stress reduction? | 72% |
| In the last 12 months, have you been treated or diagnosed by a professional for | |
|     Anxiety? | 22% |
|     Depression? | 18% |
|     Panic attacks? | 11% |
|     Migraine headaches? | 10% |
|     ADHD? | 7% |
|     OCD? | 3% |

| Have you ever required psychological or mental health services from any of the following? | |
|---|---|
| Counselor/Therapist/Psychologist? | 40% |
| Psychiatrist? | 15% |
| From other medical providers such as a physician or nurse practitioner? | 18% |
| Have you ever required psychological or mental health services from your current college or university's Counseling or Health Service? | 20% |
| In the last 12 months, has stress affected your academic performance? | 34% |
| In the last 12 months, has anxiety affected your academic performance? | 26% |
| In the last 12 months, has depression affected your academic performance? | 18% |
| In the last 12 months, has Internet use/computer games affected your academic performance? | 10% |
| In the last 12 months, have roommate difficulties affected your academic performance? | 9% |
| In the last 12 months, have finances affected your academic performance? | 7% |
| In the last 12 months, has homesickness affected your academic performance? | 5% |
| Percent of respondents who said they had transferred colleges within the last 12 months: | 13% |

# LEARNING TO COPE, IF STILL FEELING BLUE

Amid all the hubbub and excitement of the first few months of school, there may come a time when you catch yourself feeling lonely, sad or anxious, and are unable to shake it off. These experiences are actually quite common, but the worrisome feelings should subside as you spend more time in school and begin to settle in. If, after a few weeks at school, you find yourself feeling really down, overwhelmed or tense, or you find yourself having trouble sleeping, going to class, making friends, relating to others or managing in general, don't wait too long to reach out. (Same, if you see a friend grappling with these issues.)

Speak to a family member, an R.A. or an adviser or someone at the campus counseling service. (Nearly every college has one.) They can help you decide what further steps you can take to feel better so that you can effectively cope with life on campus! There are people all around you who can provide help and support. It is really important to get help before you feel too down or get too far behind in your work.

Consider having a conversation as well with your friends and family back home, if you think they can help. Here, too, are some outside resources you might also want to explore:
https://www.settogo.org/cardstack/getting-help
https://seizetheawkward.org

*Dr. Victor Schwartz is the chief medical officer of The Jed Foundation, which works to support mental health in teens and young adults and helps prepare teens for college. He is also a clinical associate professor of psychiatry at the New York University School of Medicine.*

**BE OKAY WITH LEANING ON PEOPLE.** I can remember the specific moment that was my lowest moment at college. It was the middle of February and I had just asked the athletic trainer for the women's rowing team to look at my hip, which was bothering me. She didn't know what was wrong. This was also the week I had a bout with food poisoning that left me puking in my room all day. So, physically, I felt terrible. I was no longer puking, so I still had to go to practice but still couldn't eat real food. When I got back to my room, I just started sobbing. I was just thinking, *my hip is never going to heal, I'm never going to be able to row again, I feel terrible. Now I have practice, and I don't know I'm going to be able to make it through that because I haven't eaten in 24 hours.* It just sucked.

But my roommate was in our room when I walked in. I was not expecting her to be there, so I was just sobbing, a complete mess. I never cry so when I came in, she as like 'oh my gosh are you okay? And she gave me a giant hug and I just realized there are really people who are there to take care of you. Also, my Residential College Advisor happened to see me walking to my room and texted me to say, "Hey, do you want to get dinner and talk?" At dinner, he also kind of reassured me. Even at my lowest point, there were people looking out for me, and it was really nice, and it helped me get though that day and work out all my anxiety.

—*ANONYMOUS*
*PRINCETON UNIVERSITY, SOPHOMORE*

# WHEN YOU GET KNOCKED DOWN, DON'T STAY DOWN

As a freshman I always thought I would graduate in four years with my colleagues and be a nurse working in a prestigious hospital in New York City. Never did I imagine failing two courses that would cost me two years, and then, finally graduating with not one, but two degrees: a Bachelor's of Science in Nursing and a Bachelor's of Arts in Business.

Would I have told my freshman self to get out of the nursing major while she still could? No. When midterms rolled around fall of freshman year, my advisor and my mother asked me if "this was what I wanted," if I "was even cut out for this?" That hit me so hard because I felt I was being challenged if I was strong enough or smart enough, and I wanted to prove all the doubters wrong.

When I failed the first nursing course of my sophomore year, I was distraught. A friend suggested I speak to the business department at my school, which had just begun a new minor called Hospital and Healthcare Management. Thus began the foundation for the minor I added, that later became my major.

Senior year, I was so close to the finish line, but then failed a mandatory course. Knocked down again, I was told I could not continue until I retook the course the following fall semester, thus pushing me back another year.

My parents told me to take the semester off and come back in the fall. I said "no" because I knew I would be too comfortable being home and wouldn't want to go back to school. I ended up turning my minor into a major in business. It wasn't easy. I had to take 6 classes that spring, an online course over the summer, and two more businesses courses the following fall, along with the repeated nursing course. All the hard work paid off, though, and I finished college on the dean's list.

My advice: though your dream may not go as planned, don't ever give up on your goals in life; just keep on fighting. Have a support system, and never give up.

   —VICTORIA MISTRETTA
     COLLEGE OF MOUNT SAINT VINCENT, GRADUATE

**IT'S OKAY TO DO SOMETHING FOR *YOU*.** I went to Dakota State to play volleyball, but I had a hip injury. So, I was done with volleyball. That spiked my depression, because volleyball was my identity. I'd played since sixth grade. I don't even know who I am without sports, because for the last eight years, I've been in some type of sport. I went to the school counselor, and she just referred me to somebody in town who just didn't understand what I was going through in losing my identity.

My bottom-of-the-barrel was mid-semester. I had class with three of my best friends every day, but they'd come over and they wouldn't even be able to wake me up because I didn't want to leave my bed. I felt terrible, and I felt sick. One of my friends would just tell me she couldn't go to class without me, so I had to get up, and she'd get me coffee. She is what got me through the semester.

I also went back and talked to my high school coaches, and I told them that I couldn't figure out what I was supposed to be doing in college. They said, "You're smart enough. You just have to want to do it." Before, I was motivated by the fact that, if I didn't get the grades, I couldn't play sports. Now, I had to be my own motivation. I started school with D's and F's. Now, I'm an A-B, couple-of-C's student. Looking at where I started, I thought I'd never finish college, but now, in less than two years, I'm going to graduate.

—*MORGAN KREIN*
*DAKOTA STATE UNIVERSITY, JUNIOR*

# SHOULD YOU TRANSFER?

*Ideally, your college experience has been everything you crave and the thought of transferring has never entered your head. But things happen, and there's no shame in switching schools. Surveys show that more than a third of college students transfer, and nearly half of those do it more than once.*

*If you're mulling that route, you're not alone – and these next few pages are for you. No one wants to jump ship too early. Life's most rewarding experiences sometimes just need time to marinate, and life at the next college may just replace the headaches you have now for new ones. On the other hand, there's no point in clinging to something that makes you miserable.*

*Anyone hoping to transfer, or just hoping to keep that option open for a few more months, should know this: take easy classes your first semester, since those grades will matter. This is no time to be taking advanced physics with all the pre-meds.*

**YOUR ADVISOR IS NOT ALWAYS GOING TO BE YOUR FAVORITE PERSON** – mine pushed me hard because she knew I could do it. She didn't put me in 17 or 18 credits to watch me fail. She knew that I was a kid who would thrive on that level of busyness. When my advisor found out I was transferring, she cried with me, but she made sure everything was organized for a smooth transition.

Transferring was probably one of the scariest things in my life, but both advisors – at my old school and my new one – were so willing to help me get to where I wanted to go. One of the best things I did was to make friends with my advisor.
—*KENDRA KLUMB*
*UNIVERSITY OF SIOUX FALLS, JUNIOR*

**I BEGAN MY FRESHMAN YEAR AT BROOKLYN COLLEGE AS A TRANSFER STUDENT** after graduating from Kingsborough Community College the prior spring. My first year in a senior-level college proved to be quite a challenge. However, what helped me survive was that I took a much lighter course load. As a first-semester student, I took a regular course load of four classes. This turned out to be a bad decision, as I ended the semester with a 2.75 GPA. Moving forward, I became a part-time student taking only two courses. This slowed my progress toward graduation, but it proved to be the best decision I ever made. Since I took fewer classes, I had more time to complete all my readings on time, and this ultimately helped me perform better on exams.
—*ANONYMOUS*
*BROOKLYN COLLEGE, GRADUATE*

# IS TRANSFER THE ANSWER?

So you're already at a four-year institution and maybe you're thinking of transferring to another college or university. Before you decide, make sure you're doing this for the right reasons. Remember that the grass is not always greener on the other side. Some students who end up transferring like their new university – and some do not. Here are some suggestions:

If you really feel that the institution you're in is not the best fit for you, or you're not completely happy, you have only two responsible choices: adapt and make it work, or explore transfer options.

Don't transfer solely because you are homesick, the classes are too difficult or you're having problems with your roommate – or to run from or pursue a specific relationship. You can deal with any of these in less drastic ways...visit home, challenge yourself in your classes, ask your RA for tips for dealing with your roommate, etc. If you transfer only because you hope one aspect of the experience is better, you may find other things at the new place that you don't like as much.

Transferring to a new university is tough, and can be harder than starting college in the first place. Everything will work somewhat differently than what you've already gotten used to. You'll need to establish new networks of friends and peers – with students who have already made friendships and had common experiences, learn about new course requirements, find new student organizations, etc. Many transfer students end up taking 5 years or more to graduate, because inevitably the transfer process sets them back a few terms.

Of course, there are some valid reasons to transfer... Check any of these that apply:

☐ **A major that doesn't exist on your campus.** If you want to pursue a program of study that isn't offered at your school, you don't have a lot of options. However, don't get hung up on the specific major, because as long as you take the right classes,

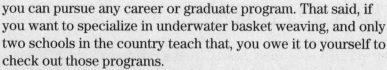

you can pursue any career or graduate program. That said, if you want to specialize in underwater basket weaving, and only two schools in the country teach that, you owe it to yourself to check out those programs.

☐ **A specific professor with whom you want to study or work.** Well, you can't very well get that person to switch to *your* university. However, you may have equally renowned faculty in your major at your current institution.

☐ **A financial incentive.** This could be because of a new scholarship, or because you were recruited as an athlete. But be sure also to check out the scholarships for students that continue on at your institution; you may be surprised at what you find there, or by doing a web search for scholarships.

☐ **Family obligations.** If your family needs you at home to take care of a relative or to help out with another matter, you may be better off taking a temporary leave of absence from college. Transferring to be close to home may not solve your problem because you still will not be able to focus on your classes.

In any case, before you apply to transfer, see your academic adviser to discuss the process…who knows? There may even be a reason to stay at your university that you haven't thought of yet. If you do decide to transfer – talk to the admissions office and academic adviser of the college you want to transfer to, to make sure that you meet all of their requirements. You'll also have to think about living arrangements…if you've signed a lease near the school you're leaving, you'll have to break it. You may have a hard time finding housing at your new institution. Once you transfer, make sure you go to the transfer orientation, which will help you transition to your new university.

Remember, think twice before you transfer…but if you go that route, make sure it's for the right reasons. The last thing you want is to get buyer's remorse once you transfer and not be able to come back.

*Scott C. Silverman, Ed.D., is the Associate Dean of the Emeritus Lifelong Learning Program at Santa Monica College, California's #1 transfer college for 27 years.*

# SHOULD I STAY...

**FIRST YEAR IS A HUGE ADJUSTMENT.** Give it a FULL year and really put yourself out there. I had always lived in the same hometown and had the same friends for 18 years leading up to college. So the process of actually making new friends seemed daunting – don't people just automatically know that I'm nice and friendly and fun to be around? After my first semester I had decided I was done trying. I couldn't find "my people" that I really related to and who seemed to share my interests and personality type. My parents urged me to give it one more semester of really trying to put myself out there and do different intramural sports as well as attend different club meetings or on-campus events, to truly find my group. Sure enough, I was able to find a crew of my close girlfriends who became my best friends throughout the rest of my college career and whom I lived with senior year.

I almost transferred during my freshman year but stuck it out and am so glad I did. I made lifelong friends and met my soon-to-be husband! People, I realized, aren't just going to come up to you and say, "Hey, wanna be friends?" You have to put in some effort and attend on-campus events to find those students who have similar interests to you. You don't need to have 80 million friends: just a solid crew of 3 to 5 is enough to help you feel more confident.

    —*T.B.*
      *BOSTON COLLEGE, GRADUATE*

# ...OR SHOULD I GO?

**MY CLOSEST FRIEND DROPPED OUT.** Talking to her while she was going through it, I could tell that one of the biggest problems she was having with the whole thing is, 'How are people going to think of me when I drop out? Are they going to see me as weak? Are my parents going to be mad at me?' And she was especially thinking, "Why can't I do this? Why can't I just finish school like everyone else?" And she soon realized that the University of Pittsburgh just wasn't for her.

She felt that she didn't fit with Pitt mentally and physically and on all sorts of levels. So when she dropped out, she took a year off, and now she's going to a local community college, commuting from home, and working at the same time. I think it's suiting her a lot better.
> —*ANONYMOUS*
> *UNIVERSITY OF PITTSBURGH, GRADUATE*

**I'M FROM NEW YORK** and I went to a very rural, small, homogeneous southern school my freshman year. It was a bit of a culture shock. I was in classes with white, upper-middle-class kids and that was it. On your tour they say it's diverse, but I don't know what their definition of that is; it's not the New York definition. I didn't realize how much it would affect me, not having access to plays and restaurants and jazz clubs. You had to really travel if you wanted to do anything that would stimulate you. I knew by November that it was not where I wanted to spend my college life. People make you think your decision to pick a college is the end-all of your entire life.

Find a place that looks interesting, and figure out what's important to you before you check out a college. Don't be influenced by a beautiful campus or the nice people in your tour. Expect that you're going to spend four years there, but know that if you don't, it's not jail; you can transfer. College is about *you*, not the school.
> —*HANNAH SMITH*
> *HARVARD UNIVERSITY, JUNIOR*

"*I can't decide if freshman year was the worst year of my life ...
or the best.*"

# More Wisdom: Good Stuff That Doesn't Fit Anywhere Else

*S*ome advice refuses to be categorized. I mean, what is with this human obsession to put everything into a box? Doesn't it rob things of their natural, mysterious wonder and beauty? If thoughts like this appeal to you, maybe try legal methods of mind expansion or Philosophy 101. Seriously though, not all wisdom fits neatly into defined chapters. Here's "the best of the rest," as they say.

**BE ADVENTUROUS.** Be open to doing things outside of your comfort zone.
—*J.V.*
*THE COLLEGE OF WILLIAM & MARY, GRADUATE*

**DON'T TAKE YOURSELF SO SERIOUSLY.**
—*TREVOR*
*AMHERST COLLEGE, GRADUATE*

**IF YOU DON'T HAVE AN OPENNESS TO THE SITUATION,** you're going to have trouble. You're going to meet people of different backgrounds and beliefs, some people who have been coddled and some people who haven't. You need an openness to learn and an openness to accept. If you don't have that, you won't do very well. If you do, your experience will be a lot better.

> —*ZACH FRIEND*
> *UNIVERSITY OF CALIFORNIA AT SANTA CRUZ, GRADUATE*

• • • • • • • •

**IF YOU'RE NOT CAREFUL,** the first year of college will be the most unhealthy year of your entire life. The food is bad for you, you're probably not exercising as much as you were in high school, you drink tons of caffeine and even more alcohol, and you don't sleep. Freshman year, try to remember to sleep more and exercise more. That way you'll be a fully functioning human being. Sometimes, it's hard to pass up parties, but remember that there will be other nights and other funny stories. Choose your night.

> —*SUMMER J.*
> *UNIVERSITY OF VIRGINIA, SENIOR*

• • • • • • • •

**IF SOMETHING HISTORIC HAPPENS ON CAMPUS, ROLL WITH IT** and embrace it. We made it to the Final Four and that will probably end up being the best month of my college career. I watched the games at the student center with over 2,000 other students. It was so packed you couldn't even move. We won a game on a buzzer-beater and everyone went ballistic – yelling, hugging people you don't know, high-fiving everyone. Campus was electric. Cars were honking their horns. There was an amazing sense of community. We will go down as one of the greatest Cinderella teams in history and I can always say I was there for it all.

> —*ANONYMOUS*
> *LOYOLA UNIVERSITY IN CHICAGO, SOPHOMORE*

**KNOW WHAT YOU WANT TO DO** when you go to college. I didn't know and I didn't care. I didn't go to many classes; I just spent my time meeting people and going to parties. I did everything you weren't supposed to do: I signed up for hard classes, I didn't go to them, and I went out every night. When I was 18, I acted a lot younger.
—*A.G.S.*
*UNIVERSITY OF TENNESSEE, DID NOT GRADUATE*

• • • • • • • •

**HAVE YOUR FUN,** but realize you're here to get an education (and, hopefully, a degree!) Make it all worthwhile – academics and social life.
—*KHALIL SULLIVAN*
*PRINCETON UNIVERSITY, JUNIOR*

• • • • • • • •

**I WOULD WANT PEOPLE TO KNOW HOW MUCH THEY'RE GOING TO LEARN.** Not just academically, but about themselves. You grow so much in such a short amount of time. You discover what you're truly passionate about and who you want to be in the world. Even if you leave college without thinking of it as "the good old days," it's going to be a big piece of your life that determines what path you take, and who you are, for the future.
—*L.G.*
*BUCKNELL UNIVERSITY, GRADUATE*

• • • • • • • •

**KNOW WHICH CLASSES TO SKIP,** and which classes not to skip. This is really a key point, because some professors don't care one way or another if you show up for class. All they care about is your test and homework performance. There are other professors who are sticklers for attendance, and even if you are an A student you can end up with a C, because of poor attendance.
—*TONYA BANKS*
*MIAMI UNIVERSITY, GRADUATE*

Don't set your mind on anything the first year. Explore. That's what it's about.
—*M.M.*
*NEW YORK UNIVERSITY, SENIOR*

# THEY'RE NOT ON THE SCHOOL PAYROLL BUT THEY CAN TEACH YOU PLENTY

Here's the best piece of advice I think I got in four years: At the end of my freshman year, I set up a meeting with a professor who had befriended me. I had been considering taking more classes over the summer to get ahead towards my degree (yes, I was a little nerd) and so I asked, "Is the quality of the courses the same as during the year? Do the same professors teach during the summer?" He said, "The professors are the same, but the courses are not as good." He paused for a second to enjoy the look of confusion on my face. "It's the students that are generally worse. During the summer, there are a lot of high school students, trying to put something on their résumé. You learn from your peers more than from the professor, you know."

My professor's advice was excellent – the people I met at college were so exceptional and taught me so much, everything from literature to physics.

—NOAH HELMAN
HARVARD COLLEGE, GRADUATE

**SLEEP EARLY AND OFTEN.** Don't stay up till 2 A.M. because you'll never get up for your 8 A.M. class. Eat early and often.
Don't skip breakfast, and eat three meals a day.
Drink – but not too early and not too often.
— C.B.

* * * * * * * *

**IT'S HARD TO REMEMBER BACK TO FRESHMAN YEAR.** There's a lesson there: It will pass, good and bad.
—LINDSEY SHULTZ
CARNEGIE MELLON UNIVERSITY, SENIOR

**BE FRIENDS WITH THE STAFF.** They can help you out and open up a lot of resources to you but they won't if they don't know you. So, introduce yourself, ask them questions and get to know them because they are great for mentoring.
—*CINDI CALVANESE,*
*BLOOMFIELD COLLEGE, GRADUATE*

• • • • • • • •

**FORM HABITS THAT WILL TRANSLATE** into career traits after your schooling is complete. This does not have to be stressful. It can be simplified:

1) Find a place that's just yours where you can study comfortably.
2) Get up early a few days a week and walk, jog, or practice something physical.
3) Do something at least one day a week that's for someone else – visit a facility where you can volunteer (not with a bunch of friends; just you.)
4) Write in a journal. Give yourself time to reflect and see things through someone else's eyes.

If you get into these habits, it will carry you not only through your first year, but also through your whole college career. You'll amaze yourself at how consistent you can be. And the carryover of these habits will frame your post-school life for success, no matter what you choose to do.
—*TREVOR*
*AMHERST COLLEGE, GRADUATE*

• • • • • • • • •

**MY FRESHMAN YEAR WAS GOOD, BAD, EVERYTHING** you could possibly imagine. The bad parts were adjusting, then readjusting, then readjusting again to leaving home and being on your own and making your life work. There was a lot to be exposed to really fast.
—*J.P.G.*
*UNIVERSITY OF PENNSYLVANIA, SOPHOMORE*

> Never be lazy. College only happens once and it's not long enough, so take advantage of it.
> —*KERRY*
> *GEORGETOWN UNIVERSITY, GRADUATE*

**EVERYONE SEARCHES FOR AN IDENTITY THEIR FRESHMAN YEAR;** that's one of your biggest struggles.
—*RYAN A. BROWN*
*UNIVERSITY OF NORTH CAROLINA AT CHAPEL HILL, GRADUATE*

. . . . . . . . .

**NETWORK, INCREASE YOUR CONTACTS AND MEET PEOPLE,** to take advantage of your college resources and the opportunities they provide. I did *none* of that as a student. I avoided those things like the plague either through fear or through not understanding what these things would really do for me or out of spite because I was too busy being a Scrooge-kind of person around campus, being like, "Oh, this place is awful!" But what I can now say is how difficult things have been because I didn't do those things. I've had to build a network from scratch because I left college with no networks and no contacts. I'm not pulling my hair out or crying over doing that now, but I would likely be a lot closer to my personal finish line had I been doing that all throughout college. It didn't mean anything to 18-year-old me. It's probably not going to mean anything to 18-year-old you, but your 22-year-old you will thank you for it.
—*DYLAN KESELMAN*
*SCHOOL OF VISUAL ARTS, GRADUATE*

# COLLEGE CHANGES YOU

The college experience helped me become a leader in so many ways. I came out of high school, shy like no other, unsure of myself, quite insecure. College allowed me to find out who I am, my potential to be someone great, and put my insecurities out at the curb. I am able to voice my opinion, speak in public places, and lead a group without feeling unsure of myself. College is what you make it!
—*VIVIAN ORIAKU*
*UNIVERSITY OF MIAMI, GRADUATE*

**WHAT I NEGLECTED MY FRESHMAN YEAR** was taking advice from professors. In high school, I always felt like my teachers didn't know what they were talking about. But the professors really do know what they're talking about, and not just in their fields. When they give you advice, listen to it. I didn't take the advice of people who could've helped me. Most freshmen have this attitude: "I got to college, so why do I need you now?" Your pride and self-confidence get in the way of reevaluating the situation you're in. That's what it comes down to. You've got to shed your attitude; it really gets in the way.
—*ZAK AMCHISLAVSKY*
*GEORGETOWN UNIVERSITY, SENIOR*

**TRULY NO ONE CARES WHAT YOU DO.** People are so wrapped up in their own lives and own dramas that no one has the time to hyper-analyze anyone else's behavior. Just do what you want to do.
—*SIMONE POLICANO*
*YALE UNIVERSITY, GRADUATE*

# WHEN ASKING FOR A LETTER OF RECOMMENDATION

Ask at least 2 weeks in advance, and try to give four weeks' notice, or more…seriously! Sometimes professors may not be able to respond to your email quickly, or they may *want* to write a letter but then forget to do it. Once you get someone to agree, occasional gentle reminders may be in order. You probably need to send the individual your résumé and a description of what you're applying for – and potentially meet up to discuss details before the letter can be written.

*Scott C. Silverman*

I learned that college is like a big high school. It's just older people, who take being immature to another level.

—*M.G.*
*VALDOSTA STATE*
*UNIVERSITY, SENIOR*

**THE HARDEST PART OF MY FRESHMAN YEAR** was to let go of my former morals, friends, and hobbies in order to develop and grow. I was so afraid that in letting go of these things, I was going to lose myself.

—*ANNIE VERNA*
*UNIVERSITY OF NORTH CAROLINA AT GREENSBORO, SOPHOMORE*

• • • • • • • •

**COLLEGE IS DIVERSE.** Be open to new experiences. Don't judge people on whether or not they get wasted on the weekends. That's just one aspect of a person.

—*ERIC MCINTOSH*
*UNIVERSITY OF NORTH CAROLINA AT CHAPEL HILL, JUNIOR*

• • • • • • • •

**I RECOMMEND TAKING A YEAR OFF BEFORE STARTING COLLEGE.** It gives a fantastic perspective on why you need to be sitting in classes day after day.

—*LEAH PRICE*
*GEORGETOWN UNIVERSITY, SOPHOMORE*

# FOOTBALL FIRSTS

1. Gatorade was named for the University of Florida (football) Gators, for whom it was developed in 1965. Coach Ray Graves's Florida team – powered by the potion concocted by a UF med school professor – came from behind to defeat heavily-favored Louisiana State in 102-degree heat, and a legend was born.

2. The football huddle originated at Gallaudet University, a liberal arts college for the deaf, when the football team found that opposing teams were reading their signed messages and intercepting plays.

**REMEMBER, EVERYONE ELSE IS IN THE SAME BOAT AS YOU.**
College is your first taste of freedom, but it comes
with a lot of responsibility. No freshman has it all
figured out, so if you find people that act like they
do, they're drunk or lying.
> —ANONYMOUS
> UNION COLLEGE

* * * * * * * *

" You can graduate with decent
grades, you can do nothing and
just get four years older, or you
can suck the marrow out of your
university and garner all the
knowledge, academic and other,
that comes your way. The choice
and your future are in your
hands. "
> —ADAM
> ELON UNIVERSITY, SOPHOMORE

* * * * * * * *

**IF YOU ARE FIRST IN YOUR FAMILY TO BE COLLEGE-BOUND,**
**MAKE THEM PROUD.** This is your chance to prove you
can do it, prove that they've raised you well. Set
a great example for future generations and never
look down on those not fortunate enough to have
had such an opportunity. Never forget where you
came from.
> —ANONYMOUS
> COLLEGE ON THE EAST COAST, GRADUATE

# WHAT MAKES COLLEGE, COLLEGE

The experience of leaving my freshman year of college is among the most memorable times of my life, along with graduating from high school. Coming to college, I was scared shitless and had no idea how I was going to survive. In May, the heat hit me hard as I was packing up my life into a few duffel bags and sweeping out the room that witnessed my first attempts at independence. I peeled off the walls the pictures of people I once saw every day and swore always to be best friends with, who became people I only talked to once in a while on IM. It sounds sad, but my high school friends and I had gone our separate ways and discovered new lives with people we once called strangers. With these strangers I now had inside jokes, crazy blurry memories, and new pictures to plaster on my wall. Not to say that college is always amazing: the food sucks, your roommate will smell, your professor can be an asshole, there are morning classes, and the guy you can't believe you hooked up with will live down the hall all semester long. It's what makes college, college. With all the bad, there is the good. With all your worries and all your fears, freshman year won't suck that bad – it might even be the best year of your life.

—KAREN
STATE UNIVERSITY OF NEW YORK AT NEW PALTZ, SOPHOMORE

**I SAW A GUY THROW HIS PHONE AT A WALL** to demonstrate the strength of his phone case. The phone exploded. Weird stuff is going to happen, you'll get into some arguments, but never put yourself or your equipment at risk just to prove a point or look cool.

—R.S.
GUILFORD COLLEGE, GRADUATE

**DO RANDOM ACTS OF KINDNESS WHEN ABLE.** People at college are really into themselves a lot of the time. You don't always need to be in competition with everyone. Do nice things for others. I was really stressed out one day at the library and I went to go print something out and when I came back there was a flower on my laptop. I never found out who did it and no one ever spoke up. I looked around to see if anyone was peeking, and no one else had a flower on their desk. It was just a random act of kindness that was really sweet.
—GRETA
NORTHERN ARIZONA UNIVERSITY, SENIOR

" All the trouble I got into, all the bad things that came from college, came from the social gatherings. All the good things came from people I met in the classrooms. "
—J.H.
WIDENER UNIVERSITY, GRADUATE

**DON'T TALK BAD ABOUT ANYONE.** My dad told me that when I was in high school and I stuck with it. No one has a bad thing to say about you if you don't say bad things about them. If they do, you realize they're not worth your time.
—CASEY
GEORGETOWN UNIVERSITY, SENIOR

**I took a gap year** before college and I think more people should do it. But only do it if you have something to do – don't just bum around on your parents' couch. That's not going to add a lot of value to your life. I had two jobs during that time and the experience of working hard and having those jobs has given me a lot of confidence coming to college. It's also way less scary to graduate because I know I can live by myself and cook for myself and pay my bills and find an apartment. If I could do it when I was 18, I can do it now!

Taking a gap year is great because you know you're going to college after – it's very low risk. You can do whatever you want to do; use the time to do what YOU want to do. Also, it's great because you'll be 21 one year before everyone else is in your class!
— *Catie*
*Harvard College, Senior*

• • • • • • • •

**Take a break when you can.** If you can sneak in a rest, take it while you can, because you don't get naps in the real world.
— *Taylor Ellingson*
*Northern State University (S. Dakota), Senior*

# WHERE FAVORITE COLLEGE MOVIES WERE REALLY SHOT

|  | SET AT | FILMED AT |
| --- | --- | --- |
| **BRING IT ON** | Rancho Carne High School | San Diego State University |
| **ANIMAL HOUSE** | Faber College | University of Oregon |
| **GOOD WILL HUNTING** | The Massachusetts Institute of Technology | MIT & Harvard |
| **CLUELESS** | Beverly Hills High School | Occidental College |
| **PITCH PERFECT** | Barden University | Louisiana State University |
| **THE SOCIAL NETWORK** | Harvard University | Johns Hopkins University |
| **OLD SCHOOL** | Harrison University | USC, UCLA, and Harvard University |
| **LOVE STORY** | Harvard University | Fordham University |
| **LIFE OF THE PARTY** | Decatur University | The Twelve Oaks Bed & Breakfast, and a warehouse in Decatur, GA |
| **REVENGE OF THE NERDS** | Adams College | The University of Arizona |

*Jon Barr is an LA-based writer & comedian, and a graduate of New York University's Tisch School of the Arts.*

# THE ESSENTIAL FRESHMAN FILL-IN LIST

Some of these answers you'll find in your new-student orientation pack or handbook, or on the college website. The rest you'll have to discover for yourself – sort of like a first-semester treasure hunt!

**PLACES**
Best study spot _____
Best computer lab _____
Best coffee_____
Best late-night food _____
Best inexpensive date location _____
Best pizza place that delivers _____

**PEOPLE**
For help with rules and requirements _____
For help dealing with stress _____
For help when you lose your key and get locked out _____
For answers about student activities _____
For late-night philosophical discussions _____
For fun and laughs _____

**ACTIVITIES**
To do when you're homesick _____
To do when you're stressed out _____
To do when you need to be healthier _____
To do when you want to meet new people _____
To do around town before you graduate and move on _____

**GOALS**
Fast-forward four years from now when you might be graduating. Reflect on what would make you most proud about your college experience. What do you see as the highlights? Jot those dreams down and any other wishes you have for yourself here where you can refer to them for added motivation. Then, revise as needed.

_____
_____
_____
_____
_____
_____

# APPENDICES

## Useful Websites

**SCHOLARSHIPS:**
Search The College Board's website for scholarships at https://bigfuture.collegeboard.org/scholarship-search

Free Application for Federal Student Aid (FAFSA): www.fafsa.ed.gov

**QUESTIONS ABOUT ACADEMICS:**
The College Board on AP credit policy: https://apstudent.collegeboard.org/creditandplacement/search-credit-policies

International Baccalaureate credits and programs: https://www.ibo.org/

**OPPORTUNITIES TO GET INVOLVED**
Volunteer Match: https://www.volunteermatch.org/

Idealist.org, "Action without Borders": https://www.idealist.org/en/?type=JOB

**HELP WITH PERSONAL ISSUES**
The Jed Foundation's ULifeline project, an online resource center for college student mental health and emotional well-being, at www.ulifeline.org/main/Home.html and Settogo.org, a guide to making the transition to college and adulthood.

LdPride.net, for information about learning styles and Multiple Intelligence – helpful for everyone, but especially people with learning disabilities and attention deficit disorder. www.ldpride.net

First-generation students: https://www.settogo.org/first-in-your-family-to-go-to-college/

**HAZING**
Stats on hazing fatalities compiled from data maintained by Professor Hank Nuwer of the Pulliam School of Journalism at Franklin College in Indiana, http://www.hanknuwer.com/hazing-deaths

State hazing laws: https://hazingprevention.org/home/hazing/statelaws/

Two organizations that work to prevent hazing are https://www.stophazing.org/ and https://hazingprevention.org/

**INFO ON SEXUAL ASSAULT**
Two national organizations working all-out on this topic are End Rape on Campus http://endrapeoncampus.org/ and Know Your IX https://www.knowyourix.org/.

**FREE SPEECH ON CAMPUS**
American Civil Liberties Union: https://www.aclu.org/other/speech-campus

**ABOUT THE FAMILY EDUCATIONAL RIGHTS AND PRIVACY ACT**
Consult the U.S. Department of Education to learn more about this act and how it safeguards your educational records at: www2.ed.gov/policy/gen/guid/fpco/ferpa/index.html

## List of Resources on Accommodations

**US Department of Education Office for Civil Rights**
https://www2.ed.gov/about/offices/list/ocr/transition.html
- At the federal level, OCR oversees access and accommodations for students, and investigates complaints of discrimination based on disability.
- OCR offers detailed information for students moving from high school to college, and explains which laws govern accessibility for students at the postsecondary level.
- If you have a question about the law or whether your school is complying with accommodations requirements, OCR offers a hotline. Leave a message and someone will get back to you within a few days. 1 (800) 421-3481.

**NCCSD: National Center for College Students with Disabilities**
http://www.nccsdonline.org/
- Information for incoming and current college students, parents, tips for how to handle times when things aren't going well and legal resources are all available on the Center's "clearinghouse and resource" library page: https://www.nccsdclearinghouse.org/.
- NCCSD lists national and student organizations as well as federal agencies related to disability and higher ed: https://www.nccsdclearinghouse.org/national-resources.html

**AHEAD: Association on Higher Education and Disability**
https://www.ahead.org/professional-resources/accommodations
- Access to some of the information on the website requires a membership in AHEAD.

Also, many college sites have dedicated areas with information for students with disabilities. Check them out, too.

# CREDITS/SOURCES

Visit HowISurvived.com to view all hyperlinks and explore source material further:

**CHAPTER 1:**
p. 6: Vitez, Kaitlyn, "Open 101: An Action Plan for Affordable Textbooks," *The Student PIRGs*, Jan. 25, 2018.
p. 11: Duncan Niederlitz, "The Best Bike Lock," *Wirecutter*, July 5, 2018.

**CHAPTER 2:**
p. 42: Douglas Belkin, "Colleges Bend the Rules for More Students, Given Them Extra Help," *Wall Street Journal*, May 24, 2018; and "Students with Disabilities," U.S. Department of Education, National Center for Education Statistics, (2016). Digest of Education Statistics, 2015 (2016-014) Ch. 3.

p. 44: Jan Hoffman, "Campuses Debate Rising Demands for 'Comfort Animals,'" *New York Times*, Oct. 4, 2015; and Consent decree entered into by the University of Nebraska at Kearney in response to government lawsuit brought on behalf of Brittany Hamilton and other students with emotional support animals, Sept. 5, 2015.

p. 46: U.S. Department of Justice, "ADA Requirements: Service Animals," Civil Rights Division, Disability Rights Section, accessed on Jan. 7, 2019; and Jacquie Brennan and Vinh Nhuyen, ed. "Service Animals and Emotional Support Animals," A.D.A. National Network, 2014; and Dr. C.W. Von Bergen, "Emotional Support Animals, Service Animals, and Pets on Campus," *Administrative Issues Journal*, Vol. 5, no. 1 (2015).

**CHAPTER 3:**
p. 54: Jacob Gershman, "How Bad is the Jacob Glut? Half Your Staff Must be Renamed," *Wall Street Journal*, p. 1, Oct 4 2018; and "Popular Baby Names," Social Security Administration, 2001.

**CHAPTER 5:**
p. 95: Washington & Lee University's online chronology, 1804.
p. 98: National Retail Federation, "Back to School and College Spending to Reach $82.8 Billion," July 12, 2018.
p. 101: Springfield College website; Southern Vermont College online history, and CollegeExpress.com's 2010 list.

**CHAPTER 6:**
p. 130: Kelsey Gee, "New Data Track Foreign Students," *Wall Street Journal*, Nov. 1, 2018, p. B6; and Jie Zong and Jeanne Batalova, "International Students in the United States," Migration Policy Institute, May 9, 2018.

**CHAPTER 7:**
p. 158: Jane E. Brody, "An Unsung Key to College Success: Sleep," *New York Times*, Aug 14. 2018; and Dr. Monica E. Hartmann and Dr. J. Roxanne Prichard, "Calculating the Contribution of Sleep Problems to Undergraduates' Academic Success," *Sleep Health* 4, Issue 5: 463 – 471, Oct. 2018.

**CHAPTER 8:**
p. 173: Trip Gabriel, "To Stop Cheats, Colleges Learn Their Trickery," *New York Times*, July 5, 2010.
p. 185: 2018 National College Health Assessment II.
p. 198: College websites for Reed College, New College of Florida, Evergreen State University, Prescott College, Alverno College, Antioch University, Hampshire College, and Brown University.

**CHAPTER 9:**
p. 215: Club listings for Kutztown University Medieval Renaissance Club, Students for an Orwellian Society, Williams College Beekeeping Club, and the University of Pennsylvania's Disney A Cappella.
p. 223: Megan Gibson, "SlutWalk: I am Woman: Hear Me Roar," *Time Magazine*, Aug. 12, 2011; and Jessica Valenti, "SlutWalks and the Future of Feminism," *Madison.com*, June 8, 2011.

**CHAPTER 10:**
p. 249: Chris Hubbell, "Rescue a Laptop from Water Damage," *Geeks.Online*, Aug. 24, 2015.

**CHAPTER 11:**
p. 255: Sallie Mae, "How America Pays for College 2018," Conducted by Ipsos Public Affairs, Oct. 18, 2018.
p. 271: McGraw-Hill and MMR Research Associates' "2018 McGraw-Hill Education Future Workforce Survey," June 28, 2018.
p. 274: 2018 National College Health Assessment II; and Collin W. Smith, "Effects of Employment on Student Academic Success," Brigham Young University Employment Services, Dec. 2016.
p. 275: Tamar Lewin, "Parents' Financial Support May Not Help College Grades," *New York Times*, Jan. 14, 2013.
p. 277: Julian Aiken, "A List of Unusual Things You Can Check out from the Library," *Yale Law School's Lillian Goldman Law Library News and Blogs*, Aug. 25, 2016, accessed on Jan. 7, 2019; and Cindy Butor, "18 Weird Things You can Borrow from your Local Library," *BookRiot*, Sept. 27, 2017; and Bestcollegesonline.com, "Ten Colleges with Successful Pet Therapy Programs," *Deaf Dogs Rock*, accessed Jan. 7, 2019.

**CHAPTER 12:**
p. 294: 2018 National College Health Assessment II.
p. 295: Dr. Catharine Paddock, "'Freshman 15' Just a Math, Study," *Medical News Today*, Nov. 2, 2011.

**CHAPTER 13:**
p. 300: Fred M. Hechinger, "About Education. Oberlin: Pointed Way 150 Years Ago," *New York Times*, April 26, 1983, p. 7.
p. 302: Cindy, Dampier, "Canada Goose Coats Targeted in a String of Chicago Robberies," *Chicago Tribune*, Jan. 24, 2019.
p. 318: Chris Lesinski, "Mix Your Own Laundry Detergent – Mom Tip," *HackCollege.com*, June 23, 2009.

**CHAPTER 14:**
p. 337, Jeremy Bauer-Wolf, "Free Speech Advocate Silenced," *Inside Higher Ed*, Oct. 6, 2017.

**CHAPTER 15:**
p. 347: "Digest of Education Statistics," National Center for Education Statistics, Table 303.70, showing total undergraduate fall enrollment in degree-granting post-secondary institutions; and Hampshire College, Common Data Set 2016-2017, p. 3.
p. 365: Martin A. Monto and Anna G. Carey. "A New Standard of Sexual Behavior? Are Claims Associated with the 'Hookup Culture' Supported by General Social Survey Data?" *Journal of Sex Research*, April 2014; and 2018 National College Health Assessment II.
p. 371: 2018 National College Health Assessment II.

**CHAPTER 16:**
p. 389, p. 395 and p. 397: National College Health Assessment II.
p. 389: Mary Beth Marklein, "College Freshman Study Booze More Than Books," *USA Today*, March 11, 2009.

**CHAPTER 17:**
p. 412 and p. 415: Thom Patterson, "What to Know Before Pledging a Fraternity or Sorority," *CNN*, Aug. 22, 2018.
p. 413: Snopes.com, "Seuss and Vonnegut," accessed Jan. 8, 2019.

**CHAPTER 18:**
p. 425. College websites for The Citadel, Reed College, Mitchell College, Muhlenberg College, University of Montana; and Lorin Eleni Gil, "Navatek Donates Catamaran to Hawaii-Pacific University," *Pacific Business News*, April 25, 2016.
p. 426: Kathy Kehrli, "The Most Popular Spring Break Destinations Revealed," *TravelMag*, Feb. 29, 2016.
p. 433: U.S. Department of State, accessed on Feb. 10, 2019, https://studyabroad. state.gov/value-study-abroad/study-abroad-data and "Open Doors 2018," Institute of International Education, Nov. 13 2018.
p. 436: "Find Your Opportunity," Cornell University website, accessed on Feb. 15, 2019.

**CHAPTER 19:**
p. 451: Kate Taylor, "Five Harvard Friends, and a Frank Talk About How They Got In," The *New York Times*, Oct. 31, 2018.

**CHAPTER 20:**
p. 470-471: National College Health Assessment II.
p. 476: Valerie Strauss, "Why So Many College Students Decide to Transfer," *Washington Post*, Jan. 29, 2017; and National College Health Assessment II.

**CHAPTER 21:**
p. 490: Joe Kays and Arline Phillips-Han, "Gatorade: The Idea That Launched an Industry," *Explore*, accessed on Jan. 8, 2019; and Arika Okrent, "The True Origin of the Football Huddle," *The Week*, Feb. 2, 2014.

# Special Thanks

Thanks to our intrepid "headhunters" for going out to find so many respondents from around the country with interesting advice to share:

| | |
|---|---|
| Jonathan Barr | Allison Mollenkamp |
| Sophia Cai | Catherine Oriel |
| Dominique Carson | Jessica Reyes |
| Jordan Cohen | Peg Rosen |
| Louise Connelly | Wendy Royston |
| Kristin Danley-Greiner | Allison Stalberg |
| Miriam Diaz-Gilbert | Kara Stevick |
| Raquel Harrah | Anthony Wallace |

And, from previous editions:

| | |
|---|---|
| Jamie Allen | Lisa Powell |
| Helen Bond | Beshaleba Rodell |
| Cindy Ferraino | Kerry Rogers |
| Brandi Fowler | Staci Siegel |
| Chelsee Lowe | Annie Stone |
| Andrea Nackenson | Andrea Syrtash |
| Adam Pollock | Beth Turney |

Thanks to our assistant, Miri Greidi, for her expert contributions to the book every step of the way and for her boundless efforts to keep us all organized. The real credit for this book, of course, goes to all the people whose experiences and collective wisdom make up this guide. There are too many of you to thank individually, but you know who you are.

# ADVICE FROM:

Albany State University
American University
Amherst College
Anderson University
Arizona State University
Auburn University
Barnard College
Baylor University
Biola University
Bloomfield College
Bloomsburg University
Boston College
Boston University
Bowdoin College
Bowling Green State University
Brooklyn College
Brown University
Bryn Mawr College
Bucknell University
California Polytechnic State University at San Luis Obispo
California State University
California State University, Fullerton
Calvin College
Carnegie Mellon University
Central Bible College
Chapman University
Claremont McKenna College
Clemson University
Colby College
College of Mount Saint Vincent
College of New Jersey
College of Southern Idaho
Columbia University
Cornell College
Cornell University
CUNY Brooklyn College
Dakota State University
Dartmouth College
DePaul University
Diablo Valley College
Drexel University
Duke University
Elon University
Emory University
Fairleigh Dickinson University
Florida A&M University
Florida State University
Foothill College
Fordham University

Franklin and Marshall College
Frostburg State University
George Washington University
Georgetown University
Georgia Institute of Technology
Georgia State University
Gonzaga University
Guilford College
Hamilton College
Harvard College
Harvard University
Howard University
Hunter College
Illinois Wesleyan University
Indiana University
Iowa Central Community College
James Madison University
John Jay College of Criminal Justice
Johns Hopkins University
Kean University
Kenyon College
Kingsborough Community College
Kutztown University
Lehigh University
Long Island University
Louisiana State University
Loyola University in Chicago
Macaulay Honors College at CUNY Hunter
Marist College
Massachusetts Institute of Technology
McGill University
Meredith College
Miami University
Millersville University
Mississippi State University
Missouri State University
Montclair State University
Moorhead State University
Mount Holyoke College
New York University
North Carolina State University
Northern Arizona University
Northern Illinois University
Northern State University (S. Dakota)
Northwestern University
Oglethorpe University
Olin College
Oxford College
Parsons School of Design
Pennsylvania State University

Princeton University
Purdue University
Queens University
Rhodes College
Rice University
Riverside Community College
Rutgers University
San Diego State University
San Francisco State University
San Jose State University
Santa Barbara City College
Santa Clara University
School of Visual Arts
Sonoma State University
South Dakota State University
Spring Hill College
St. Francis College
St. John's University
St. Joseph's
Stanford University
State University of New York at Albany
State University of New York at Binghamton
State University of New York at Buffalo
State University of New York at Geneseo
State University of New York at New Paltz
Suffolk University
Susquehanna University
Syracuse University
Temple University
Texas State University
The College of William & Mary
The Jewish Theological Seminary
Trinity University
Tufts University
Union College
United States Military Academy at West Point
University College–Salford (England)
University of Alabama
University of Arizona
University of Bridgeport
University of California at Berkeley
University of California at Irvine
University of California at Los Angeles
University of California at Santa Barbara
University of California at Santa Cruz
University of Chicago
University of Colorado
University of Colorado at Colorado Springs
University of Delaware
University of Florida
University of Georgia

University of Illinois
University of Illinois at Urbana-Champaign
University of Maryland
University of Maryland–College Park
University of Miami
University of Michigan
University of Missouri
University of Nebraska
University of New Hampshire
University of New Mexico
University of North Carolina
University of North Carolina at Chapel Hill
University of North Carolina at Greensboro
University of Notre Dame
University of Oregon
University of Pennsylvania
University of Pittsburgh
University of Rhode Island
University of Richmond
University of Rochester
University of Saint Mary
University of Sioux Falls
University of South Dakota
University of South Florida
University of Tennessee
University of Tennessee at Knoxville
University of Tennessee at Martin
University of Texas
University of Texas at Austin
University of the Sciences in Philadelphia
University of Toronto
University of Tulsa
University of Virginia
University of West Georgia
University of Wisconsin at Madison
Upper Iowa University
Valdosta State University
Vanderbilt University
Villa Julie College
Villanova University
Wake Forest University
Washington and Lee University
Wellesley College
Wesleyan University
Western Carolina University
Western Illinois University
Western Washington University
Widener University
Williams College
Xavier University
Yale University
Youngstown State University

# About the Contributors

**ALICIA ADAMCZYK** is a New York-based writer who specializes in topics ranging from investing and health care to the costs of college and managing student loans. She dreams of owning a pug someday.

**REBECCA R. AYARS** is a Connecticut-based writer who enjoys exploring stories about the arts, wildlife, and sometimes, fellow humans.

**JON BARR** is an LA-based writer and comedian, and a graduate from New York University's Tisch School of the Arts. He recommends you be wary of dining hall pizza.

**VICTOR BERNABEI** is a Connecticut-based passport agent and travel blogger who loves getting lost at home and abroad.

**LIAM BODURTHA** is a college student in New York, who creates apps for the company he founded, Innovation Apps, LLC. He dreams of having his own army of robots someday.

**VAL BODURTHA** is an award-winning author and comedian whose debut novel, written when she was 17, won a Silver Medal at the 2018 Benjamin Franklin Awards. She is a recent graduate of the University of Chicago, where she studied classics and statistics and served as Production Manager for Off-Off Campus, the oldest collegiate sketch and improv troupe in America. She has had three of her plays produced and three screenplays turned into short films, two of which she also directed. Her latest project is a comedic short featuring Paul Giamatti.

**RICH BRAHAM** is the father of Marquise Braham, a Penn State Altoona freshman who suffered emotional and psychological effects from hazing, ultimately taking his own life in 2014.

**SOPHIA CAI** is a freelance journalist based in New Jersey, focused on immigration, housing, and sports. As the co-Vice President of the University Press Club, a selective group of freelance journalists attending Princeton University, she strings for several outlets and has been published by the Trenton Times, Hopewell Express and Asian Correspondent. Currently a sophomore, she is studying International Affairs and Public Policy, while pursuing a Journalism Certificate, and competing on the Lightweight Women's Rowing team.

**LOUISE CONNELLY** is a journalist based in New York City. She graduated from Princeton University, where she spent her freshman year writing for the Daily Princetonian, the Nassau Weekly, and the University Press Club.

**LEE DESSER** is a Career Coach at UC San Diego. She earned a Master's of Education from the University of Southern California (USC). Lee has worked in career services at University of Southern California, Middlebury, and UC Berkeley. Lee writes on higher education issues and has a passion for improving student services and advocating for students. Feel free to reach her on LinkedIn at https://www.linkedin.com/in/lmdesser/.

**MIRIAM DÍAZ-GILBERT** is an independent scholar, author, freelance writer, book reviewer, and adjunct professor. She was the director of a university writing center who taught college students, including freshmen, for more than two decades. In 2008, she authored "English for Pharmacy Writing and Oral Communication," a textbook published by Lippincott Williams & Wilkins. When not writing or teaching, she's running ultra-marathons, rock climbing, snowshoeing, baking bread, knitting scarves, and tending to her garden. See www.miriamdiazgilbert.com.

**DR. CLARICE FORD** is the Vice Chancellor for Student Affairs at the University of Illinois Springfield. She is as an educational leader, consultant, author, minister, and speaker. Ford holds a doctorate degree in Educational Leadership from Fielding University and a Master's degrees in Multicultural/Diversity Education from Antioch University and in Religious Education from Lincoln Seminary.

**PAMELA M. GOLUBSKI, Ph.D.,** has many years of experience in the areas of student academic and career advising, mentoring, specialized programming, teaching, training, onboarding, first-year experience, accreditation, and assessment in higher education. She holds a Ph.D. in Instructional Management, an M.S. in Educational Counseling, and a B.S. in Management.

**THOMAS J. GRITES** serves as assistant provost at Stockton University in Galloway, NJ. He has been directly involved in the academic advising process in higher education for over 40 years, and has served as a consultant, program evaluator, and faculty development workshop leader to more than 120 different campuses. He was instrumental in forming the National Academic Advising Association (NACADA) and was its president for two terms.

Grites earned bachelor's and master's degrees from Illinois State University and completed his doctoral work at the University of Maryland. Both institutions honored him with Distinguished Alumni awards, and he was inducted into the College of Education Hall of Fame at Illinois State. Reach Tom at: gritest@stockton.edu.

**STEPHEN GRUVER** is the father of Maxwell R. Gruver, the 18-year-old aspiring journalist who died in September 2017, one month after beginning his freshman year at Louisiana State University, in an alcohol-related hazing incident at the fraternity where he was pledging. A passage Max had written in his journal about how God sometimes does bad things "to ultimately create good," found after his death, inspired Steve and Max's mother, Rae Ann, to start the Max Gruver Foundation to combat excessive alcohol consumption, bullying and hazing in college. They also helped get a law passed, named after their son, that makes hazing a felony in Louisiana, which they hope will become a model for other states.

**DOUGLAS HASTY** is the First Year Experience Librarian with Florida International University Libraries in Miami. He has been with the university since 1990. Douglas earned his B.A. in History from Guilford College in Greensboro, NC, and his MLS at the University of North Carolina – Greensboro. He is currently pursuing a doctorate degree in Higher Education Administration at Florida International University. He is active in a number of ALA groups and divisions' committees and the Florida ACRL Chapter. See http://douglashasty.com and you can contact Douglas at hastyd@fiu.edu.

**KRISTIN HUSSEY** lives with her husband and children in Connecticut, where she freelances for the New York Times, when she is not carpooling. She almost didn't graduate from college because she flunked gym.

**JUSTIN LONG** received his Bachelors of Science in Education and Masters of Science in College Student Personnel at The University of Southern Mississippi. He served as a Resident Assistant for two years and a Hall Director for three years. He currently works at The University of Southern Mississippi in the Department of Residence Life as Associate Director for Residence Education & Student Relations.

**CATHERINE ORIEL** is a student at George Washington University, studying Journalism & Mass Communication. She has a passion for investigate reporting, writing features and storytelling. Other interests include poetry, traveling, photography and interior design.

**JIM PIAZZA** is the father of Timothy Piazza, the fraternity pledge killed in February 2017 at the Beta Theta Pi Fraternity at Penn State. Jim has become an avid anti-hazing advocate and is a regular speaker on hazing and other safety matters at universities and among various Greek Life and other organizations known for hazing. Jim and his wife Evelyn live in New Jersey with their other son Michael.

**PAULOMI RAO** is a senior at Dartmouth fascinated by the intersection of international rights, sustainability, and the private sector. At school, she is a former varsity rower, current writer for The Dartmouth, America's oldest college newspaper, and a War and Peace Fellow through the John Sloan Dickey Center. Most recently, she was selected to attend a trip to Doha, Qatar, sponsored by the Embassy of Qatar.

**JESSICA REYES** graduated with a B.A. in English Writing from the University of Pittsburgh, but considers herself an adventurer first and writer second.

**PEG ROSEN** writes about education and health from Montclair, New Jersey.

**DR. VICTOR SCHWARTZ** is a clinical associate professor of psychiatry at the New York University School of Medicine with over 25 years of experience working in college mental health. He was previously medical director of NYU's Counseling Service and established a counseling center at Yeshiva University, where he subsequently served as the University Dean of Students. He currently serves as chief medical officer at The Jed Foundation, which works to support mental health in teens and young adults and helps prepare teens for college. He has also served as an adviser to HBO, MTV, the NBA, NFL, and NCAA and is a member of the National Council for Suicide Prevention. He is a distinguished life fellow of the American Psychiatric Association.

**ERICA SIEGEL** is the Assistant Dean of Communications and Outreach at Columbia University's James H. and Christine Turk Berick Center for Student Advising. She earned her undergraduate degree from Columbia in Russian literature and stayed on to complete her Ph.D there. She taught in Columbia University's undergraduate Core Curriculum before joining the Berick Center, where, among other responsibilities, she helps students in Columbia's College and Engineering School navigate four years of their undergraduate experience.

**PEYVAND MIRZADEH SILVERMAN, DVM** is the lead veterinarian with the Los Angeles office of the ASPCA. She earned her DVM at Western University, in Pomona, CA in 2011. Peyvand has worked both in private practice and shelter animal care. As she was growing up in Iran, she always had a fondness for animals, fostering strays and adopting any animal that needed her help, including dogs, chickens, ducks, other birds and reptiles. Together with her husband Scott (arguably the neediest stray of all), they are actively raising many foster animals, several pets, and two amazing kids!

**TATUM THOMAS, PhD,** is the Senior Associate Dean of Student Affairs at Columbia University's School of Professional Studies. Dr. Thomas is responsible for the strategic direction of all aspects of student affairs. She envisions quality programs and services for pre-collegiate, graduate, undergraduate, and life-long learners, including admissions, advising, residential operations, student governance, student life, and student success. In previous roles with NYU since 2005, Dr. Thomas directed the advisement process for both undergraduate and graduate students.

Dr. Thomas holds a Ph.D. from the Chicago School of Professional Psychology, an M.S.Ed. with a focus on Higher Education Administration from Baruch College of the City University of New York, and a B.A. from Marymount Manhattan College. She is pursuing a Certificate in Management Excellence with the Harvard Business School. She can be reached at tatum.thomas@columbia.edu.

**ANTHONY WALLACE** is a Phoenix based writer and thinker who recently left a college campus with a degree in Philosophy from Northern Arizona University in snowy Flagstaff. He is interested in just about everything but is particularly fond of plane crash documentaries, British art shows, and the Arizona Diamondbacks.

**DR. MICHELLE T. WILLIAMS** is dedicated to empowerment through education. She has developed retention and support programs for academically at-risk, first generation, and minority students at the high school and college levels. Her expertise lies in the development and implementation of mentor training frameworks to be used in educational settings. Dr. Williams earned both her undergraduate and graduate degrees from Temple University, and her Doctorate in Educational Leadership from Saint Joseph's University. You can reach her at drmtwilliams@gmail.com.

# ABOUT THE EDITOR

**ALISON LEIGH COWAN** spent 27 years on staff as a reporter and editor for the New York Times before leaving for new adventures in 2015. At the paper, she published roughly 1,800 articles on everything from public corruption to corn hustling, working her way up from a lowly copygirl (when that term still applied) up through the reporting and editing ranks. Along the way, she picked up a degree in philosophy from Princeton University and a master's in business from Harvard Business School, both of which she remains grateful for and uses every day.

These days, she does research for books and projects that interest her. C-Span recently featured her for work she's done on behalf of two Revolutionary War heroines who deserved to be better recognized for their service. On the side, Alison teaches English as a second language in Stamford, Connecticut, where she lives with her husband Steve and family dog, ZuZu. She is a longtime board member of the School for Ethics and Global Leadership in Washington, D.C. and a founding member of the board that mentors the Princeton University Press Club. She credits Yadin Kaufmann, a co-creator of this book, for introducing her to that heady band of student journalists, launching her career and altering her life's path.

When not chasing stories or pursuing lost causes, Alison is probably working on her Scrabble game as a confirmed Scrabbaholic. Follow her on Twitter @cowannyt or challenge her to a match @ cowan82 on Facebook.

# About the Special Contributors

**FRANCES NORTHCUTT, Ed.M.,** remembers that it was her work-study job at the Wesleyan University campus post office that first inspired her to seek a career in student affairs. She loved working at the post office window, where she explained all the complicated postage options to students, faculty, and staff, and made sure that care packages were delivered promptly. During her senior year, she made the move from the post office to the registrar's office. She also helped to start a peer advising program.

After completing her B.A. with honors in English, Fran struck out for the West Coast and became an academic advisor and admissions reader at the University of California, Berkeley. Later, she advised students and taught college skills courses at the University of the Sciences in Philadelphia. At night, she studied at Temple University and earned a master's degree in Higher Education Administration. She then became an honors adviser and admissions reader for the Macaulay Honors College of the City University of New York. Currently, she is the coordinator for academic advisement and exchange programs at the Cooper Union School of Art. Fran lives in Manhattan with her husband and daughters.

**SCOTT C. SILVERMAN, Ed.D.** is the Associate Dean of the Emeritus Lifelong Learning Program at Santa Monica College, California's #1 transfer college for 27 years. He has worked in student and academic affairs for over 17 years, mainly in programs directly serving first-year students. He coordinated new student orientation and first-year programming, advised student organizations, planned campus activities, and ran the Honors program at the University of California, Riverside, where he earned a B.S. and M.S. in Environmental Science. In 2007, Scott earned an Ed.D. in Higher Education Administration from the University of Southern California.

As a student, Scott was involved in multiple student organizations, student government, peer mentoring, and community activities, including non-profit work. Scott's a big believer in the power students have to make a difference on campus and in the community - and he's seen it happen firsthand! Follow Scott on Twitter @ScottCSilverman.

## About the Illustrator

**LISA ROTHSTEIN** began her freshman year at Brown University at age 16, and has enjoyed reliving it while illustrating this book. Lisa had made money during college as a street performer, hard-boiled egg peeler, and nude art model, before being recruited on campus by Madison Avenue advertising agency Young & Rubicam. Today, Lisa is an international brand strategist, speaker and cartoonist whose work has appeared in The New Yorker, bestselling books, and marketing campaigns. She has written and illustrated for Pearson Education and the N.Y.C. Department of Education. She lives in San Diego with her husband, Jim Benson, a television historian and radio talk show host, and Casey, their rescue terrier of indeterminate origin. For more, please visit www.lisarothstein.com/cartoons.

## About the Series Creators

**MARK BERNSTEIN** graduated from the Wharton School of the University of Pennsylvania and later from NYU School of Law. Since college he helped launch CNN.com, helped start the nation's leading volunteerism not-for-profit and has still stayed friends with many friends from freshman year. While at Penn, Mark survived by starting a business that provided freshmen with "survival kits" consisting of unhealthy food purchased by parents, who were coping with the absence of their kids.

**YADIN KAUFMANN** graduated from Princeton University, Harvard Law School and the Harvard Graduate School of Arts and Sciences. Since college he's been helping entrepreneurs start technology companies, and started two non-profit organizations. While at Princeton, he was involved in journalism and started a student agency to publish a book he wrote. He survived his freshman year by chugging Hershey's syrup, straight up. Yadin and his wife Lori – whom he met during her freshman year! – wrote *The Boston Ice Cream Lover's Guide*.